B

Fire

Justice Under Law

Justice Under Fire
THE ABUSE OF CIVIL LIBERTIES
IN NORTHERN IRELAND

Anthony Jennings, LL.B.

*of Gray's Inn and the Inn of Court
of Northern Ireland, Barrister,*

EDITOR

PLUTO  PRESS

London • Winchester, Mass

This edition first published 1990 by Pluto Press
345 Archway Road, London N6 5AA
and 8 Winchester Place, Winchester
MA 01890, USA

First published 1988 by Pluto Press

British Library Cataloguing in Publication Data

Justice under fire. — 2nd ed
   1. Northern Ireland. Government. Emergency powers
I. Jennings, Anthony, *1960–*
354.416

   ISBN 0–7453–0415–X

Library of Congress Cataloging-in-Publication Data

Justice under fire: the abuse of civil liberties in Northern Ireland
   / edited by Anthony Jennings. — [Rev.]
      p.   cm.
   Includes bibliographical references.
   ISBN 0–7453–0415–X
   1. Civil rights—Northern Ireland.   2. War and emergency powers–
–Northern Ireland.   3. Northern Ireland—Politics and
government—1969–   I. Jennings, Anthony, LL.B.
KDE420.J87   1990
342.416'085—dc20
[344.160285]   89–26566
                                                              CIP

Printed in Great Britain
by Billing and Sons Ltd, Worcester

For Nan

Contents

Tables

Figures

Contributors

Kevin Boyle is Professor of Law at University College, Galway and founder of Article 19. He has acted for a number of Northern Ireland complainants in proceedings at the European Commission and Court of Human Rights. He is co-author with Tom Hadden and Paddy Hillyard of *Law and State: The Case of Northern Ireland* (1975) and *Ten Years On in Northern Ireland* (1980). He is co-author with Tom Hadden of *Ireland: A Positive Proposal* (1985).

Colm Campbell is a solicitor and holder of the Cobden Trust Research Studentship in Emergency Law at Queen's University Belfast.

Steven Greer is Lecturer in Law at the University of Bristol. He was the Cobden Trust Research Student at Queen's University Belfast between 1983 and 1985. He has written a number of articles on emergency law for legal and current affairs journals.

Tom Hadden is part-time Professor of Law at Queen's University Belfast. He is co-author with Paddy Hillyard of *Justice in Northern Ireland: A Study in Social Confidence* (1973).

Peter Hall is a barrister practising in England and Northern Ireland.

Paddy Hillyard is Senior Lecturer in Social Administration at the University of Bristol. He is an executive member of the NCCL.

Anthony Jennings is a barrister practising in England and Northern Ireland. He has written articles on emergency law in Northern Ireland for legal and current affairs journals and for the *Guardian* and the *Independent*.

Dermot P.J. Walsh is a barrister and Lecturer in Law at University College, Cork. He has written extensively on the emergency legislation in Northern Ireland including *The Use and Abuse of Emergency Legislation in Northern Ireland* (1983).

Antony White is a barrister practising in London. He is co-author with Steven Greer of *Abolishing the Diplock Courts* (1986).

Acknowledgements

I would like to thank the following for their help and assistance in preparing this book:

Lord Lowry C.J. and his staff in Belfast for providing me with transcripts of judgments of a number of unreported cases; Pat Finuccin for the papers in the Norah McCabe case; Jonathan Rosenhead for providing me with a number of invaluable documents on baton rounds; the *Guardian* library for always supplying copies of newspaper articles; the Irish Information Partnership for data; Tom Hadden, Paddy Hillyard and Steven Greer for helping in pulling the loose ends together; Sally Miller and Donna Jennings for typing my contributions; Rick Scannell for preparing the index; Sarah Stewart for her impeccable copyediting; Anne Beech for her eternal patience; Linda Briggs and Elaine Donaldson for their work on the final stages of production; and finally Mum, Jackie, Sharon, Mark, Marie and my colleagues and friends for their good-humoured encouragement.

The Appendices on pp. 213–385 are reproduced with kind permission of HMSO.

Table of Statutes

Table of Cases

Abbreviations

AC	Appeal Cases
All ER	All England Law Reports
BNIL	Bulletin of Northern Ireland Law
CAR	Criminal Appeal Reports
CLA	Criminal Law Act
CLR	Criminal Law Review
DPP	Director of Public Prosecutions
DUP	Democratic Unionist Party
EPA	Emergency Provisions Act
HOSB	Home Office Statistical Bulletin
INLA	Irish National Liberation Army
IR	Irish Reports
IRA	Irish Republican Army
LQR	Law Quarterly Review
NI	Northern Ireland Law Reports
NIJB	Northern Ireland Judgment Bulletin
NILQ	Northern Ireland Legal Quarterly
NLJ	New Law Journal
OUP	Official Unionist Party
PACE	Police and Criminal Evidence Act
PTA	Prevention of Terrorism Act
QB	Queen's Bench Division Reports
RIC	Royal Irish Constabulary
RUC	Royal Ulster Constabulary
SAS	Special Air Service
SDLP	Social Democratic and Labour Party
SSU	Special Support Unit
UDA	Ulster Defence Association
UDR	Ulster Defence Regiment
UFF	Ulster Freedom Fighters
UVF	Ulster Volunteer Force
WLR	Weekly Law Reports

' "Amid the clash of arms the laws are silent":[1] so Cicero exclaimed over 2000 years ago. During the greatest conflict in our history Lord Atkin bravely ventured to contradict this assertion. Now, too, peace, order, and society itself are under fierce and constant attack and this is why we must remember Lord Atkin's famous dictum: "In this country, amid the clash of arms the laws are not silent. They may change, but they speak the same language in war as in peace."[2]

'This war is being waged by organisations which style themselves armies and observe military procedures, but it has not invaded, and will not be allowed to invade, the courts. The rule of law has prevailed and will continue to prevail there.'[3]

Lord Lowry C.J.

'...the law should be used as just another weapon in the government's arsenal, and in this case it becomes little more than a propaganda cover for the disposal of unwanted members of the public. For this to happen efficiently, the activities of the legal services have to be tied into the war effort in as discreet a way as possible.'[4]

Brigadier Frank Kitson

1. Cic. pro Milone 4.10.
2. *Liversidge v. Anderson* (1942) A.C. 206, 244.
3. *R. v. Gibney* (1983) 13 NIJB 7–8.
4. p. 69, *Low Intensity Operations: Subversion, Insurgency and Peacekeeping* (London: Faber & Faber 1971).

Preface to the 1990 Edition

People crushed by law have no hopes but from power. If laws are their enemies, they will be enemies to laws; and those, who have much to hope and nothing to lose, will always be dangerous, more or less.

Edmund Burke (1777)

When this book was first published in October 1988 many of the contributors felt that the abuses of civil liberties in Northern Ireland had reached their highwatermark. The government has obviously not been deterred by that feeling and therefore a lengthy review of the changes over the last year is required for the paperback edition. Perhaps the two most disturbing developments have been the extent to which Northern Ireland has once again been used, in relation to the abolition of the right to silence, as a training ground for policies to be implemented in Britain at a later date, and the way supposedly 'exceptional' powers are finding their way into the 'ordinary' criminal law in both Northern Ireland and England and Wales.

Security Review

In October 1988 the government announced a major security review of Northern Ireland. This included a media ban on all interviews with the IRA, INLA, Sinn Féin, UVF, UFF, UDA and their 'supporters'. The government relied on s.29 of the Broadcasting Act 1981 and clauses in the BBC's charter. The ban only applies to radio and television and was severely criticised in many circles on the basis that it amounted to a considerable fetter on press freedom and that some of the organisations, for example, Sinn Féin, are not illegal. Perhaps the most disturbing aspect of the ban is that it will lead to increased self-censorship and a disturbing tendency to see anyone critical of Britain's role in Northern Ireland as thereby providing 'support' for Sinn Féin or others.[1] It is ironic that, prior to the release of the 'Guildford Four', a radio programme and a pop song were not broadcast as a result of the media ban.

The most fundamental change announced by the government was the abolition of the 'right to silence' in both Northern Ireland and

England and Wales for *all* criminal offences. The 'reform' was introduced in Northern Ireland by statutory instrument (NI/SI No. 20, 1988/1989) in December 1988, without proper parliamentary debate, and it will be introduced in a restricted form in due course in England and Wales.

This move, in relation to England and Wales, was recommended by the Criminal Law Revision Committee in 1972[2] but was disapproved of by the Royal Commission on Criminal Procedure in 1981.[3] The change will allow a court to draw an adverse inference from an accused's silence in four circumstances:

1. When there is a 'prima facie' evidence against a defendant;
2. in 'ambush defence' cases;
3. when a defendant fails to explain a specific fact, e.g. a piece of forensic evidence;
4. when a defendant fails to give an account of his presence at a particular place.[4]

The *Independent*[5] claimed that the judiciary in Northern Ireland was 'strongly resisting' this change and possible reforms concerning detention periods for Prevention of Terrorism Act suspects. It was claimed that several senior Northern Ireland judges had personally told Tom King of their 'strong disapproval' of the abolition of the right to silence.

It is feared that the abolition of the right to silence will enable future courts to overcome problems with 'supporting evidence' in relation to the use of supergrasses as described in Chapter 4. Undoubtedly, the change goes a long way to alter the accusatorial nature of the British criminal trial and to some extent shift the burden of proof on to a defendant.

Amnesty International

Amnesty International's 1988 report on Northern Ireland severely criticised the role of supergrasses in the early 1980s.[6] The report made the following recommendations:[7]

- No future prosecutions based upon the uncorroborated evidence of a supergrass; this proposal should be incorporated in legislation;
- time limits on the gap between remand in custody and trial (see s.3 Northern Ireland (Emergency Provisions) Act 1987, Appendix II);
- the avoidance of using voluntary bills of indictment;
- a review of the maximum number of defendants in each trial (see para. 172, Baker Report, below);

- full disclosure of inducements offered to and accepted by a super-grass.

The Report also described the law governing the use of lethal force as 'inadequate'.[8] The organisation was further concerned that 'some of the killings by the security forces may have resulted from a deliberate policy at some official level to eliminate, or permit elimination of, rather than to arrest individuals whom they identified as members of armed opposition groups'.[9]

Amnesty also believed that, regarding the 1982 killings, the official investigative procedures had 'failed to eliminate the possibility that they (the six men) were killed with premeditation as a result of operations deliberately planned to this end'.[10]

John Stalker Revisited

In the extended paperback of his book, John Stalker examined a central question arising from the affair: 'Was he pushed or did he fall?' Stalker argued that there had for some time been an interest in his affairs but it only became real and urgent after he delivered his interim report. As he said:[11]

I believe that in April 1986 a Government decision was made to end my involvement in the enquiry. A decision of this importance I feel sure would be unlikely to have been made at anything less than the highest level. The advantages of my report were now out-weighed by the disadvantages, and I had in short become an embarrassment.

Stalker believed his suspension was important in gaining valuable breathing space for the RUC to deal with the loyalist marches of the summer of 1986 and to ensure the continuation of the Anglo-Irish Agreement. As Stalker concluded: 'I believe ... that I was on the threshold of causing a major police scandal and political row that would have resulted in several resignations and general mayhem.'[12]

In March 1989, 18 junior RUC Officers were reprimanded for their involvement in the Stalker affair. John Stalker must have wondered whether it had all been worth it.

Increased Acquittal Rate

In September 1988 no evidence was offered against a soldier, David Holden, in Belfast magistrates' court for the unlawful killing of Aidan McAnespie. This brings the total number of members of the security forces prosecuted for killings whilst on duty and involving firearms to 22, and the acquittal rate to 91 per cent.

By the autumn of 1989, 307 individuals, 167 of them civilians, had been killed by the security forces in Northern Ireland since 1969 (this does not include the three members of the IRA killed in Gibraltar).[13]

Death on the Rock[14]

On 6 September 1988 an inquest opened in Gibraltar into the killings by the SAS on 6 March 1988 of Mairead Farrell, Daniel McCann and Sean Savage.

Eighteen witnesses (seven from the army, eight from the security services and three Gibraltar Special Branch officers) gave evidence from behind a curtain and using letters of the alphabet instead of their names.

It was argued on behalf of the British government that the three deceased were part of an IRA Active Service Unit which was going to detonate a bomb in the centre of Gibraltar on 8 March when the changing of the guard ceremony would be taking place. It was apparently thought that the bomb had been brought across the border by the group and would be detonated by remote control.

MI5 officer 'O' described the three deceased as 'dangerous terrorists', almost certainly armed, and likely to use their weapons if challenged by the security forces. It was also apparently believed that the bomb would be detonated if the three were confronted.

Mr 'O' admitted that there were three major inaccuracies in the authorities' intelligence. The three were unarmed, the suspect car in the centre of Gibraltar did not contain a bomb and the 64 kilos of Semtex explosives found in Spain two days later had no remote control device but a timer mechanism.

The point of 'Operation Flavius' was supposedly to arrest the suspects, and the police had accordingly issued rules of engagement before the operation began, similar in terms to the army's 'Yellow Card'.

Home Office pathologist, Alan Watson, told the court that Farrell had three bullet wounds to the back and four to her face, and McCann had two wounds to the head and two to the back. Savage had been shot 16 times, including five shots to the head and the neck and five shots to the back. Professor Watson was not given the opportunity of examining the deceased's clothing or other forensic reports. This problem was encountered in Northern Ireland by John Stalker and in Gibraltar it hampered the task of deciding if the deceased were shot while on the ground.

The injury to McCann's head suggested to Professor Watson that he was initially shot in the back and then in the head while, quite possibly, lying on the ground. Farrell had also probably been shot while on the ground or very close to it. Savage had been shot in the head while on the ground. His body was 'riddled with bullets' and he looked to Professor Watson to have been the subject of 'a frenzied attack'.

All of the SAS men were to deny that any of the three were shot while on the ground and, of course, if they had been, it would make a nonsense of the government's assertion that the SAS had been exercising reasonable force. It was argued by the families' solicitor, Paddy McGrory, that the deceased had been executed in 'traditional' SAS fashion.

David Prior, a Scotland Yard forensic expert, told the inquest that Farrell had been shot from as close as 3 ft, and Savage from as close as 4 ft 6 ins.

Soldiers A and B told the court that they followed the three as they headed towards the border and then split up by the petrol station: Savage heading back towards the town centre. Soldiers A and B shot Farrell and McCann and soldiers C and D walked after Savage and shot him after apparently shouting a warning. All three were alleged to have made 'violent movements' which indicated that they were going for a weapon or a detonating button and so they were shot.

A number of key witnesses gave an account considerably at variance with the official story. Stephen and Lucinda Bullock and Diana Treacy said that soldiers C and D *chased* after Savage: an account denied by the soldiers.

Josie Celecia saw Farrell and McCann being shot while they were on the ground, and Carmen Proetta said both were shot after raising their hands and then shot again while on the ground.

Bank clerk Kenneth Asquez had initially made an unsigned statement saying that he saw Savage shot by men wearing berets who said they were police officers. One of them shot Savage as he placed his foot on Savage's neck/chest. Asquez withdrew this statement in court eventually, saying that he had made it because of pressure from a representative from the *Death on the Rock* television programme. Asquez said he probably obtained the details in his statement from the press, but as the coroner pointed out, the evidence about the berets and the men shouting that they were policemen was accepted by the soldiers but had never appeared in the press or on television.

The jury retired on 30 September 1988. After six hours' deliberation the coroner, Felix Pizzarelo, brought the jury back into the court and asked them if there was any prospect of a unanimous verdict. The jury said 'no' and the coroner told them that he would accept a majority verdict of ten to one or nine to two, but the foreman said the jury was deadlocked. The jury returned after a further 1 hour 45 minutes with a verdict of lawful killing in all three cases by a majority of nine to two.

The verdict was far from satisfactory from the government's point of view. A jury in one of the most loyal corners of Britain's influence had been clearly divided, and only returned a verdict by a majority. The inquest also failed to answer many important questions, largely as a consequence of the public interest immunity certificates issued at the beginning of the inquest. Were the authorities really taken by surprise by the arrival of the three in Gibraltar? Why were they not arrested at the Spanish border? What role did the Spanish police play in the surveillance and how extensive was it? If the intention was to arrest the suspects, why were soldiers and, in particular, the SAS used? Why was the area around the suspect bomb not cleared if there was a genuine fear of detonation? Why would the three be carrying a detonator two days before the planned attack? Who really pressurised Kenneth Asquez? As the deceased were unarmed and did not possess a detonating device, what were the 'violent movements' that led to their being shot?

In March 1989 highly placed sources in Spain's Foreign Intelligence Brigade claimed that British Intelligence knew that the three were not carrying arms and had no explosives in Gibraltar when they were shot. As Miguel Martin, president of the Professional Policemen's Union (SPP) said: 'We knew that the explosives weren't in Gibraltar.'[15] This later developed into an open row between Spain and Britain, with Spain's Interior Minister, José Corcuera, claiming that the British government had concealed evidence from, and deliberately misled, the Gibraltar inquest.

Coroner's Courts in Northern Ireland

One interesting aspect of the Gibraltar inquest is that it would have proceeded very differently had it taken place in Northern Ireland.

In Northern Ireland, a coroner is obliged to hold an inquest with a jury if the death occurred in prison or if there is reason to suspect that the death occurred 'in circumstances the continuance or possible recurrence of which is prejudicial to the health or safety of the public or any section of the public'.[16] In the case of Julie Livingstone,[17] her death by a plastic bullet was not considered to fall within the ambit of the section by the Belfast coroner, but his decision was quashed on appeal by the High Court, and a jury subsequently decided that Julie Livingstone was 'an innocent victim'.

The selection of jurors is also an important source of difference between Northern Ireland and England and Wales. In Northern Ireland senior RUC officers select the jury[18] but in England and Wales the jury is summoned at random in a way similar to the procedure at the Crown Court.[19]

Rule 9(2) of the Coroners (Practice and Procedure) (Amendment) Rules 1980 provides that people suspected of causing a death, charged or likely to be charged with an offence relating to the death, should not be compelled to give evidence at the inquest. This rule clearly provides the coroner with a discretion in the matter, but this discretion has increasingly been exercised to prevent the members of the security forces directly responsible for the death from giving evidence. Had this rule existed in Gibraltar, it may well have resulted in the SAS men's not giving evidence and their statements being read to the jury despite the protests of the family of the deceased.

In December 1988 the Northern Ireland Court of Appeal, Lord Hutton C.J. presiding, overturned the decision of the Belfast coroner, presiding over the inquests into the death in 1982 of Eugene Toman, Sean Burns and Gervais McKerr, that the police officers involved did not have to give evidence. The Court of Appeal accepted that this was an important point of law rather than procedure and that the RUC men still had the protection of the right against self-incrimination. In England and Wales statements can only be read by agreement or where the witness is genuinely unavailable.[20]

In England and Wales the coroner is obliged to examine on oath all persons whom he thinks it 'expedient' to concerning the death in question.[21] In Northern Ireland, since 1980, this provision has been removed[22] thus preventing the family of the deceased attempting to insist that material witnesses be called.

The Coroners Act (Northern Ireland) 1959 removed the power of the coroner's inquest to commit people for trial or to name those responsible for unlawful killings.[23] Until 1980, an open verdict was the only method of indicating that someone other than the deceased was responsible for the death. However, following a recommendation for England and Wales by the Broderick Report,[24] the open verdict was abolished in Northern Ireland in 1980 and the jury was only permitted to make limited 'findings' as to the cause of death. In England and Wales, and indeed in Gibraltar, juries can still return unlawful killing or open verdicts.[25] The then Lord Chancellor, Lord Hailsham, regarded the existence of such verdicts in Northern Ireland as 'a potent source of difficulty'.[26]

Excessive delays between death and inquest are frequent in Northern Ireland and a source of much bitterness. The first of the inquests into the six deaths in 1982, the subject of the Stalker/Sampson inquiry, only commenced in 1988 and was then adjourned. In England and Wales inquests are formally opened and then continued when the authorities have completed their investigations[27] whereas in Northern Ireland the practice has developed of not opening the inquest until the authorities indicate that they are ready.

Inquests can be highly expensive for the families involved, yet legal aid is not available in the UK even though provisions in the Legal Aid Act 1974 would allow this.[28] In view of the frequency of controversial deaths which come before the coroner's courts in Northern Ireland and the social background of many of the families involved, the absence of legal aid is all the more harsh.

European Court Ruling

During the passage of the Prevention of Terrorism Bill the European Court of Human Rights gave its ruling in the case of *Brogan and Others v. UK*.[29] The court held that although the detention provisions in section 12 of the 1984 Act were inspired by 'the legitimate aim of protecting the community from terrorism', detention for 4 days and 6 hours in police custody without an appearance before a judge or other judicial officer breached Article 5(3) of the European Convention.

The government only had three possible responses to the ruling: reduce the maximum period of detention, introduce a judicial element into the detention process or derogate from the Convention under Article 15. The government would not consider the first option and, after alleged complaints from senior judges in Northern Ireland, decided not to follow the second. The government therefore had, embarrassingly, to decide to derogate from the Convention. It first did this in relation to Northern Ireland in 1957 but withdrew all of its derogations in 1984 on the somewhat optimistic basis that none of the emergency legislation infringed the Convention. As the Prevention of Terrorism Act applies to the whole of the UK, there may be some difficulty arguing that in Britain there is, under Article 15, a 'public emergency threatening the life of the nation'.[30]

The UK has been found to be in violation of the European Convention more times than any other signatory. The UK has been brought before the European Court on 31 occasions since 1950 and found to have violated the Convention on 21 occasions. The Committee of Ministers of the Council of Europe has also found that the UK breached the Convention a further 37 times in the same period.[31]

Prevention of Terrorism Act 1989

The Prevention of Terrorism (Temporary Provisions) Act 1989 received the Royal Assent in March of that year. The expression 'Temporary Provisions' is highly misleading as the Act no longer has a maximum lifespan like its 1984 predecessor, but is instead subject to annual renewal. A copy of the new Act is contained in Appendix IV.

The new Act re-enacts many of the provisions of the 1984 Act and introduces powers in a number of new areas. The provisions concerning proscription (section 1), arrest (section 14), detention periods (section 14(4),(5), schedule 3) and port powers (section 16) are largely the same as under the 1984 Act. Despite the recommendation of Lord Colville, the power to make exclusion orders (sections 4–8) is retained, as is the offence of withholding information (section 18).

The Act borrows heavily from the Drug Trafficking Act 1986 in seeking to tackle the problem of 'laundered' terrorist funds (sections 10–13). Two disturbing effects of the new provisions are the burden they place on a defendant of showing that the funds concerned are not connected with terrorism and the extent to which financial institutions are given virtual 'carte blanche' to pass information on about 'suspect' customers.

New investigatory powers concerning documents (section 17, schedule 7) are largely modelled on the Police and Criminal Evidence Act 1984. However, the use of production orders in 'urgent cases', and also when the Secretary of State considers it 'necessary', remove the safeguard of judicial scrutiny present under PACE 1984.

A new power to order someone to remain in a specified part of premises or a vehicle, while they are being searched for munitions, transmitters or scanning receivers, is contained in section 21, and effectively amends existing provisions in the EPA 1987. This section also gives the security forces power to keep a person in those premises or vehicles, and creates a new offence of wilfully disobeying an order to stay in a particular part of premises or in a vehicle. This provision seeks to avoid the County Court decision in *Oscar and Toner v. Chief Constable RUC and Ministry of Defence*) (1987) which held that the detaining of a family for four hours during a search was false imprisonment, and also the remarks of the House of Lords in *Murray v. Ministry of Defence*[32] in a similar vein.

The Act also reduces the normal remission from one half to one third for those sentences of more than five years' imprisonment for a scheduled offence (section 22). This means that those convicted of such offences are at a considerable disadvantage to those serving a sentence in England and Wales and, in particular, convicted Republican activists in England and Wales.

The Police and Criminal Evidence (Northern Ireland) Order 1989

This Order became law at 2 a.m. on 17 July 1989 after just one and a half hours' allocated debate. The Order contains many of the provisions of PACE 1984 but extends powers in a number of key areas. The Order ostensibly only applies to 'ordinary crime' and therefore provisions concerning access to a solicitor (article 59) and tape-recorded interviews (article 60) do not apply to 'terrorist suspects'. There is also no provision, as exists in England and Wales, for legal aid for police-station consultations with solicitors.

The Order extends the grounds on which a search warrant can be obtained (article 10) and also defines a mouth swab as a non-intimate sample (article 63) although it is defined under PACE 1984 as an intimate sample which cannot be obtained without a suspect's consent. As Alex Carlisle MP remarked: 'Why is the mouth an intimate orifice in Liverpool, but not in Belfast?'[33]

Section 32 of the Criminal Justice Act 1988 allows witnesses who are outside the UK, or who are under 14, and give evidence in relation to certain offences listed in the section, to do so through a television link. Article 81 preserves the provision in relation to children under 14 but stipulates that the witness must be in Northern Ireland and extends it to cover any witness who 'will not give evidence through fear'. The article also gives the Secretary of State power to extend coverage to any witness who is in Britain or outside the UK. The Minister of State, Ian Stewart, hinted that this extension of powers may be introduced in Britain.

Article 81 will apply to those who appear in no-jury courts and it will allow future supergrasses to give evidence from a safe haven abroad and without having to appear in court.

Bullets Above the Law

In June 1989 the British Army confirmed that plastic bullets were being issued to the UDR and that training for some units in the use of such weapons had already started.[34] The decision provoked nationalist protests on both sides of the border as the almost exlusively loyalist UDR is the least acceptable of the three security forces in Northern Ireland. Around 54,000 baton rounds have been fired since 1973 and over 400 people have been seriously injured by them.

In north Belfast in the early hours of 9 August 1989, 15-year-old Seamus Duffy became the fourteenth person to be killed by a plastic bullet in Northern Ireland.[35]

Security Force Leaks

In September 1989 John Stevens, Deputy Chief Constable of Cambridgeshire, was appointed to investigate leaks from the security forces to loyalist paramilitaries. Two members of the UDR were charged with killing a Catholic who had been targeted as an active Republican by a leaked security force document. Sixteen members of the UDR have been convicted of sectarian killings to date and over 100 retired or serving members of the regiment have been convicted of a number of serious offences. The leaks, which quite quickly became a flood, threatened the stability of the Anglo-Irish Agreement and added support to those who believed in close collusion between the security forces and loyalist paramilitaries.[36]

Colville Review

Viscount Colville, who has previously reviewed the workings of the Prevention of Terrorism Act 1984 as it operated in 1987 and 1988, has also produced reviews of the 1987 and 1988 operation of the Emergency Provisions Acts 1978 and 1987.[37] His review of the E.P.A. is annual and the Act is due for renewal in 1992.

In his reviews of the E.P.A., Viscount Colville does not recommend any substantial reforms of the Acts, although he does recommend a number of minor changes which have not as yet been implemented. If this experience is anything to go by, the provisions concerning arrest, detention, interrogation and no-jury courts will be renewed in 1992.

Emergency Law Figures

In July 1989 the government published statistics on the operation of the emergency legislation.[38]

Table 1. Cases in which offences were 'certified out' of no-jury courts

1985	74%
1986	61%
1987	56%
1988	52%

Table 2. Acquittal rate in no-jury trials

1985	50%
1986	43%
1987	42%
1988	37%

Table 3. Those arrested under sections 11, 13 and 14 E.P.A. who were eventually charged

1985	17%
1986	17%
1987	9%
1988	3%

Table 4. Delay under 1987 Act in detained persons' access to a solicitor

1987	55%
1988	60%

A factor that should be borne in mind when considering the 'certifying out' figures is that a number of serious offences, which may take place in 'non-terrorist' circumstances, cannot be 'certified out'. It is also a matter of concern that the percentage of successful applications has fallen by 22 per cent since 1985 and now stands at just over 50 per cent. A recommendation by Viscount Colville in his 1988 report to alleviate this problem was subsequently withdrawn in his 1989 report.

Despite a healthy acquittal rate in the mid-1980s, there has been a drop of 13 per cent since 1985 and the figure seems to be returning to the worrying level of the early 1980s.

The arrest and charge figures illustrate the extent to which arrests in Northern Ireland are quite often a purely intelligence-gathering exercise. Moreover, the introduction of the requirement of reasonable suspicion in mid-1987 does not seem to have improved the position.

The fact that last year over 60 per cent of those who supposedly have a right to consult a solicitor have had their right to do so delayed questions the extent to which this is an effective right in Northern Ireland. The potential for injustice is all the greater with the abolition of the right to silence.

'The Guildford Four'

In October 1989 the Court of Appeal quashed the convictions of Paul Hill, Patrick Armstrong, Gerard Conlon and Carole Richardson for the Guildford and Woolwich pub bombings in 1974. The prosecution told the court that five Surrey police officers had fabricated evidence and lied during the original trial in 1975. A full judicial inquiry by ex-Court of Appeal judge Sir John May will examine the whole affair. It was a dark day indeed for British justice.[39]

Amid the clash of arms in Northern Ireland the law's silence is on occasions deafening. The laws in Northern Ireland patently do not speak the same language in war as in peace and increasingly they have become just another weapon in the government's arsenal.[40]

Anthony Jennings
Middle Temple
London EC4
February 1990

Notes

1. See *Daily Telegraph*, 17 October 1988. See also changes in the rules of evidence and reduction in the right to trial by jury in England and Wales in the Criminal Justice Act 1988.
2. 11th Report, Evidence (General), cmnd. 4991 (1972). See also Chapter 1, P. Mirfield 'Confessions' (London: Sweet and Maxwell, 1985).
3. Cmnd. 8092.
4. *Guardian*, 21 October 1988.
5. 28 December 1988.
6. *Northern Ireland: Killings by the Security Forces and 'Supergrass' Trials.*
7. Ibid., p. 83.
8. Ibid., p. 59.
9. Ibid.
10. Ibid., p. 60.
11. J. Stalker, *Stalker* (London: Penguin, 1988), p. 264.
12. Ibid., p. 268.
13. See *Ambush: the War between the SAS and the IRA*, J. Adams, R. Morgan and A. Bambridge (London: Pan Books, 1988). See pp. 193–4 for a copy of the rules of engagement issued to the SAS in Gibraltar.
14. See *Independent*, 6 September–1 October 1988. See also *Investigating Lethal Shootings: the Gibraltar Inquest* (Eur 42/02/89) by Amnesty International and *The Gibraltar Report* by NCCL. Also see *The Windlesham/Rampton Report on 'Death on the Rock'*, Lord Windlesham and Richard Rampton (London: Faber, 1989). The programme received a well-deserved BAFTA award in March 1989 and the ceremony did not fall foul of the media ban.
15. *Independent*, 16 March 1989.
16. Coroners Act (Northern Ireland) 1959, S.18; for England and Wales see Coroners (Amendment) Act 1926, S.13.
17. See Chapter 6.
18. Coroners Act (Northern Ireland) 1959, S.18(1).
19. Coroners' Juries Act 1983, S.3A.
20. Coroners Rules 1984, rule 37.
21. Coroners Act 1887, S.4.
22. Coroners (Practice and Procedure) (Amendment) Rules 1980 (sro No. 444) rule 8(1).
23. For England and Wales see Criminal Law Act 1977, S.56(1).
24. (1971) cmnd. 4810.

25.   Coroners Rules 1984, rule 42, schedule 4, form 22.

26.   14 March 1983, see Chapter 5, p. 112, supra.

27.   Coroners (Practice and Procedure) Rules 1963, rule 12.

28.   Schedule 7.

29.   *Independent*, 30 November 1988, 21 October 1989.

30.   See Chapter 1 and R. Beddard, *Human Rights in Europe*, supra.

31.   *Independent*, 30 November 1988.

32.   (1988) 2 All ER 521.

33.   H.C. Debs., vol. 157, col. 166.

34.   *Guardian*, 15 June 1989.

35.   *Independent*, 10 August 1989.

36.   *Independent*, 19 September 1989.

37.   *Report on the Operation in 1987 of the Northern Ireland (Emergency Provisions) Acts 1978 and 1987* (1988), *Report on the Operation in 1988 of the Northern Ireland (Emergency Provisions) Acts 1978 and 1987* (1989).

38.   Press release 28 July 1989 (L 56/89) by Northern Ireland Office. Section 11 EPA 1978 was repealed in June 1987.

39.   *Independent*, 20 and 21 October 1989; *Sunday Correspondent*, 22 October 1989.

40.   I would like to thank Louise McKeon for typing this foreword and for her continuing help and encouragement.

Preface to the 1988 Edition

Since the commencement of the disturbances in Northern Ireland in 1969 a number of emergency legal measures have been introduced and 'law and order' strategies have been employed in an effort to 'improve' the administration of justice in Northern Ireland.

Britain has always reacted to violence in Ireland with a crude mixture of open displays of force and poor attempts to deal with an intractable problem within the confines of the rule of law. In reality both policies are designed to achieve the same end: the elimination of the perceived threat to law and order. Ireland is, of course, not the sole beneficiary of Britain's enlightened interpretation of the rule of law; India, Palestine, Aden and others were recipients of different mixtures of the same potion.

Since 1973 Britain has decided to concentrate on defeating political violence with legal initiatives falling short of martial law and with the operation of time-honoured policing and counterinsurgency strategies.

Chapter 1 analyses the background to the conflict and provides an overview of various initiatives that have been introduced since 1969. The wide powers of arrest and interrogation, with particular reference to the Prevention of Terrorism Acts, are examined in detail in subsequent chapters. The abolition of trial by jury and the birth of the no-jury 'Diplock courts' has been one of the most important 'reforms' in Northern Ireland since 1969 and Chapter 3 questions the original rationale for abolishing such a 'bulwark of the constitution'. The emergence of the supergrass system in the early 1980s is one of the most important developments in the Diplock courts and Chapter 4 assesses its contribution to justice in Northern Ireland. The use of lead and plastic bullets by the security forces is examined, with particular reference to the growth of the shoot to kill policy, in Chapters 5 and 6. The final chapter examines the social and political implications of the use of emergency law.

Each author asks whether particular policies represent a systematic abuse of civil liberties. Can an 'emergency' such as the situation in Northern Ireland ever justify such inroads into personal freedom? Are reforms feasible? Whilst each author has a deep concern for the many abuses of civil liberties that have occurred in Northern Ireland, each chapter represents the views of the individual author.

None of the contributors to this book would suggest that the removal of the emergency legal system and its counterpart, counterinsurgency policies, would automatically bring peace and justice to Northern Ireland. The law is, of course, but a reflection of the political and economic forces controlling the particular state and this is nowhere more true than in Northern Ireland. Nevertheless, it is equally naïve to greet abuses of personal freedom simply with cant calls for the abolition of an illegal state. The acceptance of a need for a political solution to the problems of Northern Ireland does not preclude demands for the removal of the abuses that represent an insult to the very concept of the rule of law.

Anthony Jennings
August 1987
Middle Temple, London

TOM HADDEN, KEVIN BOYLE
and COLM CAMPBELL

Emergency Law in Northern Ireland: The Context

The list of abuses arising out of the current emergency in Northern Ireland is well known. There have been repeated allegations of unlawful killings by the security forces, of torture during interrogation, of widespread and random arrests, of 'assembly line' justice and show trials, of mass detention without trial and of systematic ill-treatment of prisoners. Some of these practices, such as internment, the use of special courts and the use of 'supergrass' evidence, have been deliberately adopted by the authorities and justified as a reasonable response to the emergency. Others have been denied or attributed to culpable, though understandable, failures by individual soldiers and policemen. But almost all have been criticised or condemned by a series of governmental and unofficial international inquiries.

How far are these criticisms and condemnations justified? Has there been a systematic disregard of basic human rights by the security forces and the courts in Northern Ireland or merely the occasional violation of accepted rules by individuals acting under stress, as happens in every jurisdiction? How frequent and how serious have the violations of human rights and the miscarriages of justice been in Northern Ireland in comparison with those in similar jurisdictions? How many, if any, of the practices that have been deliberately introduced have been justified by the exigencies of the emergency? And how might the situation be improved?

This book is an attempt to answer these questions in respect of a series of abuses which are allegedly still continuing in Northern Ireland. None of these practices, however, have arisen in isolation. To understand what has been happening, we must examine the development of the emergency and the policies which have been adopted by the authorities. Then, if a fair judgement is to be made, some general standards must be established for assessing the seriousness and frequency of any abuses and the legality of any systematic departure from normal standards in policing and the administration of justice.

The Immediate Context

The underlying cause of the continuing emergency in Northern Ireland is the unresolved dispute over its legitimacy and government.[1] Northern Ireland was created in 1921 by a pragmatic British decision to partition Ireland in response to the fact that while in the whole of Ireland a substantial majority of the population clearly wanted independence, in the six north-eastern counties an equally substantial majority wanted to remain British. For the next 50 years, Northern Ireland was governed by the Unionist Party in the exclusive interest of the majority community. From time to time there was a resumption of military activity by the Irish Republican Army, whose members in both parts of Ireland claimed to be pursuing the legitimate goal of expelling the British from any part of Ireland. But these campaigns and the repeated assertions by politicians in the Republic of jurisdiction over Northern Ireland regardless of the wishes of the majority of its inhabitants merely served to reinforce the determination of the Unionists to maintain their separate status and their domination over the minority Nationalist community. Since partition little has changed in these basic allegiances. Within Northern Ireland there are currently almost one million Protestants, almost all of whom want to remain British and are passionately opposed to the reunification of Ireland, and more than half a million Catholics, most of whom aspire to eventual reunification.

The current emergency commenced in 1969 when a civil rights campaign on behalf of the Catholic minority, which had experienced systematic discrimination and exclusion from power within Northern Ireland, degenerated into sectarian strife. Since then there has been a continuing series of alleged and proven abuses by the police and the British army and in the administration of justice. Most of these may be directly related to a corresponding series of distinctive periods in security policy, as illustrated in Table 1.1.

From Civil Rights to Sectarian Strife: 1969–71

In the initial period of civil rights agitation and counter-demonstrations by Loyalists, the control of public order was the exclusive responsibility of the largely Protestant Royal Ulster Constabulary and its part-time auxiliary force, the B Specials. Under the Public Order Act (Northern Ireland) 1951 and the effectively permanent Civil Authorities (Special Powers) Act (Northern Ireland) 1922–33 very broad powers to control demonstrations, to search, arrest and question and ultimately to intern without trial were available to these forces and to the Minister of Home

Affairs.[2] These powers were used in a sectarian manner, notably to ban civil rights marches and to intern leading Republicans in 1969. There were a number of unprovoked incursions into Catholic areas by members of the RUC and the B Specials, as confirmed by the Cameron Report in 1969.[3] Certain units of the B Specials were accused of indiscipline, and, although its actions were later justified by the Scarman Report, the RUC was found to have indiscriminately used firearms during the serious sectarian riots of August 1969.[4]

Following the deployment of British troops in August 1969 and the publication of the Hunt Report[5] in October of that year, the British government disbanded the B Specials. They were replaced by a new local auxiliary force, the Ulster Defence Regiment (UDR), which operated under the direct control of the British army. To prevent future 'indiscipline', the RUC was trained in the latest British techniques of riot control. At the same time, the government established an explicitly independent Director of Public Prosecutions to ensure the impartial administration of justice.[6] Despite these reforms, however, no prosecutions were initiated against those responsible for the incursions into Catholic areas and for the indiscriminate shootings, partly as a result of what a senior investigating officer from Britain called 'a conspiracy of silence' within the police and partly as a result of the very lengthy proceedings of the Scarman Tribunal.

The Period of Shared Control – From Sectarian Strife to Guerrilla Warfare: 1969-72

During the period from the deployment of the British army in 1969 until the imposition of direct rule in March 1972, control of security policies was shared by the RUC, which was subject to the Unionist government, and the army, subject to the British government. This system of dual control led to increasing strains and tensions between the two security forces, between their corresponding governments, and, not least, between the security forces and the Catholic community.

To begin with, the relationship between the army and the Catholic community began to deteriorate. There were increasing complaints of indiscriminate searching and general harassment in areas where the army was in effective control, notably during and after what became known as the Falls curfew in July 1970. This contributed to the re-emergence of the IRA as the defenders of the Catholic enclaves both from the Loyalists and from the army. Then, the shooting dead of two youths, Beattie and Cusack, during a riot in Derry in July 1971 and the subsequent refusal of the authorities to appoint a public inquiry led to the withdrawal of the newly-formed Social Democratic and Labour Party (SDLP) from the Stormont Parliament.

Table 1.1 An Overview of Security Policies, 1968–83

Dates	Period	Official policy	Legal basis	Actual operation	Abuses	Action taken
1968–9	Civil rights demonstrations	Policing by RUC and B Specials	Special Powers Act; Public Order Acts	Sectarian approach to marches and demonstrations	Attacks on Catholic areas	Cameron Report (1969); Scarman Inquiry (1969–72)
1969–71	From riots to terrorism	Joint control by army and RUC; B Specials replaced by UDR	No change	Main army presence in Catholic areas	Increasing harassment; Falls curfew; Beattie/Cusack deaths	Hunt Report (1969); MacDermott Report (1971)
1971–2	Initial internment operation	Elimination of IRA by arrest and internment of all leaders and activists	No change; review body appointed to hear appeals	Selection by RUC Special Branch, implementation by army; no-go areas established	Indiscriminate arrest and internment of Republicans; five techniques and general ill-treatment; Bloody Sunday	Compton Report (1971); Parker Report (1972); Widgery Inquiry (1972); eventual decision to take control by direct rule; Diplock Report (1972)
1972–5	Internment and Diplock courts	Putting all terrorists behind bars, where possible by trial, if not by internment	Detention Order 1972; Emergency Provisions Act 1973 and 1975; Prevention of Terrorism Act	Catholic areas policed by army; RUC limited to Protestant areas; grant of special category status	Mass screenings and harassment in Catholic areas	Gardiner Report (1975) recommends ending of internment

Table 1.1 An Overview of Security Policies, 1968–83 (continued)

Dates	Period	Official policy	Legal basis	Actual operation	Abuses	Action taken
1976–80	Criminalisation and Ulsterisation	Trial of all terrorists as criminals in Diplock courts; phasing out of special category status; increasing control by RUC; undercover operations by army and SAS	Prevention of Terrorism Act 1976; Emergency Provisions Act 1978	Interrogation centres in Castlereagh and Armagh; widespread arrests of both Republican and Loyalist suspects for interrogation and intelligence gathering	Beatings during interrogation; disputed army shootings	Shackleton Review (1978); Amnesty Report (1978); Bennett Report (1979); new code for interrogation
1980–1	Hunger strikes	Front line riot control by RUC; no concessions to political prisoners	No change	Huge increase in use of plastic bullet	Disputed plastic bullet deaths	None
1981–5	Supergrasses and 'shoot to kill'	Use of 'converted terrorists' to secure arrest of leadership; transfer of undercover operations to RUC	No change	Use of arrest and interrogation in search for informers	Bribery of suspects; disputed RUC/UDR shootings	Jellicoe Review (1983); Baker Review (1984). Stalker/Sampson inquiry (1985–88)

The most disastrous result of the practice of dual control was the mass internment operation of August 1971. The RUC Special Branch prepared the lists of those to be detained, but the actual arrests were carried out by the army. There were immediate and widespread complaints about the discriminatory use of internment against Republicans, about the failure to distinguish between involvement in political campaigns and involvement in violent activity, and about the systematic ill-treatment of suspects during the initial arrest operation. Of particular concern was the use of the so-called 'five techniques'—wall-standing, hooding, continuous noise, deprivation of food and deprivation of sleep—which were used on some suspects during prolonged interrogations, and which appeared to have been planned by the army on the basis of previous operations in Aden and elsewhere.[7]

The Compton Committee report concluded that the five techniques and other practices constituted ill-treatment but not torture.[8] The ensuing Parker Committee concluded that they were unlawful, though a majority of its members recommended that they be formally legitimised.[9] This recommendation was rejected by the British government in March 1972 when it was announced that the five techniques were to be abandoned.[10] At subsequent proceedings before the European Commission on Human Rights, however, it was held that the techniques did constitute torture, and that inhuman and degrading treatment had been used during other interrogations by the police in the autumn of 1971.[11]

The period culminated in the 'Bloody Sunday' episode of January 1972, when 13 civilians were shot dead by soldiers of the Parachute Regiment in Derry following the break-up of a civil rights march. The Widgery Committee inquiry concluded that most of the victims were innocent and that at least in some cases the shootings were reckless, thus indicating that there was a *prima facie* case of murder or manslaughter.[12] Despite these clear findings that many of the practices adopted by the police and the army at this time were unlawful no prosecutions were initiated, although compensation was paid to a substantial number of those affected. (No figures are available for compensation paid by the Northern Ireland Office and the Ministry of Defence in court settlement of claims arising from death or injury involving the security forces. £110 million has been paid since 1972 under the Criminal Injuries Compensation Scheme (New Ireland Forum, *The Cost of Violence arising from the Northern Ireland Crisis since 1969*, Dublin 1984).)

The Period of Army Supremacy – The Diplock Strategy: 1972-5

The fact that the security forces had clearly failed to stem the rising tide of IRA terrorism was of more pressing concern to the British government than the dubious legality of their methods. The international repercussions of the Bloody Sunday killings and the realisation that the Unionist regime could only be sustained by even greater repression eventually led to the imposition of direct rule from London. The British government initially required only the transfer of responsibility for all aspects of security and the administration of justice. But when this limitation of its constitutional authority was rejected by the Unionists, the British government was fully prepared to suspend the powers of the Stormont Parliament and to take over the government of Northern Ireland. It immediately appointed a committee chaired by Lord Diplock to review all aspects of security law and policy. After a brief investigation in which the views of the British army were apparently accepted without question, the committee recommended not only the continuation of internment without trial but also the establishment of a new system of special courts in which convictions could more readily be obtained.[13]

This dual strategy was based on two simple but apparently conflicting propositions: first, that a system of administrative detention was essential if known terrorists were to be put behind bars, since witnesses and jurors were being intimidated and judges in Northern Ireland had been refusing to admit confessions obtained during prolonged and psychologically oppressive interrogation of the kind developed by the army; and second, that it was nonetheless desirable to deal with as many cases as possible through a judicial system, even if some of the ordinary rules of criminal procedure had to be suspended, since judicial convictions were more generally acceptable than detention without trial. A new package of powers of arrest and interrogation was accordingly recommended to enable the army to arrest and establish the identity of possible suspects and to hold those who might have to be interned for up to 72 hours pending a decision on prosecution, internment or release. In addition, the committee recommended the suspension of jury trial for 'terrorist offences' on the grounds that in a number of recent cases largely Protestant juries had brought in perverse acquittals in cases against Loyalist paramilitaries. The committee also recommended that the rules of evidence be altered to allow convictions to be based on confessions obtained by the army's new interrogation techniques. This package was duly enacted in the Northern Ireland (Emergency Provisions) Act 1973.[14]

The new system of internment under effective army control did not solve the problem of terrorism.[15] The number of terrorist incidents and sectarian murders reached a peak in 1972 and 1973. Though large numbers of IRA activists were identified and interned, the techniques of mass screening and regular house searches by which army intelligence was obtained so alienated the Catholic community in the areas of intensive army activity that a continuing flow of new recruits was ensured. The fact that the principal impact of these military security techniques was in Catholic areas, while the RUC continued to operate the 'reformed' criminal justice system in most Protestant areas exacerbated the feeling of discrimination and alienation among most Nationalists. There was also considerable opposition, within the legal profession and generally, to the attempt to make the system of internment more acceptable by the introduction of supposedly 'judicial' review tribunals which in reality rubber-stamped the decisions of the security authorities.

The Gardiner Committee, appointed by the incoming Labour government in 1974, eventually concluded that internment could not be maintained as a long-term policy and that all terrorist suspects should be dealt with as ordinary criminals in the Diplock courts rather than as politically motivated offenders in a non-judicial system of detention. It also recommended that the 'special category' status, equivalent to that of prisoners of war, which had been granted both to internees and to those convicted in Diplock courts, should be phased out.[16] The implementation of these recommendations was delayed by the extension of the IRA campaign in Britain, notably in a series of pub bombings in Birmingham and elsewhere, and by the introduction of the Prevention of Terrorism (Temporary Provisions) Act 1974 throughout the United Kingdom. But the new Gardiner strategy of 'criminalisation' and its implications for the relative positions of the police and the army were accepted, despite some opposition from the army.[17] The last internees were released at the end of 1975.

The Beginnings of Police Primacy – Criminalisation and Ulsterisation: 1976–81

The new strategy of police primacy was implemented gradually. The most immediate consequence of the abandonment of internment was that suspected terrorists could be dealt with only by obtaining convictions in Diplock courts. Since witnesses and informants could not be expected to give evidence in open court, increasing reliance was placed on obtaining confessions from those suspected of involvement.

Two new interrogation centres were opened in Castlereagh in Belfast and at Gough Barracks in Armagh, where suspects were subjected to persistent and prolonged questioning. The Northern Ireland (Emergency Provisions) Act authorised detention with a view to interrogation for 72 hours. The extended period of detention of up to seven days authorised under the Prevention of Terrorism Act was also used in selected cases to increase the pressure on suspects. Numerous complaints of beatings and ill-treatment in these centres soon emerged, but were initially dismissed as mere propaganda. It was not until 1978, following the report of an Amnesty International inquiry and public statements of concern by some police surgeons, that an official inquiry was ordered. The resulting report of the Bennett Committee on Police Interrogation Procedures in Northern Ireland, though not permitted to deal with individual complaints, found that there was clear evidence that injuries which could not have been self-inflicted had been sustained by those under interrogation and recommended the introduction of strict internal controls on interrogation procedures.[18]

The introduction of these administrative controls during 1979 and an increased commitment to their enforcement on the part of senior officers led to a dramatic decline in the number and seriousness of complaints. A few prosecutions of police interrogators were initiated but none were successful. A number of confessions obtained by physical violence were also rejected as inadmissible in Diplock trials. But, for the most part, the confessions obtained by prolonged interrogation continued to be accepted as the sole or primary basis for convictions.

By 1978 another aspect of the criminalisation policy was beginning to create serious problems. Most of the IRA members convicted in Diplock courts after 1976 refused to accept the status of ordinary criminals in prison, notably by refusing to work or to wear prison clothes.[19] When they were denied their own clothes, they went 'on the blanket'. When the authorities responded by refusing to allow them to take their daily exercise and by denying them other facilities, the prisoners retaliated by smearing their cells with excrement in the so-called 'dirty protest'. Finally, they resorted to the traditional and ultimate method of Irish protest, the hunger strike. Ten of the protesters died during 1981.

The stubborn refusal of the British government to make any concessions to the demands by the prisoners for some recognition of their political motivation, despite repeated pleas from Catholic Church leaders and other intermediaries, caused great resentment among a large section of the Catholic community in Northern Ireland. One of the hunger strikers, Bobby Sands, was elected to the Westminster Parliament in a by-election in Fermanagh and South Tyrone in April 1981 and two others were elected to the Dail in the Republic in June 1981. There was also a major resurgence in the level of street protest, rioting and terrorist activity, and in the use of plastic bullets by the RUC and army.[20] Though the European Commission on Human Rights rejected the case taken on behalf of some of the prisoners, it was openly critical of the inflexible approach taken by the authorities.[21] The hunger strike was eventually abandoned. But some of the demands of the protesters, notably the right to wear civilian clothes and a measure of segregation, were conceded. The political, economic and social costs of attempting to treat the IRA and other paramilitaries as if they were ordinary criminals and of ignoring their obvious political motivation turned out to be considerably greater, notably in the resurgence of Provisional Sinn Fein as a major political force in Northern Ireland, than the supposed advantage of criminalisation as a means of deterring actual or potential terrorists.

The second element in the strategy of police primacy was a gradual reduction in army numbers and an increased reliance on the RUC as the frontline force, both in respect of public disorder and of terrorist activity. Greater use was also made of the locally recruited UDR. The total number of British soldiers in Northern Ireland declined from a peak of more than 16,000 (for a brief period more than 23,000) in 1973 to fewer than 10,000 by 1981. The numbers in the RUC and RUC Reserve rose from some 7,000 in 1973 to some 12,000 in 1981, while those in the UDR remained roughly constant, though with a much higher proportion of full-time members.[22]

This shift in responsibilities was accompanied by an increased emphasis by the army on undercover surveillance and preventive action. For a brief period in 1977 and 1978 it appeared to be pursuing a policy of shooting terrorist suspects dead in planned ambushes. Ten people, of whom three turned out to be innocent civilians, were shot dead by undercover army patrols.[23] After widespread protests this 'alternative' to reliance on the Diplock courts, in so far as it was a deliberate policy, appears to have been at least temporarily abandoned. The progressive reduction in the role and in the effective power of the army nonetheless contributed substantially to the restoration of a kind of normality.

The Supergrass System and Shooting to Kill: 1982-8

The most recent phase in security policy has been dominated by the use of 'supergrass' evidence and by renewed allegations of a shoot to kill policy by the RUC.

The decision to rely on evidence from first hand informers, or 'converted terrorists', as a means not only of identifying but also of securing convictions against others was almost certainly related to the perceived difficulty in obtaining confessions following the implementation of the Bennett recommendations. The search for knowledgeable members of the main terrorist groups—the IRA, INLA and UVF—who would be prepared to give evidence against their colleagues in exchange for an indemnity and a 'new life' seems to have begun as early as 1981.[24] By 1982 more than 20 potential supergrasses had been recruited and a series of mass trials of those identified by them began in 1983, as described in Chapter 4. As with previous strategies, however, the unrestrained reliance on this new weapon and the lack of concern by the authorities with safeguards against real or perceived abuses raised increasing doubts in large sections of both communities as to the legitimacy of the supergrass system. Many of those charged or convicted on supergrass evidence were eventually released, often after very lengthy periods in custody, either because of the withdrawal of the supergrass's evidence, or because of its rejection by the trial judge or on appeal.

Linked to the general policy of police primacy and army withdrawal was the re-emergence of an apparent shoot to kill strategy. A specially trained RUC undercover squad, similar to those developed by the army in the late 1970s, was established in 1982 and soon became involved in a series of incidents in which suspected terrorists were shot dead in disputed circumstances, as described in Chapter 5.[25] After widespread public disquiet a number of prosecutions were initiated. Though none resulted in a conviction, sufficient evidence was found of pre-planning and of a deliberate attempt to suppress relevant evidence on the part of senior RUC officers to require the appointment of a further investigation, known as the Stalker-Sampson Inquiry. Despite the Inquiry's recommendations, the Attorney General refused to institute any prosecutions.

After sustained pressure from many quarters, the government agreed to undertake a general review of the Northern Ireland (Emergency Provisions) Act. The Baker Report, published in 1984, recommended some minor changes in the law. Notable amongst its suggestions were: the introduction of a reasonable suspicion for certain arrest and search powers; the 'alteration' of the test for the admission of confessions; and the repeal of the most general power to arrest for interrogation (though the wider power under the Prevention of Terrorism (Temporary Provisions) Act 1984 remained available).[26]

These minor reforms were eventually enacted in the Northern Ireland (Emergency Provisions) Act 1987. In addition, a small increase in the number of cases which could be tried by jury was permitted. But no change was made in the underlying structure of emergency powers in Northern Ireland. In essence, they remain as they were under the initial Northern Ireland (Emergency Provisions) Act 1973 and the earlier Special Powers Acts.

Defeating or Sustaining Terrorism?
This brief survey indicates that the pattern of abuses in Northern Ireland is far from fortuitous, and can be directly related to successive phases in security policy. It does not necessarily follow that all or any of the

abuses were deliberately planned. Any or all of them may have arisen from a lack of control by senior officers over soldiers and policemen acting under considerable stress, both in terms of their personal safety and of pressure to produce results. An assessment of the level of responsibility for each particular abuse can only be made after an exhaustive review of the evidence, much of which is, in most cases, unobtainable. Here we can make only a tentative general assessment of the development of security policies.

The most significant feature of the successive phases and failures in security policy is perhaps the apparent belief among many senior commanders that if only the right security policy could be identified and carried out without external interference, terrorists on both sides could be defeated.[27] As each policy has been marred and eventually frustrated by the gradual revelation of the abuses, the authorities have been persuaded that some new policy — internment, interrogation in depth, the use of supergrasses, or even shooting to kill — would do the trick. Yet the new policies have accordingly been implemented with little or no concern to foresee and control possible abuses, with the invariable result of their accompaniment by a new set of abuses. This has in turn confirmed the deeply-felt view among those from whom the terrorists are recruited and supported that the security forces are incapable of acting fairly and that the administration of justice is inherently corrupt. It should be noted that this feeling extends both to the British army and to the locally recruited RUC and UDR, both of which are almost exclusively Protestant, though under the policy of Ulsterisation the focus of complaint has recently shifted away from the British army and onto the RUC and UDR.

This basic problem has been ignored by the many official reviews of security policy in Northern Ireland. The Diplock Committee, the Gardiner Commission and, most recently, the Baker Review have reiterated their belief in the essential soundness of the legal structures in dealing with terrorism and have emphasised the high degree of confidence in the Northern Ireland judiciary allegedly held by all sections of the community. As a result of this fundamental misconception, the reviews failed to recommend the kind of measures to control potential and actual abuse that were and remain necessary to alter the perceptions of the minority community and to build the kind of cross-communal confidence which the committees have posited. As a result, they too have played a part in sustaining one of the most important psychological weapons of those Nationalists committed to achieving their political objectives by violent means. Only in the aftermath of the report of the New Ireland Forum in 1984 and the Anglo-Irish Agreement in 1985 have the authorities begun to take more seriously the need to face up to these problems, though that in itself will not make their resolution any easier.

The Historical Dimension

None of this is in any way new in the context of British rule in Ireland. Most of the problems and most of the military and legal responses that have been described have a long if undistinguished history. The current emergency legislation, in particular, may be traced back to earlier legal precedents.[28]

Non-jury Courts

The difficulty of dealing with politically motivated violence in ordinary courts has plagued successive governments for centuries. In the eighteenth and early nineteenth centuries, the reluctance of local magistrates and juries to enter convictions in such cases led to the periodic suspension of jury trial. Eventually, under the Criminal Law and Procedure (Ireland) Act 1887, permanent special provisions in relation to jury trial were introduced. Under this legislation any area could be 'proclaimed' and relevant cases could then either be transferred to other parts of the country or else be tried before a special jury whose members were subject to a higher rateable value qualification. Many areas in the south and west of Ireland were so proclaimed in 1918 and 1919.

Similar government fears about the reliability of juries in the Irish Free State led to the enactment of the Public Safety Act 1927 which authorised the creation of a non-jury military Special Court, though in fact no such court was established. Then, under the Juries Protection Act 1929, special provisions were made for the protection of jurors. This did not resolve the problem, and so, during much of the 1930s, politically motivated offenders in Ireland were tried not by judge and jury but, in accordance with the constitutional amendment introduced by the Constitution (Amendment No. 17) Act 1931, by the Constitution (Special Powers) Tribunal composed of army officers. Two years after this tribunal was abolished, permanent provisions were introduced in the Offences against the State Act 1939 authorising the establishment of a non-jury Special Criminal Court composed either of army officers or of civilian lawyers appointed by the government. This court, with a bench composed exclusively of army officers, functioned in the years 1939–46 and 1961–2. In addition, a separate jury-less military court was established under the wartime Emergency Powers Acts and the Orders made under them and operated in the years 1940–3.

In 1972 the Special Criminal Court, now composed entirely of judges or retired judges, was re-established. It has been sitting in permanent session since then. The justification that has been advanced for its continued operation, as in the case of the Diplock courts in Northern Ireland, is a combination of the alleged risk of intimidation of jurors and the fear that the ambiguous attitude among ordinary members of the public towards politically motivated violence will result in unjustified acquittals.

In Northern Ireland similar concerns about the reliability of juries led to the enactment of the short-lived Criminal Procedure Act (Northern Ireland) 1922, which made similar provision for a special non-jury court. At the same time, the Civil Authorities (Special Powers) Acts (Northern Ireland) 1922–33 created special courts of summary jurisdiction to try those accused of offences against the regulations made under the Act. Their procedures were derived from the provisions of the Restoration of Order in Ireland Act 1920 and the regulations made under it, though the sentencing power of the Northern Ireland summary courts was considerably greater than that of the equivalent courts established under the earlier Act. Despite the precedents, however, it was not until the introduction of the Diplock courts in 1973 that non-jury trial on indictment became a standard procedure in Northern Ireland.

Special Powers

Many of the more general provisions of current emergency legislation in Northern Ireland may also be traced back to earlier statutes. The current powers of arrest, search, temporary detention (for interrogation), and internment along with numerous ancillary powers, such as the requisitioning of property and the closing of roads are broadly the same as those originally provided throughout Britain and Ireland under the Defence of the Realm Acts passed at the outbreak and during the course of the First World War and in the regulations made under them. In addition, in Ireland only, a number of more draconian regulations were in force. When, in 1920, these provisions were about to be repealed in Britain, their continued operation and extension in Ireland was provided for in the Restoration of Order in Ireland Act 1920. With the creation of Northern Ireland the following year, they were again reenacted under the Civil Authorities (Special Powers) Act (Northern Ireland) 1922, which was regularly renewed and eventually made permanent in 1933. In the Irish Free State similar powers were provided in the early Public Safety Acts and were subsequently made permanent in the Offences Against the State Act 1939.

These early statutes also contain a power to exclude named persons from specified areas which is similar to those incorporated in the Prevention of Terrorism (Temporary Provisions) Acts. Such powers were provided, and were used, under the Defence of the Realm Acts. Numerous exclusion orders were made in Northern Ireland in the 1920s and 1930s under the Special Powers Acts.[29] In the Irish Free State, deportations were ordered by military courts during the civil war in 1922-3, while the short-lived Public Safety Act 1927 provided for the making of 'expulsion orders' against Irish citizens. In Britain similar powers were incorporated in the Prevention of Violence (Temporary Provisions) Act 1939.

These provisions were deliberately drafted to exclude, in so far as possible, any risk of judicial challenge. For the most part this exclusion proved remarkably effective. Both in pre-partition Ireland and in Northern Ireland the courts have consistently held that their jurisdiction to review emergency powers is extremely limited.[30] In the Irish Free State and subsequently in the Irish Republic under the present constitution, introduced in 1937, the judiciary has on occasions taken a more stringent approach.[31] But in all the jurisdictions under discussion the government and the legislature have regularly responded to any judicial intervention by immediate legislation designed to fill any 'gaps' that have been created by judgments in test cases.[32] The practical effect of what little judicial intervention there has been has thus been minimised.

Martial Law
In some areas of emergency law, earlier and more draconian precedents have not been followed. From 1918 to 1921, and subsequently during the Irish civil war, widespread use was made of various forms of martial law. Under the Defence of the Realm Acts and Regulations, as applied in Ireland, provision was made for the appointment of Competent Military Authorities with power to order the trial by court martial of those accused of offences against the regulations. Under this system of what might be called statutory martial law, the powers of the Competent Military Authority extended to the banning of meetings, the imposition of restrictions on transport, and control over the availability of firearms. The Army Council was also given special powers, in this case the power (subject to the approval of the Secretary of State for War) to designate districts as Special Military Areas, within which additional restrictions could be imposed.

Under the Restoration of Order in Ireland Act, the jurisdiction of these statutory courts martial was extended to most ordinary crimes. But the principal value of this legislation to the authorities was, of course, political. In the latter part of 1920, what appears to have been a deliberate policy of exacting reprisals for the killing of soldiers and policemen was adopted. During the course of these reprisals perhaps 100 people, many of them innocent civilians, were killed and parts of urban areas were razed. In December 1920 a separate proclamation of martial law was made in parts of southern and south-western Ireland under what has variously been claimed to be a common law and a prerogative right.[33] Official reprisals were instigated in these areas and separate martial law regulations promulgated: the death penalty, for example, was imposed for those found carrying arms and a separate network of military courts was put into operation. Numerous IRA suspects were tried and convicted and several were executed under this non-statutory system of martial law. But its relationship with the pre-existing statutory system and with the ordinary courts was never finally clarified; the truce of July 1921 and the Anglo-Irish Treaty of December 1921 intervened to terminate, if not to resolve, the serious constitutional conflict which arose between the two systems in July of that year.[34]

During the Irish civil war a similar non-statutory system of martial law was put into operation. Thousands of suspected activists were interned by the military authorities. Military courts were established and 77 people were executed, with perhaps twice as many killed in unofficial reprisals.[35] Though parliamentary approval was given to some of these measures, there was no statutory authority for them.

Comparisons can readily be drawn between the British system of statutory martial law and the measures adopted in the south of Ireland in the 1930s and 1940s. The powers of the Constitution (Special Powers) Tribunal extended not only, as noted above, to the trial of offences, but also to the closing of premises and the proscribing and seizure of publications. In effect, the measure was, as one writer has described it, 'a new form of martial law'.[36] In the 1940s the Emergency Powers Acts and Orders made under them provided a battery of powers scarcely less sweeping than those incorporated in the Defence of the Realm Acts and Regulations, powers which were extensively used against IRA suspects. Those accused of breaches of the Emergency Powers Orders were frequently tried by the Special Criminal Court. Bearing in mind the composition of the court at that time, this was virtual trial by court martial. The simultaneous functioning of the Special Criminal Court and the Military Court in the years 1940–3 mirrored the parallel operation of courts martial under the Restoration of Order in Ireland Act and non-statutory martial law military courts in 1920–1.

No equivalent system of statutory or non-statutory martial law has ever been put into operation in Northern Ireland, either before or after 1969. However, under the Civil Authorities (Special Powers) Acts (Northern Ireland) 1922–33 and the regulations made under them, many of the powers which had formed the substance of statutory martial law under the Defence of the Realm Acts and the Restoration of Order in Ireland Act 1920 became exercisable by the Minister for Home Affairs. He in turn was authorised to delegate the exercise of these powers to RUC officers and did so in several instances. Thus it was that the framework of a potential police state was created. The dangers inherent in such a system were well illustrated by the markedly partisan application of these measures, particularly in the early years of the state. To take a more recent case, it is arguable that when the army imposed a temporary curfew in the Lower Falls area of Belfast in 1970 it was asserting a common law form of martial law, though the precedent was not followed.[37]

Arguably, also, the right of soldiers to shoot and kill in defence of themselves and others can be asserted as a form of martial law rather than merely the exercise of the statutory right under the Criminal Law Act 1967 to use reasonable force to prevent a crime. But no formal claims of this kind have yet been asserted by or on behalf of the army in Northern Ireland, and no attempt has been made to establish any system of military courts. All the powers exercised by the army have been exercised on the basis of express statutory authority and the jurisdiction of the ordinary courts to rule on the validity of what has been done in particular cases has never been questioned. To this extent the army in Northern Ireland may claim to be acting within the ordinary law. In any event, it is clear that the powers currently granted to the army are very much less far-reaching than those granted to both the British and the Irish armies in the 1920s.

The point of this brief account is not to claim that past precedents in any way justify present legislation. But it does help to place the current emergency in context and focuses attention on a possible standard by which the powers and practices of the security forces might be judged. Any historical comparison, however, is bound to be somewhat unsatisfactory; generally acceptable standards have changed since the 1920s. A more relevant comparison is that between current practices in Northern Ireland and today's internationally accepted standards.

The International Legal Context

The natural reaction of governments throughout the world when faced with disorders and insurrection is to introduce a battery of emergency powers. Wherever they are felt, pressures similar to those in Northern Ireland regularly produce allegations and denials of abuses. Internal disorder, guerrilla warfare, and protests against security forces can be found in recent emergencies throughout the world, from colonial conflicts such as those in Kenya, Aden and Algeria and racial conflicts such as those in Rhodesia/Zimbabwe and South Africa, to political conflicts between right and left such as those in Turkey, Chile and other Latin American states, and outbreaks of political terrorism such as those in West Germany and Italy. How does the situation in Northern Ireland compare with these and other emergencies?

Factual Comparisons

An attempt to make international comparisons of this kind raises obvious factual problems. It is difficult enough to assess the frequency and seriousness of alleged abuses even within Northern Ireland, let alone in other countries. Because allegations of improper practices and unlawful conduct play an important part in 'propaganda warfare' statistics on abuses are often unreliable, inflated by the opposition, and minimised by the government in power.

Equally difficult is determining the basis of any comparison. How is one to compare the incidence of allegedly unlawful killings by the security forces in Northern Ireland, for example, with 'disappearances' of the kind widely reported in Latin America, notably in Argentina and Chile? In this respect, it might be argued, the alleged incidents in Northern Ireland are less serious; almost without exception, they have involved disputes about the legitimacy of shooting to kill during riots and confrontations with suspected terrorists rather than the deliberate abductions and killings involved in a typical 'disappearance'. On the other hand, such disputed killings have been relatively frequent in Northern Ireland: there have been more than 100 seriously disputed killings out of a total population of only one and a half million, compared with a reported figure for Argentina of some 6,000 'disappearances' out of a total population of 24 million.[38] As for the allegations of the injustice of the Diplock courts, it could be said that these are minor on the international scale, in that the complaints have centred on the acceptability of the evidence and procedures employed rather than on the number of false convictions. Within Western democracies, however, the charge of injustice is more grave, not least because it is levelled at a part of the UK, a country which prides itself on maintaining the highest standards of justice.

Legal Comparisons

In the face of these difficulties, most commentators and human rights agencies have preferred to measure the conduct of the security forces and the courts in particular countries against an absolute legal standard. But even this approach raises contentious legal issues. What is the proper standard against which the performance of the security forces and the courts in Northern Ireland – and perhaps also of those involved in terrorist activity – should be judged? Is it that of the ordinary common law as developed to deal with essentially peaceful conditions in Britain? Is it some lesser standard applicable to states of emergency? Or is it the law of war, as is occasionally claimed on behalf both of the security forces and of their paramilitary opponents? The answer to those questions depends in turn on how the conflict in Northern Ireland is categorised. Are the activities of the IRA, the INLA and their Loyalist counterparts to be treated as ordinary crimes, as politically motivated crimes, or as the legitimate actions of 'freedom fighters'?

These questions have been addressed by international lawyers through cases brought under the Geneva Conventions of 1949 and the Additional Protocols of 1977, and the European Convention on Human Rights. What the Conventions offer is a definition of various levels of international and internal conflicts and a standard of treatment for those involved in the conflicts. Here as elsewhere, however, the standards for Northern Ireland have proven elusive.

The Geneva Conventions
The purpose of the initial Geneva Conventions of 1949 was to prescribe minimum standards for the treatment of combatants and non-combatants in international warfare.[39] Combatant status may be claimed by those engaged in an international conflict only if an identifiable uniform is worn and an identifying mark carried. Combatants who are captured are entitled to prisoner of war status, which gives them protection from ill-treatment and punishment during detention and a right to release on the cessation of hostilities. On the other hand, under the Convention, combatants may be shot without warning while on active service. Non-combatants, including those convicted as rebels, are entitled to be treated humanely and without discrimination and must not be subjected to outrages on their personal dignity or to inhuman or degrading treatment.

These rules are drawn up with traditional methods of international warfare in mind. They do not deal satisfactorily with guerrilla warfare or non-international conflicts, particularly those arising out of claims for self-determination by those dominated by a foreign or colonial power. In 1977 two additional Protocols were eventually agreed to extend the right of combatant status to guerrillas or freedom fighters in both international and non-international conflicts. Protocol I applies not only to international conflicts but to those in which 'peoples are fighting against colonial domination and alien occupation and against racist regimes in exercise of their right to self-determination'. Combatants for this purpose need only produce their weapons immediately before going into action, carry their arms openly during each engagement and submit to effective military discipline.

Protocol II applies to non-international armed conflicts, but expressly excludes 'situations of internal disturbances and tensions, such as riots, isolated and sporadic acts of violence and other acts of a similar nature'.

Those who wish to claim combatant status must show that they belong to a 'dissident armed force or other organised armed group which under responsible command exercises such control over part of a territory as to enable it to carry out sustained and concerted military operations'. Under this Protocol those who have ceased to take part in hostilities are entitled to certain fundamental guarantees, including the right not to be subjected to violence, cruel treatment, collective punishment, acts of terrorism, outrages upon personal dignity, or threats of the same. The Protocol stipulates that 'those who are deprived of their liberty for reasons related to the armed conflict, whether they are interned or detained' are entitled to minimum standards of treatment; those who are prosecuted for criminal offences related to the conflict are entitled to certain basic procedural safeguards.

It is not certain that any of these provisions can properly be applied to the conflict in Northern Ireland. Clearly, the conflict does not fall into the category of traditional international war as defined by the original Conventions. The IRA and INLA would presumably claim to qualify as combatants under Protocol I on the ground that they are engaged in a struggle against colonial domination and alien occupation. But in order to make good this claim, it would also be necessary to show that Northern Ireland is not a legitimate political unit, a task which would be difficult since the people of Northern Ireland have never been denied the right of self-determination and have consistently exercised it in support of continued union with Britain.

Alternatively, the IRA and INLA might seek to qualify under Protocol II. They would find it difficult, however, to persuade an impartial tribunal that they meet the requirements of responsible command and territorial control, though this might have been possible for a time during 1972 and 1973 when 'no go' areas were established in Belfast and Derry. Even if they satisfied these criteria, however, they would not thereby under Protocol II be entitled to claim prisoner of war status for those convicted in the Diplock courts, since prosecution and conviction of those engaged in a relevant internal conflict are clearly permitted under the Protocol and since the procedures in those courts do not infringe the basic standards of the Protocol. It should be noted that in considering the claim of IRA prisoners engaged in the dirty protest to be exempt from ordinary prison rules the European Commission on Human Rights explicitly held that a right to special treatment could not be derived from the existing norms of international law.[40]

The European Convention and States of Emergency
The European Convention on Human Rights takes a rather different approach. It does not seek to provide any specific rights for those

involved in internal rebellion or insurgency. On the contrary, it permits member states to derogate from some of the rights and freedoms protected under the Convention if there is a public emergency which threatens the life of the nation. Since Britain became one of the founding signatories of the European Convention on Human Rights, the conflict in Northern Ireland has been almost continuously on the agenda of the Commission and the Court at Strasbourg. Among the first derogations from the Convention was a notice from the United Kingdom in respect of Northern Ireland. The derogation first notified in 1957 was withdrawn in 1984. Northern Ireland has thus been formally treated as the site of a public emergency and, over the effective life of the Convention, excluded from one or other of the Convention's major protections due to a 'public emergency affecting the life of the nation'.[41]

The jurisprudence of the Commission and Court of Human Rights has established the following characteristics of an emergency where article 15 of the Convention is invoked: (i) the emergency must be actual or imminent; (ii) its effects must involve the whole nation; (iii) the continuance of the organised life of the community must be threatened; and (iv) the crisis or danger must be exceptional in that the normal measures or restrictions, permitted by the Convention for the maintenance of public safety, health, and order, are plainly inadequate.[42]

It does not follow, however, that the proclamation of a public emergency either absolves governments from their obligations under the Convention or removes the element of international supervision. It is clear from the jurisprudence of the Convention that the Commission and Court consider themselves empowered to review the entitlement of a state to derogate from protected rights in the first place and to determine, given that derogation is justifiable, whether the state has taken such measures only 'to the extent strictly required by the exigencies of the situation'. The emergency in Northern Ireland therefore has not prevented important proceedings under the Convention.[43]

Under article 15 of the Convention a state's powers in an emergency are also limited through the concept of non-derogable rights. Thus, article 3 (prohibition on torture), article 4 (forced labour), article 7 (retroactive penal law), article 41 (discrimination), and article 2 (the right to life except 'in respect of deaths resulting from lawful acts of war') may not be derogated from in any circumstances. Basic individual rights are thereby expected to be respected by Convention signatories, no matter how compelling their national security considerations may be.

The Commission and the Court have been asked to rule on the legitimacy of particular measures and practices in Northern Ireland on a number of occasions since 1969. Certain interrogation practices were judged to infringe the absolutely protected right not to be subjected to torture or cruel or inhuman treatment.[44] It was also decided, however, that conditions in the early 1970s did constitute an emergency. Moreover, it was decided that the government was justified in introducing internment without trial, that the refusal to grant special category status to IRA prisoners convicted in the Diplock courts and the treatment of those who as a result engaged in the 'dirty protest' was not a breach of the Convention, and that likewise the use of plastic bullets did not in itself constitute a breach.[45]

The possibility that the Commission and the Court would rule again on Northern Ireland was raised in 1984, when the United Kingdom withdrew all its derogations under the Convention on the (disputable) ground that none of the current provisions of the Northern Ireland (Emergency Provisions) Act and related legislation infringe the Convention.[46] However, even if it were held that some of the provisions did infringe the normal protections of the Convention, it remains open to the government to enter a new derogation under article 15. This would clearly be required, for example, if detention without trial were reintroduced. But the European Commission and Court would then ultimately have to rule, should proceedings be brought, on whether the derogation was justified by reference to the current circumstances in Northern Ireland. While it is open to the Commission and Court to take a different view on whether conditions still constitute an emergency, it is unlikely that they would do so.

Parallel with its commitments under the European Convention on Human Rights, the British government is a party to the United Nations Covenant on Civil and Political Rights. On ratifying this Covenant in 1976, the British government entered a derogation in respect of the Northern Ireland situation. This derogation was also withdrawn in 1984. As a result, it is worth noting, Northern Ireland is no longer officially designated under the international instruments as a territory where 'a public emergency threatening the life of the nation' exists.

The Political Dimension

Considerable room for argument exists on the standards by which the current emergency provisions in Northern Ireland should be judged. Under international law, states are not always required to observe the same standards in dealing with terrorism and other forms of political violence which may properly be held to justify the declaration of an emergency as they are required to observe in normal circumstances. While Britain's maintenance of a full range of emergency powers might be justified in international law, it may be, practically speaking, unwise.

Whatever the formal legal position, the political impact of maintaining any particular form of emergency law must be taken into account.

In revolutionary conflicts, as in wars, winning is unfortunately almost always more important to governments than adhering to the laws of insurrection or warfare. The problem in Northern Ireland, however, is that the authorities are seeking to secure the consent of a substantial minority to a particular constitutional regime. In such cases the advantage is more likely to lie with a strategy of adhering as closely as possible to ordinary standards of policing and justice while maintaining reasonable security and order and the pursuit of practical political measures, with a view to removing the underlying causes of the political violence.

It would not be appropriate in this book to embark on a discussion of the kind of political measures which might assist in achieving a solution to the Northern Ireland problem. Some of the contributors would favour measures which accept that there are two communities in Northern Ireland with divergent communal identities and aspirations. But there are many ways in which such objectives might be pursued, as may be seen from the somewhat different strategies adopted in the New Ireland Forum Report in 1984 and in the Anglo-Irish Agreement in 1985. For present purposes it is sufficient to emphasise that security measures alone cannot resolve the Northern Ireland problem and that one of the most important standards by which security policies and emergency laws must be judged is the contribution which they make to facilitating the development of a generally acceptable political solution.

Notes

1. For a more detailed account see K. Boyle and T. Hadden, *Ireland: A Positive Proposal* (Penguin, 1985).
2. For a general account see Twining *et al.*, *Emergency Powers: A Fresh Start* (Fabian Society, 1973).
3. *Disturbances in Northern Ireland*, Cmnd. 532 (Belfast: HMSO, 1969).
4. *Violence and Civil Disturbances in Northern Ireland in 1969*, Cmnd. 566 (Belfast: HMSO 1972).
5. *Report of the Advisory Committee on Police in Northern Ireland*, Cmnd. 535 (Belfast: HMSO, 1969).
6. *Report of the Working Party on Public Prosecutions*, Cmnd. 554 (Belfast: HMSO, 1971).
7. Reviewed in the *Report of the European Commission on Human Rights: Ireland v. United Kingdom of Great Britain and Northern Ireland* (Application No. 5310/71) (1976).
8. *Report of the enquiry into allegations against the security forces of physical brutality in Northern Ireland arising out of events on 9 August 1971*, Cmnd. 4823 (HMSO, 1971).
9. *Report of the Committee of Privy Counsellors appointed to consider authorised procedures*

for the interrogation of persons suspected of terrorism, Cmnd. 4901 (HMSO, 1972).

10.   *House of Commons Debates,* vol. 832, col. 743 (2 March 1972).

11.   *Ireland v. United Kingdom of Great Britain and Northern Ireland* (Application No. 5310/71) (1976); in subsequent proceedings before the European Court of Human Rights it was held that the treatment constituted inhuman and degrading treatment rather than torture (judgment delivered 18 January 1978).

12.   *Report of the tribunal appointed to inquire into events on Sunday, 30th January 1972 which led to loss of life in connection with the procession in Londonderry on that day,* HC 220 (HMSO, 1972). See *Ireland v. U.K.,* European Commission on Human Rights Collection of Decisions 41, pp. 12–13, 32–41, 85.

13.   *Report of the commission to consider legal procedures to deal with terrorist activities in Northern Ireland,* Cmnd. 5185 (HMSO, 1972), paras. 58–92.

14.   Subsequently re-enacted with amendments as the Northern Ireland (Emergency Provisions) Act 1978. See Appendices I and II.

15.   For a general account see K. Boyle, T. Hadden and P. Hillyard, *Law and State: the Case of Northern Ireland* (Martin Robertson, 1975).

16.   *Report of a committee to consider, in the context of civil liberties and human rights, measures to deal with terrorism in Northern Ireland,* Cmnd. 5847 (HMSO, 1975).

17.   D. Hamill, *Pig in the Middle* (Methuen, 1985).

18.   Cmnd. 7497 (HMSO, 1979); most of the committee's recommendations were accepted. See *Action to be taken on the recommendations of the committee of inquiry into interrogation procedures in Northern Ireland* (Northern Ireland Office 29 June 1979).

19.   For a detailed account of these events see K. Boyle, T. Hadden, and P. Hillyard, *Ten Years On in Northern Ireland* (Cobden Trust, 1980) Ch. 7.

20.   In 1980 a total of 1,231 plastic bullets were fired. The corresponding figure for the period January to October 1981 was 29,658. Almost 17,000 of these were fired in May 1981, the month in which Bobby Sands died (Hansard, vol. 13, written answers, 19 November 1981, col. 200).

21.   *McFeely v. United Kingdom of Great Britain and Northern Ireland* (Application No. 8317/78 (1980). See D. Beresford, *Ten Men Dead* (Grafton Books, 1987).

22.   K. Boyle *et al., Ten Years On,* p. 25.

23.   Ibid., p. 28.

24.   For a general account see S. Greer, 'Supergrasses and the legal system in Britain and Northern Ireland', *Law Quarterly Review* 198 (1986).

25.   For a detailed account see *Shoot to Kill? International Lawyers Inquiry into the Lethal Use of Firearms by the Security Forces In Northern Ireland* (Mercier Press, 1985).

26.   *Review of the Northern Ireland (Emergency Provisions) Act 1978,* Cmnd. 9222 (HMSO, 1984).

27.   See generally D. Hamill, *Pig in the Middle.*

28.   This section is based on unpublished work by Colm Campbell.

29.   See National Council of Civil Liberties, *A Commission of inquiry appointed to examine the purpose and effects of the Civil Authorities (Special Powers) Acts (Northern Ireland) 1922 and 1933* (1936, reprinted 1972).

30.   See for example, *Liversidge v. Anderson (1942)* Appeal Cases 206; *R. v. Governor of Belfast Prison, ex parte O'Hanlon* (1922) 56 Irish Law Times Reports 170; *McEldowney v. Forde* (1969) 3 Weekly Law Reports 179.

31.   See *R. (O'Brien) v. Military Governor, North Dublin Union* (1924) 1 Irish Reports

32; *Lynch v. Fitzgerald* (1938) Irish Reports 382; *The State (Burke) v. Lennon and Attorney General* (1940) 1 Irish Reports 136.

32.   O'Brien's case (ibid.) led to the enactment of the Public Safety (Emergency Powers) Act 1923 and the Public Safety (Emergency Powers) (No. 2) Act 1923, Burke's case (ibid.) was followed by the Offences Against the State (Amendment) Act 1940 (see *In re Article 26 and the Offences Against the State (Amendment) Bill 1940* (1940) IR 470), and *Hume and Others v. Londonderry Justices* (1972) NI Reports 91 was followed by the Northern Ireland Act 1972. See K. Boyle, 'Human Rights and the Northern Ireland Emergency', in J.A. Andrews (ed) *Human Rights in Criminal Procedure* (Martinus Nijhoff, 1982), pp. 144–65.

33.   For a general discussion of these theories see S. Greer, 'Military Intervention in Civil Disturbances: the legal basis reconsidered', *Public Law* 573 (1983).

34.   *R. v. Allen* (1921) 2 IR 241 and *Egan v. Macready* (1921) 1 IR 265. For a historical account of the effects of these conflicting decisions see C. Townshend, *The British Campaign in Ireland 1919–1921* (Oxford University Press, 1975) pp. 146–7, 194–5.

35.   See R. Fanning, *Independent Ireland* (Helicon Press, 1983) p. 21.

36.   L. Kohn, *The Constitution of the Irish Free State* (Allen & Unwin, 1932) p. 156.

37.   C. Palley, 'The Evolution, Disintegration and Possible Reconstruction of the Northern Ireland Constitution', I *Anglo-American Law Review* (1972) p. 368, fn. 214.

38.   See Amnesty International USA, *'Disappearances' — A Workbook* (1981) p.15.

39.   For a general account see G. Schwarzenberger, *The Law of Armed Conflict*, vol. 1 (London: Stevens, 1968); K. Vasak, *The International Dimensions of Human Rights*, vol. 1 (Paris: UNESCO, 1982) pp.190–212.

40.   Application No. 8317/78 Partial Decision of the Commission on Admissibility (1980) 3 European Human Rights Reports 161.

41.   The texts of the notices of derogation are gathered in *Standing Advisory Committee on Human Rights, The Protection of Human Rights by Law in Northern Ireland*, Cmnd. 7009 (HMSO, 1977).

42.   Lawless Case, *1960 Year Book of the European Convention on Human Rights* 492 (European Commission on Human Rights); *Regina v. Deery* (1977) N.I. 164, 166; see also Buergenthal, 'To Respect and To Ensure: State Obligations and Permissible Derogations', in L. Henkin (ed) *The International Bill of Rights* 72 (1981).

43.   K. Boyle and H. Hannum, 'Ireland in Strasbourg: An Analysis of Northern Irish Proceedings before the European Commission of Human Rights', 7 *Irish Jurist* 392 (1976); K. Boyle, 'Human Rights and Political Resolution in Northern Ireland', 9 *Yale Journal of World Public Order* 165 (1982).

44.   *Ireland v. United Kingdom* (1978) 2 European Human Rights Reports 1.

45.   The finding on internment is contained in *Ireland v. United Kingdom*, above; on special category status in Application No. 8317/78, *McFeely v. United Kingdom* 3 European Human Rights Reports 161; on plastic bullets in Application No. 10044/82, *Stewart v. United Kingdom*.

46.   It is doubtful whether the arrest powers under s.11 of the Northern Ireland (Emergency Provisions) Act 1978 conformed with the requirements of article 5 of the Convention; though the section has been repealed under the Northern Ireland (Emergency Provisions) Act 1987, a challenge to the validity of the equivalent power under s.12 of the Prevention of Terrorism (Temporary

Provisions) Act 1984 has recently been upheld by the European Commission on Human Rights and referred to the European Court of Human Rights, *Brogan and Others v. United Kingdom*, application no. 11209/84.

2

DERMOT P.J. WALSH

Arrest and Interrogation

Arrest in the Criminal Process

The power of arrest without warrant has been vested by the common law in both citizens and the police for hundreds of years. The universal availability of the power, its long history, and the frequency of its use have combined to obscure its significance. For the individual, after all, arrest represents a fundamental invasion of the most basic freedom. Without liberty, we lose the freedoms normally held by citizens in a democratic society. Unquestionably, such deprivation is occasionally necessary in the interests of society as a whole. But left in the wrong hands, the power of arrest can be used as an instrument of arbitrary repression and partisan politics. The question is that of balance — between the desirability of making this power available for the social good, and the need to ensure that it is not abused.

This balance has been best achieved by the common law. It both provides the general power of arrest necessary for public safety, and defines the limitations on the use of that power to safeguard the rights of the individual. Arrests must be made on 'reasonable' grounds, and suspects are entitled to protection while in police custody. Most importantly, the common law arrest power is intended to bring an individual to trial. Intervening police behaviour after the arrest is not meant to influence the outcome of any subsequent trial. The guilt or innocence of a suspect is determined in court; the common law arrest power is simply a means of getting a suspect before the court.

Since the troubles, this balance has been overturned in two ways, both to the profound detriment of individual rights. First, the common law has been misused to give increased powers to the security forces. Secondly, and more crucially, special statutory powers have been enacted which sidestep and override the protections offered to the individual by the common law. In a climate in which conviction of

27

suspected 'terrorists' is the paramount aim, both arrest and interrogation have been turned into a process in which the suspect is virtually convicted before entering the courtroom. Sponsored by the executive authorities and tacitly encouraged by the judiciary, the security forces have succeeded in corrupting the criminal justice process in Northern Ireland.

The Common Law Power

Section 2 of the Criminal Law Act (Northern Ireland) 1967 now embodies the common law arrest power. Under section 2, any individual may arrest another where it is reasonably suspected that an arrestable offence has been, or is being, committed. The power is only slightly broader if the arrestor is a police constable. While a citizen can only make an arrest if the offence has taken, or is in the process of taking, place, the police can arrest if a suspect is about to commit an arrestable offence.[1]

The key to this general power are the definitions of a 'reasonable' suspicion and an 'arrestable' offence. The power of arrest applies only where there are objective reasons for such an action. There are a few specific powers for relatively trivial offences,[2] but even these depend on the commission of a criminal offence and a reasonable suspicion on the part of the arrestor. In essence, no one could be arrested on a whim. The individual making the arrest had to have objective grounds for his or her action. As if to emphasise this point, the common law required the arrestor to inform the prisoner of the nature of the offence which had given rise to the arrest.[3]

Once an arrest had been effected lawfully the common law obliged the arrestor to bring the prisoner before a court as soon as reasonably practicable.[4] Today article 131 of the Magistrates' Court (Northern Ireland) Order 1981 makes the same provision, and sets the maximum delay before court appearance at 48 hours after the arrest. Although this provision concerns the treatment of a prisoner after arrest it reveals much about the true nature and purpose of arrest as developed by the common law. It was not a power to be used simply to place an individual under the care, custody and control of the arrestor. It was not to be resorted to for punitive or preventive purposes nor even to facilitate the accumulation of evidence. Its sole objective was to make an individual amenable to the court to answer for the serious offence which he is reasonably suspected of having committed.[5] In article 131, the only variation permitted is when evidence comes to light in the interval between the arrest and court appearance which dissipates any reasonable suspicion against the prisoner; in this event he or she should be released immediately.

The common law, then, confined a broad power to a single, narrow objective. But this does not mean that it cannot be altered by legislation for purposes other than those for which it was intended — to permit arrest for preventive, punitive, or investigatory purposes, for example. In Northern Ireland this course of action has become quite common. Section 2 of the CLA has been used, in conjunction with the Emergency Powers Act, to allow the RUC a free hand in its interrogation practices. Going back further, regulations made under the Civil Authorities (Special Powers) Act 1922 created powers of arrest which were in no way related to the initiation of criminal prosecution. Regulation 10, for instance, empowered any officer of the RUC to arrest without warrant and detain for up to 48 hours any person for the purpose of interrogation (with the proviso that the arrest helped preserve peace and maintained order). This power had nothing to do with making a suspect amenable to the courts; the arrested person did not even have to be reasonably suspected of a criminal offence or brought before a competent judicial authority. It was simply a means of placing individuals at the disposal of the RUC to facilitate intelligence gathering.[6]

The common law-based powers represent the first formal step in the criminal justice process, the central object of which is to convict the guilty and acquit the innocent. Here we find the inevitable problem of providing sufficient safeguards for the accused while allowing necessary, coercive investigative powers for the prosecution.[7] Whether both sides are favoured equally or one is favoured more than the other depends in part on the power of arrest and the manner in which it is used. It is at this stage that the new arrest powers can begin to play a markedly partisan role.

What happens at the arrest stage, and between arrest and the first court appearance, fundamentally affects the relevance and outcome of the judicial proceedings.[8] A full-time, organised and resourced police force vested with the responsibility of investigating and detecting criminal offenders can use arrest more effectively and decisively than individual citizens. They can use it, as they are meant to, to make suspected offenders amenable to the courts. But they can also use it to control the direction and outcome of the trial itself. The judiciary has fashioned controls over the police arrest and detention stage to protect the accused in the trial process. This becomes clear upon an examination of the most significant of these controls: the rules on the admissibility of confessions and the Judges Rules.

Until 1973, when it was amended, the common law test on the admissibility of confessions in a criminal trial stipulated that a confession would only be admissible if it had been given voluntarily. That is, it had not been obtained by fear of prejudice or hope of advantage exercised or held out by a person in authority, or by oppression.[9] If a police constable used physical force, verbal threats, bribes or long periods of questioning on the prisoner in order to extract a confession, that confession would not be admitted in evidence at the subsequent trial.[10] Often, if a confession was ruled inadmissible at the trial, the other evidence was insufficient to justify a conviction, and the suspect was acquitted. The judiciary, therefore, ensured that police action at the arrest and detention stage became a vital factor in court proceedings.

The degree to which judges controlled police action varied considerably until the mid-1960s. Some judges objected if a constable attempted to question a prisoner before bringing him or her to court. Others complained that prisoners had not been asked about certain matters before being brought to court. The frustration of the Chief Constable of Birmingham over this inconsistency led to the elaboration of further judicial controls and a tightening of the bond between the arrest and detention stage and the trial itself. These controls are popularly known as the Judges Rules.

The Judges Rules have since been amended and supplemented by administrative directions, but their objective remains the same. They provide additional safeguards for the prisoner in the interval between the arrest and the first court appearance. These safeguards are designed to ensure the suspect's well-being during this period and to prevent the police from tricking or coercing the suspect into making an inculpatory admission. If the police breach these formal rules in the course of taking a confession from the prisoner, the judge has a discretion to exclude it.[11] The burden is on the police, therefore, to display the qualities of fairness and impartiality that are the foundation of public confidence in the criminal process.

Special Powers of Arrest

Normal powers of arrest obligate the police to act within the constraints set by the common law. Under statutorily-created special powers of arrest, there are no such restrictions. If the legislature, for example, acting on the direction of the executive, conferred a power of arrest for questioning on the police, it would be equipping them to act in a capacity unrelated to the criminal process. First of all, the point of such legislation would be to make a suspect amenable to the police for questioning, not to the court for trial. Secondly, because the question of which individuals would be vulnerable to such a power would have been decided by the executive in the formulation of the terms of that power, the police would be, to this extent, acting as an agent of executive authority. This does not mean that the police are not also agents of, and accountable to, the law. But a police decision to arrest an individual under such a statutorily-endowed power would be primarily dictated by executive authority, nor by the requirements of the criminal justice system.

It is essential to grasp this crucial distinction between the two types of powers. When a police constable is exercising his common law-based power he is participating in the criminal process; the content of the power he is exercising and the controls surrounding it have evolved as an integral part of that process. They have been developed not just to make a suspect amenable to the courts but also to provide him or her with essential safeguards during the trial.[12] When a constable is exercising a specially created power of arrest for questioning he is engaged in an entirely different enterprise. This power has not been developed in the context of the criminal process. It has not been geared to provide the suspect with the safeguards he requires to ensure that he will get a fair trial. It has been devised for a different purpose altogether – a purpose for which it is not necessary to include such restrictions and controls because a trial is not the ultimate objective of the arrest. The corruption of the criminal justice process is therefore inherent in the structure and aims of the statutory special powers.

Arrest Powers in Northern Ireland

The Northern Ireland police have been equipped with both types of arrest power almost since the founding of the statelet. The common law-based power is now in section 2 CLA, while the special arrest powers have been contained in the Northern Ireland (Emergency Provisions) Act 1978 (as amended by the 1987 Act) and the Prevention of Terrorism (Temporary Provisions) Act 1984. These special powers can only be described as otiose. They have been framed and judicially interpreted in the broadest of terms; the resulting eclipse of the freedom of the individual cannot be justified by the nature of the violence they were intended to combat. Furthermore, the manner in which they have been used and abused by the RUC has corrupted the image, credibility and fairness of the whole criminal process, and thereby provoked more hostility, alienation and violence than they prevent.

The three primary powers of arrest have been found in section 11 EPA, section 12(1)(b) PTA and section 14 EPA. Although it was repealed by the Northern Ireland (Emergency Provisions) Act 1987, section 11 EPA is still relevant historically, and because the interpretations based upon it continue to be applied today. It empowered a constable to arrest without warrant any person whom he suspected of being a terrorist, and to hold that person in police custody for up to 72 hours. Like section

11, section 12(1)(b) PTA is a questioning power. It empowers a constable to arrest any person whom he reasonably suspects is or has been concerned in the commission, preparation or instigation of acts of terrorism. Here, however, the suspect can be held for up to 48 hours, followed by up to five more days if sanctioned by the Secretary of State. In contrast to both of these, section 14 EPA does not focus on terrorism, but includes a wider scope of arrest powers to encompass the arrest of anyone suspected of having committed, in the process of committing, or about to commit an offence of any nature. It, too, has been amended by the 1987 Act — in this case, to require 'reasonable suspicion' before an arrest. But as we will see, despite these changes, section 11 and the original version of section 14 for all intents and purposes remain in effect.

The Questioning Powers

Section 11 was introduced initially to facilitate detention without trial as provided for in section 12 of and schedule 1 to the EPA. It enabled the RUC to arrest and question an individual to vet his or her suitability for a much longer period of executive detention.[13] The aim was explicitly not bringing a suspect before the court; section 11(3) EPA made it clear that the requirement to bring an arrested individual before the court as soon as practicable did not apply. In fact, section 13 EPA provides a special power to arrest terrorist suspects for the purpose of bringing them before the courts. This power is very similar to, but slightly broader, than section 2 CLA.

In *re McElduff*[14] the court considered the scope of a power very similar to section 11 EPA 1978. The ramifications of this decision extend beyond the use of section 11 to the other powers of arrest and detention, but for our current purposes, the issue was whether a constable needed only a suspicion as opposed to a reasonable suspicion to effect an arrest. Mr Justice McGonigal ruled that 'the court can only enquire into the existence of the suspicion in the mind of the constable and whether the suspicion was an honest one.' If, therefore, a constable honestly believed that everyone living in a certain neighbourhood were terrorists simply because they lived there he could quite legitimately arrest any one of them — or all of them — under section 11. The reasonableness of the belief is irrelevant.

The scope for arbitrary arrest under section 11 was enhanced by the decision of the House of Lords in *McKee v. The Chief Constable for Northern Ireland.*[15] In this case the arresting officer, as is normal, was instructed by his superior to arrest the plaintiff under section 11 as he was suspected of being a terrorist. The arresting officer did not have access to his superior's information which had given rise to the suspicion; he was acting simply on instructions. The House of Lords held that the word of the superior was sufficient to create the necessary suspicion in the mind of the arresting officer and, therefore, the arrest was valid as the relevant suspicion was that of the arresting officer alone. It was no function of the court to examine the information on which the superior was acting to test whether his suspicion was genuine or not. The RUC, therefore, was in a position to block judicial review of this arrest power by using the simple expedient of a superior telling a subordinate that an individual was suspected of being a terrorist and instructing him to arrest him. This amounts to a virtually uncontrollable power of arrest as the courts cannot question in any sense the nature of the suspicion against the individual.

Section 12(1)(b) was enacted hastily, without any significant consideration of its potential impact.[16] Despite the similarity of its wording to section 11, its aim was different. The objective of section 12 was to place suspected terrorists in the custody and control of the RUC. Although the ultimate purpose of this detention was not clarified, section 12(6) PTA overrules the requirement to bring a suspected arrested under section 12(1)(b) before the court as soon as reasonably practicable. This suggests that the power was not originally intended to make suspected terrorists amenable to the court, and that the more likely object was to make the suspect amenable to the RUC for general intelligence gathering about terrorist organisations and the vetting of the suspect's suitability for an exclusion order.[17]

By excluding the requirement to bring the suspect before a competent judicial authority as soon as reasonably practicable, and by extending the arrest powers to the vague concept of 'suspected terrorist activity' as opposed to a specific criminal offence, the legislature has conferred exceptionally broad powers on the police. Through its interpretations of these provisions, the judiciary has given the RUC even greater scope. The net effect of these judicial interpretations is to make it extremely difficult to challenge the legality of the use of these powers in any particular case. That in turn enables the RUC to use them as instruments of arbitrary repression and control.

The Arrest Power

The power of arrest provided for by section 14 EPA is a different creation altogether. It empowers a member of H.M. Forces − the army in practice − to arrest anyone suspected of having committed, committing or being about to commit an offence. The nature of the offence itself is irrelevant; it can be a motor traffic offence or an attempted murder. The terms of the power relieves the soldier of the common law requirements of a valid arrest and require him to hand the prisoner over to the RUC or release him or her within four hours of the arrest. The justification for it was to enable soldiers to arrest offenders in dangerous areas where the RUC could not operate.[18] Significantly, the power arises only where an individual is suspected of committing an offence – not where he is merely suspected of being a terrorist. Its object, therefore, was to make suspected offenders amenable to the RUC so that they could initiate the criminal process against them. In other words, unlike section 11 EPA and section 12(1)(b) PTA, it was not a power of arrest for questioning.

Together, these three sections gave the security forces the power to arrest who they liked and when they liked with virtual impunity. The crucial protections of the individual under the common law were neatly swept away. There was no obligation to have a 'reasonable suspicion' of a crime, and no pressing need to bring a suspect to court. RUC arrests were, therefore, largely removed from the criminal justice system.

In 1987, the Northern Ireland (Emergency Provisions) Act repealed section 11 EPA on the recommendation of the Baker Report. It also added the word 'reasonable' to sections 13 and 14 of the EPA. Do these changes, coupled with the apparent safeguards in section 12(1)(b), represent added protection for the individual? Practice and the decision in *ex-parte Lynch*[19] suggest otherwise.

In *ex-parte Lynch*, the Northern Ireland Court of Appeal ruled that it would be sufficient for a constable effecting an arrest under section 12(1)(b) to have a general suspicion that the individual was somehow involved in terrorist activity. That he did not know the nature of the activity nor the extent to which the individual was involved was irrelevant; the RUC could use section 12(1)(b) as a means of starting its investigation into these matters.

The decision shows the weakness of the principle of 'reasonableness' when it is applied to a general concept such as terrorism instead of a specific criminal offence. In fact *Lynch* renders the term virtually meaningless. Despite the repeal of section 11, moreover, the breadth of the interpretation given to the word 'suspicion' in *re McElduff* will probably apply to section 12(1)(b) and sections 13 and 14. It would appear, therefore, that the inclusion of the term 'reasonable' in sections 13 and 14 of the 1978 EPA is simply a façade to mask the conduct of business as usual.

Emergency Arrest Powers in Practice

In considering the abuse of these powers, section 11 EPA and section 12(1)(b) PTA can be taken together. While they were designed to accommodate very different objectives, section 11 EPA and its predecessors were never confined to the detention without trial scheme. In any case, detention without trial has not been resorted to since 1975 whereas the section 11 power was applied, on average, 2,000 times a year between 1975 and 1980. Both it and section 12(1)(b) PTA were used for intelligence gathering purposes and for bringing suspects before the courts on criminal charges.[20]

Arrest for Intelligence Gathering
Of the two powers, section 11 EPA has been the more frequently employed for intelligence purposes. About three-quarters of all those arrested under it have been released without charge; about 55 per cent of those arrested under section 12 were released. This in itself does not establish that both powers were used primarily for intelligence gathering. The results of a survey carried out in 1981, however, suggest that this was the case.[21]

The survey showed that a large majority of those arrested under either provision and released without charge were never suspected of active involvement in specific terrorist activity. Their questioning in custody did not revolve around their suspected terrorism. On the contrary, it focused on a mixture of details of the prisoner's personal life, family, associates, interests, movements, organisations and individuals in his or her area and so on. The object seemed to be to build up and maintain an intelligence file on the individual and the community in which he or she lived. Many claimed that the RUC pressured them to collaborate through bribery or methods ranging from playing on the suspect's financial and domestic difficulties, threatening him or her with serious criminal charges, repeated arrests, the arrest and charging of weaker members of the family, taking children into care and so on. Many also complained, particularly during the hunger strikes, of being kept in police custody for days without being questioned at all, the implication being that they were detained for preventive or punitive purposes. The dominant objective, however, was intelligence gathering – to be achieved regardless of the degree to which the law was bent.

The RUC, of course, has not been the only section of the security forces to employ the law so flexibly. In the early 1970s the army embarked on a prolonged, massive intelligence operation.[22] Instrumental in this process was section 14 EPA[23] which was used to arrest and detain individuals for four hours of questioning aimed at the accumulation of banks of low-level intelligence. There was rarely any suggestion that the individuals arrested were suspected of any criminal offence. Indeed, figures released by the Ministry of Defence in response to a parliamentary question reveal that out of 1,504 such arrests between

Figure 2.1
Arrests under the Northern Ireland (Emergency Provisions) Act 1978
and the Prevention of Terrorism Act 1976

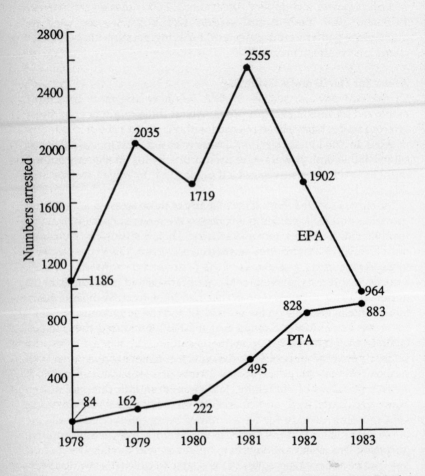

Source: *Review of the operation of the Northern Ireland (Emergency Provisions) Act 1978*, Cmnd. 9222 (HMSO, 1984) Appendix M, p. 164.

June 1980 and May 1981, only 418 were actually handed over to the RUC; the remainder were released without charge.

The official justification for using arrest as a means of intelligence gathering has always been the overriding need to combat terrorism. The authorities take the view that the RUC needs a constant flow of reliable information on terrorist membership, organisation, activities, plans and resources in order to save lives and avoid injury. They point to the success of the supergrass phenomenon in putting large numbers of suspects behind bars as a direct result of the RUC intelligence gathering operations. When asked if these ends cannot be achieved through normal police methods they respond that large sections of the community are either afraid or unwilling to cooperate in these matters making it impossible for the RUC to gather the information it needs through normal police channels.[24] Emergency arrest powers, therefore, are crucial.

This official attitude is dominated by a preoccupation with security. The test is how many individuals are arrested, how much intelligence is gathered, how many individuals are brought to trial, how many convictions are secured and so on. Little thought is given to the propriety or legality of the methods used to achieve those ends and the damaging side effects that they produce. The executive, Parliament, the police authority and numerous official inquiries into police use of emergency powers have all refused to accept that there is any real cause for concern in the nature of these powers and the manner in which they are employed. They have remained unmoved by the fact that section 11 EPA was regularly used for a purpose other than that for which it was conferred, that the army's use of section 14 EPA for screening purposes is of dubious legality and that section 11 EPA was, and section 12(1)(b) PTA is,[25] almost certainly used to arrest thousands of people who are not genuinely suspected of being involved in terrorist activity.

Arrest Leading to Trial
An even greater indictment of the institutions of justice is the manner in which the emergency powers have been used to bring suspects to trial. Prior to 1975 the army, backed by the detention without trial procedures, was the principal means of combating 'terrorism'. From the mid-1970s onwards, however, the authorities dropped detention without trial in favour of securing convictions and lengthy prison sentences in the courts, and the judicial process became the frontline in the fight against 'terrorism'.[26] This imposed a heavy onus on the RUC to make suspects amenable to the courts. Their task was made slightly easier by a new power of arrest, introduced in section 13 EPA, which empowered any constable to arrest without warrant any person

whom he suspected of committing, having committed or being about to commit a scheduled offence or an offence under the Act which is not a scheduled offence. This meant, in short, that there was no longer any need for a constable to have reasonable grounds upon which to arrest.

But this question of 'reasonable' grounds applied only to arrest, not to an appearance before the court. Although the suspect was required to be brought before a competent judicial authority within 48 hours, an arrest simply on the basis of a constable's 'reasonable' suspicion did not guarantee that there would be sufficient grounds to bring the suspect before the courts. It was anticipated, therefore, that while the suspect was in custody the RUC would attempt to obtain enough evidence to justify specific charges and possibly a conviction. There was always the danger, however, that statements induced from the suspect would be rendered useless at the subsequent trial because they were taken in circumstances which breached the rules on the admissibility of confessions or the Judges Rules. In other words, the common law restrictions on arrest and questioning which ensured a fair trial would defeat the government's objective. This danger was easily averted, however, by a simple statutory provision.

Section 8 EPA provided that any statement made by the accused would be admissible in evidence in the Diplock courts if it was relevant and if the prosecution could satisfy the judge that it was not extracted by torture or inhuman or degrading treatment. Judicial interpretations of this provision have made it abundantly clear that its effect is to render admissible much of what would have been previously inadmissible under the common law test.[27] In *R. v. McCormick*,[28] for example, McGonigal L.J. ruled that the use of a moderate degree of physical ill-treatment to obtain a confession would not render the statement automatically inadmissible. In *R. v. Halloran*,[29] Lord Lowry C.J. stopped short of condoning ill-treatment, but made it clear that the use of lengthy, persistent and even intensive interrogation was acceptable.[30] Subsequent cases have permitted the use of bribes and threats. The judiciary has retained the common law discretion to exclude confessions on the grounds that their prejudicial effect outweighs their probative value. At the same time, however, it has declared that the discretion could not be used to defeat the intention of section 8.[31] The cumulative effect of these judicial interpretations is that the RUC can subject a prisoner to lengthy, repetitive and debilitating interrogations, threats, bribes, trickery, verbal abuse and possibly even a moderate degree of physical ill-treatment to obtain a confession without that confession being ruled inadmissible.

No confession taken under these conditions would be admissible under the common law rules. In one quick step, a simple statutory provision had eliminated vital safeguards over the arrest and detention process. For the suspected terrorist the implications are much more serious than the prospect of rougher treatment in police custody. By curtailing a suspect's protection at the arrest and detention stage, the authorities have tipped the delicate balance of justice fundamentally in favour of the prosecution and diminished, from the moment of the arrest, the possibility of a fair trial. Unhappily, the EPA 1987 has failed to address this problem. Its clarifications will do no more than confirm in statute what the judges have already confirmed. The Act cannot be seen as a step forward for defendants.

With the addition of section 8 EPA to section 2 CLA and section 13 EPA, the RUC was essentially free to do what it liked in the interrogation room. But it was still obligated to bring the prisoner before a court as soon as reasonably practicable and not more than 48 hours after arrest. This imposed an important constraint on the length of time a suspect could be questioned. The RUC dodged these controls by using section 11 EPA and section 12(1)(b) PTA instead of section 2 CLA and section 13 EPA to bring suspects before the courts. In its evidence to the Bennett Committee, the RUC openly admitted its policy of arresting terrorist suspects under these general powers even where they were caught in the act of committing a specific offence.[32] A survey of all suspects tried in the Diplock courts in the first three months of 1981 revealed that more than four times as many were arrested under the former powers than under section 2 CLA and section 13 EPA.[33] This was so despite the fact that it was obvious in many cases that the RUC had sufficient grounds for a reasonable suspicion that the suspect had committed a specific arrestable offence.

The draconian section 12(1)(b) was a particular RUC favourite. It was seen to be more productive in extracting confessions than other sections, presumably because it permitted the suspect's detention for a maximum of seven days instead of three. Surprisingly, it was little used until 1980; the severity of the interrogation techniques adopted prior to that date apparently sufficed to produce confessions within the three days permitted by section 11. When public pressure forced the RUC to tone down these techniques, it had to resort to more time-consuming methods of bribery and psychological pressure, and for this it needed the extra time permitted by section 12(1)(b) PTA. As a result, the use of this power rocketed after 1980 while section 11 EPA fell into decline. More and more suspects are now arriving in the Diplock courts having been arrested and interrogated under section 12(1)(b) PTA, but the judges still ignore this perversion of the criminal process.

The logic behind this arrest policy is not difficult to identify. It enables the RUC to subject suspects to longer periods of intense interrogation and frees them from the requirements of the Judges Rules.[34] It serves the double purpose of intelligence gathering and extracting confessions which will be sufficient to secure convictions against the suspects in the Diplock courts. For the suspect, however, it represents a further obstacle to be overcome in the struggle for a fair trial. Instead of innocence or guilt being established in a courtroom, the suspect is essentially tried in police custody. The one-sided nature of this contest is illustrated by the manner in which the RUC process prisoners arrested under section 11 EPA and section 12(1)(b) PTA.

The two special police interrogation centres at Castlereagh and at Gough Barracks, Armagh, are capable of coping with large numbers of prisoners for extended periods of time. On arrival the prisoner is stripped of all personal belongings and put in a small rectangular cell containing nothing but a bed and a chair. This is where the prisoner eats, sleeps and lives for up to seven days. During this time prisoners are given nothing with which to occupy their minds or pass the time between interrogation sessions. They receive no visits from the outside world apart from a possible visit from their solicitor, which is permissible after a minimum of 48 hours in custody and usually only if the prisoner has made a confession. Medical supervision is provided by the police.

Interrogation is highly organised. Normally, prisoners are interrogated three or four times a day, each session lasting an average of two to three hours. These are conducted by rotating teams of two detectives in small rectangular rooms containing only a table and three chairs. There is no independent monitoring of the interrogations although they can be watched by uniformed police officers on closed-circuit television. This regime is devised to isolate the prisoner, to make him feel cut off, lonely and vulnerable, and very much in the custody and control of the RUC. In this state he is easy prey to the confession hunters. If the prisoner succumbs and makes an inculpatory statement he is as good as convicted. Continuous monitoring of Diplock trials has revealed that about 90 per cent of defendants made confessions during interrogation, while in 75 to 80 per cent of cases the prosecution evidence was based either wholly or substantially on confessions.[35]

Successful challenges to the admissibility of such confessions are conspicuous by their rare occurrence. The reluctance of judges to accept that a confession may have been extracted by torture or inhuman or degrading treatment renders it virtually pointless for defendants even to attempt a challenge; for all intents and purposes, they are convicted when they leave the police station.[36] The gravity of this situation is indicated by the fact that about 10,000 individuals have been convicted mainly on confession evidence in the Diplock courts.

The few examples of successful challenges illustrate the lengths to which a defendant who has made a confession must go to free himself from the conveyor belt leading to conviction. In *R. v. Brophy*,[37] for example, the accused claimed that he had been subjected to an intolerable degree of maltreatment ranging from being physically punched to being sexually assaulted. Medical evidence supported many of his claims. Nevertheless the judge was reluctant to believe him. Only the exceptional astuteness and memory of the defendant, combined with very unsatisfactory RUC evidence, ultimately persuaded the judge to exclude the confession. The defendant had been careful to memorise the identities of his interrogating officers and the various times at which they interrogated and ill-treated him. At his trial he was able to point out the culprits, who happened to be present in the courtroom. It transpired that some of them were not even on record as having interviewed him. They claimed that they were engaged in other activities at the time making it impossible for them to have interviewed Brophy. When their duty roster was checked, however, not only were these claims proved false but it chanced that they were all free and available at Castlereagh at exactly the times Brophy claimed they had interrogated and ill-treated him. The coincidences were so great that the judge had no alternative but to accept that there was sufficient truth in Brophy's account to exclude his confession.

The vast majority of detainees, however, invariably find that their word that a confession was forcibly extracted from them is overruled in favour of detectives' claims that they acted like perfect gentlemen. Even where the judges accept that there has been abuse they are reluctant to exclude the confession. In *R. v. Tohill*[38] the trial judge accepted in evidence a statement taken from a 15-year-old who had been arrested at 3:30 a.m. and, in the judge's words, subjected to four hours of intensive interrogation during which the detectives became angry, expressed their disbelief in forceful language, and reduced the boy to tears on several occasions. Also in *R. v. McKearney*[39] the trial judge excluded a confession of membership of the IRA made by the accused in the first 14 interviews because he found that the accused had been subjected to torture and inhuman and degrading treatment. He proceeded to admit a confession of attempted murder made in interviews 15 and 16 on the grounds that the effects of the earlier treatment had dissipated by this stage — despite the fact that only a few hours had elapsed between the confessions and that the accused remained in the same police station under the custody and control of the same police officers. Even the judiciary's discretion to exclude evidence is not put to good use. In *R. v. Culbert*[40] the Court of Appeal ruled that the failure of the police to comply with the Bennett recommendations, which were aimed at protecting those in police custody against physical ill-treatment, was not sufficient to take the resulting confession into the grey area where the judge might exercise his discretion to exclude.

It was never intended that section 11 EPA and section 12(1)(b) PTA arrest powers should be used as a regular procedure for bringing suspects to trial. Judicial inquiries into emergency legislation and RUC interrogation practices acknowlege the reshaping of the law. But none has considered the extent to which it deprives the suspect of a fair trial, let alone actually condemn it. Even judges who are traditionally zealous in upholding and protecting the integrity and justice of the criminal process have bent to the demands of the RUC. Every year they convict between 500 and 1,000 individuals who arrive in their courts carrying the guilt of a confession delivered after being arrested under sections 11 or 12(1)(b) and subjected to intensive interrogation in Castlereagh and Gough. Nor have they seen fit to question the propriety or legality of this practice. The RUC has been allowed to take virtual control of the criminal process by effectively discarding sections 2 CLA and 13 EPA in favour of sections 11 EPA and 12(1)(b) PTA.

The RUC's Accountability to the Law
Just because the confessions obtained by the RUC's uncivilised methods of arrest and interrogation are acceptable as evidence in the Diplock courts does not mean that it is beyond the reach of the law. Each individual constable and the force as a whole are, theoretically, subject to the law in exactly the same manner and to the same extent as any other individual.[41] If a suspect is assaulted in an attempt to extract a confession, that is no less a criminal offence because it was inflicted following arrest under section 11 EPA or section 12(1)(b) PTA. The police officers involved can be charged and tried in the same manner as any other person accused of committing the same offence. Reality, however, does not match up to the theory. In practice, the RUC operates as though it were above the law.

When detention without trial was phased out in 1975 intense political pressure was applied to the RUC to apprehend and secure convictions against a steady flow of terrorist suspects. Specially constructed inter-rogation centres, more staff, emergency powers of arrest, amended rules on the admissibility of confessions, no-jury courts and the goodwill of political and judicial authority were placed at their disposal. The RUC responded by embarking on a programme of arrest and interrogations which can only be described as barbaric.[42] It was not long before the volume of formal complaints of serious physical assault and battery in RUC custody rocketed.[43]

Police doctors working in the interrogation centres drew up a report detailing the nature and extent of suspects' injuries. The report was suppressed, provoking a resignation from the Police Authority. Ultimately the chief medical officer at Gough, Dr Robert Irwin, became so alarmed at the injuries and exasperated at official inaction that he expressed his concern publicly. This prompted his vilification in a malicious press compaign (which many believed to have been instigated by the authorities), and he was forced to resign. Meanwhile individual members of the Police Authority, political representatives and church leaders were becoming more vocal in their concern. The authorities, by their continued inaction, seemed to be condoning what was happening in the interrogation centres.

Not until Amnesty International investigated the situation and declared that 'maltreatment of suspected terrorists by the RUC has taken place with sufficient frequency to warrant the establishing of a public inquiry to investigate it'[44] did the government feel compelled to act. It did not set out to investigate the truth of the allegations, but its inquiry into RUC interrogation and complaints procedures[45] concluded that prisoners had received injuries in police custody which were not self-inflicted.[46]

By 1979, when the Bennett Committee reported, more than 1,600 formal complaints of assault and battery had been lodged. Many of these complaints were backed up by independent medical evidence. None the less, not a single RUC officer has been convicted. In fact, none has been charged. The Director of Public Prosecutions, an independent prosecution authority established in 1972, is responsible for directing criminal prosecutions of this nature. Yet there has not been a single test case. In his evidence to the Bennett Committee, the DPP claimed that he applied no special principles in cases against the security forces; his uniform approach, he said, was to assess whether the evidence was such as to give reasonable prospects of conviction.[47] It is strange, therefore, that he has been willing to prefer charges against 'terrorist' suspects in cases where the only evidence against them is the word of an RUC officer but has consistently refused to prefer charges against an RUC officer where the evidence consists of the word of a suspect and independent medical testimony. It is difficult not to conclude that the DPP, in these matters, is bending, consciously or unconsciously, to the wishes of the government in allowing the RUC a free hand. Whatever the explanation the result has been that the RUC has been seen to be a force above the law when arresting and interrogating paramilitary suspects.

Conclusion

The security forces' powers of arrest and interrogation were conferred for the purpose of gathering intelligence from suspected terrorists. Why, then, has the RUC been allowed to arrest and question people whom it did not genuinely suspect of terrorism? Why are individuals held for questioning about the minutiae of their family lives? Why has the RUC been able to use the emergency powers to bring suspects before the courts on specific charges when ordinary powers could, and should, have been used? In short, why has the RUC been allowed to dictate its terms in the criminal justice process?

One answer is that the security forces are simply doing the job that the executive wants them to do. It is no secret that since 1975, the executive has preferred the police and the justice system to the army as the primary weapons against 'terrorism'. If the RUC interprets and applies its powers to suit itself, the executive will not interfere. It has never demonstrated any overt concern at the prospect of the RUC overstepping the legal boundaries of the emergency powers. On the contrary, it has supported police methods which increase the flow of information on terrorist organisations and produce large numbers of charges and convictions for terrorist offences. Claims of RUC abuses are regarded by the executive as a matter for the courts. There is little point, therefore, in lobbying the executive to take effective measures to protect the fundamental freedoms of the individual against RUC excesses.

If the executive has provided the impetus, the judiciary, by default if not actively, has created an environment in which the security forces can call the shots in the criminal process. Traditionally, it has created controls over arrest and detention procedures to ensure that they do not prejudice the prospects of a fair trial. What better opportunity to apply this zealousness than the current situation in Northern Ireland? The RUC may act with the blessings of executive authority, but its methods are not necessarily lawful. The police are bound to act within the ambit of the legal powers conferred on them at common law and by statutes. But even here, to say nothing of curtailing the use of the emergency powers, the judiciary has failed to act.

The effects of this failure have been felt at every stage in the arrest-to-trial process. For all intents and purposes, the RUC is free to decide who to arrest, under what emergency powers to arrest them so as to bring them to trial, and how to extract confessions in the interrogation room — in other words, to obtain convictions at almost any cost. By its inactivity and by its interpretations, the judiciary has effectively abdicated its control over the criminal justice process to the RUC. It has tarnished its image of independence and impartiality, and prompted an increasingly widespread view that the judiciary is subservient to the wishes of the executive. Most importantly, it has left the individual without effective lawful means of redress against oppressive police practices.[48]

Notes

1. Section 2(4).
2. For example, breach of the peace.
3. *Christie v. Leachinsky* (1947) A.C. 573. For the current position in Britain, however, see Police and Criminal Evidence Act, 1984, s.28.
4. *Dunne v. Clinton* (1930) I.R. 1.
5. For a discussion on the purposes of arrest see *The People v. Shaw* (1982) I.R. 1.
6. See Mr Justice McGonigal in *In re McElduff* (1972) N.I., 1 at p. 9.
7. For a discussion on this see Packer, *The Limits of the Criminal Sanction* (Stanford University Press, 1969).
8. For an analysis of the impact of the pre-trial procedure on a fair trial see Douwe Korff, *The Diplock Courts in Northern Ireland: A Fair Trial?* (SIM Special, 1984).
9. See Cross, *Evidence* (5th edn) (Butterworths, 1983) pp. 534–51. For the current position in Britain see Police and Criminal Evidence Act 1984, s.76, s.78.
10. Archbold, *Criminal Pleading, Evidence and Practice* (42nd edn) (Butterworths, 1985) paras. 15:45–15:54.
11. *R. v. Clarke* (1973) N.I. 45, at p. 58.
12. See Lord Hailsham in *DPP v. Ping Lin* (1976) A.C.574, p. 600.
13. *Report of the Committee of Inquiry into Police Interrogation Procedures in Northern Ireland* (The Bennett Report) Cmnd. 7497 (London: HMSO) para. 66.
14. (1972) N.I. 1.
15. (1985) 1 All E.R. 1.
16. See Chapter 7.
17. See C. Walker, *The Prevention of Terrorism in British Law* (Manchester University Press, 1986).
18. *Report of the Commission to consider legal procedures to deal with terrorist activities in Northern Ireland* (The Diplock Report) Cmnd. 5185 (London: HMSO) para. 49.
19. (1980) N.I. 126.
20. See D. Walsh, *The Use and Abuse of Emergency Legislation in Northern Ireland* (Cobden Trust, 1983).
21. Walsh, 'Arrest and Interrogation: Northern Ireland 1981', in *Journal of Law and Society* (1981) vol. 9, p. 37.
22. K. Boyle, T. Hadden and P. Hillyard, *Law and State: The Case of Northern Ireland* (Martin Robertson, Law in Society, 1975) pp. 43-6.
23. It first appeared as section 12 EPA 1973.
24. Bennett Report. See also Cmnd. 9222 (The Baker Report).
25. See Chapter 7.
26. K. Boyle, T. Hadden and P. Hillyard, *Ten Years On in Northern Ireland: The Legal Response to Political Violence* (Cobden Trust, 1980) ch. 4.
27. For discussion see Greer, 'The Admissibility of Confessions under the Northern Ireland (Emergency Provisions) Act 1978', 31 NILQ (1980) pp. 217–24.
28. (1977) N.I. 105.
29. (1979) 2 NIJB (CA).
30. See also *R.v. Hetherington* (1975) N.I. 160.
31. *R. v. McCormick*, supra; also *R. v. Milne* (1978) N.I. 110 and *R. v. McCracken* (unreported, 1975).

32.　Bennett Report, para. 70.

33.　Walsh, *Emergency Legislation*, ch. 2.

34.　For a discussion on the regulations governing the treatment of a suspect in police custody under the emergency provisions see Douwe Korff, *The Diplock Courts*, ch. 2.

35.　See K. Boyle *et al.*, *Ten Years On*, and Walsh, *Emergency Legislation*.

36.　This is the central thrust of Korff's analysis.

37.　(1980) 4 NIJB.

38.　(1974) NIJB.

39.　Unreported, 1978.

40.　(1982) NIJB (CA).

41.　*R. v. Metropolitan Police Commissioner, ex-parte Blackburn* (1968) 2 QB 118.

42.　For an excellent account of this saga see P. Taylor, *Beating the Terrorists? Interrogation in Omagh, Gough and Castlereagh* (Penguin Special, 1980).

43.　This was not the first time that the RUC had resorted to the systematic use of physical ill-treatment to extract information from suspects in their custody. Following the internment operation in 1971 selected suspects were subjected to the 'five techniques' by the Special Branch. This included long periods of wall-standing, food and sleep deprivation and subjection to continuous noise. See Compton Report (Cmnd. 4823) and the Parker Report (Cmnd. 4901). The British government was found guilty of using inhuman and degrading treatment on suspects in police custody by the European Court of Human Rights in a case in police custody by the European Court of Human Rights in a case brought by the Irish government, *Ireland v. U.K.* (Application No. 5310/71).

44.　Amnesty International, *Report of a Mission to Northern Ireland in 1978*.

45.　Bennett Committee.

46.　Bennett Report, para. 163.

47.　Ibid., para. 371.

48.　The Northern Ireland (Emergency Provisions) Act 1987 puts into statutory form a number of the recommendations of Sir George Baker (*Review of the Northern Ireland [Emergency Provisions] Act 1978*, Cmnd. 9222, 1984). Section 5 amends section 8 of the 1978 Act to make it clear that a confession will be inadmissible if an accused is subjected to the use or threat of violence (see *R. v. McCormick* and *R. v. Halloran*). It is also made clear that a discretion exists to exclude a confession in the interests of fairness to the defendant or in the interests of justice (see *R. v. Hetherington, supra*). Sections 14 and 15 introduce in broadly similar terms the protections contained in sections 56 and 58 of the Police and Criminal Evidence Act 1984. Sections 13 and 14 of the 1978 Act are amended to require reasonable suspicion. Section 11 of the 1978 Act is repealed. See Appendix II.

3

STEVEN GREER and ANTONY WHITE

A Return to Trial by Jury

Following the suspension of the Stormont Parliament and the imposition of direct rule in 1972, the Heath government decided to investigate politically acceptable alternatives to internment. In the words of the Northern Ireland Secretary, William Whitelaw, the question was 'whether changes should be made in the administration of justice in order to deal more effectively with terrorism without using internment under the Special Powers Act'.[1] To this end, Whitelaw announced on 18 October 1972 the appointment of a commission chaired by Lord Diplock.

The Diplock Commission recommended that jury trial should be suspended for certain terrorist offences; when it came to such cases, trial by jury was no longer practicable. The Commission gave two reasons for this view: first, jurors could be threatened and intimidated; and secondly, there was the risk that Loyalist defendants would be perversely acquitted by what were then predominantly Protestant juries. Its report, published in December 1972, concluded *inter alia* that 'the jury system as a means for trying terrorist crime is under strain. It may not yet have broken down, but we think that the time is already ripe to forestall its doing so.'[2]

The bulk of the Commission's recommendations were incorporated into the Northern Ireland (Emergency Provisions) Bill 1973. After impassioned debates in the House of Commons the Bill became law. Section 2(1) of the Northern Ireland (Emergency Provisions) Act 1973 (the EPA) provided that the trial on indictment of 'scheduled' offences should be by a judge sitting without a jury. Offences scheduled in the Act include murder, manslaughter, most offences of violence against the person, arson, malicious damage, riot, firearms and explosives offences, armed robbery, aggravated burglary and a string of other offences thought likely to be committed, in the main, by paramilitaries or their sympathisers. The Act also empowered the Attorney General to certify that particular cases of murder, manslaughter and offences against the person should not be treated as scheduled and should, therefore, be tried by jury. This is known as 'certifying out'.

Parliament assumed that the Emergency Provisions Act was a temporary measure. As such the Act contained a provision requiring the legislature to reconsider every year whether or not it was still required. These 'renewal debates' soon became a rubber-stamping exercise: poorly attended and usually starting late at night, they made little or no serious attempt to examine dispassionately the implications which changes in the day-to-day affairs of Northern Ireland had for the Act's detailed provisions. And, like the Parliamentary debates and reviews that followed in the years after the passage of the EPA, the renewal debates failed to challenge, and even condoned, trial without jury.

In January 1975 the Gardiner Committee, set up to consider whether the EPA had achieved the correct balance between dealing with terrorism and preserving civil liberties, reported 'that trial by jury is the best form of trial for serious cases and that it should be restored in Northern Ireland as soon as this becomes possible'.[3] However, the Committee assumed that if juries were restored they would be intimidated and cause delay. Accordingly, it recommended that the jury-less Diplock courts should remain.

The EPA 1973 was slightly amended in 1975 and largely re-enacted in a consolidating statute, the Northern Ireland (Emergency Provisions) Act 1978, at the impetus of the Labour government. Section 2 of the 1973 Act became Section 7 of the 1978 Act.

On 8 April 1983 Sir George Baker, a retired president of the Family Division of the High Court, was appointed to review the operation of the EPA. Apart from a few minor concessions to the Act's critics, the Baker Report, published in 1984, endorsed all the major derogations from normal legal standards which had been on the statute book since 1973. With respect to scheduled offences Sir George declared: 'The time is not ripe for the return of jury trial....'[4]

On 15 November 1985 British Prime Minister Margaret Thatcher and Irish Prime Minister Dr Garret Fitzgerald signed the Anglo-Irish Agreement at Hillsborough in Northern Ireland. Amongst other things the accord recognised the importance of public confidence in the administration of justice in Northern Ireland and indicated that the Intergovernmental Conference established on this occasion would consider various measures to give it 'substantial expression'.[5] The prospect of a return to jury trial has, however, been given short shrift by both governments. The British administration continues to justify its support for non-jury trial on the traditional intimidation grounds.[6] The Irish government presides over a criminal justice system which also includes trial by non-jury, three-judge courts for offences scheduled in the Offences Against the State Act 1939. It is, therefore, hardly in a position to lecture the British about the absence of jury trial in the north.

In January 1986, under pressure to make some concessions following the completion of the Baker review of the EPA, and in view of the Anglo-Irish Agreement, Parliament extended the Attorney General's certifying out discretion to include kidnapping, false imprisonment, certain offences under the Firearms (NI) Order 1981, and some scheduled offences which are triable summarily or carry a maximum sentence of less than five years.[7] In May 1987 a new EPA was passed which made some comparatively minor alterations to the 1978 Act. As far as the mode of trial was concerned the only change was a modest extension of the certifying out power to include blackmail. In the debates various alternatives were suggested by the Labour opposition and Mr Enoch Powell to achieve the transference of more cases from the Diplock to the jury system, but without success. The proposed modifications included inverting the certifying discretion to one which required cases to be certified in, and giving magistrates and the DPP for Northern Ireland a role in determining the mode of trial in individual cases. There have been plenty of pious affirmations from the government of the desirability of returning to jury trial as soon as this becomes possible.[8] It would appear, however, that there is little prospect of any significant steps in this direction in the foreseeable future.

Since the signing of the Anglo-Irish Agreement, speculation on the nature of the courts which should try scheduled offences in Northern Ireland has centred on whether they should be composed of one judge, or, as in the Special Criminal Court in the Irish Republic, three. Cross-border security courts trying certain offences committed on either side of the border and composed of judges from both the six and the 26 counties have also been suggested.[9] To be feasible each proposal would require additional judicial appointments in Northern Ireland, and to be acceptable to the Intergovernmental Conference, a significant proportion of these would have to be drawn from the minority community.

The difference between a collegiate and a single judge Diplock court is, at best, marginal. The central argument against the suspension of jury trial concerns the nature of the institution which took its place — a judicial tribunal — rather than the number of those involved. Numbers are not unimportant but it is debatable whether on the key questions of fact three judicial heads are much better than one. Certainly they are a lot less desirable than twelve non-judicial ones. In one sense the introduction of collegiate courts would be even less welcome than no change at all since it gives the appearance of progress without the substance. The risk is that such a departure would further delay rather than advance the return of the jury since the authorities are likely to treat the collegiate court as a significant concession whose appearance can be regarded as closing the debate for the foreseeable future.

Trial by jury has continued in Northern Ireland since 1973 for non-scheduled indictable offences, some civil cases and in the coroners'court. Until August 1987 it played a significant role in the civil courts but the civil jury has now been abolished for the trial of civil injuries and personal accident cases.[10]

What was originally enacted as a temporary response to an emergency situation has now been law for some 15 years. Non-jury trial has become, for a whole generation of both lawyers and the public, the accepted mode of trial for a vitally important set of serious offences. The conclusion of the Diplock Commission that the alleged problems of juror intimidation and perverse acquittals could be dealt with only by the removal of jury trial has been endorsed by the Gardiner and Baker Reports and has become the received wisdom both in and outside Parliament. According to Lord Devlin, trial by jury is 'the lamp that shows freedom lives'.[11] If so, that lamp was extinguished for over 10,000 Diplock defendants in Northern Ireland between October 1973 and December 1986.[12]

The purpose of this chapter is to consider the circumstances in which trial by jury was suspended for scheduled offences, to examine the effect this has had on the standard of justice administered in Northern Ireland, and, despite the hostile official climate, to suggest a package of reforms which would facilitate its speedy return.

The Importance of the Jury

The jury system was introduced to Ireland together with other features of Anglo-Norman law in the late twelfth century. Originally, jurors were in effect witnesses who brought their personal knowledge of the case to bear on the question before the court. As the system evolved the jury came to play its modern role as an independent arbiter between conflicting witnesses.[13] Trial by jury became an integral part of the legal tradition which both parts of Ireland inherited when the island was partitioned in 1921.[14]

Trial by jury is the traditional and accepted mode of trial for serious offences in the English-speaking world. It is the cornerstone around which the modern law of evidence and trial procedure has developed. The jury occupies this central position not by chance or historical accident but because it both ensures the existence of certain highly advantageous features in the administration of justice, and because it expresses fundamental political values. Historically, the jury has stood between the might of the state and the vulnerability of the individual.

Sir William Blackstone, for example, recently described by Lord Denning as 'the greatest exponent of the common law we have ever had',[15] wrote in the seventeenth century:

> Trial by jury ever has been, and I trust ever will be, looked upon as the glory of the English law.... The liberties of England cannot but subsist so long as this palladium of liberty remains sacred and inviolate, not only from all open attacks (which none will be so hardy as to make), but also from all secret machinations, which may sap and undermine it by introducing new and arbitrary methods of trial.[16]

Technical and Procedural Safeguards

In every jury trial there is a fundamental division of labour. The judge rules upon and gives guidance on the law which the jury must (in theory) accept. The facts of the case are for the jury alone to determine. The prosecution must prove its allegations so that the jury is sure of the accused's guilt. The juror's oath concludes: '... and give a true verdict *according to the evidence*'.[17] The evidence means the admissible evidence. Here the division of functions is vital. It is for the judge to decide whether evidence is admissible and if certain evidence is ruled inadmissible the jury hears nothing of it. The question of admissibility is decided in the jury's absence.

The rules of evidence seek to exclude irrelevant evidence or evidence which is prejudicial to the accused and does not assist in proving whether or not he or she committed the crime charged. Certain types of evidence which have proved unreliable during the evolution of the common law are also excluded. For example, if a man is charged with indecent assault, as a general principle the judge would rule inadmissible the fact that the same man had been caught in possession of a revolver the day before, or the fact that he had on two previous occasions held up the postman at knife-point. The jury would not be helped in reaching a decision on the accused's guilt or innocence by hearing these other discreditable and prejudicial details. In this way the judge is able to ensure that the jury's decision is reached only on the basis of evidence which is relevant and probative.

The most common dispute is over the admissibility of a confession which the prosecution allege the accused has made. In the common law the prosecution had the burden of showing that any confession which it wished to use in evidence was given voluntarily.[18] In Northern Ireland the EPA altered this rule to place a burden on the accused who wishes to challenge the admissibility of a confession. By section 8(2) of the 1978 Act the defence must adduce prima facie evidence 'that the accused was subjected to torture or to inhuman or degrading treatment in order to induce him to make the statement'. The common law rule has in its turn been altered for England and Wales by s.76 of the Police and Criminal Evidence Act 1984. This provides that the prosecution must show beyond reasonable doubt that a confession which is tendered as evidence against an accused was not obtained by oppression or conduct likely to make it unreliable. But unlike the EPA, PACE does not appear to impose on the defence a burden of raising a prima facie case against admissibility. Provided 'it is represented to the court' that the confession was obtained in violation of the s.76 admissibility tests, the burden of proof rests with the prosecution.[19]

The departure from the common law test of admissibility occasioned by the EPA has been cogently criticised[20] but the vital point in the Diplock courts is procedural. In jury trials the question of admissibility is decided in the absence of the jury. The judge decides the point at a 'trial within a trial' or a 'voir dire'.[21] In the Diplock courts, the same procedure is applied insofar as it is possible to do so. However, the judge cannot decide the question of admissibility without hearing, or at least being aware of, the evidence on which he has to rule. Should he rule it inadmissible, he has to attempt to put it out of his mind where he, as it were, 'swops hats' and becomes the trier of fact. It would be very difficult for a judge genuinely not to be influenced by the fact that the accused had confessed, even though the circumstances of the confession rendered it inadmissible.[22]

Section 8(2)(b) of the 1978 Act, which could provide a similar safeguard to that ensured in a jury trial by the voir dire, appears to receive little use.[23] This provision gives a judge a discretion, after ruling a statement to be inadmissible, to order that the trial re-start before a different judge with the inadmissible evidence excluded.

In addition to the safeguards lost due to the unreality of the voir dire in the Diplock courts, there are a number of related disadvantages for the accused. In jury trials if a defendant fails to have a confession ruled inadmissible in the voir dire he or she can nonetheless adduce the same evidence as to the circumstances of the confession to the jury with the intention of showing that even though the confession is admissible, little weight should be attached to it.[24] In the House of Commons debate on the 1973 Emergency Provisions Bill the Attorney General of the day asserted[25] that the judge in a jury-less court would be able to reconsider the circumstances of an alleged confession, which he had earlier ruled to be admissible, when considering the weight to be attached to it. Plainly, there is little scope for a defendant to seek to persuade a judge, who has already ruled that the circumstances of a confession do not render it inadmissible, that such circumstances nevertheless detract from its weight.[26]

Another procedural disadvantage which only arises where there is no jury concerns the possible inclusion of inadmissible evidence in the 'committal papers'. As a rule, the trial of a person charged with a serious offence is preceded by committal proceedings in the magistrates court, the purpose of which is to ascertain whether there is sufficient evidence to warrant a full trial. The papers prepared by the prosecution for committal proceedings frequently contain inadmissible evidence, for example, police interviews with the accused which either mention his or her criminal record or include questions about other offences with which the accused is not charged. In a jury trial it does not matter if the trial judge sees such evidence in the committal papers; the jury which decides the issue of guilt or innocence will not. In the Diplock court, however, if the trial judge sees such inadmissible evidence, it is seen by the trier of fact. This is grossly unfair to the accused.[27] As Walsh points out,[28] this particular problem is exacerbated where, as in certain of Northern Ireland's supergrass cases,[29] the 'voluntary bill of indictment' procedure was used and committal proceedings dispensed with.[30]

Perhaps the most telling procedural inadequacy of the Diplock courts concerns the uncorroborated evidence of an accomplice. In essence this is the evidence given for the prosecution by a person who played a part in the crime or crimes with which the accused is charged, which is not supported by any independent evidence implicating the accused. The experience of the common law is that such uncorroborated evidence is not reliable. In a trial by jury in which an accomplice of the accused gives evidence against him or her the judge must warn the jury that although they *may* convict on the accomplice's evidence, it is dangerous to do so unless it is corroborated.[31] Thus convictions based upon the uncorroborated evidence of accomplices are not legally prohibited, but the accomplice evidence rule is clearly based upon the assumption that there is a jury to be warned and upon the separation of functions which this implies. It is difficult to accept that this rule is satisfactorily fulfilled merely by a judge as arbiter of law warning himself in his alter ego as arbiter of fact – a problem which arises in its most acute form when the accomplice in question is a supergrass. This, however, is the way in which the Northern Ireland courts have interpreted it.[32]

The division of functions between judge and jury in jury trials also entrusts to the jury the vital task of assessing the credibility of witnesses. The common sense with which a jury approaches the question of whether or not to believe a witness is one of its greatest values. Whereas a judge's legal training will lead him or her to concentrate on inconsistencies or the lack of them, a jury will take an overall view of a witness, bearing in mind his or her demeanour, attitude and so on. The accused in a Diplock court is thus deprived of the debates in what Lord Devlin has called 'a little parliament'.[33]

The presence of the jury in the common law tradition further protects the accused − in this case, from trial by the mass media. This is achieved through the operation of the contempt of court laws. As a very general proposition, it is a contempt of court to publish material which creates a substantial risk that the course of justice in particular legal proceedings will be seriously impeded or prejudiced.[34] However, in deciding whether published material creates a substantial risk of justice being impeded or prejudiced a different standard is applied depending on whether or not a jury is involved.[35] What this means in practice is that the press and others feel able to publish far more damning and prejudicial views on matters coming before the Diplock courts than would be the case if a jury were used.

Gifford refers to a statement made by the Chief Constable of the RUC while the first of the trials in Northern Ireland's supergrass system was being heard.[36] This contained a justification of the supergrass policy and emphasised its importance. The trial judge, Mr Justice Murray, took the view that this would probably have amounted to a contempt of court had a jury been sitting but he asserted that it had not influenced his decision. No doubt an honest attempt was made to ignore the statement but it is impossible to say whether or not it was successful.[37]

Another safeguard built into the system of trial by jury is that the jurors come fresh to each trial. A judge might well be prone to weary cynicism when yet another defendant claims, for example, to have been coerced by the police into making a confession. A fresh jury will give the matter very serious consideration indeed. Sir George Baker captures this concept of 'case-hardening' in a few words: 'the judge has heard it all before; therefore he does not believe the accused; therefore he is or becomes prosecution-minded or more prosecution-minded.'[38]

The case-hardening thesis is supported by official statistics.[39] These show that the average acquittal rate in contested Diplock cases is lower than that of contested non-scheduled cases tried by jury in Northern Ireland. In the 1974–86 period 55 per cent of Crown Court defendants who pleaded not guilty were acquitted by juries whereas only 33 per cent of Diplock defendants who pleaded not guilty were acquitted. Without the high acquittal rate of 58 per cent, including convictions quashed on appeal in the supergrass trials between 1983 and 1986, the overall Diplock acquittal rate would have been lower still.[40]

Nevertheless this fact has not dissuaded some from continuing to assert that the quality of justice dispensed by the Diplock courts is as good as, if not better than, that obtained from juries. Sir George Baker and others have remarked upon the absence from the Diplock system of notorious and widely recognised miscarriages of justice.[41] Some have even drawn favourable contrasts with the Guildford, Woolwich and Birmingham bomb trials, each of which involved a jury. There is a superficial plausibility to these arguments but it dissolves on closer inspection. The central problem in the Birmingham, Guildford and Woolwich cases lay in the failure of the court to expose the flaws in the expert evidence to the jury and in the failure of the wider criminal justice system to review satisfactorily the original decisions of the respective juries.[42] The anti-Irish hysteria encouraged by certain sections of the press was hardly conducive to dispassionate verdicts either. It is also instructive to examine more closely the term 'miscarriage of justice'. This can mean that the manifestly innocent have been wrongly convicted against the evidence, as many would argue the Birmingham defendants were. It can also, however, refer to convictions in circumstances where the standard of proof has been altered so that it is legally easier than under usual conditions to prove guilt, as in the Diplock system. It must be conceded that there have not been any miscarriages of justice in the Diplock system in the first sense. This is true by definition. There have been no public campaigns in respect of Diplock defendants comparable to those mounted for the Birmingham and Guildford accused. But this does not mean that innocent people have not been wrongly convicted. It is easier for the prosecution to prove guilt in the Diplock system compared with the trial of non-scheduled indictable offences, a result primarily of the absence of the jury and the different rules governing the admissibility of confessions. After all, the whole purpose of Lord Diplock's inquiry was to make recommendations as to how convictions in terrorist cases could be obtained more readily.

Political Safeguards

In addition to bringing a fresh set of minds to the courtroom juries have such obvious qualities as the fact that they contain people of both sexes. The Northern Ireland judiciary is exclusively male.[43] Jurors generally live on salaries or state benefits amounting to a mere fraction of a judge's income, and they come from every walk of life, from all backgrounds and classes. These facts indicate what is arguably the most important aspect of the jury system — their essentially political rather than legal advantage.

Jury service is the only opportunity for ordinary men and women to exercise direct power in matters of state. This is particularly significant in Northern Ireland where, in contrast with the rest of the UK, all magistrates are trained lawyers rather than lay persons. Lord Devlin puts the point eloquently:

> The jury is the means by which the people play a direct part in the application of the law.... Remember too that judges are part of the establishment. Blackstone called them 'a select body of men'. Their decisions, he wrote, 'in spite of their own natural integrity will have frequently an involuntary bias towards their own rank and dignity.' Rank and dignity are no longer what count. But there is still the like divide between the people who settle what is to happen to others and the people who have things settled for them. In our society in the great questions of personal liberty it is the governed who decide: this is what the jury system means. It is idle to suppose that there will not be times when the governors think that the governed are foolish and unreasonable.[44]

The removal of this vital element of self-government and public participation in the criminal justice process is fundamentally undesirable. In so far as it stems from the view that the people are not fit to decide important issues, it is also arrogant. As Mr A.W. (now Lord) Stallard said in the Committee debates on the 1973 Bill:

> We have seen this constant lobbying, this kind of pressure, being built up to do something about juries because they are composed in the main of people like us, ordinary people who really ought not to be involved, some of them say, as the ordinary workers do not know enough to be able to make a rational judgment; we are all a bit thick and ought therefore to leave it to professionals.[45]

The trial of scheduled offences by jury would also bring the public, including people who support paramilitary organisations, directly into contact with the reality of the violence which is being carried out ostensibly on their behalf.

It is essential in any society, particularly in a divided society like Northern Ireland, that the legal system has the confidence of the public. The importance of this was stressed by Lord Diplock himself in 1973 in the House of Lords:

> The courts of Northern Ireland have a reputation, and have maintained throughout these troubles a reputation, for impartiality.... It is essential in the happier future that we all hope is coming for

Northern Ireland that nothing will have happened which will sully that reputation.[46]

Yet, as Harvey points out:

> Lord Diplock made the greatest contribution of any one person to the weakening of public trust and respect for the courts and judiciary of Northern Ireland. While certain individual judges still command considerable respect in the legal community and further afield, the courts in which they sit do not.[47]

Research conducted by Boyle, Hadden and Hillyard and by Walsh confirms the suggestion that the introduction of the Diplock courts has further weakened the confidence of certain sections of the public in the administration of justice.[48] Above all, the Diplock courts undermine public confidence in the criminal justice system because they remove the most important basis for it − the public's own participation in the justice system as jurors.

Sir George Baker's analysis of the public confidence issue is weak. He states:

> One consequence of the suspension of jury trial is that in the public eye the judiciary assumed total responsibility for all apparent miscarriages of justice ... the judge all too easily became identified with the security forces ... it is a view we received on all sides.[49]

This view is then dismissed in five words: 'This assumes miscarriages of justice.' It does not. It records unease about *apparent* miscarriages of justice. Public confidence stems from the second half of the old adage 'Justice must not only be done. It must also be seen to be done.' Baker seems unduly confident of the former and unconcerned with the latter.

Arguably one important factor undermining public confidence in the Diplock courts is the significant number of 'ordinary offences', i.e. those which are not connected with the current civil unrest and which would normally be tried by jury, which have fallen into the Diplock catch-net. This is the result of assigning, as the EPA does, a list of crimes ('scheduled offences') to be tried by the non-jury courts irrespective of the motivation or associations of the person committing them, a problem predicted by the Labour opposition in 1973.[50] Walsh estimates that some 40 per cent of offences tried in the Diplock courts in 1981 were unrelated to terrorist activities.[51]

Baker accepted the injustice of trying non-terrorist offenders in the Diplock courts and made a number of recommendations as to how such cases could be 'certified out', i.e. authorised by the Attorney General to be tried by jury.[52] Although these suggestions are to be welcomed as far as they go, their underlying premise is highly unsatisfactory. It is inconsistent to suggest that those for whom the Diplock courts were designed get a fair trial, yet 'ordinary' criminals who end up there due to quirks of the scheduling system do not. A trial procedure does not become fair because it is politically expedient.

The history of security force defendant trials in the Diplock courts has particularly damaged the reputation of the justice system. According to a 1985 estimate, 284 people have been killed by either police officers or soldiers in Northern Ireland since the current troubles began.[53] While the circumstances of many of these deaths have been bitterly disputed, there have been few prosecutions and few convictions. The controversy about the legality of many of these fatal shootings has tended to centre around prosecution policy[54] and the way in which the courts have applied the relevant law.[55] The law states that 'A person may use such force as is reasonable in the circumstances in the prevention of crime, or in effecting or assisting in the lawful arrest of offenders or of persons unlawfully at large.'[56] In the Diplock courts, the judge decides whether in a particular case the fatal force used was 'reasonable in the circumstances'. This is a question which, perhaps more than any other, should be decided by the public on whose behalf the agencies of law enforcement operate rather than by another employee of the state.

Justifications for the Suspension of Trial by Jury in 1973

The Diplock Report conceded its own lack of facts and figures concerning intimidation, perverse verdicts and the anticipated collapse of the Northern Irish jury system. 'It is fair to say,' the report read,

> that we have not had our attention drawn to complaints of convictions that were plainly perverse and complaints of acquittals which were plainly perverse are rare.... The threat of intimidation of witnesses which we have already described extends also to jurors, though not to the same extent.[57]

The complete absence of any systematic data on the extent of the two alleged problems of perverse verdicts and juror intimidation provoked critical comment both inside and outside Parliament. Lord Diplock's reply in the House of Lords was: 'When I see a fire starting, and indeed we saw a fire starting then, I send for the fire brigade, not a statistician.'[58] A pragmatic approach, it might be thought, but should a judge be quite so contemptuous of calls for the evidence on which he bases his judgment?

Since the Diplock Report disclosed no adequate grounds for dispensing with trial by jury[59] the Parliamentary debates must be considered in order to assess the evidence and arguments on which the decision was taken. It is noteworthy that all the debates took place in the House of Commons. Disappointingly, given the House of Lords' deserved reputation for producing a high standard of debate, the clause in the 1973 Bill which suspended the right to trial by jury for scheduled offences received virtually no discussion whatever in this chamber. Lord Gardiner conceded at the outset on behalf of the Opposition: 'We are persuaded by the Diplock Commission's Report that the case for not having juries is made out.'[60] Lord Hailsham, the Lord Chancellor, claimed to have 'some startling figures'[61] and 'quite voluminous'[62] evidence to support the government's case. However, he declined to give details in the debate and refused a written request from the National Council of Civil Liberties that the figures be made available.

The debates in the House of Commons, in contrast, were stormy. The Attorney General, Sir Peter (now Lord) Rawlinson, provided the focus by stating during the debate on the second reading that the government was concerned about two matters: 'First, the intimidation of jurors; secondly, verdicts and jury disagreements running – I put it no higher – contrary to the evidence.'[63] Throughout the debates such verdicts and disagreements were referred to as 'perverse'. Opposition MPs lost no time in pressing for definite evidence of intimidation or perverse juries. Mr William (now Viscount) Whitelaw accepted that the Opposition was right to press for such evidence and passed the task to the Attorney General. He also conceded that up to that point the evidence might not have been sufficient to justify the step proposed but stated that he must have regard to 'what might happen in the future'.[64] Pressed to disclose whether there had been any definite examples of juries having returned perverse verdicts the Secretary of State would go no further than to say that 'some of the verdicts given had been rather hard to understand'.[65]

Bernadette Devlin forcefully expressed the dissatisfaction felt by Opposition MPs of all parties:

> We have not heard from the government, and certainly not from Lord Diplock, one concrete point of evidence to show that it is necessary for this step to be taken. We have heard of packed juries. But where is the statistical evidence? How many packed juries have there been? What is the percentage of juries that have been packed one way or the other? If there have been perverse judgments, convictions or acquittals, what is the percentage?[66]

Winding up the second-reading debate, the Attorney General for the first time descended to detail. He gave a vague and anecdotal list of instances of the intimidation of jurors.[67] One of the few specific cases to which he referred was an example of witness, not juror, intimidation. As though conscious of the inadequacy of his evidence, the Attorney General explained that information was very hard to come by.[68] This is plainly unsatisfactory. First of all, the government shouldered the burden of proving the necessity of the suspension of trial by jury and this burden cannot be discharged with inadequate evidence. The inadequacy of the evidence is not reduced by claiming that it was hard to obtain. Secondly, there is no single self-evident reason why evidence was hard to obtain. One possible reason is that it did not exist.

The Attorney General then dealt with the question of 'perverse' verdicts. Again he resorted to an anecdotal list.[69] It may be that his desire to simplify examples led to them being unsatisfactory. One glaring example of perversity was, he suggested, as follows: 'a leader of a UDA unit was identified as taking part in the armed robbery of a Post Office — result of the case, acquittal.'[70]

It is astonishing to find a lawyer stating that an acquittal in a case which turned on identification evidence was obviously perverse. The unreliability of identification evidence has been extensively catalogued[71] and there are rules of law and practice which seek to prevent unsafe convictions being based upon it.[72] It is a question for the jury whether evidence of identification is reliable. Merely because they decide that it is not in a particular case does not make the acquittal perverse. Moreover, the assumption made in each case cited by the Attorney General as an example of a perverse acquittal is that certain facts were established, but this is not the case. In criminal trials the judge makes no findings of fact. The jury considers the version of the facts put forward by the prosecution against the evidence adduced in support. If they think the prosecution evidence is unreliable or inadequate, they must acquit.

The unsatisfactory nature of the evidence presented by the government at the second-reading debate gave the 1973 Bill a hotly contested Committee stage. Shortly after the session began Mr Kevin McNamara highlighted an important inconsistency in the government's approach. The Prime Minister and the Secretary of State had earlier in the year given the House figures for the number of convictions for criminal offences relating to terrorism which were said to be so impressive that they 'spoke for themselves'.[73] Mr McNamara agreed, but offered a different interpretation of what they said: 'They speak in many cases of the strength and courage of the juries of Northern Ireland and the strength of the jury system in Northern Ireland.'[74] Mr Peter Archer demanded to know if there was any actual evidence of juror intimidation.[75] Regarding the Attorney General's point that evidence of intimidation was hard to come by since those jurors who had been intimidated would be too frightened to complain, he said:

> It is a little like arguing that people who have been liquidated by Daleks are not likely to complain afterwards about their liquidation and to go on from that to argue that the fact that no one has ever complained of being liquidated by Daleks is a positive argument in favour of the proposition that people are liquidated by Daleks.[76]

The Attorney General replied to these criticisms by stating that the upsurge in Loyalist violence since the Diplock Report had been accompanied by an increase in perverse verdicts and that this had been the basis of the anxieties expressed to Diplock.[77] The Reverend Ian Paisley was clearly angered by this explanation and demanded further details before he would accept that the majority of Protestants serving on juries in Northern Ireland were not doing their duty.[78]

In reply the Attorney General related brief details of four 'perverse' acquittals.[79] Two of these involved allegations of the intimidation of witnesses, one had to do with a defendant who appeared to have been acquitted after raising the defence of duress, and the last hinged on identification evidence. Then he reported the views of the prosecuting bar in Northern Ireland that the time had come to eliminate jury trials.[80] The Reverend Ian Paisley made the obvious but telling criticism of such 'evidence': 'Of course the prosecutor is annoyed when he does not get a verdict.... I can well understand a Crown prosecutor not liking a verdict. But I do not think that that establishes the argument that juries should be done away with.'[81]

After praying in aid 'the urgent representations' of a single Belfast solicitor,[82] the Attorney General candidly admitted that he had no 'actual numbers' and turned to the pressures imposed upon the jury system by the property qualification for jury service which, he said, was 'more likely to draw people from a section of society which may not be anxious or may not be prepared to bring in the verdict which they clearly and truthfully should do'.[83] The weakness of this explanation scarcely needs pointing out; if the property qualification caused problems, the answer should have been its reform or abolition, not the jettisoning of the jury.

The committee stage concluded with Mr Merlyn Rees declaring that the Opposition had 'listened carefully' to the government's case but were still 'not convinced'.[84] When it came to the vote the committee split right down the middle (12:12) on the jury suspending clause. Such unlikely bedfellows as the Reverend Ian Paisley and Mr Gerry Fitt found themselves in the 'Noes' lobby. The decision was therefore in the hands of the Chairman (Harold Gurden) who used his casting vote in favour of the clause. When voting Mr Gurden said that he was merely fulfilling the Parliamentary custom that the chair's casting vote should be in favour of the status quo,[85] and that he understood this to mean in favour of the clause under discussion. However, as Mr A. W. Stallard noted later, the custom was uncertain; many members took the view that the status quo in question should have been the retention of trial by jury.[86] It is disturbing that the removal of the right to trial by jury involved such an uncertain Parliamentary procedure.

In the final debate on the third reading, the Attorney General gave brief details of further examples of intimidation or perverse verdicts. On this occasion the list was longer, but it remained anecdotal.[87] Again, the 'perverse' juries were sometimes those confronted with a case turning on identification evidence, and there was still no indication of the extent of the alleged problem even though the obvious question, asked repeatedly in the months since the publication of the Diplock Report, was 'in how many cases does this problem occur?'

The Attorney General asserted that 50 per cent of those on the jury panel applied successfully to be excused using 'every possible excuse'.[88] The source of this figure was not given. In any event there is no obvious inference to be drawn. One study in Birmingham, for example, found that a 'sizeable proportion' of prospective jurors applied to be excused.[89] Surely before an institution as important as trial by jury is removed, there should be a better basis than that of untested conclusions drawn from unsubstantiated figures.

Reference was made to the views of the DPP for Northern Ireland[90] and to the problem of the courts and public galleries being packed with 'bully boys'.[91] The former are further views of professional prosecutors while the latter is an example of what Mr Silkin called 'an ample generalisation in exchange for our request for particularity'.[92] The fact that it was expressed as a generality does not mean that the problem did not exist, but it does mean that no effort was made to discover how serious or widespread a problem it was before the draconian step of jury suspension was taken. The 'bully boy' difficulty also occurs in England[93] but no one would seriously suggest that the jury be abolished because of it, certainly not until a full study of its dimensions had been carried out. As one MP said during the Committee stage: 'The … impression that I got … was that … this step would never be taken here but that it was good enough for Northern Ireland.'[94]

At the end of the third-reading debate the opponents of the Bill were still not convinced that the government had made out a case for the suspension of jury trial.[95] Without doubt, the evidence adduced in 1973 to justify the suspension of jury trial for scheduled offences was seriously deficient.

Perverse Acquittals and Intimidation Reconsidered

Little fresh evidence concerning perverse acquittals and the intimidation of jurors in Northern Ireland in trials relating to the unfolding disorder of the 1969–73 period has since come to light. Three studies, *Justice in Northern Ireland: A Study in Social Confidence*[96] by Hadden and Hillyard, *Law and State: The Case of Northern Ireland*[97] by Boyle, Hadden and Hillyard and *Prosecutions in Northern Ireland*[98] by the Law Officers' Department, lend support to the perverse acquittals thesis. The relevant sections in each study were based on surveys of all criminal cases heard between January and June 1973 by the Belfast City Commission, the forerunner of the Belfast Crown Court, which tried serious offences committed in the Belfast area.

Until 1974 there was a property qualification for jury service in Northern Ireland. Only those paying rates of at least £20 annually for real estate in a city, 'county of a city' or urban district not in such a county and at least £16 elsewhere were eligible. Not surprisingly, disproportionately more Protestants than Catholics were able to fulfil these requirements and, although increases in the rateable valuation of property in Northern Ireland since this provision was enacted in 1926[99] progressively brought the less well-off within reach of a jury summons, the jury remained a largely male, middle-aged, middle-class Protestant institution until 1974. Subject to certain exemptions (e.g. teachers, lawyers, doctors, nurses) and disqualifications (e.g. persons recently or currently imprisoned) the Juries (NI) Order 1974 made everyone in Northern Ireland between 18 and 70 whose name appears on the electoral register liable to serve on a jury. It is ironic that this change occurred only a year after the suspension of jury trial for scheduled offences. Had it been introduced instead of the Diplock courts it could have made a major contribution towards reducing the likelihood of sectarian verdicts, whether or not they were, in fact, a serious problem.

Importantly, attention has focused on allegedly perverse *acquittals* rather than perverse *verdicts*, which would include perverse convictions. It has been argued that trial judges could and did prevent the latter by directing juries to acquit or declaring that there was 'no case to answer'.[100] This may be true but the lack of official concern with the possibility of perverse convictions reveals a preoccupation with punishment which is consistent with other conviction-maximising aspects of the Diplock process. There is no evidence to suggest that juries perversely acquitted all Protestants in all criminal cases tried in Northern Ireland since partition. However, the Boyle, Hadden and Hillyard and the Law Officers' figures appear to show an identifiable difference in acquittal rates between Protestants and Catholics tried by the Belfast City Commission between January and June 1973 and it seems that this difference is due, at least partly, to jury bias. The most plausible explanation for the apparent bias of at least some juries in favour of Loyalist defendants is that there was a widespread belief in the Unionist community at the time that Loyalist violence was essentially defensive and reactive.[101] It was, therefore, partially excusable, whereas Nationalist violence was completely unjustified, threatened the very stability of the status quo and required convictions in a greater number of cases.

Two caveats must be observed concerning the perverse acquittals claim, however. First, it has been argued that leading prosecution counsels in the early 1970s were closely identified with the Unionist cause and may have mounted much less convincing prosecutions of Loyalist than of Nationalist defendants charged with similar offences. The higher acquittal rate for Loyalists may, therefore, be due to defects in prosecution practice rather than to jury bias.[102] Second, internment, which was used almost exclusively against Nationalists, may have distorted the figures. Nationalist suspects against whom the evidence was weak may have been dealt with via internment with the result that only the more compelling Nationalist cases reached the courts.[103]

As far as intimidation of jurors is concerned the evidence has never advanced beyond hearsay. There are simply no available figures whatsoever. This does not mean that there was no intimidation of jurors in Northern Ireland from 1969 to 1973. What it does mean is that, in the absence of any solid evidence, the extent to which it was a problem remains in considerable doubt. Unquestionably, jurors were vulnerable to intimidation from paramilitary organisations prior to the introduction of the Diplock courts. But it does not follow from this that suspending jury trial was the only or most appropriate response. A significant shortcoming of the case in favour of the Diplock courts is that no serious consideration was ever given by the authorities to ways in which jurors could be protected from intimidation, e.g. by concealing their identity from the public at every stage in the trial process.

The intimidation thesis seems to have attracted more than its fair share of highly suspect, if not entirely spurious, arguments. One notable example is the parallel drawn between the intimidation of witnesses and that of jurors. The Gardiner Committee reported in 1975 that, between 1 January 1972 and 31 August 1974, '482 ... civilian witnesses to murder and other terrorist offences were either too afraid to make any statement at all or, having made a statement implicating an individual were so afraid that they refused in any circumstances to give evidence in court.'[104]

If this was the case with respect to witnesses, it has been suggested, the same must have been true of jurors. Why, then, are there no comparable figures? The flaw in this line of reasoning is that despite concrete evidence of the risk to civilian witnesses, prohibiting them from testifying for their own protection was never seriously countenanced by the government. Yet on the basis of rumour and supposition devoid of a single statistic, trial by jury was suspended. The explanation appears to lie once more in the conviction orientation of the Diplock process. Since civilian witnesses may have a role to play in securing convictions, the authorities clearly consider it inexpedient to deprive the courts of their assistance. Juries, as argued above, may be less willing to convict than judges and are, therefore, a hindrance to a conviction-oriented system. It would seem, therefore, that the risks to which jurors were allegedly exposed in the early 1970s conveniently rationalised an exercise in conviction-maximisation at the expense of defendants' rights.

A Proposal for the Restoration of Jury Trial to Scheduled Offences

It is clear that the evidence concerning perverse acquittals and juror intimidation cannot sustain the case for the suspension of jury trial for scheduled offences. The jury should, therefore, be restored to the trial of these offences forthwith. Three broad principles should be observed to make the trial process both safer and fairer.

First, all scheduled offence trials should begin in Belfast before a jury. Separate jury panels should be selected for scheduled offence cases from all the jury books in Northern Ireland in accordance with the procedure governed by the Juries (NI) Order 1974 which makes everyone in Northern Ireland between 18 and 70 whose name appears on the electoral register liable to a jury summons (subject to the standard exemptions and disqualifications). If either defence or prosecution in any scheduled case could prove that it was more likely than not that an attempt had been made to intimidate anyone whose name appeared on the scheduled offence jury panel list, whether by opponents or associates of the accused, the trial should be re-started before a different judge and a fresh jury. If intimidation was proved to have recurred the trial should automatically be conducted by a judge sitting without a jury. For ease of reference this could be known as 'Contingent Jury Trial'.[105] If the other proposals suggested below were also implemented, the probability of the non-jury option being exercised would be extremely low.

Second, the random and democratic element in the selection of jurors established by the Juries (NI) Order 1974 should be extended by abolishing the prosecution's right to 'stand by' and by limiting the number of peremptory challenges, to be exercisable by the defence, to three per defendant. Defence counsel in Northern Ireland currently possess the right to object to the empanelling of twelve jurors per defendant in non-scheduled criminal trials on indictment without having to give reasons.[106] The prosecution has no such 'peremptory challenges' but can 'stand by' any number of jurors, i.e. have them go to the end of the queue without having to show cause. It would be fairer if each had exactly the same opportunities to influence the selection of jurors in the courtroom. The best way this can be achieved is for defence and prosecution to be given the same number of peremptory challenges with no right to stand by available to the prosecution.[107]

Thirdly, jurors in scheduled offence trials should be anonymous to all but a skeleton staff of Belfast court officials.[108] Lawyers for both defence and prosecution and the public should be denied access to the scheduled offence jury panel lists. Prospective jurors need not know until they have arrived at the Crumlin Road Courthouse in Belfast whether they have been called for a scheduled or non-scheduled case. In order to conceal scheduled offence jurors from the public a jury panel room common for all scheduled cases should be provided to which, apart from these jurors, only selected court officials would have access. The summoning of these jurors to particular trials should be by number only and the jury box and all other parts of the court-house between it and the panel room should be hidden from public view. Court administrators should look favourably upon applications for exclusion from jury service for scheduled offences made by people living in those parts of Northern Ireland in which Loyalist and Republican paramilitaries wield considerable influence. Persons having served on a jury in a scheduled case should be excused any further jury service as of right.

The suggestion that a scheduled offence jury should be anonymous has been greeted with dismay in certain quarters. In the Committee debates on the Northern Ireland (Emergency Provisions) Bill 1987, Mr Enoch Powell, for example, referred to it as a 'fancy device' which amounted to a 'contradiction in terms'.[109] Others have suggested that it amounts to a serious derogation from the rights of an accused. However, a recent High Court decision on the anonymity of magistrates tends to support the view that the non-disclosure of jurors' identity is an acceptable modification of normal procedures in exceptional circumstances such as the trial of scheduled offences. In *R. v. Felixstowe Justices, ex-p. Leigh*,[110] a journalist challenged the legality of a policy adopted by magistrates at Felixstowe, Ipswich and Woodbridge which involved withholding the names of justices from the press and public during and after hearings. It was held that this was contrary to the principle of open justice and an 'unwarranted and an unlawful obstruction to the right to know who sits in judgment'. The court nevertheless accepted that 'a clerk to justices would ... act with justification in refusing during and after a hearing to give the name of one of the justices to a person who the clerk reasonably believes requires that information solely for mischievous purposes.'[111]

What was deemed objectionable about the policy in question was its blanket nature. It covered all cases irrespective of whether there were risks to the bench or not. A resolution of the Council of Magistrates Association of July 1985, which was endorsed by the Press Council, was quoted without comment in the course of judgment. On the issue of exceptions to the disclosure of identity rule it is more detailed than the High Court decision but entirely consistent with it. It states:

> Names should be withheld where there are substantial grounds for belief that the magistrates concerned, or members of their families, or other associates might in consequence of the proceedings be subject to violence or harassment. Examples are where defendants are believed to be members of terrorist groups, or other organisations habitually using violence or harassment to achieve or publicise their objectives.[112]

If the names of justices may lawfully be withheld in cases involving terrorist groups in England, why not the names of jurors in similar cases in Northern Ireland? The proposals offered here go further in recommending a jury concealed from the public and press galleries. This is, however, merely an extension of the anonymity principle which is justified in the circumstances. An anonymous and partially concealed jury is better than no jury at all.

Conclusion

The pivotal position of the jury in the British and Irish systems of criminal justice is not a matter of historical accident. It is a recognition of the advantages which jury trial ensures. Any interference with jury trial, however temporary, therefore, should require convincing justifications rooted in solid and compelling evidence.

An examination of the Parliamentary debates shows that the evidence which was presented to justify the introduction of jury-less Diplock courts in Northern Ireland in 1973 was seriously deficient. At most, it indicated that eligibility for jury service should have been democratised, the selection of juries randomised and the identity of jurors concealed. Ironically, in 1974, the first two of these principles were introduced to those parts of the jury system left unaffected by the EPA but the implications of these changes for the Diplock system were never adequately considered by Parliament.

Years after the introduction of the Diplock courts politically motivated violence remains a feature of life in Northern Ireland. Alterations in the pattern of violence can be attributed to the complex interaction of security policies with internal self-initiated changes by the paramilitary organisations themselves, but it is clear that the Diplock process has not succeeded in its aim of bringing peace and stability to Northern Ireland. Indeed it can be argued that, on the contrary, the Diplock courts have fuelled the sense of injustice which has sustained the present conflict. A full return to jury trial, modified for scheduled offences in the manner suggested, would be a significant and essential step in the direction of stability and democratic law enforcement which should precede or accompany more wide-ranging political change.

Notes

For a more detailed account of the issues discussed in this chapter see S.C. Greer and A. White, *Abolishing the Diplock Courts: The Case for Restoring Jury Trial to Scheduled Offences in Northern Ireland* (The Cobden Trust, 1986).

1.   Mr William (now Viscount) Whitelaw, Secretary of State for Northern Ireland, H.C. Debs., vol. 855, col. 276.

2.   *Report of the Commission to Consider Legal Procedures to Deal with Terrorist Activities in Northern Ireland* (The Diplock Report) Cmnd. 5185 (London: HMSO, 1972) para. 37. It is noteworthy that Lord Diplock alone of the Commission members visited Northern Ireland and his meetings there were restricted to 'members of the security forces on the ground' (para. 4).

3.   *Report of a Committee to Consider, in the Context of Civil Liberties and Human Rights, Measures to Deal with Terrorism in Northern Ireland* (The Gardiner Report) Cmnd. 5847 (London: HMSO, 1975) para. 26.

4.   *Review of the Operation of the Northern Ireland (Emergency Provisions) Act 1978* (The Baker Report) Cmnd. 9222 (London: HMSO, 1984) p. 139.

5.   *Agreement between the Government of the United Kingdom of Great Britain and Northern Ireland and the Government of the Republic of Ireland,* November 1985, Cmnd. 9657 (London: HMSO) art. 8.

6.   See for example the remarks of the Solicitor General, Sir Patrick Mayhew, in the Committee debates on the NIEPA 1987 (Parl. Debs. Standing Committee D, 19 February 1987, col. 312).

7.   Northern Ireland (Emergency Provisions) Act 1978 (Amendment) Order 1986, SI No. 75.

8.   For example, Mayhew, Committee debates, supra.

9.   Cmnd. 9657, art. 8.

10. Jury Trial (Amendment) (Northern Ireland) Order 1987.

11. P. Devlin, *Trial by Jury* (Stevens, 1956) p. 164.

12. The Baker Report (Appendix H) and *Judicial Statistics for Northern Ireland* 1985 and 1986.

13. See for example W.R. Cornish, *The Jury* (Penguin, 1968) and Devlin, *Trial by Jury*, for further details.

14. The suspension of jury trial in Northern Ireland is not unprecedented. Immediately prior to partition all imprisonable offences in Ireland were triable by court martial (by virtue of the Restoration of Order in Ireland Act 1920, s.1(2)). The Prevention of Crime (Ireland) Act suspended jury trial in 1882 (see C. Townshend, *Political Violence in Ireland: Government and Resistance Since 1848* (Clarendon, 1984)).

15. A.T. Denning, *What Next in the Law* (Butterworths, 1982) p. 13.

16. *Commentaries*, Book iv, p. 350.

17. This is true of both the old form of the oath and also of the new simpler form used since 3 December 1984. See Practice Direction (Crime: Jury Oath) [1984].

18. See Judges Rules 1964, principle (e), approved in e.g. *R. v. Harz & Power* [1967] 1 AC 760; *DPP v. Ping Lin* [1976] AC 574.

19. See V. Bevan and K. Lidstone, *A Guide to the Police and Criminal Evidence Act 1984* (Butterworths, 1985) p. 297. See also the wider discretion to exclude evidence contained in s. 78.

20. See especially D.P.J. Walsh, *The Use and Abuse of Emergency Legislation in Northern Ireland* (The Cobden Trust, 1983) pp. 46–53, and Chapter 2 herein.

21. *R. v. Francis* (1959) 43 Cr. App. R. 174.

22. See J.D. Jackson, *Northern Ireland Supplement to Cross on Evidence (5th edn)* (SLS, 1983) p. 13. See also Walsh, *Emergency Legislation*, p. 99.

23. Walsh, *Emergency Legislation*, p. 99.

24. *R. v. Murray* [1951] 1 KB 391.

25. H.C. Debs., vol. 855, col. 388.

26. See D.S. Greer, *The Admissibility of Confessions Under the Northern Ireland (Emergency Provisions) Act* (1980) 31 NILQ 205, 207.

27. A number of experienced Belfast solicitors have expressed their continuing concern about the inclusion of such inadmissible evidence in the papers read by the judge in scheduled offence cases (Interviews by authors in Belfast, 28 February 1985–1 March 1985).

28. Walsh, *Emergency Legislation*, pp. 86, 90.

29. See Chapter 4 and S.C. Greer, 'Supergrasses and the Legal System in Britain and Northern Ireland' (1986) LQR 198 and 'The Rise and Fall of the Northern Ireland Supergrass System' (1987) CLR 663.

30. See T. Gifford, *Supergrasses: The Use of Accomplice Evidence in Northern Ireland* (The Cobden Trust, 1984) para. 89.

31. *Davies v. DPP* [1954] AC 378.

32. *R. v. Graham* (1983) 7 NIJB; *R. v. Gibney* (1983) 13 NIJB; *R. v. Donnelly* (1983) (unreported); *R. v. McCormick* (1982) 3 NIJB.

33. Devlin, *Trial by Jury*, p. 66.

34. Contempt of Court Act 1981, ss. 1 and 2.

35. See *Arlidge and Eady on Contempt* (Sweet & Maxwell, 1982) pp. 112–13.

36. Gifford, *Supergrasses*, para. 43.

37. In *Attorney General v. BBC* [1981] AC 303, Viscount Dilhorne said: 'It is

sometimes asserted that no judge will be influenced in his judgment by anything said by the media and consequently that the need to prevent the publication of matter prejudicial to the hearing of a case only exists where the decision rests with laymen. This claim to judicial superiority over human frailty is one that I find some difficulty in accepting.... It should, I think, be recognised that a man may not be able to put that which he has seen, heard or read entirely out of his mind and that he may be subconsciously affected by it.'

38. Baker report, para. 122.
39. *Judicial Statistics for Northern Ireland*, 1973–86.
40. See Walsh, *Emergency Legislation*.
41. Baker Report, para. 125
42. For further details see C. Mullin, *Error of Judgment* (Poolbeg, 1987); R. Kee, *Trial and Error: The Maguires, the Guildford Pub Bombings and British Justice* (Hamish Hamilton, 1986).
43. The gender used in this chapter is, therefore, deliberate.
44. P. Devlin, *The Judge* (Oxford University Press, 1979) pp. 127–130.
45. Parl. Debs. Standing Committee B, vol. 2, 1972–3, col. 53.
46. H.L. Debs., vol. 344, col. 705.
47. R. Harvey, *Diplock and the Assault on Civil Liberties* (Haldane Society of Socialist Lawyers, 1980) p. 34.
48. Walsh, *Emergency Legislation*, p. 119; Boyle, Hadden and Hillyard, *Law and State: The Case of Northern Ireland* (Martin Robertson, 1975) ch. 7.
49. Baker Report, para. 108, quoting from *Diplock and the Assault on Civil Liberties*.
50. Mr Peter Archer. Parl. Debs. Standing Committee B, vol. 2, col. 62, 1972–3.
51. Walsh, *Emergency Legislation*, pp. 16, 59–60.
52. Baker Report, paras. 130–51. The mere extension of the power to certify out is insufficient. As Walsh discovered (p. 82) the present power is not used to the full by the Attorney General although suitable cases have arisen.
53. D. Roche, 'Patterns of Violence in Northern Ireland in 1984', *Fortnight*, no. 218. See also Chapters 5 and 6.
54. See S.C. Greer and T. Jennings, 'Political Expediency in Plastic Bullet Cases', *Fortnight*, no. 221, p. 8.
55. See T. Hadden, 'When is it Murder to Shoot to Kill?', *Fortnight*, no. 218. Also A. Jennings, 'Northern Ireland: The Legal Control of the Use of Lethal Force', (1985) *New Law Journal*, vol. 135, 921.
56. Criminal Law Act (Northern Ireland) 1967, S.3(1). This is the same provision as that applicable in England and Wales.
57. Diplock Report, paras. 35 and 36.
58. H.L. Debs., vol. 344, col. 706.
59. Only seven paragraphs out of 119 refer to the jury question.
60. H.L. Debs., vol. 344, col. 697. A notable exception was Lord Brockway's contribution at the Committee Stage (H.L. Debs., vol. 344, cols. 1411–13).
61. Ibid., col. 714.
62. Ibid., col. 693.
63. H.C. Debs., vol. 855., col. 380.
64. Ibid., cols. 281–2.
65. Ibid., col. 282.
66. Ibid., col. 305.
67. Ibid., cols. 380–1.

68. Ibid., col. 383.
69. Ibid., cols. 381–3.
70. Ibid., col. 382.
71. See for example the *Eleventh Report of the Criminal Law Revision Committee* (the Devlin Committee Report) Cmnd. 338, 1976; *Cross On Evidence* (6th edn) (Butterworths, 1985) pp. 44–8.
72. *R. v. Turnbull* [1977] QB 224.
73. The Prime Minister said: 'since the beginning of the year ... there were 157 convictions for specific criminal offences relating to terrorism. These figures speak for themselves', H.C. Debs., vol. 853, cols. 1323 and 1553.
74. Parl. Debs. Standing Committee B, 1972–3, vol. 2, col. 29.
75. Ibid., col. 66.
76. Ibid., col. 63.
77. Ibid., cols. 69–70.
78. Ibid., cols. 85–90.
79. Ibid., cols. 70–1.
80. Ibid., col. 71.
81. Ibid., col. 89.
82. Ibid., col. 71.
83. Ibid., col. 73.
84. Ibid., col. 94.
85. Ibid., cols. 95–7.
86. Ibid., col. 97.
87. H.C. Debs., vol. 859, cols. 765–6.
88. Ibid., col. 767.
89. J. Baldwin and M. McConville, *Jury Trials* (Clarendon, 1979) p. 90. One of the authors of this chapter knows of trials at the Old Bailey in which a dozen or more jury panel members requested to be, and were, excused for reasons ranging from pre-arranged holidays to hardship for the self-employed.
90. H.C. Debs., vol. 859, cols. 767–9.
91. Ibid., vol. 855, col. 381.
92. Ibid., vol. 859, col. 738.
93. The newspapers provide frequent examples. On 12 September 1984 a trial at Manchester Crown Court of three policemen was stopped after two jurors reported that they had been photographed as they left the court (*The Times*, 13 September 1984). One of the authors has seen a trial at the Old Bailey in which an application was made to the trial judge to exclude certain persons from the public gallery.
94. Mr A.W. Stallard. Parl. Debs. Standing Committee B, 1972–3, vol. 2, col. 52.
95. H.C. Debs., vol. 859, col. 775.
96. Cobden Trust, 1973.
97. Martin Robertson, 1975.
98. HMSO, 1974.
99. The Jury Laws Amendment Act (NI) 1926.
100. Diplock Report, para. 35.
101. Such views persist. Mr Cecil Walker in the December 1984 EPA renewal debate claimed that 'Loyalist Terrorism was very much reactive' (H.C. Debs., vol. 70, col. 634).
102. Baker Report, para. 100.

103. Boyle *et al.*, *Law and State*, p. 75.
104. Para. 27.
105. The idea is not a new one. It was raised in wider form as an amendment to the 1973 Bill by Sam Silkin MP. Baker Report, para. 151, also gives cautious support.
106. Juries Act (NI) 1953, s. 9 (1).
107. At common law an accused was allowed 35 peremptory challenges. This was reduced to 20 in 1825. The Criminal Justice Act 1948 reduced the number to seven and the present entitlement of three was set by the Criminal Law Act 1977, s.43. It is disturbing that the Criminal Justice Bill, before Parliament at the time of writing, envisages the abolition of the peremptory challenge in England and Wales with no corresponding reduction in the right to stand by. It is of the greatest importance that some limited provision be made for both defence and prosecution to eliminate jurors from the panel for undisclosed reasons. In certain cases the exercise of such rights may result in a more racially or sexually balanced jury or may exclude prospective jurors who are prejudiced against one side or the other. In other trials it may help reassure the defendant, who generally needs more reassurance than the prosecution, and indeed the public at large, that at least in the selection of jurors the dice are not loaded.
108. See A. Jennings and D. Wolchover, 'Northern Ireland: Star Chamber versus the Gang of Twelve', NLJ 3 August and 10 August 1984.
109. Parl. Debs. Standing Committee D, 19 Febuary 1987, col. 285.
110. [1987] 1 All E.R. 551.
111. Ibid., p. 561 d.
112. Ibid., p. 556 c–d.

4

STEVEN GREER

The Supergrass System

On 21 November 1981, Christopher Black from the Ardoyne area of Belfast was arrested in the north of the city after having participated in an IRA roadblock staged for publicity purposes. After two days of silence in police custody, he began to make the first of a large number of statements implicating himself and others in a catalogue of IRA-related offences. On 24 November, he was granted immunity from prosecution. In the trial that followed, which ran from December 1982 through August 1983, he gave evidence against 38 accused, 35 of whom were convicted.

The trial signalled the launching of a distinct counterinsurgency initiative: the supergrass system. In essence, it was a method of securing the prosecution and conviction of large numbers of allegedly key members of paramilitary organisations for a huge range of offences on the basis of evidence given by alleged accomplices in a series of mass trials. These proceedings quickly became public dramas and were, in certain quarters, denounced as 'show trials'. In the ten years prior to Black's arrest, there had been at least four paramilitary supergrasses.[1] But with Black's appearance, the trickle became a flood. Between November 1981 and November 1983, at least seven Loyalist and 18 Republican supergrasses were responsible for nearly 600 people being arrested and charged with offences connected with paramilitary activities in Northern Ireland.[2]

Several of these defendants were shunted from one supergrass to another as a result either of having been acquitted in one case or of having the evidence against them retracted. Three of the accused in the Kirkpatrick trial, for example, were implicated by five successive supergrasses and spent almost four years in custody before being found guilty of any offence, then only to be acquitted on appeal. This state of affairs has given credence to the accusation that the supergrass system has facilitated a form of 'internment by remand'.[3]

73

Fifteen of the supergrasses retracted their evidence before the trials in which they were involved began or before they were concluded. In the case involving UDA informer James Williamson, charges were withdrawn against all but two accused who had made confessions. As the following table shows, in the ten supergrass trials to date, 55 per cent, or 120 out of 217, of defendants tried at first instance were convicted or pleaded guilty. However, in the five cases in which appeals were lodged, 67 out of the 74 convictions appealed against were quashed. In the opinion of the trial court, or courts, of the 50 outstanding convictions, 48 involved alleged confessions and admissions; in the other two, the accomplice evidence was corroborated by forensic evidence. The overall conviction rate for the ten trials, then, taking the appeal verdicts into account, stands at 42 per cent.

Only two new supergrasses have appeared since November 1983. One of these, Eamonn Collins, withdrew his evidence within a fortnight in March 1985, and the DPP for Northern Ireland decided in October 1986 to drop charges against those implicated by the other, Angela Whoriskey, a year after the initial arrests. Meanwhile, Diplock trials continued. Those tried on the evidence of an alleged accomplice in 1983, 1984 and 1985 accounted for only 12 per cent of the total number of defendants in no-jury trials during this period.[4] Nevertheless, this does not detract from the significance of the supergrass system as a prosecution initiative carefully targeted at the alleged 'godfathers of terrorism'.

The nickname 'grass' for an informer seems to derive from the Cockney rhyming slang 'grasshopper-copper', but it may also owe something to the popular song 'Whispering Grass', and to the term 'snake in the grass'. Whatever the derivation, the actual word 'supergrass' was first coined by journalists in the early 1970s to describe a succession of London bank robbers who not only informed on suspects, but took the next step to enter the witness box to testify against them. As a policy, the supergrass system is not limited to Northern Ireland: supergrasses from illegal paramilitary organisations have also been used by the authorities in Germany and Italy.[5]

Apart from the large number of defendants involved in supergrass cases, three main features distinguish the supergrass from the usual accomplice who decides to give evidence for the prosecution. First, almost without exception, supergrass witnesses in the UK have been the products of deliberate law enforcement initiatives directed either at organised crime, mostly in the south of England, or at paramilitary activity in Northern Ireland. Secondly, they have been deeply involved

Table 4.1 The Supergrass System—The Statistics

Supergrass In order of completion of trials at first instance	Position regarding own offences	No. prosecuted	No. tried	No. convicted at first instance	No. convicted on uncorroborated accomplice evidence at first instance	Type of corroboration in opinion of trial court(s) ('confessions' includes alleged admissions)	No. appealing against conviction	No. of convictions quashed
Joseph Bennett (UVF)	Immunity	16	16	14	11	1 forensic 2 confessions	14	14
Christopher Black (IRA)	Immunity	38	38	35	18	2 forensic 15 confessions	22	18
Kevin McGrady (IRA)	Serving life for murder and other offences	10	10	7	2	5 confessions	3	2
Jackie Grimley (INLA)	Immunity	22	21[(1)]	14[(2)]	—	11 confessions	—	—
John Morgan (IRA)	Immunity	5	5	—	—	—	—	—
Robert Quigley (IRA)	Immunity	16	11[(3)]	10	8	2 confessions	8	8
Raymond Gilmour (IRA)	Immunity	35	35	—	—	—	—	—
James Crockard (UVF)	Serving life for murder and other offences	29	29	8	—	8 confessions	—	—
William 'Budgie' Allen (UVF)	Released in April '86[(4)]	25	25	5	—	5 confessions	—	—
Harry Kirkpatrick (INLA)	3 life sentences	27	27	27	25	2 confessions	27	25
Totals		223	217	120	64	50 confessions 3 forensic	74	67

Total number of convictions outstanding after appeal verdicts: 50
(1) 1 did not answer bail. (2) including 3 guilty pleas. (3) 4 sent for re-trial but released without having been tried when appeal verdict in trial of other 11 delivered. 1 no case to answer.
(4) by the exercise of the Royal prerogative after having served 2 years of a 14 year prison sentence for robbery and other offences.

in these serious violent crimes. Thirdly, in almost every case, they have been motivated by a highly developed sense of self-interest. Other accomplices turning Queen's evidence, by contrast, may emerge anywhere in the UK, may have committed any type of offence involving more than one participant and may take this step at the impetus of any one or more of a variety of motives including genuine contrition, the desire for revenge, or the hope of obtaining some personal advantage, e.g. leniency in punishment, immunity from prosecution or a financial or other material reward.

The prosecuting authorities in Northern Ireland maintain that the closed and secretive nature of paramilitary organisations precludes recourse to normal investigative policing and that if those who have been active in such organisations are prepared to testify it would be wrong for charges not to be preferred on their evidence.[6] Officially, the initiative in each case comes from the suspect, who voluntarily decides, usually after having been arrested, to testify for the Crown. Because the law enforcement process is deemed to be greatly facilitated by such decisions, certain rewards, e.g. police protection from potentially vengeful ex-comrades, immunity from prosecution,[7] help in securing a reduced sentence or early release from prison,[8] luxurious prison cells[9] and in some cases new identities and new lives elsewhere,[10] are considered appropriate. These, it is said, are agreed on a case by case basis and the allegation that the use of supergrasses has ever amounted to a prosecution 'strategy' or 'system' has been vigorously denied.[11]

The available evidence throws considerable doubt on this view. The fact that so many supergrasses appeared over a comparatively short period of time in Northern Ireland suggests that a deliberate shift in prosecution policy occurred in the early 1980s. The key elements facilitating this change appear to be (a) alterations in interrogation priorities to give greater prominence to inducements and threats at the expense of questions with a neutral fact-finding purpose, and (b) advance manpower and finance authorised at a high level for the sort of deals which have been made. Moreover, evidence from supergrasses who have retracted their statements supports the view that the prospect of turning Queen's evidence is usually first mooted by the police rather than the suspect.[12]

In attempting to understand Northern Ireland's supergrass phenomenon it is important to answer a number of central questions. How have the judges in these cases applied the relevant law? How and why did the system emerge and develop as it did? What contrasts and comparisons can be drawn between it and the supergrass experience in England? Finally, what contribution has it made towards the construction of a peaceful and stable society in Northern Ireland?

The Law on Accomplice Evidence

There is no law on supergrass trials as such. Since the first English supergrass case was heard on appeal in 1975,[13] it has been clear that the standard law on accomplice evidence applies. This law has three principal facets. The 'accomplice evidence rule' obliges judges to warn juries of the dangers of convicting an accused on uncorroborated accomplice evidence in any case where an accomplice testifies for the prosecution.[14] If the warning is omitted any convictions secured are likely to be quashed on appeal unless no substantial miscarriage of justice is deemed to have occurred.[15] Second, a number of rules deal with the credibility required of accomplice evidence in order for convictions to be justified. Third, other rules govern what constitutes corroboration. The judgments delivered in several of Northern Ireland's supergrass cases and in another Diplock trial involving the evidence of an accomplice, *R. v. McCormick*,[16] have contributed to the development of each of these areas.

The Accomplice Evidence Rule

The accomplice evidence rule is based upon the premise that accomplices as a class of witness are inherently untrustworthy and that their evidence, in consequence, must be presumed to be unreliable: hence the emphasis on corroboration. The following dangers have traditionally been cited.[17] First, an accomplice-witness is, by definition, a criminal, and therefore a person of bad character whose evidence is 'not entitled to the same consideration as the evidence of a clean man, free from infamy'.[18] Second, he or she may fabricate chunks of his or her 'evidence'. Third, the accomplice may tell the truth about the incidents in question but substitute the names of innocent people, or suspects whom the police are especially anxious to see convicted, for those who actually took part. Fourth, the accomplice-witness may tell the truth about the offences and implicate those who were genuinely involved but change the roles to cast him- or herself in the most favourable light and the others in the worst. Fifth, spurious plausibility could be accorded to false accomplice evidence by virtue of the accomplice's familiarity with the details of the crime or crimes.

All these dangers are particularly acute with respect to supergrasses. Each has been involved in serious and mostly violent crime and is, therefore, of unusually 'bad character' even compared with other possible accomplice-witnesses. The pressure to tell a story sufficiently appealing to the prosecuting authorities to attract the various rewards on offer is also likely to be more intense than with most other accomplices turning Queen's evidence. There is, in addition, ample time and opportunity during the many months spent in police 'protective custody' for false evidence to be rehearsed in preparation for a convincing courtroom appearance.

The mandatory nature of the accomplice evidence warning has led to a bizarre practice in Northern Ireland, where since 1973 a list of offences contained in a schedule to the Northern Ireland (Emergency Provisions) Act 1973 and usually associated with the activities of paramilitary organisations ('scheduled offences') have been tried by the non-jury 'Diplock' courts. Since the judges in these trials are required to discharge the functions of 'tribunal of fact' and 'tribunal of law', the judiciary in Northern Ireland has assumed that the accomplice evidence rule obliges the judge trying a scheduled offence case to issue the danger warning to himself.[19] However, since the accomplice evidence rule is based upon the assumption that there is a jury, and upon the separation of identities and functions which this implies, it is not at all clear that this is a legitimate interpretation.

A jury brings to every criminal trial the benefit of a collective decision about guilt or innocence. This collective process, in contrast to the one-person decision of the Diplock courts, is particularly important where the outcome of a trial hinges upon the uncorroborated evidence of an accomplice because where this is the case reasonable people are likely to disagree about whether or not it represents the truth. Indeed, it could even be argued that the accomplice evidence rule is designed to put pressure on juries *not* to convict in such circumstances because it strengthens the doubts of those who would have been reluctant to convict in the first place. At the very least, the rule can provoke an intense discussion about the justice of convicting without corroboration. In fact the available evidence suggests that juries tend to acquit when the only evidence against an accused is the uncorroborated testimony of a supergrass.[20] It would seem that disagreement amongst jurors as to whether the supergrass's evidence should be trusted or not indicates that reasonable doubt persists and, therefore, that guilt has not been proved to the requisite standard.

In Northern Ireland's first three supergrass trials – *R. v. Graham*[21] (the Bennett case), *R. v. Donnelly*[22] (the Black case) and, *R. v. Gibney*[23] (the McGrady case) – 61 per cent of those convicted were found guilty on the uncorroborated evidence of the accomplice-witnesses concerned. It is generally agreed that in discharging their function of tribunal of fact judges in Northern Ireland's Diplock courts must act as a 'reasonable jury'.[24] But if this concept bears any relation to the behaviour of actual juries then the trial judges in these three cases fell far short of the appropriate standard.

This shortcoming could have been avoided if the judiciary in Northern

Ireland had interpreted the accomplice evidence rule more restrictively. It can be plausibly argued that the logic of the principles underpinning the rule requires judges, in the absence of a jury, not to convict upon uncorroborated accomplice evidence in trials on indictment since this is the only appropriate alternative safeguard to a jury's evaluation. In *R. v. Graham*,[25] the first supergrass case in Northern Ireland to be heard on appeal, the Northern Ireland Court of Appeal implicitly dismissed this argument. Although quashing all 14 convictions because of the manner in which the trial judge had assessed the credibility of the accomplice evidence, Lord Lowry stated: 'the evidence of a largely uncorroborated accomplice of bad character who has a lot to gain by giving evidence can still be accepted.'[26]

Interestingly, many other countries, including some which do not subscribe to the liberal-democratic conception of the rule of law, legally prohibit convictions based solely on the evidence of an accomplice. In the USSR, for example, the evidence of an accomplice is not sufficient for a conviction unless confirmed by other evidence even though all serious criminal offences are tried by a judge and two lay assessors.[27]

The Credibility Requirement

In any criminal trial the vital question which the tribunal of fact (normally the jury, but in a Diplock trial, the judge) must answer is: does the totality of the evidence establish the guilt of the accused beyond reasonable doubt? It is generally the case that, where it is called, the evidence of an accomplice will constitute the principal evidence for the prosecution. Consequently, the verdict in such cases will normally hinge upon whether the tribunal of fact believes the evidence. In such circumstances the only line of defence open to the accused is to attempt to discredit the accomplice-witness. It is at this point that the inherent weaknesses of a supergrass's evidence should enter the equation. The independent evidence in any given trial on the evidence of an accomplice, e.g. a confession,[28] may, nonetheless, be taken as proving guilt beyond reasonable doubt by itself, and may, therefore, justify a conviction even where the accomplice evidence is deemed untrustworthy.[29] But where it is an issue, the credibility of the accomplice's testimony must be considered in the light of all the evidence in the case[30] including his or her personal credibility and character,[31] his or her demeanour in the witness box and the circumstances which led him or her to become a prosecution witness.[32]

In the Bennett case[33] the Northern Ireland Court of Appeal held that the trial judge, Mr Justice Murray, had overestimated the degree to which items of independent evidence implicating none or only a few of the defendants were capable of enhancing the general credibility of the accomplice evidence. The court also declared that the judge had placed unwarranted significance on the failure of the defendants to testify on their own behalf. In the view of the Court of Appeal, when the credibility of a 'suspect witness'[34] is called into question by the defence, as in this case, his or her evidence will rarely if ever be so compelling as to require the defendants to testify or suffer adverse consequences if they do not.

The decision in the Bennett appeal, while valid and welcome in other respects, contributes little towards redressing the imbalance against the accused in non-jury supergrass trials. The elaborate discussion about the degree to which the general credibility of the accomplice evidence can be enhanced by independent evidence which at most only implicates some defendants merely means that if they want their decisions to stand on appeal, Diplock judges cannot state in their judgments that they regard such evidence as 'crucially' supporting the accomplice evidence or as a 'best test' of its credibility. They could, of course, continue to take this view whilst refraining from admitting to it. Similarly, in affirming that defendants will rarely, if ever, be penalised for failing to testify on their own behalf in an accomplice evidence case, the Northern Ireland Court of Appeal has eliminated one of the factors which judges can explicitly bring to bear upon their decisions. But because it does not appear in the written judgment does not necessarily mean that the failure to testify has not entered into the decision.

The credibility of accomplice evidence was also at the heart of the Black, Quigley and Kirkpatrick appeals. Delivering the judgment of the Northern Ireland Court of Appeal in the Black case, for example, Lord Lowry, the Lord Chief Justice, said that Mr Justice Kelly's view of Black as 'one of the best witnesses I have ever heard' was 'a very ambitious and generous claim' reached at 'an unusually early stage' of the trial after which the trial judge 'found it very difficult to attach credence to any evidence which conflicted with Black's or to any interpretation of the evidence which cast doubt on Black's correctness'.[35] Despite his 'undoubted acumen, his great experience and the enormous care which he took over this case', the trial judge had 'greatly overestimated the honesty *as a witness* (he had made no mistake about his previous character as a man) of the accomplice Black'.[36] The Northern Ireland Court of Appeal concluded that the appellants had successfully shown that there were many inconsistencies in Black's evidence not fairly attributable to genuine mistake or lapse of memory which Mr Justice Kelly may have overlooked or not assessed properly. All the convictions appealed against which depended purely on Black's testimony were, therefore, quashed. Four others supported by corroboration, a confession and an admission, plus two involving forensic evidence, were upheld.

Corroboration

The leading case on what constitutes corroboration of accomplice evidence is *R. v. Baskerville*. The then Lord Chief Justice, Lord Reading, stated:

> We hold that the evidence in corroboration must be independent testimony which affects the accused by connecting or tending to connect him with the crime. In other words it must be evidence which implicates him, that is, which confirms in some material particular not only the evidence that the crime has been committed, but also that the prisoner committed it....[37]

His Lordship also approved *R. v. Noakes*[38] which decided that the evidence of one accomplice cannot corroborate another but in *DPP v. Kilbourne*[39] and *DPP v. Boardman*[40] the House of Lords rejected this view and held that accomplices can corroborate one another providing they give independent evidence of separate incidents and the circumstances exclude the danger of a jointly fabricated story.

The most significant component of the *Baskerville* test is the requirement that corroborative evidence must *implicate* the accused in the offence with which he or she is charged by confirming in a material particular that he or she committed it. Lord Reading understood this to include circumstantial evidence. As he remarked: 'The corroboration need not be direct evidence that the accused committed the crime; it is sufficient if it is merely circumstantial evidence of his connection with the crime.'[41]

By and large since *Baskerville* the courts have applied Lord Reading's interpretation of the 'implicates' requirement. In the McGrady case, for example, Lord Lowry said:

> Corroboration is independent testimony which affects the accused by connecting or tending to connect him with the crime.... It can include an admissible oral or written statement made by that accused. Independent evidence which tends to confirm the truth of the suspect witness's evidence in a material respect may help the tribunal of fact to assess the giver of the evidence but it is not corroboration unless it satisfies the test defined above.[42]

Other evidence which tends to verify the truth of those parts of the accomplice evidence which do not implicate the accused is termed 'supportive evidence'.

In *R. v. McCormick*[43] the Northern Ireland Court of Appeal departed from Lord Reading's broad approach by adding a further distinction to that already widely recognised between 'corroborating' and 'supporting' evidence. Delivering the judgment of the court the Lord Chief Justice, Lord Lowry, held that evidence which may be corroborative in the *Baskerville* sense may still not justify a conviction if the tribunal of fact considers the credibility of the accomplice evidence to be such that a higher than usual calibre of corroboration is required.

A detective sergeant in the Special Branch of the RUC was charged with a number of scheduled offences ranging from armed robbery to the murder of an RUC sergeant. The Crown case was based upon the testimony of Anthony O'Doherty, a paid police informer, then serving an 18 year prison sentence for his part in some of the offences with which the defendant was charged. The judge, Mr Justice Murray, held that it would be 'highly dangerous and wrong to convict the accused on any of the crimes charged against him on the evidence of O'Doherty unless that evidence is supported by clear and compelling corroboration'.[44]

Mr Justice Murray inferred that discrepancies between the defendant's evidence and that of other witnesses indicated that the accused was lying and that taken together these things amounted to corroboration of the necessary standard. The defendant had found himself in a worsening financial situation at the time of the robbery. He made a statement admitting buying a van and claiming that O'Doherty, the accomplice-witness, gave him 'Nan's money', some £600 or £700, to purchase the van. Mrs McLaughlin ('Nan') denied in evidence that she had parted with such a sum. He denied possessing a hand grenade while his landlady had found one in his room and a Detective-Sergeant gave evidence that he had taken one from a police security cabinet. O'Doherty alleged that a hand grenade was used in a robbery which he claimed he and the accused committed. An entry in the defendant's official diary referred to his having met O'Doherty on the day the robbery of which McCormick was eventually convicted was carried out.

The Northern Ireland Court of Appeal overturned the conviction on the grounds that in the circumstances the discrepancies between McCormick's evidence and that of other witnesses did not justify the inference that he had lied to conceal his guilt and, though the meeting between O'Doherty and McCormick recorded in the appellant's official diary could give rise to suspicion, and suspicion could in certain circumstances afford corroboration, it also admitted an innocent interpretation. Since O'Doherty was a paid police informer and McCormick was his 'handler' the two had a legitimate reason for being together. The judge, therefore, 'lacked the cogent and compelling corroboration which he declared to be indispensable to a finding of guilty'.[45]

Since the Northern Ireland Court of Appeal accepted the trial judge's conclusion that O'Doherty's evidence required 'clear and compelling corroboration' the decision would appear to amount to no more than a disagreement with Mr Justice Murray concerning whether these criteria had been fulfilled.[46] But there is more to it than that. By endorsing the trial judge's assessment that a high standard of corroboration was required in this case the Northern Ireland Court of Appeal has affirmed that the credibility of accomplice evidence and the 'implicates' requirement can stand in inverse relation. It would appear that, in some cases, the lower the credibility of the informer, the stricter the corroboration test. At a certain point on this continuum, to be determined by the view the tribunal of fact takes of the credibility of the accomplice evidence, circumstantial evidence of the sort which was presented against McCormick will not be considered corroborative. Unfortunately Lord Lowry did not make clear whether the Court of Appeal's decision rested solely upon the trial judge's view that the evidence of the *particular* accomplice in question required especially compelling corroboration or whether there is, or should be, a rebuttable presumption that the evidence of *certain classes of accomplice*, for example those whose cooperation clearly stems from inducement rather than remorse, cannot be sufficient to sustain a conviction without independent evidence which is corroborative in the higher sense.

The McCormick case raises a further query. In terms of character, motivation and performance in the witness box (with the possible exception of Christopher Black and Jackie Grimley, at opposite ends of the spectrum) there was very little to distinguish O'Doherty from any of the supergrasses. Yet, far from requiring 'clear and compelling corroboration', the judges in the Bennett, Black and McGrady cases based 61 per cent of the convictions on the uncorroborated testimony of these witnesses. Two of these judges were none other than Mr Justice Murray and Lord Lowry.

The Origins of the Supergrass System

The use of accomplice evidence as a method of controlling violent political unrest is not new to Ireland. In both the United Irishmen and Fenian uprisings in the eighteenth and nineteenth centuries, respectively, the authorities relied heavily for convictions on those prepared to betray their comrades in arms.[47] But the use of supergrasses in the 1980s as a routine method of dealing with large numbers of terrorist suspects developed out of the unique succession of counterinsurgency initiatives introduced since the early 1970s to control the violence of Loyalist and particularly Republican paramilitary organisations.

The intervention of the British army in August 1969 failed to quell the sectarian disturbances which had erupted in Northern Ireland in the previous year.[48] In August 1971, with the agreement of the Westminster cabinet, the Unionist government introduced internment without trial as authorised by the Civil Authorities (Special Powers) Act (NI) 1922. This resulted in a dramatic escalation in the intensity of the conflict. By March 1972 it was clear that the Unionist regime had lost control of public order; the British government suspended the Stormont Parliament and executive and undertook direct responsibility for the affairs of Northern Ireland.

A Commission of Inquiry chaired by Lord Diplock was appointed in October 1972 to examine 'whether changes should be made in the administration of justice in order to deal more effectively with terrorism without using internment under the Special Powers Act'.[49] A package of measures was proposed, the bulk of which were enacted in the Northern Ireland (Emergency Provisions) Act 1973 (the 'EPA'). Police and army powers to stop and question, search and seize, and arrest and detain were extended, the law was altered in order to facilitate convictions on confessions extracted in special anti-terrorist centres and jury trial was suspended for a list of mostly violent offences contained in a schedule to the Act ('Scheduled offences').

Following the enactment of the EPA the use of internment was greatly reduced in favour of imprisonment by the courts rather than by executive decision.[50] The police, therefore, came under increased pressure to show a satisfactory conviction rate,[51] especially after internment was discontinued in 1975.[52] Until the advent of the supergrass strategy the critical point in the Diplock process was whether a suspect confessed or not. Only 32 confessions out of nearly 4,000 were declared inadmissible by the courts between 1976 and 1980,[53] and 75 to 80 per cent of the 93 per cent conviction rate in scheduled offence cases in the first six months of 1978, a not untypical period, rested on confessions alone.[54]

The drive for confessions occasioned a flood of complaints about the physical abuse of suspects in interrogation centres.[55] In 1978, Amnesty International confirmed that many of these allegations were justified.[56] In 1979, the report of the Bennett Inquiry outlined several ways in which the opportunities for physical ill-treatment could be curtailed, e.g. that the right of access to a solicitor should be absolute after 48 hours without prejudice to prior access, that medical checks should be carried out at least every 24 hours, that a closed circuit television system should be installed in interrogation centres to monitor interviews, that each suspect should be provided with a printed notice of his or her rights on arrival at the police station and that a formal code of conduct for interviewing officers should be incorporated into the RUC Code.[57] The number of complaints from suspects concerning physical abuse dropped dramatically shortly after the publication of Bennett's conclusions and recommendations.[58]

The Bennett Report appears to have made the extraction of confessions much more difficult. The policy of securing convictions on confession alone consequently lost the viability it once had, a fact which seems to have prompted the security forces to concentrate their efforts on enlisting the services of informers.[59] While the quest for informers has been an integral part of law enforcement the world over since time immemorial, and a particularly favoured method of countering politically motivated violence in Ireland,[60] the objective in Northern Ireland in the early 1980s seems to have been not only to garner low-grade intelligence but also to cultivate a batch of high-powered accomplice-witnesses who would be prepared to testify in court against those suspected of being the big fish in the Republican and Loyalist paramilitary organisations. It seems inconceivable that the financial and manpower resources which this has required[61] were not authorised at the executive level in advance rather than, as the authorities maintain, agreed on a case to case basis as each 'converted terrorist' came forward. For this reason alone the term 'supergrass system' is not inappropriate.

The Supergrass System in the Ascendancy: The Bennett, Black and McGrady Cases

The first three supergrass cases established several important benchmarks which seemed to bode well for the future promotion of the supergrass system but which, in retrospect, seem to have contained the seeds of its subsequent decline.

First, and of greatest importance, 88 per cent of the 64 accused in these three trials were found guilty. This seemed to indicate that the courts were prepared to cooperate with the supergrass strategy more or less as it stood,[62] thereby making it a highly efficient method of obtaining convictions. Second, the fact that 61 per cent of these convictions were secured on the uncorroborated evidence of the supergrasses suggested that at least some judges would not require much independent evidence in order to arrive at guilty verdicts. This was particularly encouraging from the point of view of the security forces since it tended to vindicate the decision to concentrate resources into the cultivation of supergrass evidence at the expense of the accumulation of evidence from the normal range of sources. Third, the Bennett, Black and McGrady cases showed that judges were prepared to trust the supergrass's uncorroborated evidence despite the fact that both it and other aspects of the prosecution case in each trial contained serious specific flaws, in addition to those generally associated with the evidence of supergrasses.

The Bennett Case

The arrest of Christopher Black is generally taken as signalling the start of the supergrass system. But before the trial of those charged on his testimony was finished, 14 of the 16 defendants prosecuted on the evidence of UVF supergrass Joseph Bennett were convicted.

Bennett had a significant criminal record even before he became involved in the activities of the proscribed Ulster Volunteer Force in 1972. In August of that year he was arrested and charged with possession of guns, ammunition and explosives but was released on compassionate bail in December on the grounds that his wife was terminally ill with cancer. Following her death in April 1973 he absconded and was re-arrested in March 1974. The house in which he was then living was found to contain a considerable quantity of firearms and explosives. He was sentenced to twelve years' imprisonment but, under the standard remission arrangements,[63] he served only six, during the last year and a half of which he acted as the UVF Commander of compound 21 in the Maze Prison. Following his release in 1980 he became a UVF Company Commander in the Sandy Row area of Belfast but was subsequently sentenced to death in his absence by a UVF Court Martial for stealing money from his employer. In May 1982 he was arrested following the armed robbery of a post office in Killinchy, Co. Down, during which the elderly postmistress was brutally murdered. Bennett denied having inflicted the fatal knife wounds but admitted having been armed with a loaded gun. While in custody he realised his dilemma. As he later told the court:

> I was inside for life or sentence of death outside....The future was bleak. The police offered a third alternative.... My life depended on impressing the police and on my first day in custody I mentioned immunity.... There was a strong incentive to cooperate.... At the end of the day my usefulness to the police would be measured in the number of men I put away.[64]

Despite his involvement in the Killinchy murder and seven other serious crimes before the court Bennett was guaranteed complete immunity for his own offences in return for his testimony. The trial judge Mr Justice Murray declared that he was a 'ruthless, resourceful criminal whose criminal acts extended to the use of his dead father's police uniform to carry out daring armed robberies from which considerable sums of money were stolen and divided amongst himself and his accomplices'.[65] The judge also concluded that Bennett's dominant motive in giving evidence was to avoid a second long prison sentence.[66]

Bennett achieved this aim in 1983. But in February 1986 he was convicted in England of armed robbery. Several guns found in his Midlands home had been licensed in Northern Ireland, alerting the police to his identity. The RUC and Special Branch, it appears, had supplied Bennett with new documents under a new name, including a passport and birth certificate, and had provided a furnished house and a job following the Belfast trial.[67] This was, no doubt, an expensive undertaking – and all for a man whose cooperation with the prosecuting authorities in Northern Ireland had led to a protracted trial which ended in quashed convictions for all the accused and whose gratitude for his own good fortune was expressed in a rapid return to violent crime a few hundred miles from his original area of operation.

It is possible to identify other flaws in Mr Justice Murray's assessment of Bennett's credibility apart from those upon which the Northern Ireland Court of Appeal based its decision. Most seriously, he accepted that Bennett had committed perjury during the course of the trial, yet felt this did not sufficiently damage his credibility to warrant acquitting the twelve who were convicted on the uncorroborated accomplice evidence. A cheque for £200 bearing Bennett's signature was produced in court which Bennett had previously denied having endorsed. Mr Justice Murray stated: 'I have to say, and say clearly, that Mr. Boal [defence QC] has convinced me that Bennett told a lie about it. I think that must be so but it seems to me to be clear that it was an extraneous matter entirely as the evidence emerged.'[68] But how is it possible to be sure of guilt beyond reasonable doubt where the evidence of such a witness is completely uncorroborated?

The Black Case

Christopher Black joined the IRA in 1975. He was arrested in December of the same year and convicted of attempted robbery. Having served the customary 50 per cent of his ten year prison sentence, he was released in December 1980 and immediately rejoined the IRA. According to Mr Justice Kelly, the judge at the trial of those charged on his evidence, he was 'up to his neck in terrorist activity throughout 1981',[69] playing a major role in a catalogue of violent incidents. The judge also stated that Black's overriding motive in deciding to give evidence was, as with Bennett, the desire to evade a second term of imprisonment.

The scale of the Black trial was staggering. Thirty-eight defendants were seated in rows around three sides of the courtroom guarded by a score of prison officers and police some of whom were heavily armed. The indictment contained 184 charges based on 45 separate incidents and the trial lasted from December 1982 to August 1983, occupying 120 court sitting days. The committal proceedings, the 'preliminary inquiry', had been avoided by the DPP by obtaining a Bill of Indictment from the High Court, a controversial and rarely used procedure[70] which spared Black the ordeal of having to give his evidence twice.[71]

Although Black was, by all accounts, an impressive witness with a phenomenal memory, serious questions were raised at the trial about the truth of many of his allegations. There were particularly acute doubts with respect to two defendants. Tobias McMahon was convicted on Black's uncorroborated evidence for his part in a conspiracy to murder and sentenced to 15 years' imprisonment. Yet Black did not name McMahon until he had spent a full nine months in protective custody, and, as he admitted in court, he and McMahon had a strong personal antipathy towards one another.[72] Joseph Kelly was convicted of membership of the IRA purely on Black's testimony although the evidence against him was extremely confused.[73] Black claimed Kelly had been with him at a training camp in Donegal in the Irish Republic in the pre-Easter period, March and April 1981. However, the indictment charged Kelly with having been at the camp between 1 June and 15 July 1981. Kelly had signed a confession admitting being at an IRA camp in Donegal in August 1981 but the admissibility and weight of this statement was contested at the trial and 40 alibi witnesses were produced to show that the defendant had been in Belfast throughout August and the pre-Easter period.

Nonetheless, Mr Justice Kelly allowed the Crown to change the dates on the indictment to 1 March to 31 August 1981. This contrasts sharply with the approach taken by the English Court of Appeal in *R. v. Thorne*[74] where a similar request was refused, and in *Thorne* the desired change was only a matter of a few days. The alibis were dismissed as being supplied by 'hardly disinterested witnesses'[75] and Kelly's account was said to reveal 'a massive lack of credibility'.[76] Although membership of an organisation proscribed by the EPA normally attracts a custodial sentence of five years or more, Kelly received a two year suspended sentence, perhaps an admission by the judge that he was not convinced beyond reasonable doubt about his guilt after all. As Gifford states: 'The problem was that if Black was shown to be embroidering his evidence or inserting wrong names or simply unreliable, about any one defendant, his unshakeable credibility, which was the sheet anchor of the judge's decision, would be undermined.'[77]

Twenty-three of those convicted in the Black trial appealed, although one, Charles McKiernan, sentenced to life imprisonment for murder, withdrew. According to Lord Lowry, who presided over the appeal hearing, the twelve who did not appeal 'could mainly be regarded as having played minor supporting parts'.[78] McMahon was amongst the 18 whose convictions were quashed, as already noted, on the grounds that Mr Justice Kelly had not given sufficient attention to the defects in Black's evidence. The Northern Ireland Court of Appeal also devoted quite a sizeable chunk of its judgment to Kelly's case, concluding that his conviction was also unsafe due to the confused evidence, particularly regarding the dates of his alleged membership of the IRA and his visit to the training camp.

The McGrady Case

Kevin McGrady joined the IRA in 1975 and had already participated in a number of serious incidents before his arrest for murder in December. The charge was dropped when a key witness withdrew his evidence, but McGrady served a three month prison sentence for having assaulted a police officer in the course of his interrogation. Following his release he went to London and then on to Amsterdam where he joined an evangelical Christian sect, claiming that he had had a religious conversion.

Unique among the supergrasses in England and Northern Ireland, McGrady gave himself up voluntarily to the police in Belfast in January 1982, maintaining that some men, including his brother Sean, had been wrongfully convicted of offences for which he had been responsible himself. He also told the court at the trial of those charged on his evidence that he felt he had to expiate his misdeeds in order to make progress in the religious sect he had joined. Following his confession, McGrady was interviewed at length by the police, during the course of which he made a number of written statements. On 26 June 1982 he pleaded guilty to 27 charges, including three murders, and was sentenced to life imprisonment.

The most remarkable feature of the McGrady supergrass trial was that despite the fact that, on a number of charges, the evidence which he gave was completely disbelieved by the presiding judge, Lord Lowry, three defendants were convicted without corroboration. Those parts of McGrady's testimony which were believed had 'the ring of authenticity',[79] the judge stated.

Referring to those offences with respect to which McGrady's testimony was rejected, Lord Lowry said:

> to have convicted on any of the counts in these groups of charges would have been a perversion of justice according to law, so contradictory, bizarre and in some respects incredible was McGrady's

evidence and so devious and deliberately evasive was his manner of giving it.[80]

In one such case, McGrady had originally implicated Eugene Pinkey for an attempted murder. But Pinkey turned out to have been in prison at the relevant time − so McGrady substituted his brother, the defendant Thomas Pinkey.[81] Perhaps even more so than with Bennett and Black the question can be asked: is it possible to be sure of guilt beyond reasonable doubt where the evidence of a witness such as McGrady is entirely uncorroborated, as it was for three of the seven defendants who were convicted? If it is, why were three others acquitted?

A subsequent decision of the Northern Ireland Court of Appeal supports the view that McGrady was an unreliable witness whose testimony deserved not to be trusted. Dismissing Sean McGrady's appeal against conviction for murder, Lord Justice Gibson and Murray J. declared that the 'new evidence' supplied by Kevin McGrady was 'quite unimpressive and indeed incredible' and irreconcilable with 'other evidence which is unshakeable and flatly contradictory'.[82] Kevin McGrady was released from prison in April 1988.

The Supergrass System in Decline

Following the McGrady case another seven supergrass trials reached a verdict. These trials featured, in chronological order, the accomplice-witnesses Jackie Grimley, John Morgan, Robert Quigley, Raymond Gilmour, James Crockard, William 'Budgie' Allen and Harry Kirkpatrick. In only two, the Quigley and Kirkpatrick trials, were convictions secured purely on the evidence of the supergrass. In the Quigley case, ten of the eleven defendants were found guilty, eight of these on uncorroborated accomplice evidence, and in the Kirkpatrick trial 25 of the 27 accused, all of whom were convicted, were found guilty at the initial trial without the supergrass's testimony being corroborated. All these uncorroborated convictions were eventually quashed on appeal.

The conviction rate for the seven trials at first instance in this second phase of the supergrass system was 42 per cent, 53 per cent of these convictions being based on uncorroborated accomplice evidence and the others resting on confessions or alleged admissions plus three guilty pleas. The main reason for these high conviction rates was the Kirkpatrick verdicts. In the six trials prior to Kirkpatrick, the conviction rate had plummeted to 29 per cent, only 22 per cent of which involved uncorroborated accomplice evidence. All the supergrass appeals have now been settled and the outcomes indicate that the critical attitude adopted by the Northern Ireland judiciary towards the evidence of supergrasses from the end of 1983 onwards has been strengthened and, if anything, become more critical.

Throughout its lifespan the supergrass system was the subject of intense public debate. Three of its features are now clear. First, the system fell into two distinct phases, one of ascendancy, covering the first three trials, and one of decline, covering the last seven and the appeal verdicts. Second, the supergrass system has, in the event, amounted to a method of obtaining confessions plus a form of quasi-internment, not only in its remand aspect, as was originally evident, but also in its conviction aspect. As already stated, one of the original complaints about the use of supergrasses in Northern Ireland was that it amounted to a form of 'internment by remand' because it involved long periods of pre-trial detention. As far as convictions are concerned, it has often been said that confessions and alleged admissions can corroborate accomplice evidence. This may be true, but such evidence can also provide a self-sufficient basis for conviction even if the accomplice evidence is entirely rejected. It has been widely reported that none of the outstanding convictions in Northern Ireland's supergrass system rest on uncorroborated accomplice evidence. This assertion is broadly accurate, but in one or two cases the reliability of the alleged admission, which has been counted as corroboration, is highly suspect. The supergrass system can, therefore, be regarded as a means of obtaining convictions on confessions and alleged admissions which might otherwise not have been forthcoming. In this respect it has remained faithful to the basic orientation of the Diplock process. On the other hand, those defendants whose convictions were quashed because their guilt rested purely on supergrass evidence were successfully taken out of circulation by what was effectively an executive decision (albeit with a temporary judicial stamp), a result analogous to internment proper. The third conclusion indicated by the figures is that the supergrass system is now undeniably dead and buried, and is highly unlikely to be resurrected. How can we explain this rise and fall pattern?

Two familiar, but unconvincing, contenders are the official view and the conspiracy theory. The former[83] goes something like this: there never was a 'supergrass system' as such because the degree of coordination and planning which this term implies was completely absent. Decisions concerning the mounting of prosecutions were taken by the prosecuting authorities on a case to case basis, in accordance with standard criminal procedure, as each 'converted terrorist' came forward. The dearth of fresh supergrasses since November 1983 is the result of a reluctance on the part of accomplices to offer their services to the Crown. All non-jury trials in the UK, including those in the Diplock courts, are decided on their individual merits by judges acting independently of each other and of the executive. Their job is to apply to proven facts technical rules and principles which are largely politically neutral. The overall outcome of the supergrass trials is merely an aggregate of differing, but mostly negative, independent judicial assessments of the credibility of the evidence of each individual supergrass. Indeed, the fact that most of the convictions secured in the supergrass trials were quashed on appeal indicates just how independent the courts in Northern Ireland are.

The official view is difficult to accept for two principal reasons. First, it defies belief to suggest that over 25 supergrasses inexplicably volunteered to turn Queen's evidence between November 1981 and November 1983 without some corresponding, and indeed prior, change on the part of the prosecuting authorities, while in the previous twelve years only a handful surfaced and over the past three years only two have made an appearance with neither lasting the course. It is also inconceivable that the financial and manpower resources which the supergrass trials required were not authorised at a senior executive level. Second, the official view leaves the sharp differences between phases one and two entirely unexplained. There is, therefore, plenty of evidence to justify the use of the term 'system'. As for the appeal decisions, a better explanation than the official one can also be found, but this is best considered later.

The 'conspiracy theory' maintains that the institutions of the state in Northern Ireland work hand in glove to maintain the status quo and defeat its principal challenger, militant Republicanism.[84] The 'independence of the judiciary', especially in the Diplock courts, is a deceit which disguises the close coordination and common purpose of the judiciary, executive and security forces. In reality, any apparent disputes between the different branches of the 'British war machine' are not disputes at all, but merely evidence of what has been 'conspired' or, alternatively, mechanisms by which counterinsurgency policy can be finely tuned. Applied to the supergrass system, this means either that quasi-internment was what the judiciary, the security forces and the government wanted all along, or that the two-phase conviction pattern is an autonomous attempt by the judiciary to rescue the supergrass system by forcing refinements at the prosecution stages. The promotion of Loyalist supergrasses tends to be seen by advocates of the conspiracy view as a ploy by the authorities to provide a veneer of even-handedness to this essentially anti-Republican initiative.

It is difficult to accept either version of the conspiracy theory. The first amounts to a claim that the executive authorities prefer to see supergrass trial defendants who were acquitted or whose convictions were quashed on the streets rather than behind bars. This is clearly absurd. While the RUC probably accept quasi-internment as a booby prize, it is obvious from the optimistic predictions made by senior police officers in 1981 that a great deal more was originally expected.[85]

The main problem with the second branch of the conspiracy theory is this: although the emergence of a refined supergrass system at some future date is not beyond the bounds of possibility – the courts have been careful not to erect any obstacles in the form of firm legal rules[86] – recent developments tend to point in the opposite direction. It is difficult to see how the sort of refinements which appear to be required by the Northern Ireland Court of Appeal, i.e. a higher calibre of supergrass evidence, more carefully mounted prosecutions and more corroboration, are possible. The attraction of the paramilitary supergrass to the prosecuting authorities in Northern Ireland appears to have depended critically upon the willingness of the courts to accept their uncorroborated testimonies, warts and all. Moreover, though there can be little doubt that while the security forces, the government and the courts see Republican paramilitary organisations as the main threat to stability and established interests in Northern Ireland, the activities of Loyalist paramilitaries are also regarded as highly prejudicial to the delicate equilibrium. The use of Loyalist supergrasses ought, therefore, to be seen as a genuine attempt to deal with 'troublesome elements' rather than as a deceitful balancing act.

There is a third, more satisfactory, explanation for the rise and fall of the supergrass system. Its initial success was underwritten by an uncritical judiciary which subsequently realised its mistake and about-turned, destroying the phenomenon it had helped create. This was achieved against the wishes of the executive authorities and, apparently, largely in response to a broadly based anti-supergrass campaign. Contrary to the official view, therefore, Northern Ireland's judges were acting together in a deeply political manner all along, but not in the crude sense alleged by the conspiracy theory. The supergrass policy was a high-cost counterinsurgency strategy in manpower, financial and propaganda terms and therefore required a high conviction rate and an appreciable reduction in the level of violence to justify its continued existence. The indispensable cooperation of the courts was faithfully rendered in the Bennett, Black and McGrady trials in 1983. But, following the McGrady case in November 1983, judges trying supergrass cases clearly became much more critical of this type of evidence than the judges in the first three trials. It is impossible to identify precisely the factors which have produced this result. It could be argued that Northern Ireland's judges, drawn largely from Unionist backgrounds,[87] recognised the dangers inherent in the disenchantment of large sections of the Loyalist community with the courts and government policy which the supergrass system inspired. The well-organised campaign by the various relatives' groups and others almost certainly had an impact even on this notoriously remote institution. Probably Lord Gifford's unofficial inquiry from October to December 1983 was of considerable influence since the report,[88] published in January 1984, demonstrated that the decisions in the Bennett, Black and McGrady cases were open to criticism on purely legal grounds.[89] These conclusions were widely anticipated throughout the autumn and winter months of 1983.

All these factors seem to have prompted the judiciary to reassess its original choice between uncritical loyalty to counterinsurgency policy as conceived by the executive and loyalty to the ideology of the rule of law. Opting for the latter was ultimately deemed to be necessary in order to limit the damage to the legal system and to reassert a much compromised judicial 'independence'. It is likely that this *volte face* on the part of the courts, rather than cajoling the security forces to smooth down its rougher edges, has wrecked the supergrass system.

The symptoms of the supergrass system's illness were clear long before the Anglo-Irish Agreement was signed in November 1985, and it is a mistake to credit the accord with the system's demise. Nevertheless, the Hillsborough agreement has tended to constrain the inauguration of a re-vamped supergrass system since it would jeopardise the cornerstone of British policy in Northern Ireland by antagonising the Dublin government. Figures from the security forces show that there is little prospect of the security advantages which might otherwise justify taking such a risk. There is also little justification for the view, which has gained some currency, that Irish pressure inspired the then British Attorney General, Sir Michael Havers, to state in March 1986[90] that it was unlikely that there would be any further prosecutions in Northern Ireland on the basis of uncorroborated accomplice evidence. All that the statement in question says on this point is that prosecutions are unlikely in the absence of both corroborative and supporting evidence. But the absence of supportive evidence has never been an issue in the Northern Irish supergrass trials. The critical point is that, by and large, supportive evidence falls far short of implicating an accused individual in a specific offence and may indicate nothing more than that the offence in question has been committed. The absence of corroborative evidence pointing to a particular defendant has always been the central issue.

A further factor making the resurrection of the supergrass system unlikely is its insignificant impact upon the pattern of politically motivated violence in Northern Ireland. Achieving a significant reduction in the level of violence was its whole *raison d'être*.

The contribution made by the supergrass system to the level of political violence in Northern Ireland is impossible to gauge accurately. The nature of the conflict has altered over the past 18 years as the result of a complex interplay between anti-terrorist policies and self-initiated changes on the part of the various paramilitary organisations. In 1977, for example, the Republican movement, which embraces both the IRA and Sinn Fein, decided to embark upon the 'ballot-armalite' strategy of increasing the emphasis on political activity while shifting paramilitary operations away from, for example, random bombings to carefully targeted killings.[91]

In fact, the number of violent incidents has declined steadily since 1976, following a dramatic decrease from 12,010 to 2,202 between 1972 and 1975. Except for a small rise in 1981, the year of the hunger strike, the number of violent deaths since 1976 has also dropped. However, the number of deaths per violent incident has grown since 1972. Deaths occurring as a result of assassinations in homes or places of work or leisure have risen as a proportion of total violent deaths – from 25 per cent in the 1969–73 period to 40 per cent in 1980–3 and 50 per cent in 1983 and 1984 – while deaths arising from riots, explosions, gun battles, cross-fire and sniper activity have declined both in proportionate and absolute terms. While the IRA has maintained a constant level of killings since 1977, the number of fatalities caused by Loyalist and other Republican paramilitary organisations has dropped.[92]

In other words, peace and stability is not being restored to Northern Ireland. Rather, the conflict is increasingly being channelled into more focused killings by both security force personnel and the IRA.[93] It is clear, therefore, that the supergrass system has not succeeded in eliminating paramilitary violence from Northern Ireland. Indeed, in overall terms, it would seem that it has promoted rather than discouraged the likelihood of further violence. Paramilitary organisations thrive upon bitterness and a sense of grievance and injustice, particularly when these sentiments are directed against authority. This hostility has apparently been nourished by the supergrass system, especially amongst the Nationalist community. In a recent poll[94] 72 per cent of Catholic respondents either disapproved or strongly disapproved of the supergrass policy whereas only 21 per cent of Protestant respondents fell into this category. In another poll[95] 57 per cent of Catholics expressed the view that the legal system in Northern Ireland dispenses justice unfairly or very unfairly. Only 9 per cent of Protestant respondents took this view. Although the statistics do not establish clear causal links between disenchantment with the supergrass strategy and support for paramilitary activities it seems reasonable to suppose that such links exist.

The parallel with internment is clear. In the early 1970s, detention without trial was seen by its advocates as a potential panacea for the mounting disorder. It is now widely recognised, however, that this security initiative resulted in the incarceration of innocent men, thus further estranging large sections of the Nationalist community from the legal process, and that this in turn dramatically increased the flow of recruits to the IRA and added fuel to an already bitter civil conflict. The supergrass system has perhaps sown the seeds for a similar harvest.

Supergrasses in England and Northern Ireland: Contrasts and Comparisons

The supergrass phenomenon in Northern Ireland shares two major features in common with its English counterpart[96] apart from those implied by the term 'supergrass'. First, the utilitarian justification for using supergrass evidence has been accepted by the courts in both places. This was expressed by Lord Justice Lawton in *R. v. Turner* and endorsed by the courts in succeeding supergrass trials. His Lordship stated:

> It is in the interests of the public that criminals be brought to justice; and the more serious the crimes the greater is the need for justice to be done. Employing Queen's evidence to accomplish this end is distasteful and has been distasteful for at least 300 years to judges, lawyers and members of the public.[97]

Second, the law on accomplice evidence in each jurisdiction is broadly the same.[98]

However, there are five major differences between supergrass policies in the two jurisdictions:

1. In England, following the Smalls case, the practice of granting supergrasses immunity from prosecution was abandoned in 1972 in favour of having such witnesses tried and sentenced before allowing them to appear for the prosecution in other trials. In Northern Ireland, on the other hand, at least 13 supergrasses[99] were offered an immunity deal between 1981 and 1983 and it is not clear that the prosecuting authorities in this jurisdiction have now rejected this way of proceeding.

2. In England and Wales the prosecution of defendants on the uncorroborated evidence of a supergrass was apparently discontinued in 1977 on the DPP's instructions;[100] in Northern Ireland it has persisted up to and including the most recent cases.

3. Several supergrass trials in Northern Ireland have been considerably larger than any seen in England despite the English Court of Appeal's advice that

No more accused should be indicted together than is necessary for the proper presentation of the prosecution's case against the principal accused. Necessity not convenience should be the guiding factor. Our experience warns us ... that in cases involving a number of accused, there is a danger that those on the fringes will be dragged down by those at the centre.[101]

4. The supergrass system in Northern Ireland emerged from a background of political instability, political violence, emergency laws, non-jury courts and a unique succession of counterinsurgency initiatives. In England it developed as a response to a regional, though nonetheless serious, professional crime problem and processed through the regular criminal justice system.
5. Public concern about the English supergrass trials diminished as the prosecuting authorities, responding to the guidelines set by the courts, eliminated its most controversial features, immunity from prosecution and prosecutions on uncorroborated accomplice evidence. This allowed a string of subsequent supergrass cases to be processed relatively smoothly through the courts.[102] In Northern Ireland, on the other hand, public disquiet was intensified by the initial rubber-stamping attitude of the judiciary which in its turn apparently forced the courts to about-turn, thus rendering the supergrass system no longer viable.

Conclusion

Northern Ireland's supergrass system is the latest in a series of controversial law enforcement initiatives introduced in the attempt to deal with the violence of Loyalist and particularly Republican paramilitary organisations. The same objective, conviction maximisation through the criminal justice system at the expense of defendants' rights, has been the dominant theme in all these strategies except internment. The supergrass policy has also had other spin-off advantages from the authorities' point of view, e.g. holding suspects on remand for long periods and sowing fear and mistrust in Loyalist and Republican communities. In the Bennett, Black and McGrady cases, the presiding judges were prepared to facilitate a high conviction rate by, on the one hand, interpreting the law on accomplice evidence narrowly, thus making the danger warning a largely empty ritual and, on the other, applying the credibility rules broadly. The result was a high conviction rate based largely on the accomplices' uncorroborated testimony. It would seem, according to the available evidence, that this would not have happened had these cases been tried by jury. The constraints upon the readiness to convict provided by the jury system could have been more

effectively reproduced in the Diplock courts if the judiciary had refused
to convict on the basis of uncorroborated accomplice evidence. It would
also be easier to regard the decision of the Northern Ireland Court of
Appeal in *McCormick* as a valid development of the corroboration rules
if the courts had applied it generally from the outset to accomplice-
witnesses of O'Doherty's calibre, a category which clearly would have
included all the supergrasses.

In promoting the supergrass system, the English policy of trying and
sentencing supergrasses before permitting them to appear as prosecution witnesses has apparently been implemented, albeit rather late in
the day. The courts in Northern Ireland have also belatedly followed
the English precedents of generally refusing to sustain convictions on
the uncorroborated evidence of supergrasses. The English Court of
Appeal's advice about limiting the size of trials has been completely
ignored.

Any contribution the supergrass system has made towards resolv-
ing the Northern Ireland conflict has been largely, if not entirely,
negative, as many predicted from the start. It has achieved little except
misery for those involved, considerable public expense and a sharpened,
and perhaps even extended, distrust of the legal system amongst certain sections of the community. It should never have happened at all,
and, indeed, there is no reason why the critical approach eventually
taken by the courts could not have been deployed to nip the whole
business in the bud at its inception. Nevertheless, the fortunes of the
supergrass system show that the government and the security forces
cannot always have things their own way. The need obviously felt by
the judiciary in Northern Ireland, even in the Diplock courts, to maintain some fidelity to the ideology of the rule of law — however
instrumental their motives — clearly imposes some limitations, however
sluggish, upon executive power. It is apparent then that official legal
rhetoric, though flawed as an account of legal reality, can sometimes
be wielded to secure worthwhile objectives against the wishes of the
executive institutions of the state, i.e. respect for due process in
preference to ultimately counterproductive crime control short cuts. It
would be a mistake, however, to exaggerate the room for manoeuvre.
The judiciary, the security forces and the government will soon establish
a new *modus vivendi* with respect to politically motivated violence in
Northern Ireland. But equally it would be a mistake to dismiss the
relative autonomy of the courts as insignificant. Their independence,
however shaky, can hardly be a matter of indifference to those whose
convictions in the supergrass system were quashed.

It seems unlikely that a supergrass system will reappear in Northern
Ireland in the foreseeable future in any form worthy of the name. Some

fresh security initiative can, therefore, be expected. What form this initiative will take is difficult to anticipate precisely, but extradition will probably play a key role. Isolated supergrass trials may occur sporadically, perhaps occasioned by a genuine *volte face* on the part of the supergrass. In such circumstances the courts may feel less compunction about convicting without corroboration. The need for a statutory corroboration requirement in non-jury trials on indictment or, better still, the return of the jury to the trial of scheduled offences, therefore, remains.[103]

Notes

1. See Workers Research Unit, *Belfast Bulletin no.11* — Supergrasses (Workers Research Unit, 1984).
2. The figure 593 for 1982–5 was given in a Commons written reply by Mr Nicholas Scott, Northern Ireland Junior Minister (House of Commons Debates, vol. 73, col.100). Accuracy is precluded by the fact that a number of supergrasses retracted their evidence before their names became public.
3. See S. Greer, 'Internment with a Judge's Stamp', *Fortnight*, no. 203, 1984; D.P.J. Walsh, *The Use and Abuse of Emergency Legislation in Northern Ireland* (The Cobden Trust, 1983) ch. 5.
4. Attorney General's statement, H.C. Debs., vol. 73, col.100.
5. See P. Hillyard and J. Percy-Smith, 'Converting Terrorists: The Use of Supergrasses in Northern Ireland', *Journal of Law and Society*, 335 (1984); *Sunday Times Colour Supplement*, 8 April 1984.
6. T. Gifford, *Supergrasses: The use of accomplice evidence in Northern Ireland* (The Cobden Trust, 1984).
7. At least twelve of the 25 supergrasses identified by Lord Gifford were granted immunity from prosecution (*Supergrasses*, p.10). For an account of the law and policy relating to the granting of immunity from prosecution see A.T.M. Smith, 'Immunity from Prosecution' (1983) CLR 299.
8. In the case of William 'Budgie' Allen, for example. See *Guardian*, 5 May 1986.
9. According to a report in *Guardian*, 11 August 1986, Northern Ireland's convicted supergrasses have been transferred from the Crumlin Road gaol in Belfast to the recently built Maghaberry prison complex 20 miles away where they are reputedly being housed in a cell block equipped with videos, TV, private bathrooms, a gym, easy chairs and a library.
10. The claim that several of Northern Ireland's supergrasses have found new lives in South Africa has been denied by the South African ambassador to the UK (*Irish News*, 13 April 1985). Indeed, the recent arrest and conviction of Joseph Bennett in the English Midlands suggests that they are all much nearer to home.
11. See the Attorney General's statement of 19 March 1986 (H.C. Debs., vol. 94, col. 187).
12. See Gifford, *Supergrasses*.
13. *R. v. Turner* (1975) 61 Cr. App. R. 67. See Lawton L. J.'s remarks on the advisable maximum number of defendants per trial.
14. *Davies v. D.P.P.* (1954) A.C. 378.

15.   S. 9 (1) Criminal Appeal (NI) Act 1968; *R. v. Thorne* (1978) 66 Cr. App. R. 6, 16.

16.   (1984) 1 NIJB (CA).

17.   See for example J.D. Heydon, 'The Corroboration of Accomplices' (1973) CLR 264; Gifford, *Supergrasses*, paras. 29 and 67.

18.   *People v. Coffey* 39 LRANS 704, 706 (1911).

19.   See e.g. *R. v. Graham* (1983) 7 NIJB p. 55.

20.   Gifford, *Supergrasses*, paras. 12–20.

21.   (1983) 7 NIJB.

22.   (1983) (unreported).

23.   (1983) 13 NIJB.

24.   See J.D. Jackson, *Northern Ireland Supplement to Cross on Evidence* (5th edn), (S.L.S., 1983) p.16.

25.   (1984) 18 NIJB (CA).

26.   Ibid., p. 23.

27.   W.E. Butler, *Soviet Law* (Butterworths, 1985) p. 318.

28.   In the Grimley supergrass trial, eleven of the 22 defendants were convicted on this basis even though the accomplice evidence was rejected.

29.   *Boardman v. D.P.P.* (1975) 60 Cr. App. R. 165, 183.

30.   *R. v. Turner* (1975) 61 Cr. App. R. 67, 84; *R. v. Graham* (1983) 7 NIJB; *A-G of Hong Kong v. Wong Muk-ping* (1987) 2 All E.R. 488, p. 68; *Cross on Evidence* (5th edn) (Butterworths, 1979) p. 208. In *R. v. Gibney* (1983) 13 NIJB Lord Lowry held that the 'great anxiety' displayed by Gibney on having been confronted with McGrady while in police custody strengthened McGrady's credibility (p. 21).

31.   *R. v. McCormick* (1984) 1 NIJB (CA) p.13.

32.   *R. v. Graham* (1983) 7 NIJB p. 56.

33.   *R. v. Graham* (1984) 18 NIJB (CA).

34.   Ibid., pp. 6–7.

35.   *R. v. Donnelly* (1986) 4 NIJB 32 (CA), p. 89.

36.   Ibid., p. 91.

37.   (1916) 2 K.B. 658, 667.

38.   (1832) 5 C. & P. 326.

39.   (1973) 57 Cr. App. R. 381.

40.   (1975) 60 Cr. App. R. 165.

41.   (1916) 2 K.B. 658, 667.

42.   (1983) 13 NIJB p. 5.

43.   (1984) 1 NIJB (CA).

44.   (1982) 3 NIJB p. 8.

45.   (1984) 1 NIJB (CA) p.12.

46.   Ibid.

47.   See for example A. Boyd, *The Informers: A Chilling Account of the Supergrasses in Northern Ireland* (Mercier Press, 1984) ch. 1 and Hillyard and Percy-Smith, 'Converting Terrorists'.

48.   For a good account of the disturbances of the late 1960s and early 1970s see *Sunday Times* Insight Team, *Ulster* (Penguin, 1972). See also A. Boyd, *Holy War in Belfast* (Grove Press, 1969); M. Farrell, *The Orange State* (2nd edn) (Pluto Press, 1980); P. Buckland, *A History of Northern Ireland* (Gill and Macmillan, 1981).

49.   Mr William Whitelaw, Secretary of State for Northern Ireland, H.C. Debs.,

vol. 855, col. 276.

50. K.Boyle, T. Hadden, and P. Hillyard, *Ten Years On in Northern Ireland: The Legal Control of Political Violence* (The Cobden Trust, 1980) p. 1.

51. Ibid., p. 40.

52. For further details see *Review of the Operation of the Northern Ireland (Emergency Provisions) Act 1978* (The Baker Report), Cmnd. 9222 (London: HMSO, 1984) para. 225.

53. See D.S. Greer, 'The Admissibility of Confessions under the Northern Ireland (Emergency Provisions) Act' (1980) 31 NILQ 205, 233.

54. *Report of the Committee of Inquiry into Police Interrogation Procedures in Northern Ireland* (The Bennett Report), Cmnd. 7497 (London: HMSO, 1979) para. 30.

55. Boyle *et al.*, *Ten Years On*, p. 39. See also *Ireland v. UK* (1976) Yearbook of European Convention on Human Rights, 512.

56. Report of an Amnesty International Mission to Northern Ireland (28 November–6 December 1977).

57. Bennett Report, para. 404.

58. Boyle *et al.*, *Ten Years On*, p. 40.

59. In his survey of 60 individuals arrested and detained under the EPA between September 1980 and June 1981 but released without charge after a period of interrogation, Walsh found that 35 per cent claimed they had been pressurised by the police to become informers (Walsh, *Emergency Legislation*, p. 68).

60. Ibid., p. 11.

61. In a written reply on 22 February 1985, the Secretary of State for Northern Ireland, Douglas Hurd, disclosed that providing protection for people who had given evidence against former accomplices in terrorist organisations had cost the taxpayer £1.3 million over the last seven years (H.C. Debs., vol. 74, col. 126).

62. In the Bennett case the judge, Mr Justice Murray, criticised the prosecution for not spelling out the details of Bennett's immunity deal (*R. v. Graham* (1983) 7 NIJB p. 23).

63. See the Baker Report, paras. 455–9.

64. *R. v. Graham* (1983) 7 NIJB pp. 25–6.

65. Ibid., p. 22.

66. Ibid., pp. 23–6.

67. See *Guardian*, 7 April 1986 and 30 July 1986.

68. *R. v. Graham* (1983) 7 NIJB p. 87. In his report Lord Gifford appears to confuse this with a sum of £600 which Bennett alleged he was given by the defendants Hewitt and Houston acting as officers for the UVF (Gifford, *Supergrasses*, para. 39). Nevertheless Gifford's conclusion that this proven lie undermined Bennett's credibility remains valid as a general point.

69. *R. v. Donnelly* (1983) (unreported) Day 1, p. 71.

70. The only other supergrass cases in which it was used were those featuring Patrick McGurk, who retracted his evidence the day the trial of those he had implicated was due to start, and Harry Kirkpatrick.

71. For a discussion of the voluntary Bill of Indictment procedure see Walsh, *Emergency Legislation*, pp. 88–90.

72. (1983) (unreported) Day 1, pp. 157–9.

73. (1983) (unreported) Day 2, pp. 9–50.

74. (1978) 66 Cr. App. R. 6.

75. (1983) (unreported) Day 2, p. 27.
76. Ibid., p. 37.
77. Gifford, *Supergrasses*, para. 52.
78. *R. v. Donnelly* (1986) (CA) supra.
79. (1983) 4 NIJB 32 (CA) p. 33.
80. Ibid., pp. 11–12.
81. Ibid., p. 29.
82. *R. v. Sean P. McGrady* (1984) 8 NIJB (CA) p. 19.
83. This view is culled from a number of sources, including media interviews with government spokesmen, statements in the House of Commons (e.g. H.C. Debs., vol. 47, col. 305 and vol. 94, cols. 187–8) and unofficial expositions of what amounts to a pro-official position (e.g. E. Graham, 'A Vital Weapon in the Anti-Terrorist Arsenal', *Fortnight*, no. 198).
84. The conspiracy view is also culled from a number of sources: statements by relatives' organisations and political parties, and various pamphlets and articles (e.g. Workers Research Unit, *Belfast Bulletin no. 4 – Supergrasses* (1984), R. McDonagh, 'Are the Judges Another Arm of British Policy?', *Fortnight*, no. 216).
85. The Chief Constable of the RUC, Sir John Hermon, stated in his annual report for 1982: 'It is clearly beyond question that the community as a whole has benefited immeasurably from this development.... The outcome is crucial to the well-being of Northern Ireland....' (pp. xi–xii).
86. There has been a reluctance, for example, to accept that the largely uncorroborated evidence of an accomplice of bad character who has a lot to gain by giving evidence is an unsafe basis for conviction in all circumstances in a non-jury court. See *R. v. Graham* (1984) 18 NIJB 23.
87. See for example the thumb-nail sketches in Workers Research Unit, *Belfast Bulletin no. 10 – Rough Justice* (1982).
88. Gifford, *Supergrasses*.
89. See also S.C. Greer, 'Supergrasses and the Legal System in Britain and Northern Ireland' (1986) L.Q.R. 198.
90. H.C. Debs., vol. 94, col. 186.
91. See *Fortnight*, no. 187, 1982.
92. These figure are taken from D. Roche, 'Patterns of Political Violence in Northern Ireland in 1984', *Fortnight*, no. 218, 1985.
93. Ibid.
94. *Fortnight*, no. 209, 1984.
95. *Belfast Telegraph*, 6 February 1985.
96. For an account of the English supergrass phenomenon see D. Seymour, 'What good have supergrasses done for anyone but themselves?', *LAG Bulletin*, December 1982. For a more detailed comparison of the use of supergrasses in England and Northern Ireland see S.C. Greer, 'Supergrasses and the Legal System'.
97. (1975) 61 Cr. App. R. 67, 79.
98. It would be exactly the same were it not for the Northern Ireland Court of Appeal decisions in *R. v. McCormick* (1984) 1 NIJB (CA) and *R. v. Graham* (1984) 16 NIJB the implications of which for the law in England and Wales are not clear.
99. Gifford, *Supergrasses*, p.10. The police have maintained that immunity is never granted to anyone who has been directly responsible for murder (para. 27).
100. *Guardian*, 29 May 1977 and 30 May 1977.

101.   *R. v. Thorne* (1978) 66 Cr. App. R. 6, 12–14. The Black trial involved 38 defendants, the Gilmour trial 35 and the Crockard case 29.
102.   Seymour, 'What good have supergrasses done?'
103.   The demand for a statutory corroboration requirement has been consistently rejected by the government (see H.C. Debs., vol. 80, col. 1009). For the case for the restoration of jury trial to scheduled offences see S.C. Greer and A. White, *Abolishing the Diplock Courts* (The Cobden Trust, 1986).

5

ANTHONY JENNINGS

Shoot to Kill:
The Final Courts of Justice[1]

> There is no shoot to kill policy, there never has been, and as far as
> I am concerned there never will be.
>   – James Prior, Secretary of State for Northern Ireland[2]

The law governing the use of lethal force has remained ostensibly
unchanged during the 'emergency'. Nevertheless, the vagueness of the
law and the attitude of the judiciary have led to a situation in which
few effective controls exist to restrict the use of firearms by the security
forces. 'Shoot to kill', a strategy of assassinating known or suspected
Republican activists through their deliberate engagement by the security
forces in armed confrontation, is the result of this indulgent attitude
of the courts towards the security forces.

Generally speaking, deadly force has been exercised in two ways.
The first is what can be termed the habitual and excessive use of force
by ordinary members of the security forces, the most common example of which is teenagers being shot and killed whilst joyriding and failing to stop at roadblocks. The second category involves the use of special
anti-terrorist squads employed to stake out and kill suspected terrorists.

As a result, over 270 individuals, at least 155 of them 'civilians',[3]
have been killed by the security forces in Northern Ireland since 1969.
Between November 1982 and February 1985 35 individuals were killed
by the security forces, 23 of them in covert operations. Only one of those
23 was not a known or suspected Republican activist. Twenty-one
members of the security forces have been prosecuted for killings using
firearms committed on duty. Only two of these individuals, as Table
5.1 shows, have been found guilty of murder or manslaughter. This
lack of accountability for these deaths, many of them taking place in
disputed circumstances (see Table 5.2), shows that the security forces
have, to a large degree, been granted the power to decide the guilt or

innocence of suspected Republican activists without recourse to the courts. Through their ability to use firearms virtually without restriction, they have become the final courts of justice.

Table 5.1 Security Force Prosecutions

Case	Victim	Verdict
Army		
R. v. Foxford[a] (1974)	Kevin Heatley	Not Guilty
R. v. Ross (1974)	Anthony Mitchell	Not Guilty
R. v. Spencer (1974)	Samuel Martin	Not Guilty
R. v. Nicholl (1975)	Alex Howell	Not Guilty
R. v. Jones (1975)	Patrick McElhone	Not Guilty
R. v. Fury (1975)	Hugh Devine	Not Guilty
R. v. Scott (1976)	Anthony Gallagher	Not Guilty
R. v. Williams (1977)	Majella O'Hare	Not Guilty
R. v. Bohan and Temperley (1979)	John Boyle	Not Guilty
R. v. Davidson[b] (1981)	Theresa Donaghey	Guilty (Manslaughter)
R. v. Bailey and Jones (1983)	Eamonn Bradley	Not Guilty
R. v. Thain (1984)	Thomas Reilly	Guilty (Murder)
RUC		
R. v. McKeown (1981)	Michael McCartan	Not Guilty
R. v. Robinson (1984)	Seamus Grew, Roddy Carroll	Not Guilty
R. v. Montgomery, Brannigan and Robinson (1984)	Gervais McKerr, Eugene Toman, Sean Burns	Not Guilty
R. v. Hegarty (1987)	John Downes	Not Guilty
UDR		
R. v. Baird (1984)	Martin Malone	Not Guilty

The acquittal rate in no-jury courts in 1981 was 33.98 per cent and 34.92 per cent in 1982 (The Baker Report, Appendix H, page 160). The acquittal rate in prosecutions of members of the security forces for killings committed whilst on duty resulting from the use of firearms is 90.5 per cent overall.

This table does not include prosecutions for offences committed whilst off duty or caused other than by the use of firearms (K. Asmal, *Shoot to Kill?*, p. 25, n. 25). Thus the convictions of four UDR men in 1986 for murdering Adrian Carroll are not included.

(a) This defendant was convicted of manslaughter by Kelly J. at first instance but his conviction was overturned on appeal by Lord Lowry C.J.
(b) Sentenced to 12 months' detention in Young Offenders' Centre, suspended for 2 years.

The Law: 'An Unlimited Licence'

It is unrealistic to expect the security forces to carry out their hazardous tasks without clear guidance on the circumstances in which it is permissible to open fire. The law has manifestly failed to provide this guidance. Its vagueness has permitted the rules governing the use of deadly force to be interpreted in a way that unduly favours the security forces. The need for effective legal controls is an urgent one.

Self-defence

The use of lethal force is governed by both the common law and statute. To rely upon the common law defence of self-defence, a person's act must be both immediately necessary and proportionate to the harm feared,[4] and it appears that the test is still an objective one.[5] The law also accepts that a person may use a pre-emptive strike against immediately threatened violence, although the force used should not be disproportionate to the harm feared.[6] This safeguard, however, has been qualified by the Privy Council:

> A person defending himself cannot weigh to a nicety the exact measure of his necessary defensive action. If a jury thought that in a moment of unexpected anguish a person attacked had only done what he honestly and instinctively thought was necessary that would be most potent evidence that only reasonable defensive action had been taken.[7]

Moreover, if an individual uses force under a mistaken and unreasonable belief that he was entitled to do so, he will be acquitted provided he genuinely laboured under this belief.[8]

Older authorities attempted to lay down specific cases in which the use of deadly force would be justified.[9] More recent authorities, however, have moved away from the precision of the old law and sought refuge in the somewhat elastic concept of reasonableness.

Where force is used to arrest and the suspect simply flees, then the case is decided under section 3(1) of the Criminal Law (Northern Ireland) Act 1967. But where a suspect offers resistance, the decision is made in accordance with the common law rules governing self-defence. Where a suspect forcibly resists a lawful arrest then fatal force may be used as a last resort.[10] The position concerning a suspect who flees but who offers no resistance is unclear. It is also arguable that as an assault is a crime, all cases of self-defence are now governed by section 3.

In the absence of any authority on the point, Professor Williams believes that if a suspect is armed then the police may open fire first.

If there appears no other way of arresting a 'dangerous suspect', then, Williams believes, the person may be shot.[11]

Criminal Law Act 1967

According to section 3(1) of the Criminal Law (Northern Ireland) Act 1967: 'A person may use such force as is reasonable in the circumstances in the prevention of crime, or in effecting or assisting in the lawful arrest of offenders or suspected offenders or of persons unlawfully at large.' This provision, which is identical to the one in England and Wales, was introduced prior to the civil disturbances in Northern Ireland. It was not designed to cover a situation where the forces of law and order permanently carried firearms. As Lord Lowry C.J. has observed: 'The security forces are operating in conditions with which the ordinary law was not designed to cope, and in regard to which there are no legal precedents.'[12]

Prior to 1967, the law required 'apparent necessity' before an officer of justice might use deadly force.[13] The previous common law rules therefore set a higher standard than section 3, although, interestingly, the British government argued before the European Commission that section 3 had the effect of requiring necessity.[14] Section 3(2) of the Act makes it clear that the statute overrides the common law rules.

It has been suggested[15] that the proper interpretation of section 3 is that it cannot be reasonable to cause death unless: (1) it was necessary to do so in order to effect the arrest or prevent the crime; and (2) the evil which would follow from failure to prevent the crime or effect the arrest is so great that a reasonable person ought to think him or herself justified in taking another's life to avert that evil.

A defendant must raise a triable issue in order to use the defence of reasonable force.[16] A defendant must put forward facts which contain the constituent elements of the defence and adduce evidence sufficient to put before the jury.

The Attorney General's Reference Case

In *The Attorney General for Northern Ireland's Reference* (No. 1 of 1975)[17] the House of Lords declined the opportunity to provide guidelines on the use of lethal force. The case arose from the acquittal of a soldier in 1975 for the murder of farmhand Patrick McElhone.[18] The accused had approached McElhone on his own farm to detain him for questioning. The soldier called on the deceased to halt, McElhone looked over his shoulder to see the accused pointing his rifle at him, and ran. At the time that the deceased was required to halt he was about eight yards from the soldier, and as McElhone ran he was shot and killed by the defendant. The deceased was clearly unarmed at the time and it was accepted at the trial that McElhone was an 'entirely innocent person who was in no way involved in terrorist activity'.

At his trial the defendant, Lance Corporal Jones, stated that when he fired he honestly and reasonably believed that he was dealing with a member of the Provisional IRA who was seeking to run away. But Jones admitted that he had no belief at all as to whether the deceased had been involved in acts of terrorism or was likely to be involved in any immediate act of terrorism. This was an important admission in view of the way Lord Diplock later approached the case in the House of Lords.

At the end of the trial, MacDermott J. acquitted the soldier of murder. One of the grounds for the acquittal was the somewhat unusual one that the defendant did not possess an intention to kill or cause grievous bodily harm. The main basis for the decision, however, was that the soldier genuinely believed that he was shooting at a fleeing suspected terrorist and that he had no alternative means of stopping the man but to shoot him.

The decision caused extreme concern in some circles, where it was perceived as giving the security forces carte blanche to shoot suspected terrorists who posed no immediate threat. The Attorney General, Sam Silkin QC, decided to refer the matter to the Northern Ireland Court of Appeal for clarification and guidance on two issues: (1) whether a crime is committed when a member of the security forces shoots to kill or seriously wound a person believed to be a member of a proscribed organisation in the course of his attempted escape; and (2) if it is a crime, is it murder or manslaughter?

In the Court of Appeal, Jones L.J. and Gibson L.J. did not express disapproval of the trial judge's finding of fact and held that there was a triable issue as to whether the Crown had proved that the defendant's use of force was unreasonable. Lord Justice McGonigal dissented. He pointed out that McElhone's failure to stop when requested to do so by the soldier could have resulted in a fine or a short prison sentence: 'this, in either case, is far removed from death or serious injury'.[19] The answer to the question of whether it was lawful to shoot a 'card carrying member' of the Provisional IRA who poses no immediate threat and who runs away, McGonigal L.J. said, is 'clearly "NO" and the force used is so manifestly disproportionate to the mischief sought to be prevented that no reasonable jury properly directed could do other than hold that the force used was excessive'.[20]

Moreover, he pointed out, the danger involved in permitting the security forces to shoot to kill outside the cases involving an immediate threat to the person is that: 'the possibilities of who may be shot legitimately are endless. It is giving an unlimited licence to the security forces.'[21] His judgment concluded: 'It is, in my opinion, the duty and responsibility of these courts to stand between those exercising such powers and the persons against whom they are exercised to ensure that those powers are not used excessively to cause unlawful harm.'[22]

A Licence to Kill

The House of Lords declined to follow McGonigal L.J.'s judgment. The Lords held that the first question contained in the reference was a question of fact for the jury and that the only question of law contained in the first part of the reference was whether there was a triable issue as to whether the prosecution had proved that the accused used unreasonable force. The answer to that question was in the affirmative.

As has been said, older authorities were unclear as to whether an 'officer of justice' was entitled to kill a fleeing suspect who offered no resistance. Lord Diplock[23] circumvented this obstacle by relying on a matter which had not been pleaded by the defence at Lance Corporal Jones' trial. Lord Diplock stated that on the facts there was material on which a jury might take the view that a defendant had reasonable grounds for the apprehension of 'imminent danger' to himself or other members of the patrol if the deceased were allowed to escape. The imminent threat posed by the deceased was that: 'if he got away, [he] was likely *sooner or later* to participate in acts of violence' (emphasis added).[24]

A soldier must consider matters of the widest import in his decision to open fire. Lord Diplock said he had to balance the risk of:

killing or wounding of the patrol by terrorists in ambush, and the effect of this success by members of the Provisional IRA in encouraging the continuance of the armed insurrection and all the misery and destruction of life and property that terrorist activity in Northern Ireland has entailed.[25]

Lord Diplock went on to propound a test of such width as to be of no practical assistance in deciding when it is permissible to open fire. The question for the jury is, he said:

Are we satisfied that no reasonable man (a) with knowledge of such facts as were known to the accused or reasonably believed by him to exist (b) in the circumstances and time available for reflection (c) could be of the opinion that the prevention of the risk of harm to which others might be exposed if the suspect were allowed to escape justified exposing the suspect to the risk of harm to him that might result from the kind of force that the accused contemplated using?[26]

Those members of the forces of law and order who would look to this case for guidance would be better advised to look elsewhere, as the House of Lords has left the law in a state of some confusion. Probably an officer of justice would be safe in shooting a fleeing suspect if he felt in immediate danger from the suspect but the criteria for deciding what amounts to 'imminent danger' are unclear. Lord Diplock's definition of 'imminent danger' is rather elastic and its implications are disturbing. Can logic permit the expression to be stretched to such an extent that it is lawful to shoot someone because at some unspecified future date he or she may be involved in acts of violence? This is, to say the least, an extreme theory of preventive policing. Even taking a less extreme view, there are still outstanding questions. What of a soldier or policeman who fears a possible danger from the suspect in the future or who seeks to arrest a person for a past murder even though the suspect poses no future threat? What degree of force may be used against a person escaping with the proceeds of a large robbery even though the suspect has not used or threatened force?

Robert Spjut[27] has argued that the courts have allowed the security forces to suppress disorder by threats. Facilitating this process is the fact that the courts have subtly eroded four principles. First, the principle of proportionate force has been developed to enhance deterrence by allowing the security forces to use lethal force not only for less than grave crimes, but also where there exists a vague notion as to what crime has been committed. Secondly, the relaxation of the requirement of an immediate threat of violence has allowed the security forces to intervene well in advance of a crime. Thirdly, the minimum force principle has been so diluted that the courts no longer consider that defendants have alternatives to using lethal force. Fourthly, the duty to minimise a confrontation has been undermined so that there are few limits on what action the security forces can take to prevent a crime or apprehend an offender or prevent his escape.

A Half-Way House

On the second point of reference, both the Court of Appeal and the House of Lords made it clear that, provided a defendant possessed the necessary intent, the offence was murder. It had been hoped that the House of Lords would follow the Australian doctrine[28] that where death results from the use of excessive force in self-defence the crime may be reduced from murder to manslaughter.[29] It has also been suggested[30] that the invidious choice the court has to make between a conviction for murder and an acquittal could be alleviated by the creation of a new offence of causing death by the unreasonable use of lethal force.

'In the Circumstances'

In deciding if the force used by an accused was 'reasonable', the courts have rendered interpretations which have been far from consistent and applied with considerable indulgence to the security forces. In *Farrell v. Ministry of Defence*[31] an unarmed man had been shot by soldiers from a rooftop after snatching a night deposit bag from a man outside a bank and his widow brought an action against the Ministry of Defence for negligence. The court must look at the circumstances of the offence, and in this case, the House of Lords held that it is the immediate circumstances of the offence, not matters leading to the incident such as the planning of the operation, that are to be taken into account. The fact, therefore, that soldiers had been positioned on a rooftop and so prevented from capturing the suspect was held not to fall within the definition of circumstances. Nevertheless, the courts have held that circumstances include the 'general wartime situation',[32] the local terrain, the fact that the area was hostile to the security forces, evidence of IRA activity and the tactic of ambush.[33]

A most important consideration from the courts' point of view is an accused's sense of duty. If a soldier reasonably thought that his actions were consistent with his duty then this will be potent evidence that he acted reasonably.[34] It has also been suggested that a member of the security forces may not foresee the likely consequences of his actions because he is trained to act instinctively.[35] Widespread judicial acceptance of such a theory, however, would effectively prevent the conviction of any member of the security forces for murder. It is disingenuous to suggest that soldiers and policemen who are trained in the use of firearms would not foresee that the likely consequence of someone being hit by a bullet from a self-loading rifle would be death or serious injury.

All soldiers in Northern Ireland are issued with instructions on the use of firearms which are contained in what is known as the 'yellow card',[36] shown here in Table 5.3. It has been pointed out that these instructions do not define the legal rights and duties of soldiers,[37] and some judges have regarded breaches of the instructions as 'irrelevant'.[38] Nonetheless, it must be of importance that soldiers and policemen fail to adhere to the standards that they have set. Perhaps if such instructions were given the force of law then they would 'ensure that firearms are not used indiscriminately'.[39]

The European Convention

Section 3 of the Criminal Law Act and its interpretation by the courts would appear to be in breach of the European Convention. Article 2 of the Convention provides that a person can use no more force than is 'absolutely necessary' for the purpose of defending a person from violence, arresting a suspect or preventing an escape or quelling a riot or insurrection.

In *Farrell v. UK*[40] the European Commission held admissible a complaint alleging that section 3 breached article 2. The case was brought by the same widow of the unarmed man mentioned above who had been shot by soldiers from a rooftop. The applicant brought an action against the Ministry of Defence claiming compensation for the death of her husband, and her claim eventually reached the House of Lords where it was dismissed.

The applicant argued that: (1) as there was no threat to the soldiers concerned, the Convention did not allow the use of fatal force to prevent crime; (2) the courts failed to draw a distinction between the case where a person is resisting arrest and where a person is fleeing from arrest without resistance; and (3) the trial judge's direction to the jury that a fleeing suspect was believed to be 'likely to commit actual crimes of violence if he succeeded in avoiding arrest' gave soldiers the power to execute summarily for crimes that might be committed in the immediate or remote future.

The applicant relied upon the trial judge's direction to the jury, which must be regarded as one of the most overt indications of the judiciary's sympathy for the security forces. Gibson L.J. told them:

> if you watch wild west films, the possy go ready to shoot their men if need be, if they don't bring them back peaceably they shoot them. And in the ultimate result if there isn't any other way open to a man it's reasonable to do it in the circumstances. Shooting may be justified as a method of arrest.[41]

Unfortunately the case did not proceed to the European Court for full argument as both sides entered into a 'friendly settlement', and the British government agreed to pay 'substantial damages' to Mrs Farrell.

It is lamentable that the security forces, operating in what has been described as a 'quasi-war situation',[42] should be expected to do so without any real guidelines on when they are permitted to open fire. The courts have attempted to maintain the pretence that as regards the taking of life the security forces are subject to the same rules as ordinary citizens,[43] whilst at the same time developing the law so as to make it unduly favourable to the security forces. The law in its present state patently fails to protect the citizen from the deliberate or reckless use of firearms by the security forces. Most disturbingly, the law's vagueness and imprecision led to the security forces being granted a virtually unlimited licence to kill.

The Forces of Law and Order

The use of undercover surveillance units and the existence of 'dirty tricks' departments is a tradition in British colonial history.[44] The SAS has operated in Northern Ireland since 1969,[45] and it was rumoured in the early 1970s that special death squads existed with instructions to assassinate top IRA leaders.[46] The revelations of the Littlejohn brothers and their alleged recruitment by British intelligence as hired assassins were viewed as confirmation of such rumours.[47] In fact, the government finally admitted that the SAS was being used in undercover operations in Northern Ireland.[48] Undercover operations were increased in an attempt to combat the growing strength of the IRA and it was revealed that every soldier in Northern Ireland was being trained in routine intelligence work.[49]

The introduction of the policy of Ulsterisation led to a lower profile for the army. Undercover operations, however, continued, and in 1976 a campaign was apparently launched in Armagh designed to destroy the local IRA hierarchy. Between late 1977 and late 1978 the number of selective assassinations increased dramatically as ten individuals were killed by the security forces in covert operations.[50] Not long before, the Secretary of State had announced that the SAS would be strengthened.[51] In his maiden speech in the House of Commons Ken Livingstone MP claimed that Captain Robert Nairac, an SAS officer killed by the IRA in 1977, had been involved in killing IRA man John Green in 1974 and the Miami showband killing in 1975. Mr Livingstone also suggested, based upon the allegations of former intelligence officers Fred Holroyd and Colin Wallace, that the security services had been involved in a number of dirty tricks operations during this period.[52]

The escalation of covert operations was due probably to the combination of two important factors. First, Labour Secretary of State Roy Mason was a hardliner in the effort to defeat the IRA. Secondly, the arrival of Major General Timothy Creasy in Northern Ireland as Commanding Officer provided an ideal military counterpart to Mason's political role. Creasy had served in Oman between 1972 and 1975 and had used the SAS extensively.

It was, however, the success of Provisional Sinn Fein in the October 1982 assembly elections that led to the full unleashing of shoot to kill operations against the Nationalist community. In December 1982 top RUC sources apparently confirmed that special anti-terrorist units were engaged in a shoot to kill policy.[53] Between 1982 and 1985, 23 individuals were shot by the security forces in covert operations.[54]

Many Unionist politicians viewed the shoot to kill policy as a welcome development and a belated indication that the security forces were prepared to 'take off the gloves' in the fight against Republican 'terrorism'. Thomas Passmore of the OUP called for the Secretary of State to 'remove the political shackles from *our* security forces' (emphasis added).[55] William Douglas of the OUP had nothing but praise for the individuals involved in these operations: 'men of that ability and accomplishment who selectively kill men who are known murderers need to be supported in every way.'[56]

Two recent murder trials, both of RUC members for murders allegedly committed on duty, illustrate, it is said, the operation of the shoot to kill policy, the inadequacies of the existing law, and the attitude of Northern Ireland's judges to the role of the security forces. The resulting acquittals raised serious questions as to the reasons for the DPP's decision to prosecute. The Nationalist community felt that they were specifically chosen because of the difficulties involved in obtaining convictions for killing suspected armed terrorists. More importantly, it was argued that the cases would portray the authorities as acting even-handedly in bringing the prosecutions, and the resulting acquittals would provide judicial endorsement of and encouragement for the RUC's fight against Republican 'terrorism'. Such allegations would, no doubt, be strenuously denied.

R. v. Robinson[57]

On the evening of 12 December 1982 Seamus Grew and Roddy Carroll were travelling in an Allegro motor car to Grew's home in Mulcreve Park, Armagh. An unmarked police surveillance vehicle intercepted the Allegro. An ex-British soldier, Constable John Robinson, got out of the car and fired 15 shots at Carroll, who was in the passenger seat. Robinson then reloaded his weapon, ran in front of the car to the driver's door and shot Grew. Both of the deceased men were unarmed.

According to a local Roman Catholic priest, Father Raymond Murray, the two men had previously been issued death threats by the security forces. Prior to the incident armed men had entered Grew's home and fired a number of shots; several UDR men were later convicted of the murder of Roddy Carroll's brother Adrian. Both Grew and Carroll were alleged to have been active members of the INLA and their deaths occurred less than a week after the Ballykelly pub bombing in which off-duty members of the security forces were killed. Responsibility for the explosion had been claimed by the INLA.

Robinson was charged with the murder of Grew. The trial commenced in March 1984 before Mr Justice MacDermott sitting without a jury. It will be remembered that MacDermott J. had acquitted the soldier charged with the murder of Patrick McElhone in 1975, and it was his judgment which set the precedent for the principle that the security forces could kill unarmed suspected terrorists who flee without resistance.

At the trial Robinson testified that he was a member of the RUC's undercover Special Support Unit. Robinson and other officers, without the permission of the Irish authorities, had followed the deceased men from a family funeral into the Irish Republic where they were returning a relative to her home. It was there, according to a police informer, that Grew and Carroll were to pick up INLA chief Dominic McGlinchey to take him back across the border.

According to the RUC version of events at the time, both men drove through a police roadblock, and injured a policeman as they did so. The Allegro was then pursued by Robinson. Robinson admitted in court that the roadblock story had been concocted after consultations with senior officers. Even when the restrictions imposed by the Official Secrets Act had been lifted and Robinson was free to tell the truth, he persisted with the roadblock story. Once again, according to the accused, this was on the advice of senior officers. The prosecution argued, however, that the invention of the roadblock story was a desperate attempt to help justify the police intervention in the incident. It was also argued that any fear that Robinson had that his life was in danger must have dissipated if he was able to reload his weapon and then pass in front of the car in order to reach Grew.

Forensic evidence at the trial showed that at the time of the shooting Grew was attempting to reverse the car with the handbrake on. Robinson had testified that he had heard gunfire from the Allegro before opening fire but forensic scientists could produce no sound from the car similar to gunshots. This ostensibly difficult point was dismissed by the learned judge with characteristic ease: 'a clinical test of that nature does not however mean that there could not have been a noise which the accused reasonably thought was a gunshot.' Forensic evidence also established that Grew could not have been shot, as Robinson claimed, through the car door; it appeared that he had in fact been shot whilst attempting to leave the car. This point was similarly swept aside by the judge: '[Robinson's] recall in relation to this part of the incident is and will remain *disturbed* and he is not lying or seeking to conceal something' (emphasis added).

In acquitting Robinson of murder, Mr Justice MacDermott said that he had 'no doubt' that the Crown had failed to satisfy him that the accused was not acting in self-defence. He went on: 'while policemen are required to act within the law they are not required to be supermen and one does not use jeweller's scales to measure what is reasonable in the circumstances.'

R. v. Montgomery and Others[58]
On 11 November 1982 Gervais McKerr was driving his car in Lurgan

in the company of Eugene Toman and Sean Burns when an RUC patrol opened fire on the car killing all of the occupants. The three deceased men were unarmed. In April 1984 three RUC men stood trial at the Belfast Crown Court for the murder of Eugene Toman. At the end of the prosecution case the trial judge, Gibson L.J., acceded to a defence submission that the three policemen had no case to answer and they were acquitted of the charge.

It was claimed that the deceased had driven through a police roadblock and refused to stop. The police opened fire on the car and the three accused claimed that they believed that fire was returned. The forensic explanation for this claim was that flashes emitted by the officers' bullets striking the car could give the appearance of fire being returned. The car then came to a halt. The officers said that they then heard the sound of a gun being cocked and they opened fire again. Toman was found lying out of the car with bullet wounds in his back. The officers had fired a total of 109 bullets, 56 of which hit the car.

The accused men were also members of the Special Support Unit. They had originally claimed to be part of an ordinary police patrol and did not disclose that the three deceased men had been under surveillance for some time. This story was changed when the accused were re-interviewed and the restrictions of the Official Secrets Act were waived. At the trial Deputy Chief Constable Michael McAtamney, who had given similar evidence at the Robinson trial, told the court that the keywords in the officers' training were: 'firepower, speed and aggression'. He added that the principle was 'once you have decided to fire, you shoot to take out your enemy.' 'Do you mean permanently out of action?' asked the judge. 'Yes,' replied McAtamney.[59]

Gibson L.J. held that the officers had acted in self-defence and had used reasonable force in attempting to effect an arrest. The accused were 'absolutely blameless', he remarked, and he asked, 'When a policeman or a soldier is ordered to arrest a dangerous criminal, and in substance, as in this case, to bring back dead or alive, how is he to consider his conduct?' Reminiscent of his 'possy' direction to the jury in the Farrell case, Gibson L.J. went one step further. He stated that the prosecution never had 'the slightest chance of sustaining a conviction', and then commended the RUC men for their 'courage and determination in bringing the three deceased men to justice; in this case, to *the final court of justice*' (emphasis added).

His remarks were greeted with outrage. Irish premier Dr Garret Fitzgerald said that they were 'entirely unacceptable; unworthy of any decent judicial authority'.[60] The Northern Ireland Bishops and the Irish Primate, Cardinal O'Fiach, issued a statement that such remarks were 'inexplicable and inexcusable'.[61] Nationalist politicians called for the judge's resignation and he took the virtually unprecedented step of calling the press into court to explain his remarks. In answer to the allegation that he had effectively endorsed a shoot to kill policy, Gibson L.J. said: 'I do not believe that on any fair interpretation; indeed, nothing was further from my mind, nor would I or any other judge contemplate for a second, that such a view was tenable.'[62] Lord Justice Gibson and his wife were killed in 1987 by an IRA bomb as they travelled into Northern Ireland from the Republic of Ireland.

On 22 August 1984 Armagh coroner Gerry Curran resigned due to 'grave irregularities' in the police files in the Grew and Carroll case.[63] The following week, acting coroner James Rodgers said he would be unable to take over the inquest due to 'professional commitments' and he too pointed to a number of differences between the police account as contained in the files and that given in court.[64] The inquest was adjourned pending an inquiry by members of the Greater Manchester Police.[65] The inquest into the deaths of McKerr, Toman and Burns was transferred to the Belfast coroner James Elliott.

The Stalker Affair[66]

John Stalker, Deputy Chief Constable of Greater Manchester, conducted an inquiry into the killings of Grew, Carroll, Toman, Burns, McKerr and Michael Tighe which all occurred in Co. Armagh within a month of each other in late 1982. (Michael Tighe and Martin McCauley were shot in a hayshed by members of the Special Support Unit whilst examining three 60 year old rifles. McCauley was subsequently tried and convicted for possessing firearms.) Before the completion of his investigations Stalker was suspended from duty pending the outcome of a number of alleged disciplinary offences. The inquiry into the killings and Stalker's activities was conducted by Colin Sampson, Chief Constable of West Yorkshire. Stalker was eventually reinstated by his police committee without any action being taken against him but he subsequently resigned from the police force. Sampson's report eventually went before the DPP for consideration.

Stalker concluded that there were grounds for charging a number of police officers, including senior RUC men, with a range of serious offences. During his investigations he had carried out forensic tests, the results of which contradicted the evidence in the Robinson and Montgomery cases. In the Tighe case it was apparently accepted that an ambush led to the 'cold blooded murder' of the wrong man, and Stalker apparently wished to interview the Chief Constable, Sir John Hermon, and one of his deputies under caution. The tapes in the Tighe case were apparently wiped clean. Stalker had also discovered that an informant was paid £2,000 after the killing of McKerr, Toman and Burns, and that the same informant was also linked to the Tighe killing. The RUC allegedly blocked his attempt to interview the informant.

Sources close to Stalker alleged that senior government officials in Belfast and London had asked him to whitewash the RUC. It was also alleged that a man in police custody had been asked by police to fabricate allegations against Stalker.[67] Moreover, sources close to him alleged that the investigation had been obstructed on a number of occasions by Sir John Hermon. Hermon apparently refused to suspend two senior RUC men following a request by Stalker, and also refused to release MI5 tapes of a surveillance bug from the scene of the Tighe killing.

The Stalker affair has remarkable parallels with a similar incident which took place in 1979. When police surgeon Robert Irwin confirmed allegations of ill-treatment of suspects in custody, the RUC told the press that Irwin was a 'drunk' who was 'sour and bitter' over the RUC's failure to investigate the rape of Mrs Irwin. Whatever the truth of the allegations against John Stalker, his credibility was irretrievably damaged. The timing of the damaging findings by Stalker and the announcement of his suspension was remarkable.

The Attorney General's Response

The Attorney General, Sir Patrick Mayhew, announced in January 1988 that eight RUC officers involved in a conspiracy to pervert the course of justice and responsible for obstructing the Stalker inquiry would not be prosecuted for reasons of 'national security'.[68] Sir Patrick stated that the decision had caused him 'the greatest anxiety' and that he had had 'to balance one harm to national security against another'. He added that 'it was not an easy consideration.'

It appears that the Stalker/Sampson inquiry had recommended a number of prosecutions but the DPP for Northern Ireland, after consultation with the Attorney General, concluded that 'it would not be proper to institute any proceedings.' There was also apparently no evidence of offences 'such as incitement to murder or of what might be described as shoot to kill'.

The Irish government greeted the announcement with 'deep dismay' and stated that they were seeking 'urgent clarification' of the decision. Ken Livingstone MP was suspended from the House of Commons after describing the Attorney General as an 'accomplice to murder'.

It is difficult to see what 'national security' interests outweigh the public interest of bringing prosecutions against those in positions of trust and power who have committed serious offences. Unfortunately, during the premiership of Mrs Thatcher the expression 'national security' has rolled off the tongues of government ministers with remarkable ease and become a byword for obsessive and dangerous secrecy. The decision undoubtedly represents a major setback to Anglo-Irish relations and another potent reason for the Nationalist community to view the police as operating beyond the reaches of the law.

The greatest repercussion of this decision is undoubtedly for the security forces. Those police officers who in future would wish to conspire with others to commit perjury and obstruct senior police officers engaged on an official inquiry will take great comfort from the Attorney General's decision.

Stalker's Response

John Stalker eventually broke his silence with a book about the affair published only a few weeks after the Attorney General's statement in the House of Commons (J. Stalker, *Stalker* (London: Harrap, 1988); extracts from the book published in the *Daily Express*, 1–5 February 1988). He confirmed that his terms of reference did not include an investigation of the existence of a shoot to kill policy. Furthermore, Stalker was given the clear impression by the Chief Constable of Northern Ireland, Sir John Hermon, that he was simply to read a few documents, write a report and suggest minor operational changes. When Stalker made it clear that this was not his intention he met with hostility and opposition. He was informed anonymously that his office and accommodation were bugged and 'it became obvious that we could not trust anyone' (p. 33). In his view key RUC officers took a conscious decision to obstruct his investigation.

A police informer turned out to be a central link in two of the incidents. On 27 October 1982 a landmine killed three RUC officers in Kinnego, Lurgan, and an informer named Toman, Burns, McKerr and McCauley as being involved in the killings. Several weeks later the first three were dead. Also, the hayshed where Tighe and McCauley had been shot had been under surveillance and was regarded as the store for the landmine that killed the three officers. Stalker believed that the files on the two prosecutions had been incompetently prepared, amounting to a 'catalogue of ineptitude' (p. 42), and as a result he 'could see why the prosecutions had failed' (p. 40). 'The killings had a common feature: each left a strong suspicion that *a type of pre-planned police ambush had occurred,* and that someone had led these men to their deaths' (p. 72) (emphasis added).

Stalker suspected the involvement of an agent provocateur in the killings and was prepared to accept that the rifles may have been planted in the hayshed by the informant or others. One key piece in the puzzle of the existence of a shoot to kill policy was the MI5 bug in the hayshed: 'I could think of no better way of proving, or disproving, this awesomely serious allegation than to obtain a copy of that tape. This issue now transcended all others' (p. 66). The Chief Constable consistently refused to hand over the tape and it was only a few days before Stalker was due to fly to Belfast to hear the tape that he was suspended from duty.

Stalker concluded that he could present extra evidence which strongly suggested that all six men had been unlawfully killed. But what of the existence of a shoot to kill policy, or rather a policy of 'shoot first, ask questions later'?

Stalker believed that:

> The circumstances of those shootings pointed to a police inclination, if not a policy, to shoot suspects dead without warning rather than to arrest them. Coming as these incidents did, so close together, the suspicion of deliberate assassination was not unreasonable….(p. 253)
> There was no written instruction, nothing pinned upon a noticeboard. But there was a clear understanding on the part of the men whose job it was to pull the trigger that that was what was expected of them (*Times*, 9 February 1988).

The *Daily Express* quoted an RUC officer who felt that the force had been made a scapegoat in the Stalker affair. He added that British intelligence agents were 'up to their necks' in the killings. Another officer revealed: 'Our operations were sanctioned at a very high level. I'm not talking about Belfast, but London. This goes all the way to the top.' He added: 'The government would not dare put the RUC on trial. There would be too many leaks about London's involvement and they would have to do a hell of a lot of explaining to Dublin.' If this is so, then the Attorney General has a most peculiar and idiosyncratic interpretation of 'national interest'.

It is difficult to treat seriously the authorities' strenuous denials that there has ever been a shoot to kill policy. It is clear that special undercover squads have existed and operated in the past. Is it therefore mere coincidence that this spate of killings followed the setting up of the specialist mobile support units in 1982? The sheer number and type of killings since that date, and the circumstances in which the specialist units operated in *R. v. Robinson* and *R. v. Montgomery*, clearly establishes that specially trained and approved squads have been carrying out a policy of creating situations in which selected suspects may be shot and killed with some semblance of justification. The fact that a large number of these incidents involved specialist units the basis of whose training is 'firepower, speed and aggression', excludes the explanation of occasional aberrations by members of the security forces operating in a situation of stress. The remarks of the trial judges in the two RUC murder trials have, no doubt, provided further official endorsement, if ever such endorsement was needed, of such a policy. The conviction in December 1984 of a young British soldier for murder has been relied upon by the authorities as evidence of the impartiality of justice in Northern Ireland. But as we will see, this case was very different from the above two trials and the young soldier may have found himself in the wrong place at the wrong time.

R. v. Thain[69]

On 14 December 1984 Private Ian Thain was convicted of the murder of Thomas Reilly, road manager of the pop group Bananarama, and was sentenced to life imprisonment. Thain was the first British soldier to be convicted of a murder committed whilst on duty, and in October 1985 the Northern Ireland Court of Appeal (Lord Lowry C.J. presiding) upheld the conviction. The case adds little to the existing law, but is of considerable interest because of the trial judge's approach to the facts.

In August 1983 the deceased was involved in an incident in West Belfast in which he assaulted a member of an army foot patrol. When the accused arrived on the scene, as part of a second foot patrol, there was pushing and verbal abuse. Reilly ran away from the patrol and a corporal told the defendant to 'get him'. Reilly was naked above the waist as he ran from the patrol. The soldier testified that he thought the deceased was involved in the incident involving the patrol, that one of the patrol had been seriously injured and that the deceased might be armed. Thain then pursued Reilly, shouting a number of warnings to halt as he ran. He said later that his shouts of 'stop or I'll shoot' were, as the judge put it, a 'bluff', and that if the deceased had failed to stop he would not have opened fire. He opened fire because, he said, the deceased had turned back slightly towards Thain and his hand disappeared from view. The accused believed that Reilly was reaching for a weapon and he fired.

What distinguishes this case from all of the other lethal force cases is that the trial judge did not believe substantial portions of the soldier's evidence. Higgins J. advanced two reasons for refusing to believe the accused: first, that immediately after the shooting Thain did not act as if the deceased had been armed; and secondly, that neither then nor in the months after the shooting did the accused ever suggest to anyone that he had fired at the deceased because he believed that he was armed with a pistol and was about to fire at him. In support of the first point the judge pointed out that after the shooting the accused failed to take precautions against Reilly who was kneeling after being shot and who was allegedly armed. Moreover, no warnings were given to colleagues as they and Thain ran towards Reilly and no search was made for the gun afterwards.

Mr Justice Higgins took the view that the defence case had been 'manufactured' and that on occasion Thain was 'untruthful and was knowingly trying to mislead the court'. Higgins J. concluded: 'Having regard to all the evidence, I simply do not accept the accused's testimony that he believed he was about to be shot at and reacted to that danger by shooting in self defence.' In the Court of Appeal Lord Lowry C.J. said that having regard to these findings of fact it might be 'perverse' to question the judge's right to be satisfied that self-defence had been disproved. The conviction was upheld.

In the course of his judgment, Lord Lowry C.J. accepted that the law governing the use of lethal force was far from clear. His Lordship suggested that 'the obvious solution to this problem, as well as some others arising on section 3(1), is for Parliament to decide what the law ought to be and to declare or amend it accordingly.'

Mr Justice Higgins' thorough and considered judgment is to be welcomed but should not be seen as indicative of the Northern Ireland judiciary's approach to the use of firearms by the security forces. This is the first case in which the trial judge has examined with such care the defendant's purported honest beliefs. The judges in Northern Ireland all too often appear to believe that a defendant's assurance that his life was in danger is sufficient in itself to justify an acquittal. Higgins J.'s approach in *R. v. Thain* may be sharply contrasted with the attitude of the trial judges in *R. v. Jones*, *R. v. Robinson* and *R. v. Montgomery*.

It is often argued in Northern Ireland that factors other than evidence play a part in such decisions. Some might argue that the contrast between Higgins J.'s judgment and those of trial judges in other lethal force cases is due to the fact that he was less readily inclined to see the security forces' point of view than other judges. This may be true, but the circumstances of the trial seem more significant: the judgment followed Gibson L.J.'s much-criticised remarks in *R. v. Montgomery*, two shoot to kill incidents earlier that month and a flood of protests from pressure groups and politicians in Ireland, Britain and abroad. Moreover, Thomas Reilly had no paramilitary connections and as the road manager of a well known pop group his killing attracted considerable adverse publicity. On the same day that he sentenced Thain, Mr Justice Higgins found UDR Corporal David Baird not guilty of the murder or manslaughter of Armagh youth Martin Malone. The judge considered that 'in the light of the situation' Baird's failure to check the safety catch on his rifle was not reckless.

Pte. Thain was released on licence from his life sentence after serving only two years and three months and was allowed to rejoin his regiment.

Conclusion

A number of factors combine to exclude mere coincidence and indicate that a shoot to kill policy has operated during particular periods. The sheer number of incidents and the circumstances in which they occurred during 1977–8 and 1982–5 points towards the deliberate planning of operations in which opportunities for the use of lethal force would arise. The fact that many of the victims were suspected Republican activists and their killers were members of specialist units points in the same direction. The use of cover stories in the two RUC trials, the involvement of senior officers and the obstruction encountered by John Stalker indicates knowledge, if not support, of these operations at a high level.

The expression 'shoot to kill' is to some extent misleading. All soldiers are taught to shoot at the largest part of a 'target' and once members of undercover squads decide to shoot, then they shoot to kill. Also, there is not, as yet, any direct evidence of a shoot to kill 'policy' in the form of a government or force instruction. Nonetheless, the security forces have reacted to the green light given by the courts with a tactic of 'shoot first, ask questions later.' This 'policy' has been employed ostensibly without dissent from on high.

No doubt, in the first four years of the disturbances in Northern Ireland, many killings by the security forces were occasional violations of accepted rules by individuals working under very difficult circumstances. Two incidents, however, turned occasional aberrations into a policy of excessive and lethal force. The state's failure to prosecute soldiers for killing 13 civilians on Bloody Sunday in 1972 marked a watershed in the Nationalist community's attitude to the security forces. Many soldiers and policemen may well have taken the view that if these soldiers were not to be prosecuted then there would be little prospect of prosecutions in other cases, especially those involving suspected Republican activists. Secondly, the virtually unlimited licence granted to the security forces in the *Attorney General's Reference Case*, as described above, undoubtedly led to a feeling that few shackles would be placed upon the security forces when it came to tackling what they perceived to be serious security threats.

One can appreciate the difficulties faced by the security forces in operating in what they perceive to be a quasi-war situation. These difficulties do not, however, justify a systematic disregard for the concept of reasonable force. It is disingenuous to employ the army in aid of the civil power, describe them as 'citizens in uniform' and then treat them as largely above the law. As the *Irish Times* has said:

There is abundant evidence that for a considerable time the RUC and the British Army have operated officially a 'shoot to kill' policy against suspected members of the Provisional IRA and the INLA. In Latin America the forces which carry out such operations have become known as 'death squads' and have incurred the odium of the civilised world.[70]

The increased use of firearms by the police in Britain and a number of recent civilian killings by the police[71] raise the question of whether the British police are soon to occupy the position of privilege the courts have accorded the security forces in Northern Ireland. Certainly when the courts come to consider the liability of the police for the use of firearms they will, sadly, look to Northern Ireland for guidance. There will, however, be one major difference between the two jurisdictions. In England police officers will be tried by a jury, not a judge sitting without a jury. For the sake of citizens in England as well as Northern Ireland, it is essential that the law be changed by statute to make it clear that the use of lethal force is only permissible when 'absolutely necessary' to protect oneself or another person.[72]

The shoot to kill policy is more militarily discreet and politically expedient than the practices of South American death squads. Rather than openly executing opponents, the security forces engage them in situations where they will be able to act with virtual impunity, always being able to fall back on the elastic concept of reasonable force.[73] But the intent — and result — are similar. If experience is anything to go by, most members of the security forces responsible for killing civilians are unlikely to be charged, those who conspire to pervert the course of justice will probably be protected by the all-embracing concept of national security, those charged are unlikely to be convicted and those unlucky enough to be convicted will probably serve only a fraction of their sentence and may be free to return to serve in the security forces. The actions of the security forces and the attitude of the judiciary only serve to compound the Nationalist community's belief that the security forces are a law unto themselves. Such an attitude helps only to sustain rather than defeat political violence. Moreover, as the spectre of the state's 'final courts of justice' looms, what little respect Nationalists have for the administration of justice in Northern Ireland subsides.

Table 5.2 Killings by the Security Forces in Disputed Circumstances, 1982–5

11 November 1982*	IRA volunteers Gervais McKerr, Eugene Toman and Sean Burns shot dead near Lurgan, Co. Armagh.
24 November 1982*	Michael Tighe shot dead by the RUC whilst innocently inspecting rifles at a farmhouse near Lurgan.
12 December 1982*	INLA members Roddy Carroll and Seamus Grew shot dead by the RUC outside Armagh.
27 December 1982	Patrick Elliot shot dead by the army during a robbery of a shop in Andersonstown, West Belfast.
19 January 1983	Francis McColgan shot by the RUC during a petrol station robbery on the Lisburn Road, Belfast.
3 February 1983*	INLA volunteer Eugene McMonagle shot by an army undercover unit in Shantallow, Derry.
16 March 1983*	William Millar shot dead by RUC undercover squad in South Belfast.
27 July 1983	Anthony O'Hare killed by the RUC whilst running away from a post office robbery in Lurgan.
30 July 1983	Martin Malone shot dead in Armagh City by a UDR patrol following an argument.
9 August 1983	Thomas Reilly shot by an army patrol in Whiterock, Belfast.
13 August 1983*	INLA volunteers Brendan Covery and Gerard Mallen killed by the RUC in a shoot-out at Dungannon, Co. Tyrone.
28 November 1983	Bridget Foster (80) killed by the RUC firing into a post office in Pomeroy, Co. Tyrone.
4 December 1983*	Colm McGirr and Brian Campbell killed by SAS at arms cache in Tyrone.
30 January 1984	Mark Marron shot dead by the army whilst joy riding in West Belfast.
21 February 1984*	INLA volunteers Declan Martin and Henry Hogan killed by the SAS in a shoot-out at Dunloy, Co. Antrim.
14 May 1984	Seamus Fitzsimmons shot by RUC during attempted robbery of Ballygalley Post Office.

15 June 1984	Paul McCann shot during exchange of gun-fire with RUC.
13 July 1984*	IRA volunteer William Price shot by the SAS in Arboe, Co. Tyrone.
12 August 1984	John Downes killed by a plastic bullet fired in West Belfast by a reserve constable later acquitted of unlawful killing.
19 October 1984*	Fred Jackson shot in crossfire between IRA and British army in East Tyrone.
2 December 1984*	IRA volunteer Tony McBride shot dead by the SAS in a gun battle near Kesh, Co. Fermanagh.
6 December 1984*	IRA volunteers Danny Docherty and William Fleming shot by the SAS in the grounds of Gransha Hospital, Derry.
17 December 1984*	IRA volunteer Sean McIlvenna killed by the RUC in Co. Armagh.
15 January 1985	Paul Kelly shot dead by the UDR whilst joy riding in West Belfast.
7 February 1985	Gerry Logue killed by the RUC whilst joy riding in West Belfast.
23 February 1985*	IRA volunteers Charles Breslin, Michael Devine and David Devine shot by the SAS in Strabane.

* indicates Security Force undercover squad

Table 5.3 'Yellow Card' (1980)†

RESTRICTED
Army Code No. 70771
Instructions for Opening Fire in Northern Ireland

General Rules
1. In all situations you are to use the minimum force necessary. FIREARMS MUST ONLY BE USED AS A LAST RESORT.
2. Your weapon must always be made safe: that is, NO live round is to be carried in the breech and in the case of automatic weapons the working parts are to be forward, unless you are ordered to carry a live round in the breech or you are about to fire.

Challenging
3. A challenge MUST be given before opening fire unless:
   a. to do so would increase the risk of death or grave injury to you or any other person.
   b. you or others in the immediate vicinity are being engaged by terrorists.
4. You are to challenge by shouting:
   'ARMY: STOP OR I FIRE' or words to that effect.

Opening Fire
5. You may only open fire against a person:
   a. if he* is committing or about to commit an act LIKELY TO ENDANGER LIFE AND THERE IS NO OTHER WAY TO PREVENT THE DANGER. The following are some examples of acts where life could be endangered, dependent always upon the circumstances:
      (1) firing or being about to fire a weapon
      (2) planting detonating or throwing an explosive device (including a petrol bomb)
      (3) deliberately driving a vehicle at a person and there is no other way of stopping him*
   b. if you know that he* has just killed or injured any person by such means and he* does not surrender if challenged and THERE IS NO OTHER WAY TO MAKE AN ARREST.

6. If you have to open fire you should:
   a. fire only aimed shots,
   b. fire no more rounds than are necessary,
   c. take all reasonable precautions not to injure anyone other than your target.

*'She' can be read instead of 'he' if applicable.

†It appears that the RUC force instructions on the use of firearms are almost identical (see *The Times*, 5 January 1983).

Source: K. Asmal (chairman), *Shoot to Kill? International Lawyers' Inquiry into the Lethal Use of Firearms by the Security Forces in Northern Ireland* (Mercier Press, 1985), pp. 75–6.

Notes

1. For a detailed account of this subject see K. Asmal (chairman), *Shoot to Kill? International Lawyers' Inquiry into the Lethal Use of Firearms by the Security Forces in Northern Ireland* (Mercier Press, 1985). See *Report of the Tribunal appointed to inquire into the events on Sunday, 30th January 1972, which led to the loss of life in connection with the procession in Londonderry that day*, by Lord Widgery, H.C. 220 (1972), for a disturbing failure to criticise the actions of soldiers in killing 13 civilians on Bloody Sunday. See *Ireland v. U.K.*, Council of Europe, European Commission of Human Rights, Collection of Decisions 41, pp. 12–13, 32–41, 85. Also see A. Jennings, 'How Facts Point to a Shoot to Kill Policy', *Independent*, 8 February 1988.

2. *Guardian*, 12 June 1984.

3. See *Shoot to Kill*, pp. 17 ff. The Irish Information Partnership define civilians as those 'without manifest connection with paramilitaries, security forces, police or prison services'.

4. See *Palmer v. R.* (1971) 55 CAR 223. See also *Attorney General's Reference (No. 2 of 1983)* (1984) 78 CAR 183, for an interesting interpretation of self-defence in relation to the use of petrol bombs.

5. *R. v. Shannon* (1980) 71 CAR 192.

6. *Devlin v. Armstrong* (1971) N.I. 13. See also Croome-Johnson J.'s direction to the jury in the Waldorf shooting case (*Guardian*, 18 and 19 October 1983).

7. Per Lord Morris of Borth-y-Gest, *Palmer v. R*, supra at 242.

8. *R. v. Williams* (G) (1984) 78 CAR 276; *R. v. Kimber* (1983) 77 CAR 225.

9. See A.V. Dicey, *Introduction to the Study of the Law of the Constitution* (8th edn), appendix iv.

10. Hale P.C. i. 481, 494, ii. 117–18. Cp.Co. Inst. iii. 56; Hawkins i c. 28 ss 17–19; Foster 270–1; Blackstone iv Comms 179; East P.C. i. 307; Stephen, H.C.L. i. 193; *Mackalley's case* (1611) 9 Co. Rep. 61b, 65b, 77 E.R. 824, 828; *R.v. Simmonds* (1965) 9 W.I.R. 95 (Jamaica).

11. *Textbook of Criminal Law* (2nd edn) (Sweet & Maxwell), p. 510.

12. *R. v. McNaughton* (1975) N.I. 203, at 208.

13. Archbold, *Criminal Pleading, Evidence and Practice* (35th edn), pp. 1008–1609. It was erroneously suggested in *Shoot to Kill* (pp. 70–2) that the law still required apparent necessity as the statute does not state that the common law is being changed. Sub-section (2) of the Act, however, specifically repeals the common law rules.

14. *Farrell v. U.K.* (application No.9013/80).

15. Smith and Hogan, *Criminal Law* (5th edn) (Butterworths) p. 325.

16. *R. v. McNaughton*, supra.

17. (1977) A.C. 105.

18. *R. v. Jones* (1975) 2 NIJB. All murder cases in Northern Ireland can be tried by a judge without a jury: s.7 Northern Ireland (Emergency Provisions) Act 1978.

19. (1976) N.I. 169 at 192.

20. At 193.

21. Ibid.

22. Ibid.

23. The late Lord Diplock is the 'author' of Northern Ireland's emergency legislation and the non-jury courts are fondly named after him. See *Report of the*

Committee to consider legal procedures to deal with terrorist activities in Northern Ireland, cmnd. 5185 (1972).

24. Supra at 135.
25. At 138.
26. At 137.
27. *Public Law*, April 1986, 38.
28. *R. v. McKay* (1957) All E.R. 648; *R. v. Howe* (1958) 100 C.L.R. 448.
29. The doctrine had previously been rejected in *Palmer v. R.* supra; *R. v. McInnes* (1971) 3 All E.R. 295.
30. T. Hadden, 'When is it murder to shoot to kill?' *Fortnight*, no. 218, p. 7.
31. (1980) 1 All E.R. 166.
32. *R. v. Jones*, supra at 18.
33. Ibid.
34. Ibid at 22. Cf. *R. v. Thomas* (1815) 4 M & S 442.
35. Ibid. *R. v. McNaughton*, supra at 208. Lord Diplock, *A.G.'s Ref.*, supra 139, said that this finding was 'consistent with the view that in the agony of the moment the accused may have acted intuitively or instinctively without foreseeing the likely consequences of his act beyond preventing the deceased from getting away'.
36. See Table 5.3.
37. Per MacDermott J., *R. v. Jones* supra, at 22.
38. Per Gibson L.J., *A.G.'s Ref.* (1976) N.I. 160 at 197.
39. Per McGonigal L.J., *A.G.'s Ref.*, supra at 189.
40. Supra.
41. *McLaughlin v. Ministry of Defence* (1977) unreported (transcript). At first instance the case was brought under the plaintiff's name at the time.
42. Per MacDermott J., *R. v. Jones* supra at 18.
43. See *Report on disturbances at Featherstone Colliery* (1893–1894) C. 7234; *Lynch v. Fitzgerald* (1938) I.R. 382, per Hanna J. According to Lord Diplock, *A.G.'s Ref.* supra 136, to describe the army as citizens in uniform is 'misleading in the circumstances in which the army is currently employed in aid of the civil power in Northern Ireland'.
44. See J. Bloch and P. Fitzgerald, *British Intelligence and Covert Action* (Brandon, 1984); C. Townshend, *Britain's Civil Wars* (Faber & Faber, 1986).
45. See T. Geraghty, *Who Dares Wins* (Fontana, 1980).
46. *The Times*, 17 May 1973.
47. *Guardian*, 9 August 1973.
48. *The Times*, 19 March 1974.
49. *Observer*, 11 August 1974.
50. See Roche, 'Patterns of Violence in Northern Ireland in 1984', *Fortnight*, no. 218, p. 10.
51. *Financial Times*, 9 June 1977.
52. *Independent*, 9 July 1987.
53. *Irish Times*, 22 December 1982.
54. Roche, 'Patterns of Violence'.
55. 'Magill', February 1983, p. 45.
56. Ibid.
57. (1984) 4 NIJB. See also *Daily Telegraph*, 21 March 1984; *Guardian*, 29 March 1984 and 6 April 1984.

58. (1984) unreported (transcript). *Guardian*, 5 June 1984.
59. *Irish News*, 5 June 1984.
60. *The Times*, 11 June 1984.
61. *Guardian*, 18 June 1984.
62. *The Times*, 12 June 1984.
63. *Guardian*, 23 August 1984.
64. *Guardian*, 4 September 1984.
65. *Guardian*, 17 September 1985.
66. *Guardian*, 3 June 1986, 8 June 1986, 11 July 1986, 12 July 1986; *Observer*, 6 July 1986, 20 July 1986, 10 August 1986, 12 October 1986. See also P. Taylor, *Stalker* (Faber & Faber, 1987); F. Doherty, *The Stalker Affair* (Mercier Press, 1986); J. Stalker, *Stalker* (Harrap, 1988).
67. *Observer*, 6 July 1986.
68. H.C.Debs., vol. 126, cols. 21–35. See also *The Times* and *Guardian*, 26 January 1988.
69. (1984), (1985) 11 NIJB 31, 76 (CA).
70. Quoted in D. Hamill, *Pig in the Middle* (Methuen, 1986) pp. 270-1.
71. See Croome-Johnson J.'s direction to the jury in the Waldorf shooting case, supra; *R. v. Chester*, *Guardian*, 3 July 1986, where a police officer was acquitted of the murder of John Shorthouse; and *R. v. Lovelock*, *Guardian*, 16 January 1987, where a police inspector was acquitted after shooting Cherry Groce. See also police stake-out and controversial shooting of robbery suspects, *Guardian*, 10 July 1987. See also killing of Aidan McAnespie and charging of soldier for unlawful killing, and shooting of three IRA activists in Gibraltar, *Independent* 22 February and 7 March 1988 respectively.
72. See criticisms and proposals for reform by Northern Ireland Standing Commission on Human Rights, Annual Report for 1983 on the Use of Firearms by the Security Forces, quoted in Asmal, *Shoot to Kill*, pp. 162–71.
73. See J. Baxter and L. Koffman (eds), *Police: the Constitution and the Community* (Professional Books, 1985) ch. 13.

6

ANTHONY JENNINGS

Bullets Above the Law[1]

> The use of baton rounds ... is strictly controlled, not only by the law
> but by orders and training.
>   — James Prior, Secretary of State for Northern Ireland

In 1986, Keith White became the first Protestant to be killed by a baton
round. His death brought the total number of people killed by rubber
and plastic bullets to 16, seven of whom were children. Yet, until the
decision to prosecute an RUC reserve constable for the unlawful killing of John Downes in August 1984,[2] not a single prosecution for these
deaths had taken place. The victims were simply seen as the unhappy,
perhaps inevitable, casualties of a war-time situation.

This chapter argues that the deaths and injuries in Northern Ireland
from rubber and plastic bullets are not inevitable. They are, rather, an
example of bad policing, and — contrary to James Prior's assertion —
of the arbitrary use of plastic bullets to subdue a recalcitrant population. Unlike the shoot to kill policy, these victims are not part of a
security force plan to search out suspected 'terrorists' with a view to
engaging them in gunfire. They are, instead, a reflection of the increasing use of excessive force, in which weapons are used not as a last but
as a first resort, and of its acceptance by the security forces and judiciary
alike.

The Development of Riot Control

The British have used force for centuries to suppress strikes and
demonstrations. In 1819 yeomanry charged a peaceful meeting calling
for parliamentary reform in what became known as the Peterloo
massacre. Eleven people were killed and 400 were injured. Perhaps the
most infamous incident in British colonial history occurred at Amritsar
in India in 1919, when troops opened fire on a peaceful meeting, killing

300 and wounding 600 in just under ten minutes.

Such crude displays of force, however, tended to attract adverse publicity. Governments instead developed what are euphemistically called 'non-lethal' forms of population control. By 1912 the Paris police had developed a form of tear gas. For Britain, non-lethal riot control technology was used extensively in the colonies in the 1950s. Worldwide, the most intense period of development occurred in the 1960s with the outbreak of civil disturbances in the USA, Paris, Latin America and Northern Ireland.

As Ackroyd *et al.*[3] point out, the state relies upon a number of justifications for the use of such weapons. First, disturbances are portrayed as 'rebellions' warranting a swift and effective response. Secondly, it is pointed out that the rioters behave a lot more badly than the forces of law and order. Thirdly, the use of non-lethal weapons is said to obviate the need for using real bullets. Lastly, the weapons are described as being 'harmless'. Non-lethal riot control involves, then, the removal of rioters from the streets, the punishment of the local populace to force them to disown the activists, and the appearance of the use of minimum force by the security forces.

History of the Baton Round

In 1958 the British government introduced a wooden baton round in Hong Kong in an attempt to quell rioting. Despite causing the death of a young girl, the wooden bullet was hailed by the authorities as a success. It was apparently considered for use in Northern Ireland but was rejected as being too dangerous.

In 1970, following a nine month crash research programme at the Chemical Defence Establishment at Porten Down, the rubber bullet was introduced in Northern Ireland. The launch of the bullet was accompanied by a press campaign designed to emphasise its purported comic and phallic qualities. At the initial press conference a journalist from the *Observer* was reported to have said: '... firing bullets made of rubber. Soon they'll be lobbing grenades full of confetti, and guns that fire rose pellets. You can't take this sort of thing seriously.'[4]

The rubber bullet that killed eleven year old Francis Rowntree in April 1972 was taken very seriously indeed. Eye witnesses claimed that the bullet in question had been doctored by having been cut in half and the remaining half replaced by a torch battery. Francis Rowntree was Northern Ireland's first rubber bullet fatality.

'Harmless Weapons'

From 1970 to 1972 surgeons at the Royal Victoria Hospital[5] in Belfast examined 90 patients who required hospital treatment as a result of being struck by rubber bullets. Eighty per cent had head injuries. Two people were blinded in both eyes and seven people lost the sight of one eye; five people had serious loss of vision in one eye, and four had their faces severely disfigured. The surgeons noted three cases of brain damage. The authorities' response was to prevent publication of the surgeons' report under the Official Secrets Act 1911.

Rubber bullets were eventually withdrawn in 1975 after 55,834 of them had been fired[6] and two more young men had been killed. According to *Jane's Infantry Weapons* (1976), this was because the disability and serious injury resulting from its use were 'not considered acceptable'.

The Plastic Bullet

The plastic bullet was introduced as a replacement for the rubber bullet in 1973. The bullet is 3½ inches long and 1½ inches in diameter and weighs approximately 135 grammes. This weapon has none of the comic pretensions of its predecessor; it leaves the nozzle of the gun at 130 to 170 mph. Despite the reasons advanced for the introduction of the plastic bullet, it proved more lethal than its rubber counterpart. Research at the US Law Enforcement Assistance Administration[7] showed that impacts with energy levels of 90 foot pounds were in the 'severe damage region'. The energy level of the plastic bullet at 50 yards is 110 foot pounds; at five yards its energy level doubles, to 210 foot pounds. As Lawrence Roche of the Royal Victoria Hospital has confirmed, 'plastic bullets tend to cause more severe injuries to the skull and brain [than rubber bullets], and therefore more deaths'.[8] Between 1975 and 1984 plastic bullets caused twelve deaths and many serious injuries. Nevertheless, the government maintains that the plastic bullet is 'the most effective means of controlling riots, consistent with the use of minimum force'.[9]

Instructions to the army on the use of plastic bullets, a copy of which can be seen in Table 6.1, are intended to limit the circumstances in which they may be fired.[10] Plastic bullets are only supposed to be fired when 'it is judged to be minimum and reasonable force in the circumstances'. The rules go on to say that baton rounds should not be fired indiscriminately but at selected targets. They should be aimed at the lower part of the body and not fired from a distance of less than 20 metres unless the safety of soldiers or others is 'seriously threatened'. In December 1984 Recorder's Court judge Sir Robert Porter criticised RUC officers for being uncertain of these rules when he awarded damages to two Belfast women who had been injured by plastic bullets in 1980.[11] Nevertheless, it is difficult to predict the weight that judges will attach to a defendant's breach of the guidelines. If the example set by the shoot to kill cases is followed it will be regarded as 'irrelevant'.[12] Certainly in *R. v. Hegarty* the police officer's breaches of instructions in shooting John Downes were not considered important by Mr Justice Hutton.

The British government claims that 'plastic bullet rounds have never been used in non-riot situations'.[13] But the number of injuries resulting from the use of baton rounds and the circumstances surrounding a number of the fatalities casts serious doubt upon the extent to which these guidelines are truly adhered to. The circumstances in which many baton round victims have met their deaths, moreover, fail to corroborate the authorities' contention that these weapons are used to protect life and that they are used against those who pose a serious threat to security.

Table 6.1 Rules for Engagement for P.V.C. Baton Rounds (Plastic Bullets)

General
1. Baton rounds may be used to disperse a crowd whenever it is judged to be minimum and reasonable force in the circumstances.
2. The rounds must be fired at selected persons and not indiscriminately at the crowd. They should be aimed so that they strike the lower part of the target's body directly (i.e. without bouncing).
3. The authority to use these rounds is delegated to the commander on the spot.

Additional Rules for the 25 Grain P.V.C. Baton Round
4. Rounds must not be fired at a range of less than 20 metres except when the safety of soldiers or others is seriously threatened.
5. The baton round was designed and produced to disperse crowds. It can also be used to prevent an escape from H.M. Prisons if it is, in the circumstances, still considered to constitute the use of minimum and reasonable force. If a prisoner can be apprehended by hand, the baton round must not be used.

Source: K. Asmal (chairman), *Shoot to Kill? International Lawyers' Inquiry into the Lethal Use of Firearms by the Security Forces in Northern Ireland* (Mercier Press, 1985), p. 63.

- In May 1981, fourteen-year-old Julie Livingstone was killed by a plastic bullet in the Lenadoon area of Belfast when the army opened fire on people protesting the death of hunger striker Francis Hughes. The army claimed that it shot in response to petrol bombs thrown by a group of youths. The inquest jury found that Julie Livingstone was an 'innocent victim'.
- Whilst returning home with a carton of milk for her mother, twelve-year-old Carol Ann Kelly was killed in the Twinbrook estate in May 1981. The army claimed that they fired two plastic bullets in response to a group of missile-throwing youths. It was not alleged that the deceased girl was involved in any rioting.
- Peter Doherty was killed in Divis flats in July 1981 by a plastic bullet fired by a Royal Marine Commando. The soldiers involved alleged that missiles were thrown by youths and residents in the flats; Mr Doherty was standing in the kitchen of his first floor flat when he was struck on the head.
- In April 1982 eleven-year-old Stephen McConomy was killed in Derry after being hit on the head by a plastic bullet; the army claimed that they had opened fire after their landrover was attacked by a group of youths. The inquest jury found that the dead boy was killed from a distance of 17 feet and that the gun responsible for his death was faulty. The jury added that there was insufficient evidence that Stephen McConomy was involved in rioting, that the soldiers were not 'in any great danger' at the time and that the deceased was killed 'without due cause'.

Table 6.2 Victims of Rubber and Plastic Bullets

Victims	Age	Date	Place
Francis Rowntree*	11	20 April 1972	West Belfast
Tobias Molloy*	18	16 July 1972	Strabane
Thomas Friel*	21	17 May 1973	Derry
Stephen Geddis	10	28 August 1975	West Belfast
Brian Stewart	13	4 October 1976	West Belfast
Michael Donnelly	21	10 August 1980	West Belfast
Paul Whitters	15	15 April 1981	Derry
Julie Livingstone	14	12 May 1981	West Belfast
Carol Ann Kelly	12	19 May 1981	West Belfast
Henry Duffy	45	22 May 1981	Derry
Norah McCabe	30	18 July 1981	West Belfast
Peter Doherty	33	24 July 1981	West Belfast
Peter McGuinness	41	9 August 1981	West Belfast
Stephen McConomy	11	16 April 1982	Derry
John Downes	22	12 August 1984	West Belfast
Keith White	20	14 April 1986	Portadown

* denotes death by rubber bullets

Despite these cases, the authorities have consistently refused to admit that the plastic bullet is used indiscriminately. When James Prior was questioned about the number of children who had been killed he said: 'if young children are asked by others to form a riot or to give protection for others in a riot, they are bound at times to get hurt.'[14] The security forces, however, have claimed that only two of the seven children killed (Brian Stewart and Paul Whitters) were involved in rioting.

The most intensive use of plastic bullets occurred during the hunger strike of 1981. In May of that year, 16,656 plastic bullets were fired compared with 1,959 fired in the previous month. Between 5 May and 6 July of the same year, 110 people received hospital treatment, 45 of them for head injuries. In that year alone seven people were killed by plastic bullets.

The Killing of Norah McCabe

One case that pours scorn upon the authorities' contention that the use of plastic bullets is both necessary and well-controlled is that of Norah McCabe.[15] It also raises a number of disturbing questions about the criteria applied in deciding to prosecute a member of the security forces for a plastic bullet killing.

Early on the morning of 8 July 1981, Belfast housewife Norah McCabe was seriously injured in an incident at the junction of Linden Street and the Falls Road in West Belfast. She died the following day from wounds which were, according to Deputy State Pathologist Derek Carson, 'entirely consistent' with having been struck on the head by a plastic bullet. At an inquest before Belfast coroner James Elliott and a jury, the RUC completely denied responsibility for Mrs McCabe's death. They did concede that an RUC patrol had passed the junction of Linden Street and the Falls Road at the time of the incident and had fired plastic bullets into adjoining streets. But they categorically denied firing any plastic bullets 'at or into Linden Street'.

The officers told the inquest that they were travelling towards the country in two police landrovers on the Falls Road on the morning in question. The death of hunger striker Joe McDonnell had just been announced and serious disturbances were expected. In charge of the patrol in the lead vehicle was West Belfast's most senior policeman, Chief Superintendent James Crutchley.

The police told the court that their journey up the Falls Road was obstructed by debris: 'the roadway was strewn with beer barrels, concrete blocks, etc.' There were apparently burning vehicles on nearby street corners and a hostile group of 70 to 80 youths. The patrol was then attacked by petrol bombs which 'rained around' the landrover.

One officer gave an account of 'twenty youths, some of whom were masked, who all had petrol bombs in their hands'. The police officers quickly formed the opinion that they were in 'a riot situation' and the order was given to open fire at '*specific targets*' (emphasis added).

The officers admitted firing plastic bullets into adjacent streets but they were adamant that 'none were fired either into Linden Street or at the junction of Falls Road/Linden Street.' An officer in the lead vehicle who had fired a plastic bullet at a masked petrol bomber added: 'I am satisfied beyond any doubt that no members of our vehicle could possibly have hit anyone at the junction of Linden Street.' Witness A, who admitted firing a plastic bullet at two petrol bombers under order from Chief Superintendent Crutchley, said under caution: 'I can categorically deny that any rubber [sic] bullets were fired at or into Linden Street by any member of my crew.'

So who did kill Norah McCabe? Hospital worker Jean Mooney had no doubt as to who was responsible. On the morning in question she had just finished saying a rosary on the Falls Road for the dead hunger striker. She had just entered Linden Street when she observed a leading police vehicle, in a convoy of two, turn as if to enter Linden Street and fire a plastic bullet from its offside porthole. She then saw Norah McCabe crumple and fall to the ground. Mooney observed no riot nor did she see any petrol bombs thrown at the RUC.

As in similar cases, the jury could have been left to decide the issue of who killed Norah McCabe by balancing the testimony of an alleged eyewitness from an area renowned for its hostility to the security forces against that of a Chief Superintendent and five other police officers. Unfortunately for the RUC, however, their ostensibly hazardous trek up the Falls Road had been filmed by a Canadian television crew. The inquest was adjourned for several months to enable the film to be traced and analysed.

The man entrusted with this task was RUC Detective Superintendent Alfred Entwhistle. Entwhistle told the inquest that the lead landrover 'braked suddenly preparatory to pulling across to the right hand side of the Falls Road' and that 'when the landrover stopped at an angle on the right hand side of the Falls Road ... a puff of smoke was seen to come from the side of the vehicle.' But where exactly had this happened? According to Detective Superintendent Entwhistle, when the lead vehicle fired the plastic bullet it 'had reached the junction of Linden Street'. He also confirmed that the video revealed 'no evidence of debris on the road nor of petrol bombs being thrown'.

The jury returned with a verdict on 21 October 1983. They found that there was 'nothing to support [the claim] that petrol bombs were thrown'. They accepted that 'at the mouth of Linden Street the leading vehicle in the patrol turned sharply to the right and stopped briefly, at which time a baton round was discharged from an offside porthole.' The jury added: 'there is no clear evidence to suggest that there was a legitimate target to be fired at in the street. Neither is there clear evidence to support that the deceased was other than an innocent party.'

One might have expected swift action from the authorities in view of the evident clash between the jury's findings and the vehement denials of the police officers. The DPP, however, announced that there would be no prosecution of any officer for involvement in the shooting or for perjury. The Attorney General, Sir Michael Havers, subsequently stated that he would not interfere with this decision, nor agree to the request of eighty MPs to hold an inquiry into the case. The RUC confirmed that there was to be no disciplinary action against any of the officers involved. Chief Superintendent Crutchley who, according to the inquest jury's findings of fact, ordered the fatal shot to be fired, has since been promoted to Assistant Chief Constable. Jim McCabe, Norah's husband, nonetheless brought a civil action against the RUC for the death of his wife. The case was settled out of court and the McCabe family was paid 'substantial damages' by the RUC.

The refusal to prosecute in the McCabe case can be contrasted with the recent decision to prosecute an RUC reservist for the unlawful killing of John Downes in August 1984. In his evidence to the Bennett Committee in 1979,[16] the DPP stated that he applied no special principles in deciding to prosecute members of the security forces. His decision was apparently based on whether the evidence gave rise to a reasonable prospect of conviction. But why has it taken 14 deaths in 15 years for such a decision to be made?

The circumstances of the Downes case, for one thing, left no alternative but to prosecute. The incident was filmed and shown around the world on the same day and it took place in what Liberal Party leader David Steel called 'a police riot'. The McCabe film, by contrast, was not seen on television until over three years after the incident. Secondly, it has been suggested that it is the prospect of an acquittal, not a conviction, which tends to motivate a security force prosecution. It appears that John Downes was shot as he attempted to strike a police officer. It would therefore be open to the accused to argue that he was using reasonable force in the defence of others, in preventing a crime or in effecting an arrest. But on the evidence presented to the inquest jury in the McCabe case, there is precious little to suggest that the person responsible could say anything to justify his actions.

The decision to prosecute in the Downes case is projected as further evidence of the even-handedness of the prosecuting authorities. But if the shoot to kill prosecutions, as we saw in the last chapter, are any guide to plastic bullet prosecutions, the selectiveness employed in choosing cases for prosecution will prove most fortuitous. Not only will officers be acquitted but they may be showered with praise and encouragement by the trial judge.

R. v. Hegarty[17]

In September 1986 reserve constable Nigel Hegarty was acquitted of the manslaughter of John Downes. It was established during the trial that the RUC had breached the regulations governing the use of plastic bullets on two counts: the accused was less than 20 metres from the deceased, and the baton round struck the upper part of Downes' body. Hegarty maintained that he fired in order to protect two RUC men whom Downes was about to hit during what was described as a 'riot' at a Sinn Fein internment rally in 1984. Mr Justice Hutton said: 'in the circumstances of sudden attacks I think it is probable that the accused did act almost instinctively to defend his comrades without having time to assess the situation in the light of his knowledge of the police regulations.'

The acquittal represented a setback for the supporters of the Anglo-Irish Agreement, who hoped that the signing of the accord would lead the Northern Irish courts to set a higher standard by which to judge the actions of the security forces. Seamus Mallon MP described the decision as 'amazing' and added, 'it will rank with hundreds of others which have brought the process of justice into disrepute and which regrettably, have diminished respect for the process of law in Northern Ireland.'

In view of the standards that have been set in the shoot to kill trials, the acquittal was not surprising. The courts appear to pay lip service to the concepts of reasonable force and necessity. In only one murder trial have the courts given more than a cursory consideration to the defendant's assurances that he acted on the spur of the moment in defence of himself or others. The key question that the court in *R. v. Hegarty* failed to consider was whether it can ever amount to reasonable force to fire a plastic bullet at the upper torso of a man who is going to strike another with no more than a stick.

Stewart v. UK

Although the courts in Britain and Northern Ireland had been, until *R. v. Hegarty*, deprived of an opportunity of considering the law in relation to the use of baton rounds, this was not the case with the European Commission on Human Rights.[18] In *Stewart v. UK* [19] the Commission was asked to consider the admissibility of a complaint made by

Kathleen Stewart, whose thirteen year old son Brian had been killed by a plastic bullet in 1976.

Mrs Stewart had originally brought a civil action against the Ministry of Defence claiming £1,000 compensation for the death of her son, but her claim was dismissed at first instance and on appeal by Lord Justice Jones. She then made a complaint to the Commission alleging that the killing of her son breached articles 2 (the right to life), 3 (the restriction on torture, inhuman and degrading treatment), and 14 (the prohibition against religious discrimination) of the European Convention for the Protection of Human Rights and Fundamental Freedoms. Article 2 of the Convention prohibits the use of lethal force unless 'absolutely necessary' in order to: defend any person from unlawful violence; effect a lawful arrest or prevent the escape of a person lawfully detained; or lawfully quell a riot or insurrection.

In the lower court the judge had found that at the time of the incident there was a riot in progress and that Brian Stewart was a participant. The judge also held that the shooting was unintentional as the soldier concerned had aimed at another rioter but had been struck by a missile and misfired.

As the Commission heard no new evidence as to the circumstances of Brian Stewart's death, it proceeded on the facts as found by the trial judge. The Commission noted that Northern Ireland is in a state of 'continuous public disturbance' and that such riots can be used as cover for sniper attacks on the security forces. The Commission accepted that the plastic bullet was 'a dangerous weapon' but the available evidence suggested that it was 'less dangerous than alleged'. The Commission held that Mrs Stewart's complaint was 'manifestly ill-founded' as her son's death 'resulted from the use of force which was no more than absolutely necessary in action lawfully taken for the purpose of quelling a riot'.

The Stewart decision is not a blanket endorsement of the use of plastic bullets, but it is unfortunate that the only case in which an inquest had found that a plastic bullet victim was a 'rioter' was selected as the test case. The Stewart case may be contrasted with the decision of the Commission in *Farrell v. UK* as described in chapter 5. That complaint, however, was successfully brought on the more restrictive grounds that section 3 of the Criminal Law (Northern Ireland) Act 1967 breached article 2 of the European Convention.

The Training Ground

It has been argued for a number of years that Northern Ireland serves as a training ground for British security forces, who might need to apply the same techniques of population control in Britain.[20] Indeed, during the 1981 riots, the government considered using plastic bullets against rioters, but the Home Secretary, William Whitelaw, said that plastic bullets would not be used in Britain as their use would 'mean inflicting injury or even death on rioters'.[21] The hypocrisy inherent in this statement (it was presumably acceptable for people in Northern Ireland to be injured, but not people in Britain) apparently filtered through; the Home Secretary later changed his mind, and senior British police officers sought advice on riot control from the RUC.

Not until the miners' strike of 1984, however, did police practices begin to mirror the Northern Ireland experience.[22] For the first time, the police, and indeed the courts, became militarised. The police were placed under national, no longer local, control, and the National Reporting Centre was used to deploy police forces, so that, for example, London police under the control of Metropolitan Police Commissioner Sir Kenneth Newman, who had been Chief Constable in Northern Ireland in the late 1970s, could be sent to Yorkshire to deal with mass pickets with which local police forces were said to be insufficiently firm. Riot control equipment such as helmets and long shields, the assembly of the police in military formation, and the charging on pickets by mounted police were other signs. As in Northern Ireland, too, 'snatch squads', small groups of police who could dart out from larger police formations, were used to make arrests in the midst of pickets.

During the dispute, the Police Federation called for all police forces in Britain to be issued with plastic bullets.[23] This call was repeated, again unsuccessfully, during the disturbances in Birmingham in 1985.[24] Following severe rioting in the Tottenham area of North London in October 1985, however, the British police were issued with plastic bullets for the first time. Sir Kenneth Newman said that he would 'not shrink' from authorising the use of plastic bullets and CS gas if he believed it to be 'a practical option for restoring peace and preventing crime and injury', and his decision was supported by the Home Secretary, Douglas Hurd.[25] Sir Kenneth Newman has confirmed in his annual report that plastic bullets are now a normal and necessary part of the British police armoury.

Future Developments
While the groundwork has been laid for the introduction of plastic bullets in Britain, such a step is likely to radically alter public perceptions of the British police. It may be, then, that the government will seek to dampen public fears by using less lethal forms of riot control. Scientists are continually developing more sophisticated forms of riot control, and these may be preferred to plastic bullets.

A sample of these 'less lethal' weapons includes:

Ultrasonic sound devices and flashing lights, already considered for use in Northern Ireland;

Stench, a grenade which gives off an obnoxious smell;

Instant Mud, a substance sprayed at rioters' feet to make them slip and fall;

Instant Banana, which, spread on the ground, makes roads impassable;

Dart Gun, a drug-filled syringe which is fired at rioters;

Taser, which gives an electric shock so powerful that the victims are paralysed until the current is turned off;

Tennis Ball, a hard plastic ball fired from a gun;

Electrified Water Jet, which fires water containing a high electrical current from a cannon; and

Photic Driver, a strobe light with oscillating sound which can produce vomiting or fits.[26]

Conclusion

It has never been proved that the use of baton rounds saves lives; in many instances, they exacerbate situations of conflict. As the Downes case illustrates, plastic bullets have become weapons of first response rather than of last resort. The circumstances surrounding the death of Norah McCabe expose the extent to which plastic bullets have come to be used as a means of inflicting summary punishment upon a recalcitrant section of the population.

The plastic bullet is an expedient panacea for an underlying problem that the government refuses to tackle. Its use is far from strictly controlled and the number of resulting deaths and injuries proves that the use of plastic bullets amounts to a systematic abuse of human rights. These weapons are not justified by the demands of the emergency and represent a profound inroad into individual liberty. Their use perpetuates a violent situation: the security forces have become so accustomed to plastic bullets that it would be difficult for them to deal with 'normal disturbances' without the use of excessive force.

The Catholic Bishops of Northern Ireland have called the use of plastic bullets 'morally indefensible'[27] and the European Parliament has twice called for them to be banned.[28] The British government should follow suit.

Notes

1.   L. Curtis, 'They Shoot Children' (pamphlet), 1982. See also T. Gifford, 'Death on the Streets of Derry' (pamphlet) 1982.

2. For a detailed criticism of the decision see S. Greer and T. Jennings, 'Political Expediency in Plastic Bullet Cases', *Fortnight*, no. 221, p. 8.

3. C. Ackroyd, K. Margolis, J. Rosenhead and T. Shallice, *The Technology of Political Control* (Pluto Press, 1980) p. 199.

4. S. Winchester, *In Holy Terror* (Faber & Faber, 1974) p. 88.

5. *Sunday Times*, May 1972.

6. For details of other years see Curtis, 'They Shoot Children', p. 38.

7. Information provided in a Parliamentary answer (H.C. Debs., vol. 924, cols. 329–32).

8. *Lancet*, 23 April 1983.

9. Lord Gowrie, H.L. Debs., vol. 424, cols. 689–90.

10. See Table 5.3.

11. *Fortnight*, no. 212, p. 17.

12. See the remarks of Lord Lowry C.J. in *R. v. McNaughton* (1975) N.I. 203, at 206; and MacDermott J. in *R. v. Jones* (1975) 2 NIJB, at 22.

13. *International League of Human Rights Submission to the UN Sub-commission on Prevention of Discrimination and Protection of Minorities*, 36th Session, 29 August 1983, in K. Asmal (chairman), *Shoot to Kill? International Lawyers' Inquiry into the Lethal Use of Firearms by the Security Forces in Northern Ireland* (Mercier Press, 1985) appendix D.

14. H.C. Debs., vol. 32, col. 1001.

15. Information on the Norah McCabe case comes from statements and papers at the inquest.

16. *Report of the Committee of Inquiry into Police Interrogation Procedures in Northern Ireland* (1979), Cmnd. 7497, para. 371.

17. (1986) 12 NIJB 25. See also *Guardian*, 25 September 1986.

18. See generally Beddard, *Human Rights and Europe* (Sweet & Maxwell, 1980) and Chapter 1.

19. Application No. 10044/82.

20. Ackroyd *et al.*, *The Technology of Political Control*.

21. *Irish News*, 6 August 1981.

22. See J. Coulter, S. Miller and M. Walker, *State of Siege* (Canary Press, 1984).

23. *Guardian*, 24 October 1984.

24. *Guardian*, 13 September 1985.

25. *The Times*, 8 October 1985 and *Guardian*, 29 May 1986. The Chief Constable of Greater Manchester, James Anderton, refused a request by his police committee to return his police force's stock of plastic bullets (*Guardian*, 4 November 1985).

26. Campaign Against Plastic Bullets, British Society for Social Responsibility in Science, London.

27. Press release, 4 July 1983.

28. Press release, 14 December 1981 and 11 October 1984.

7

PETER HALL

The Prevention of Terrorism Acts

Introduction

> These powers are draconian. In combination, they are unprecedented in peacetime. I believe they are fully justified to meet the clear and present dangers.
>
> — The Rt Hon Roy Jenkins[1]

The Prevention of Terrorism (Temporary Provisions) Act (PTA) 1974[2] is commonly assumed to have been born out of the killing of 21 people in the Birmingham pub bombings of 21 November 1974. The exercise of the powers contained in this and subsequent Acts has led to thousands of arrests, infringements of civil and human rights and the harassment of political activists.

This major piece of constitutional legislation was rushed through Parliament in 42 hours. The PTA 1974 was revised in 1976 and 1984 but the Act is in essence the same document today as it was in 1974. The 'Temporary Provisions' element of the title remains as an ironic testimony to the problem it was purportedly designed to deal with.

The PTA was an ill-conceived and hastily introduced attempt to quell growing public outrage at IRA bombings and to convince the British electorate that the 'Irish problem' was being tackled head on.

The current PTA will expire in March 1989. The British government has held regular reviews of the PTA which result in reports presented to Parliament containing proposals for future legislation. It is predetermined that every report will support 'the continuing need for legislation against terrorism'.[3] Viscount Colville of Culross QC is the most recent reviewer, his report[4] representing the first round in the lead up to the PTA 1989. Apart from the Act itself it is the most important document in the current debate surrounding the PTA.

The Act in its implementation and potential is a significant and devastating encroachment on the rights and freedoms of the citizen in the UK and has laid the foundation for similar erosions of freedom in the future. It poses fundamental questions for lawyers and politicians, democrats and human rights campaigners, socialists and libertarians.

Does the Act amount to a systematic flouting of human, civil or legal rights? Does the 'emergency' claimed by the proponents of the Act still exist, if it ever really did? If it does exist, does it justify the Act or could it be dealt with under the ordinary criminal law? Will the Act become permanent? What improvements might be made to it? These questions and others may not have clear answers but an assessment of the issues raised by them is an essential step along the path, if not to an answer, then at least to an analysis. The vehicle for the assessment must inevitably be the Acts themselves.

The Banning of Organisations

On 27 November 1974 the Home Secretary, the Rt Hon Roy Jenkins, presented the Prevention of Terrorism (Temporary Provisions) Bill for its First Reading. It was presented as, amongst other things, 'a Bill to proscribe organisations concerned in terrorism'.[5] Roy Jenkins said the following day in opening the debate on the Second Reading that 'the proscribing of named organisations is for us a wholly exceptional measure and can be justified only by a wholly exceptional situation — a clear and present danger'.[6] The proscribing of named organisations is governed by section 1.[7] Schedule 1 of the 1984 Act lists two organisations. The first is the Irish Republican Army (IRA) which was proscribed with the passing of the 1974 Act. The second is the Irish National Liberation Army (INLA) which was proscribed by statutory instrument on 3 July 1979 following the killing of Airey Neave MP in the car park of the Houses of Parliament.

Proscription in itself has always been acknowledged as a hollow measure. The force of proscription lies in its use in combination with other provisions of the Act. Mr Jenkins stated: 'I have never claimed, and do not claim now, that proscription of the IRA will of itself reduce terrorist outrages. But the public should no longer have to endure the affront of public demonstrations in support of that body.'[8] This was a reference to clause (now section) 2 which prohibits displays of support in public for a proscribed organisation.

Lord Jellicoe in his review of the PTA[9] concluded that: 'proscription had some — albeit relatively limited — beneficial effects.' He accepted that '*proscribing an organisation is unlikely to impair substantially its capacity for carrying out terrorist attacks or to deter those most deeply involved in its activities*'. (Emphasis added.) Its importance, for Jellicoe, lay in the fact that it 'enshrines in legislation public aversion to organisations which use, and espouse, violence as a means to a political end'.[10]

It would seem from the acceptance of this view that the outlawing of certain organisations has little to do with the prevention of terrorism and more to do with a propaganda war against Irish Republicanism. The transparency of the propaganda basis of the Acts was clear from the start. At the end of the Committee Stage of the Bill in 1974 Gerry Fitt MP, now Lord Fitt, moved an amendment to Schedule 1 of the Bill. At that time only the IRA was to be listed as a proscribed organisation. Fitt's amendment was a proposal to add the names of three loyalist paramilitary groups, the Ulster Freedom Fighters, the Red Hand Commandos, and the Ulster Protestant Action Group. Fitt recounted some of the recent murders in Northern Ireland for which these groups had claimed responsibility. He advised that it was 'the duty of the Government to include in the Bill all the other organisations which have been engaged in this campaign and so make it clear to every citizen of the United Kingdom that this is a fair and even handed measure'.[11]

The Home Secretary declined to take Fitt's advice, preferring his own counsel, which told him, as he told the Committee,

> We are dealing essentially with activity in this country. I do not think that we should be stampeded into adding to the list. I believe that it will prove necessary to add to it, and I have power to do so by order. *I shall not hesitate to use that power in what I might describe as an evenhanded way. There will be no question of proceeding against one side rather than the other.*[12] [Emphasis added.]

This was a curious response from the Home Secretary. First, he refers to 'activity in this country', when subsection 4 makes reference to 'terrorism occurring in the United Kingdom and connected with Northern Irish affairs'. The United Kingdom is defined as 'Great Britain and Northern Ireland'.[13] The terms of the subsection enable the Secretary of State to consider the activities of loyalist paramilitary groups in Northern Ireland. Although then, as now, sections 1 and 2 of the PTA did not extend to Northern Ireland,[14] that does not rule out an assessment of the potential threat to the remainder of the United Kingdom using evidence of paramilitary activities from the six counties.

Second, it was disingenuous of the Home Secretary to say that he would not be 'stampeded' into taking such a course when he was simultaneously asking Parliament to grant him, in great haste, 'unprecedented ... draconian ... powers' to intervene in the exercise of the freedom and right of political expression of thousands of people.

Third, the Home Secretary thought 'it will prove necessary to add' to the list of proscribed organisations. The Act was, however, supposedly designed to prevent terrorism, not to wait until it happened and then react to it as with the ordinary criminal law.[15] It would probably be fair to assume that the Home Secretary would have the benefit of police and intelligence reports when deciding on further proscriptions. It was never explained why the public admissions of sectarian killings by Loyalist paramilitary groups, mentioned by Fitt,[16] did not arouse sufficient fear of their being capable of political bombings and shootings of known Republicans on the mainland. If there were even a faint desire on the part of the Home Secretary to be evenhanded, as he protested he was, it was difficult to perceive.

Jellicoe was clearly embarrassed by the proscription powers of the Acts, stating that 'If one were starting absolutely with a clean slate, proscription would I believe be low on the list of priorities for inclusion in counter-terrorist legislation'.[17] He later added, 'The proscription provisions of the 1974 Act were introduced on an understandable wave of public resentment, and were, indeed, considered by many to be among the Act's most important provisions. *I believe that time has proved this judgement to be mistaken*'[18] (my italics). He also admitted to having 'much sympathy' with the view that proscription is an 'unacceptable infringement of freedom of speech',[19] and that the members of these organisations should be prosecuted under the normal provisions of the criminal law. Linked to this, Jellicoe accepted the need for a free and untrammelled political discussion on the progress of Northern Ireland. He further accepted that the proscription provisions presented a potential barrier to this discussion.

Colville was similarly embarrassed by the powers to ban organisations. He said of proscription, 'If it were possible, I would be happy to get rid of it altogether.'[20] Perhaps because he had 'sympathy' with the view that the PTA 'deters Irish people from expressing their political views and participating in ordinary community life in the United Kingdom',[21] Colville recommended that the power to ban groups should be subject to annual renewal and review. When considering the position of international terrorism Colville takes the view that proscription is 'too blunt and inflexible a weapon'.[22] The reality of the situation is probably that with British financial and military interests spread so widely across the world, it would be impossible to protect them from retaliatory attacks by international groups proscribed in Britain.

Jellicoe recommended that the police be issued with a circular to give them guidance on the proper use of sections 1 and 2 of the Act,[23] but he did not go on to recommend an appropriate wording for the police circular, nor did he attempt to justify why the long arm of the executive should be vested with the responsibility of determining legitimate political debate. A matter of such great constitutional importance as this one, free speech, would in most liberal democracies be the subject of legislative enactment and judicial interpretation. Indeed, countries with an executive playing this type of active policy-making role would be criticised as totalitarian if political debate were to be defined and interpreted by an internal police circular. Following the extension of the Act in 1984 to cover 'international terrorism', a circular was issued to chief constables purporting to restrict the use of the new provisions. In Northern Ireland much use is made of delegated legislation to alter the law, thus avoiding Parliamentary examination and even the limited scrutiny of political debate.[24]

Jellicoe justifies failing to deproscribe the current organisations on the assumed grounds that there would be a 'wave of public resentment',[25] but he failed to state what evidence or submissions he relied upon to determine this anticipated public reaction. Colville has an equally weak justification for not deproscribing. He gives two reasons for saying that it is 'impossible to deproscribe' the IRA and the INLA. Colville claims that the public perception following deproscription would be that the British Parliament no longer disapproved of the 'leading merchants of Irish terrorism', and that proscription deters 'parades and fund-raising'.[26]

It seems most unlikely, however, that, in deproscribing, the British Parliament would leave the impression that the IRA and INLA are no longer disapproved of. As far as fund-raising is concerned, section 10 makes it an offence and Colville proposes consideration of further measures to deal with the financing of terrorism.

Jellicoe recommended that there be no further additions to the list in schedule 1 'in the absence of a clear and demonstrable need for this'.[27] Criticism that the exercise of the proscription provisions lacks 'symmetry' or evenhandedness as regards the Loyalist and Republican paramilitaries, and is based instead on the political views or aims of the organisation, are dealt with by Jellicoe who says that 'proscription ... is based ... on their open and avowed use of violence to achieve those aims'.[28]

Jellicoe ignores the tail end of subsection (4) of the proscription provisions which contains the words 'or in promoting or encouraging it'.[29] Thus the Secretary of State can proscribe any organisation that promotes or encourages acts of terrorism perpetrated by another organisation as long as these acts occur in the United Kingdom and are connected with Northern Irish affairs. Some extreme right-wing British groups are known to have connections with Loyalist paramilitary groups who have claimed responsibility for sectarian murders in Northern Ireland. Their connections include joint military training, financial support and political encouragement.[30] Under Jellicoe's limited and mistaken interpretation of subsection (4) these groups escape his considered attention.

Colville uncritically supports the Jellicoe approach, and attempts to justify the anomaly that a Scottish resident member of a Loyalist group banned in Northern Ireland commits an offence only if s/he travels to Northern Ireland, by arguing that the Loyalist groups limit their terrorist operations to Northern Ireland.[31]

The effect of the Jellicoe–Colville argument is to provide a safe haven for Loyalist terrorists on the British mainland. In their British-based training camps they can 'commission, prepare or instigate acts of terrorism designed to put the public, or a section of the public, in fear with a view to influencing public opinion or Government policy with respect to the affairs of Northern Ireland'. It seems that as far as Jellicoe and Colville are concerned, this does not amount to a clear and demonstrable need for the proscription of Loyalist groups in Britain.

Proscription is not a new political weapon in the government's armoury.[32] In 1956 the Northern Ireland Special Powers Act 1922 Regulation 24A was amended to permit proscription of organisations. Sinn Fein, the IRA, Cumann na mBan and the Fianna na hEireann were duly proscribed. The only Loyalist organisation to be proscribed was the Ulster Volunteer Force (UVF) which was added in 1966 by a further order. By the Northern Ireland (Emergency Provisions) Act 1973[33] section 19 (now section 21 of the 1978 Act), the Secretary of State for Northern Ireland can by order proscribe 'any organisation that appears to him to be concerned in terrorism or in promoting or encouraging it'. This was incorporated, with a slight addition, into the PTA 1974. It was also an offence under the NI(EP)A 1973 Act, as later under the PTA 1974, to belong or profess to belong to a proscribed organisation or to support financially or otherwise that organisation.

Currently proscribed under schedule 2 of the NI(EP)A 1978 are: the Irish Republican Army, Cumann na mBan, Fianna na hEireann, the Red Hand Commandos (since 12 November 1973), Saor Eire, the Ulster Freedom Fighters (UFF) (since 12 November 1973), the Ulster Volunteer Force, and the Irish National Liberation Army (INLA) (since 3 July 1979). Sinn Fein was deproscribed on 16 May 1974 as was the Ulster Volunteer Force but the latter was reproscribed on 3 October 1975.

It is worth noting that the Loyalist Ulster Defence Association (UDA) is not proscribed. The UDA is a paramilitary organisation. Baker[34] noted the case for proscription but offered six reasons against it. Ostensibly the UDA is a political organisation involved in clubs, parades and political strikes, yet it is commonly perceived to operate through paramilitary fronts such as the UFF, the UVF and the Red Hand Commandos. It has had many members imprisoned for sectarian murders, firearms offences, gun-running and intimidation charges. Eleven of its members in Scotland were imprisoned in 1979 for firearms offences. The UDA always denies responsibility for sectarian murders, bombings and associated offences. UFF members when arrested often use their UDA membership to avoid responsibility for their acts.

Baker's reasons for not proscribing the UDA are as follows:

- *The UDA does not claim responsibility for acts of terrorism.* Baker fails to recognise that this is an essential activity for an organisation that uses fronts for its acts of violence, thus retaining its acceptable public image. Baker ignores the numerous examples of UDA violence, including numerous shootings and a two-day war with the British army in 1972.[35]
- *Proscription would revive interest in the UDA.* This is an argument which applies with equal force to the IRA or to those Loyalist groups that have already been proscribed.
- *It would be difficult to enforce.* No more difficult, one would imagine, than enforcing proscription against any of the organisations already banned.
- *The UDA does not represent a threat to the Roman Catholic population.* Baker relies on a UDA press statement that said it would not 'be drawn into a sectarian war, but will use every means at its disposal to eliminate those who pose a threat to the state of Ulster and all its people.' It would take an absurd level of naivety or a dangerous level of dishonesty to say that the statement does not imply the use of violence for political ends.[36] On 14 March 1988 the UDA held a press conference where it announced a resumption of the military campaign it started in the early 1970s. It claimed that despite the discovery by the RUC of a large amount of UDA arms it was better equipped than ever before.[37] Further, no comment is made on regular assurances made by the IRA and printed in *An Phoblacht*[38] that they too do not wish to be drawn into a sectarian war.
- *Proscription would drive those in the UDA involved in military activity underground, and those people would be likely to be proved to be UFF members in any event.* This objection to proscribing the UDA implies an acceptance that some, at least, of its members are involved in unlawful military activities.
- *Proscription would hinder rather than help the police at this time.* Baker does not explain why this does not apply to those groups that have already been proscribed. This merely fuels speculation that the real reason has more to do with the embarrassing overlap between membership of the UDA and the RUC, and the British Army's UDR.

It is worth noting in this context the series of unopposed raids on UDR armouries, and the weapons stolen, without resistance, from the homes of UDR members,[39] as well as Baker's failure to discover any significance in these events.

The government of the Irish Republic has had powers to proscribe organisations since 1939. The Offences Against the State Act 1939 makes it illegal to belong to, recruit for, or possess documents or publications of a 'suppressed' organisation. The IRA is proscribed in the Republic.[40]

Section 1 of the PTA 1984 sets out offences and powers in relation to proscribing organisations and belonging to or generally helping such organisations in their activities.[41] The proscription powers are governed by subsections 3, 4, 5 and 6. Parliament banned the first organisation, the IRA, but since then any consideration of proscription or deproscription has been left to the Home Secretary. Such additions are made by statutory instrument, as in the case of the banning of the INLA in 1979. There has never been a deproscription in Britain.

The wording of the PTA does not exclude the courts from examining whether the Home Secretary has exceeded the powers given in the Act. An organisation can be banned if it 'appears' to the Home Secretary that it is concerned in terrorism. This wide subjective power is theoretically capable of review if it is exercised illegally, irrationally or with procedural impropriety. A Home Secretary would undoubtedly raise the issues of public policy and state security in defence. Although success is unlikely, the issues concerning proscription might be forced into the public domain.

Before 1 January 1988, of the 6,430[42] people arrested under the Acts there had not been a single charge laid against a person under either section 1(1)(a) or (1)(c). Those subsections involve membership of and support for proscribed organisations. Subsection (1)(b) has been more widely used. Before 1 January 1988 seven people had been charged with an offence under subsection (1)(b), five of whom were acquitted, two found guilty and sentenced to imprisonment for less than one year. This subsection is breached by giving, collecting or asking for support for the resources of a proscribed organisation. Jellicoe commented that this figure (the same figures were current at the time of the report) for rate of conviction was 'disturbingly low'.[43]

What then is the purpose of these subsections? They appear on the surface to be of little value to the police or the courts, and they may in practice prove to be largely unenforceable. One of the two people found guilty under subsection (1)(b) was James Fegan,[44] who was sentenced to six months' imprisonment. He was alleged to have said, when in a public house in Glasgow, 'Support the boys' as he offered for sale posters with captions such as 'Victory to the IRA' and 'Brit thugs out.' It appears that he was a member of Provisional Sinn Fein, for whom the monies were intended. There was no evidence that the IRA, proscribed under the PTA 1974, was to receive either the purchase price of the posters or any money by way of royalties.

The subsection is an attack on the resources of a proscribed organisation. There is no measuring the actual effect of this subsection as the IRA has never been known to publish accounts. It is likely that it has had no perceptible effect on the resources of an organisation that has the material support of at least one national government and many non-governmental groups around the world. The true purpose of the subsection must be to keep from public view those who, through political work rather than military activity, wish to express their support for Irish Republicanism. The silencing of that support is one of the acknowledged reasons behind the PTA.

If conduct of this nature is thought to be so serious that it must be prosecuted, could the true purpose be expressed through the ordinary criminal law? It could, for example, come within sections 4 or 5 of the Public Order Act 1986, or section 5 of its predecessor, the 1936 Act. Under section 5 of the 1986 Act an offence is committed if 'a person ... (a) uses threatening, abusive or insulting words or behaviour, or disorderly behaviour, or (b) displays any writing, sign or other visible representation which is threatening, abusive or insulting, within the hearing or sight of a person likely to be caused harassment, alarm or distress thereby.' No doubt British courts would be only too willing, in implementing the intention of Parliament, to find posters proclaiming support for the IRA to be at least abusive or insulting, upon the evidence of a police officer that some passer-by looked alarmed or distressed upon seeing such a poster. This would be regardless of a request for funds, which no doubt would operate as an aggravating feature in the mind of the court.

The Statutory 'Defence'

Subsection (7) provides a defence to a person accused of belonging or professing to belong to a banned organisation. The defence involves the accused person being able to prove that s/he became a member before the organisation was banned *and* that s/he has not taken part in any of its activities while it has been banned. This is not much of a defence, but it looks more like a device to achieve two clear goals. First, to prevent any accusation that the government of the day was introducing retrospective legislation. Such 'legislating for history' is itself banned by parliamentary practice and frowned upon in liberal democracies. Secondly, subsection (7) allows the prosecution merely to lay the foundation with some evidence and thus reverse the presumption of innocence, allowing the courts to convict easily for membership. This subsection moves the normal and historic burden of proof from the prosecution to the accused.

A practical effect would be that a person accused under section 1(1)(a) of being a member of a banned organisation, namely the IRA, on a date unknown since 29 November 1974, would have one of two possible defences. One would be that s/he had never been a member of the organisation. Alternatively, the subsection (7) defence would entail admitting or proving membership of the IRA *predating* the 1974 Act and then going on to prove that s/he had not taken part in any of its activities at any time whilst it has been banned, that is, since 1974.

The effect of subsection (7) is not to make illegal current membership if the accused can show, to the satisfaction of a court, that s/he became a member before proscription and has not been active since proscription. Oddly, a person who joins a banned organisation since the date of proscription cannot claim passive membership as a defence. If an accused person sought to rely on subsection (7) s/he would be in the impossible position under the second limb of trying to prove a negative. It is difficult in this respect to imagine what evidence any court would accept. Evidence from inside the organisation would be impossible or would carry little weight with a tribunal of fact. That would leave the accused person with having to prove, in the case of the IRA since 1974 innocent activity since the organisation was banned.

Reliance on subsection (7) would guarantee that great prejudice would attach to an accused person for two reasons. First, any attempt to maintain the fundamental right to silence would be highly prejudicial in the face of the reversed burden of proof. Second, assuming there was an admission or sufficient proof of membership predating the ban, then the backdrop to any defence evidence would be that the accused was a member of a now banned terrorist organisation. This would inevitably be prejudicial to an accused person.

This 'defence' has never been tested in court. There is no known prosecution, or even charge, in Britain for the offence of membership of a banned organisation. This is a peculiar statistic for two reasons. First, in numerous political murder and bombing trials since 1974 accusations have been made in open court and in the media that the accused were members of the IRA, yet none of the accused have ever been charged with membership. Second, the accusation appears to be at least difficult, if not impossible, to counter owing to the considerable advantage for the prosecution.

Why has membership of the IRA never been charged in Britain? There are a number of possible reasons for not charging a person with a membership offence in Britain:

- There is considerable propaganda value in making an assertion that you are not forced to prove with hard evidence. Terrorist trials in Britain tend to provoke a flurry of fear-inducing activity by the state and the media. This includes tight security around members of the jury and body searches of members of the public. This no doubt heightens fears already created by prejudicial media coverage of the case.

- In order to prove membership there may be a risk that the identity of spies, informers or members of the security forces who engage in covert operations, would be exposed from answers given in court. It may also put the activities of the security services under further public scrutiny.

- A charge of membership would give an opportunity for the accused to create a political trial in a way not currently done.

- Convictions for membership offences would result in a clear category of political prisoners. At the moment the state denies the political status of prisoners convicted in terrorist trials and instead insists on classifying them as ordinary criminals.

In Northern Ireland the authorities are less circumspect about charging membership. Between June 1978 and the end of 1983, 537 directions to prosecute for membership were given under section 21 of the EPA 1978.[45]

Displaying Support for a Banned Organisation

Section 2 of the PTA makes it an offence to wear any item of dress, or wear, carry or display any article in public in a way or in such circumstances as to arouse reasonable apprehension that s/he is a member or supporter of a banned organisation.[46] This offence has been charged three times in the life of the PTA; two of those charges were dropped and the only conviction resulted in a fine.[47]

A person charged with displaying support for a banned organisation is, by section 2(1)(b), denied trial by jury but that does not prevent, on conviction, the possibility of being sent to prison for up to six months or being fined £2,000, or both.[48] The declared purpose of this section was to restrict the right of people 'to wear articles which are plainly IRA insignia but which fall short of the requirements for a successful prosecution under the Public Order Act'.[49] According to Harry Street, the PTA 1974 section 2 'provides a comprehensive definition of wearing a uniform', something which section 1 of the Public Order Act 1936 failed to do.[50]

One of the reported cases involved an allegation concerning the display of the '1984 Republican Resistance Calendar' in circumstances likely to arouse reasonable apprehension that the accused was a supporter of the IRA. Inside the calendar were photographs of Republican militias and various dates were noted for the deaths of IRA volunteers and successful IRA attacks. The calendar was on sale from a stall run by Sinn Fein inside a pub well known for the Republican sympathies of all who used it. One night in December 1983 it was patronised by two members of the Special Branch whose sympathies lay elsewhere. The stall-holder was arrested, interviewed, charged, convicted and fined. That calendar and calendars in other years are and have been freely on sale in shops in London.[51]

The above case is an example of the catch-all nature of this offence. Displays of support for Republicanism used to be restricted by the operation of section 1 of the Public Order Act 1936. To secure a conviction under this section the prosecution had to prove that the accused person was wearing 'a *uniform* signifying his association with any political organisation or with the promotion of any political object'.[52] A uniform was judicially considered in a case involving arrests made at an Irish Republican funeral and a protest march against internment in Northern Ireland, both in London.[53] The result was that, providing the context is correct, a black beret amounts to a uniform. This is of course subject to the wearing of such a uniform being likely to involve the risk of public disorder.[54] In not using the word 'uniform', section 2 is more widely drawn.

Section 25 of the NI(EP)A 1978 is virtually identical to section 2. The only difference is that under section 25 there is the possibility of a trial on indictment entailing the further possibility of a one-year prison sentence or an unlimited fine or both. Trial on indictment was introduced in Northern Ireland as an amendment by the NI(EP)A 1987 section 11(1) and was a direct result of the Baker review.[55] Baker, rejecting a similar suggestion from the RUC, adopted a suggestion from an unnamed source that the section 25 offences 'should become hybrid offences, that is to say, capable of being charged on indictment where by reason of other charges to be tried on indictment, this is appropriate'.

This amendment does not give an accused person any new right. A section 25 offence is likely to be tried alongside more serious scheduled offences in the judge-only Diplock courts. The practical result is that evidence in support of a banned organisation will be heard with evidence on more serious allegations. The resulting prejudicial effect of a court hearing such evidence must be seriously damaging to the prospects of a fair trial. For example, a person may face two charges, conspiracy to murder where the evidence for the prosecution comes only from a supergrass, and displaying support for a banned organisation where the evidence for the prosecution comes from a police officer present at a Republican funeral.

It was always the intention, even under section 2 of the PTA, to ensure that no one charged with such an offence would appear before a jury. In the Committee stage of the Bill in 1974, Ivor Stanbrook MP, in speaking in favour of sentences just low enough to ensure the loss of the right to trial by a jury, said, 'It might be better that the offence should be restricted to summary trial alone for practical and other reasons. That might be of greater assistance to the police than that a defendant came before a jury.'[56] Alex Lyon MP, Home Office Minister, replying on behalf of the government, revealed their thinking when he said, 'Although [trial by jury] would not be reprehensible in itself because it would be an extension of civil rights of the accused, it would give an opportunity for the accused to make his declarations in court in a way which might be even more offensive than the kind of conduct which is thought to be so reprehensible as to justify the clause in any case.'[57]

The question that must be asked of section 2 is not whether it is an unnecessary measure, but whether it is fairly administered. If one starts from the premise given by section 1 of the PTA that it is permissible to ban organisations, then it must logically follow that displays of support should be outlawed as well. If part of the test is to be 'what amounts to reasonable apprehension', who should decide that in a democracy? A magistrate, a judge or a jury? The draconian nature of the PTA can be seen not just in the measures to which it has given legislative force but also in who is allowed to decide that the law has been broken.

The Offence of Contributing Towards Political Violence

In the PTA 1976 the government introduced a new section 10 designed to punish contributions to acts of terrorism. Section 10 remains substantially unaltered in the current PTA. The section sets out a number of offences. Under section 10(1)(a) it is an offence to solicit or invite another person to give, lend or otherwise make available any money or other property intending that it shall be applied or used for or in connection with the commission, preparation or instigation of acts of terrorism connected with Northern Irish affairs. Section 10(1)(b) outlaws the receipt of such money or other property. Section 10(2) makes it an offence to give, lend or otherwise make available such money or other property knowing or suspecting the above-mentioned use. This section of the PTA, unlike sections 1 and 2, also applies to Northern Ireland.[58] Jellicoe notes that section 10 is 'far less controversial' than sections 1 and 2,[59] and Baker commented that he had received no submissions on the section.[60] It appears that there is a lacuna in the critical appreciation of this section by those who consider themselves supporters of civil rights.

Section 10 is not restricted to contributions to banned organisations but applies to terrorist groups that have not been proscribed, and to groups that act as front organisations for them, as well as those that have been banned. The essence of the section is that it is an offence to ask for, receive or give any money or other property expecting it to be used to aid terrorism connected with Northern Irish affairs. As such it is clearly much wider than section 1 and deals with an aspect of support not covered by section 2.

The statistics for persons charged under the PTA in Great Britain to 1 January 1988 are shown in table 7.1.[61]

Table 7.1 Outcome of Charges Made Under PTA (to 1 January 1988)

	Total	Dropped	Waiting	Not Guilty	Guilty
10(1)(a) soliciting	8	2	0	0	6
10(1)(b) receiving	16	3	0	3	10
10(1)(a) and (b)	25	1	0	9	15
10(1) and (2) giving	1	0	0	0	1
10(2)	6	0	2	1	3
Total	56	6	2	13	35

These statistics have been given differing treatment by Jellicoe and Colville. Jellicoe feels that they show that the section 'fills a genuine need',[62] while Colville describes their use as 'not large'.[63] Colville points out that in 1986 in the United Kingdom there were only seven charges, five of which were withdrawn, one person was still awaiting trial at the time of the report and one had not bothered to appear at court for trial.[64] Baker reported that there were only 18 directions to prosecute people in Northern Ireland under section 10(2) in the six years from 1977 to 1982.[65]

Where is the value in a series of charges that receive so little use? There appear to be two accepted areas at which this section is aimed, first, 'security' firms that operate protection rackets fronting for terrorist groups and, second, individual collections in pubs and clubs. Jellicoe received evidence that funding of terrorism came from extortion in the construction industry, bogus 'security firms' and practices in the field of gaming machines. Jellicoe feels that the police should have adequate powers to deal with the problem of extortion, and because the police and the RUC say that section 10 gives them adequate powers he recommended that it be retained.[66] He relies on the words of Sir John Hermon, Chief Constable of the RUC, who said, 'Money is a crucial factor in the continuance of terrorism ... Quite simply it finances murder and destruction. Every pound in the coffers of the paramilitary organisations is a nail in the coffin of an innocent victim of their murder gangs.'[67] Hermon announced in September 1982 that he had set up a special detective team for the purpose of investigating the extortion and protection rackets.[68] Neither Baker nor Colville mentions the results of this investigation by the specialist team.

This aspect of fund-raising is now dealt with outside the PTA. On 1 January 1988 Part III of the NI(EP)A 1987 came into effect. These eight new sections are designed to deal with the regulation of the provision of private security services. It creates offences related to running, advertising or paying for such services without a certificate issued upon application and scrutiny by the Secretary of State. Extortion enterprises can be, and always could have been, dealt with by well-established criminal charges. Section 21 of the Theft Act 1968 makes it an offence to make a demand with menaces. The demand can be for the benefit of the person making it or for another, and can be made in writing, by speech or by conduct. Menaces include words or conduct that either intimidate or influence or make someone so apprehensive as to make a person of normal stability and courage accede unwillingly to the demand.[69]

Colville concludes from the low use of section 10 charges that it is proof that it is a 'deterrent against collections for causes which are likely to be fronts for Irish terrorist organisations'.[70] He fails to say why the same set of figures do not show a poor detection rate by the police. This equally valid interpretation would, of course, contrast with the impression given in the reviews of success of the British government's war against Republicanism.

Colville argues that the section should be retained on the grounds that not to replace it might be seen to acquiesce in such fund-raising.[71] The question of acquiescence would not arise if section 10 offences could be brought within the ordinary law. Aiding or abetting an offence is as punishable as the commission of the full offence. Consequently anyone who aids or abets an act of political violence or a conspiracy to commit acts of political violence would be liable to the same punishment as the principal.[72]

Colville takes the view that it is possible that section 10 could be the only apt offence but he does not go on to give an example where it would exclusively arise.[73] In order to bring such offences within the ordinary law there has to be an actual offence and the aider or abettor must have realised that an offence was going to be committed from within a range of offences contemplated by her or him.[74] Many, if not all, offences that have been or would be charged under section 10 could be charged under the ordinary law. The lending of weapons, vehicles or premises for use in preparation or execution of terrorist attacks, or conspiracies, or the storing of firearms and explosives, can all be charged under existing criminal law.[75]

Where section 10 purports to mark an extension is where money or other property is requested, received, given or lent in anticipation that it will or may be applied or used not just for an actual commission but in the anticipation or hope of a commission, or in the preparation or the instigation of an act of political violence. The allegation could be that a person knew or hoped that they were assisting in some unspecified terrorist act or the preparation or instigation of one. Any number of examples could be given to show the danger of this section and it is one that is realised by some commentators.[76] The true danger to civil rights lies not in the use of section 10 to charge people — it would soon bring the section and the Act into disrepute if it were to be taken literally — but in its use to provide grounds for arrest and interrogation, and to terrorise the legitimate activities of an entire community fearful lest their donations and assistance to non-violent organisations be misinterpreted. This section provides a dangerous opportunity to those who seek to harass an entire community or to hinder non-violent political activity and organisation.

Colville recommends that section 10 be extended to international terrorism. This will put at risk many people and groups currently welcome in Britain who, in their own countries, are regarded as terrorists and liable to arrest, torture and execution with or without trial. The only safeguard that Colville offers for foreign political activists and freedom movements is the Attorney General's discretion not to prosecute.[77]

As with Northern Irish terrorism, international terrorism can be and is caught by the provisions of ordinary criminal law. Section 4(1) of the Explosive Substances Act 1883 makes it an offence for a person to make, possess, or control explosives in circumstances that give rise to a reasonable apprehension that it is not for a lawful purpose. The maximum sentence is 14 years. International terrorism raises the jurisdictional question of whether the lawful purpose is confined to the United Kingdom. The 1883 Act was passed as a direct result of a Fenian bombing campaign in London between 1 March 1883 and 31 January 1885. Like the PTA it was rushed through Parliament[78] as a response to the military and political support for Irish Republicanism. The English courts have attempted to lay the jurisdictional question to rest most recently in 1984 in the case of *R. v. Berry*.[79] The result is that section 4(1) is not confined to a purpose occurring in the United Kingdom nor is the lawfulness of the purpose to be constrained by an interpretation using English law.

The position is similar in relation to guns. Section 16 of the Firearms

Act 1968 makes it illegal to possess a firearm or ammunition with the intent to endanger life, the maximum sentence being life imprisonment. The same jurisdictional question arises here. The prosecution has to prove possession in the United Kingdom, but the intent can relate to anywhere in the world. A conspiracy to possess with intent to use the weapon in a kidnap in Paris satisfies section 16.[80] Under section 8 arms dealers have to hold a certificate of authorisation. Under section 5 the possession, purchase, acquisition, manufacture, sale or transfer of certain prohibited firearms is an offence punishable with up to five years in prison if done without the authority of the Secretary of State.

The ordinary criminal law can deal effectively with substantive acts of preparation in the United Kingdom for international terrorism. The only additional powers that Colville's recommendations would bring concern fund-raising. If section 10 is extended in this way many liberation movements will be at risk, as well as those in the United Kingdom who donate sums of money to them. Members of groups such as the ANC, SWAPO and the PLO will be liable under the PTA to arrest and detention even though the individuals concerned have no knowledge of terrorist acts occurring in the United Kingdom or abroad. In these circumstances, if this unnecessary and dangerous extension takes place it may not be sufficient to allow civil rights to rest on the discretion of the Attorney General not to prosecute; by that time the damage will have been done.

Colville recommends that there should be included in the PTA financial measures in addition to those already applicable to section 10. Currently, money or property in the possession or control of a person convicted under section 10 intended by them for use in an act of terrorism can be forfeited by the court.[81] Colville proposes that the police and the courts should have the power to trace, freeze and confiscate funds and other proceeds of terrorist organisations. He takes as his model the Drug Trafficking Offences Act 1987 and the legislation of a number of European countries such as West Germany, Sweden and the Republic of Ireland. In the jurisdictions that he draws on, such provisions are contained within the ordinary law.[82]

The Crime of Staying Silent

It is an offence under section 11 of the PTA for a person to have information which s/he knows or believes might be material in either preventing a terrorist act by another person or ensuring the capture, prosecution or conviction of another person for the commission, preparation or instigation of a terrorist act connected to Northern Irish affairs, and failing to disclose that information. The information must be disclosed as soon as reasonably practicable to a constable in England or Wales, or a constable or a member of the armed forces in Northern Ireland, or the Procurator Fiscal in Scotland. It is a defence under the PTA to have a reasonable excuse for failing to disclose.[83]

This offence has caused some controversy and confusion, not least amongst the authors of the major reports. Jellicoe and Baker both recommended the retention of the offence but Shackleton and, most recently, Colville argue that it should be dropped.[84]

The offence of withholding information was not contained in the original PTA but there had been attempts by backbenchers in Parliament to force an amendment. The 1974 attempt failed, but a second attempt in 1976 succeeded in persuading the government to draft a new clause for insertion in the Prevention of Terrorism Bill.[85] One reason for the government's opposing the introduction for so long was that there were already similar provisions within the law and it was not thought desirable to make further provision in special 'temporary' legislation. It was also the case that 'prior to the coming into force of section 11 the firm view of the police service was that there was no need for it and that it would be of no real assistance to them'.[86]

It is perfectly true to say that there were other similar provisions existing at the time. The Criminal Law Act (CLA) 1967 abolished the offence of misprision of felony which consisted of 'concealing or procuring the concealment of a felony known to have been committed'.[87] Section 5 of the CLA 1967 introduced the offence of withholding, for a bribe, information about a committed arrestable offence. The penalty upon conviction on indictment is a maximum two years' imprisonment. This Act did not extend to Scotland or Northern Ireland. There remains no provision in Scotland other than section 11 of the PTA. A conviction under section 11 may result in a prison sentence of up to five years and an unlimited fine.[88]

The situation in Northern Ireland is covered by the Criminal Law Act (Northern Ireland) 1967 section 5, which makes it an offence not to give information within a reasonable time to a constable where there has been an arrestable offence committed and the person knows or believes that the offence has been committed and that s/he has information which is likely to secure, or be of material assistance in ensuring, the capture, prosecution or conviction of any person for that offence.[89] It is a defence to this offence that the person had a reasonable excuse in failing to give that information. The penalty varies according to the gravity of the offence about which the person has failed to give information. If the offence carries a life sentence, the maximum sentence upon failure to give information about it makes someone liable to a maximum of 10 years' imprisonment; if 10 years, 5 years; and in all other lesser cases the maximum is 3 years.[90]

Section 11 of the PTA differs from the CLA(NI) 1967 section 5 in that: (1) it refers to acts of terrorism, although most such acts would be arrestable offences under the CLA(NI); (2) it refers to the prevention of such acts; (3) there need not have been a completed act of terrorism, as preparation or instigation will suffice; and (4) the maximum penalty is fixed at five years. Additionally, section 11 differs from the CLA 1967 section 5, which applies in England and Wales only, in that there is no requirement that there should have been a bribe, and the maximum penalty is restricted to two years' imprisonment for the section 5 offence.

Up to 1 January 1988 in Britain only 25 people had been charged with the section 11 offence and only one of these people had been charged since 1985. Five of these were dropped by the prosecution, one was still awaiting trial, six had been acquitted, and 13 people had been found guilty. Two people had been fined, eight people had received suspended prison sentences, two had been sent to prison for less than one year, and one person was sent to prison for more than one year but less than five.[91] In Northern Ireland up to 1 November 1982, section 11 accounted for 62 charges, 16 of which were dropped, another 16 were awaiting trial, 8 people had been acquitted and 22 convicted. Nineteen people received suspended prison sentences and three were given sentences of immediate custody.[92]

Colville recognises that the section is 'hardly used' and reports that the police now regard it as useful only 'where there are technical difficulties in framing a charge of more direct involvement'.[93] This reasoning is at odds with Jellicoe who argued that the figure for prosecutions was not the essential criterion, but that the purpose of the provision was to 'help the police to obtain sufficient information to prevent terrorist acts and to apprehend those responsible for committing them'.[94]

The teeth were drawn from the section 11 offence in 1984 when the PTA of that year appeared in Bill form and, following a recommendation by Jellicoe, the power of arrest for this offence was dropped.[95] Up to then section 12(1)(a) had given the power of arrest without a warrant to a constable if he had reasonable grounds for suspecting a person to be guilty of an offence under section 11. There was a further Jellicoe-inspired amendment to section 11 in that the new Bill made it clear that the information required was about the activities of third parties, clearly signifying that self-incrimination was not expected.

The section had always been the subject of criticism on the grounds that: (1) it was open to abuse by the police, who might threaten with a charge relatives of known or suspected terrorists to encourage them to tell what they knew; (2) that it was an interference with a person's right to silence as implied by the caution ('you need not say anything but if you do' etc.); (3) that it might lead to the giving of false information by those in fear of the police or with a personal motive against those on whom they 'inform'; and (4) it was adequately covered under ordinary law.

What was the reason for the repeal of the state's power of arrest under section 11? To some extent the embarrassing cogency of the criticism may have had an effect but Jellicoe concluded that 'section 11 is of genuine value, and that this value is not outweighed by the arguments of principle against it'.[96] The amendments he recommended were only 'designed to guard against the *possibility* of abuse'. Jellicoe did not report any specific incidents of abuse, but instead refers to '*potential* for abuse', the '*danger* of unfair pressure', and 'a *real danger* of the section being misused, albeit *innocently*'[97] (my emphasis).

Where did the real need for this section lie? At the time of the recommended amendments the supergrass system was at its height. The system involved using the testimony of alleged accomplices who had been paid by the police. Most of the convictions achieved with the use of such evidence were quashed but not before many people had been in prison for several years. Under the supergrass system individuals did not need the inducement of the avoidance of a section 11 charge: they were paid large sums of money, and given new identities and immunity from prosecution.[98] Further, the power of arrest was superfluous, as the holder of information that the police wanted could be arrested under sections 1, 9 or 10, or the ordinary criminal law. Consequently, the 'potential' abuses would not be stopped if someone were arrested on suspicion of membership of a proscribed organisation or of having contributed to an act of terrorism because it was believed they had the type of information covered by section 11.

The use to which section 11 can be put can be seen by the extent to which public threats of charges have been made against television and newspaper journalists. In March 1988 two armed, plain-clothed soldiers drove their car at a Republican funeral procession in Belfast. The detention and beating of the two men, but not their deaths, were filmed by television crews and photographed by journalists, and some of the footage was screened the same day on British television. When the television companies refused to hand over, without a court order, the few seconds of material that had not been broadcast, the police threatened that journalists would be arrested and charged with an offence under section 11. The television companies claimed that it was reasonable for them to withhold the film in the absence of a court order as their journalists might in future be at personal risk if they were seen to collaborate with the police. The film clips were released when the police arrived at the television studios set to arrest the journalists involved.

In 1974 there had been an unsuccessful backbench attempt to amend the PT Bill to ensure control over broadcasts concerning Northern Ireland terrorists. Since that time there has been a lengthy history of attempts to censor television companies and the press in what they report about Northern Ireland, and the extent to which they should adhere to the will of the government and the police.[99]

Colville concludes his brief discussion of section 11 with a proposal that goes much further. He notes that in Northern Ireland detainees on suspicion of terrorist acts increasingly remain silent. This deployment of the right to silence causes him concern as in his view it might lead to the breakdown of the rule of law.[100] Colville proposes that future anti-terrorist legislation should be supplemented so as to abolish the right to silence. The RUC have brought pressure to bear in respect of this proposal by indicating to Colville 'that unless they catch a terrorist in the act they find great obstacles in the way which leads to successful conviction. They say that a person who is found in any incriminating situation, but who employs his right to remain silent, should be faced with the reality that a court would be entitled to draw adverse inferences from his failure to make any explanation.'[101] There has been criticism elsewhere that when the RUC catch 'terrorists' in the act they summarily execute them.[102]

Colville, looking for precedents, relied on the Republic of Ireland's Criminal Justice Act 1984 (sections 18 and 19) which so impressed him that he appended them to his report. The main point of the sections is to allow a court to make inferences from a failure to explain incriminating circumstances or forensic material or to allow such failure to amount to corroboration. This is a clear attack on fundamental principles of law. First, it is nothing less than the abolition of the right to silence. The usual caution (mentioned above) will be ineffective. Second, any answers given may disclose any defence before trial. The disclosure will occur before charge which will permit unscrupulous police officers to know what evidence they need to fabricate. At the very least, it will present a 'danger' or 'potential' (to use Jellicoe's words in relation to section 11) for abuse.

Interestingly, Colville recognises that there could not be a 'convincing argument for such a change ... made out in Great Britain'. He does think, though, that 'in the Province the situation does not seem to be the same'.[103] The implication here is that such a repressive measure could and should be used on the Irish whereas the British would not stand for its introduction against them. As with many other measures, Ireland, and in particular the six counties, would be used to experiment with the reduction of civil rights.

The Power of Internal Political Exile

Sections 3–9[104] of the PTA provide for a system of internal political exile. It is recognised as the least defensible part of the Act and the one that most infringes civil rights. Jellicoe said, 'It is in many ways the most extreme of the Act's powers: in its effect on civil liberties [it] is ... more severe than any other power in the Act; in its procedure and principles it departs more thoroughly from the normal criminal process; ... it has led to criticism of the United Kingdom in the international forum on human rights.'[105] All attempts to justify the use of the power of exclusion founder on the rocks of government secrecy.

The power to exclude a person is given by section 3 of the PTA. This section confers on the Secretary of State the exclusion power in the broadest possible terms by allowing her or him to exercise the power 'in such way as appears ... expedient to prevent acts of terrorism'.[106] Such a power is thus allowed to go unchecked save for the implementation of other sections and subsections.

The prime limitation on a Secretary of State is section 3(4) which guarantees that each exclusion order shall expire at the end of three years. The PTA 1974 did not have this provision so that an exclusion order passed under that Act would last for an indefinite period. This provoked much criticism and the government introduced the three-year limit in the PTA 1976. The reform has a reduced effect, as section 3(5) enables the Secretary of State to make a further order following the expiry of three years. Thus if it is thought desirable permanently to exclude a certain person or persons this can still take place under the current legislation. The only effect, therefore, is to ensure a review of an exclusion order in the light of the current circumstances.[107] Like the initial making of the order, the revocation of any order can be done under the Act but only by the Secretary of State.[108]

Section 3 also limits the power to make exclusion orders to acts of terrorism 'designed to influence public opinion or Government policy with respect to affairs in Northern Ireland'. Consequently, international terrorism is not dealt with under this section of the Act but can be dealt with under the Immigration Act 1971.[109] Sections 4, 5 and 6 of the PTA 1984 provide the framework for the orders. All three sections are in roughly the same form but provide respectively for exclusions from Great Britain, Northern Ireland and the United Kingdom.[110]

A Secretary of State may make an exclusion order if s/he is satisfied that a person either 'is or has been concerned in the commission, preparation or instigation of acts of terrorism' or 'is attempting or may attempt to enter Great Britain (section 4), Northern Ireland (section 5), or Great Britain or Northern Ireland (section 6), with a view to being concerned in the commission, preparation or instigation of acts of terrorism'.[111] The order prohibits the named person from being in or entering the the area covered by the order.[112]

Under section 6 no British citizen can be excluded from the United Kingdom as a whole. Section 4 guarantees that a person 'ordinarily resident in Great Britain throughout the last three years' or who is already excluded from Northern Ireland cannot then be excluded from Great Britain in addition. Section 5 gives the same guarantee for those ordinarily resident in Northern Ireland for three years or already excluded from Great Britain.[113]

The PTA does not provide for any form of appeal through the courts but it does allow someone subject to an exclusion order to make representations to the Secretary of State.[114] If a person does not consent to removal from the specified territory or wishes to challenge the order s/he can, within seven days[115] of being served with notice of the order, make representations to the Secretary of State. There is no warning that an exclusion order is about to be made and the notice is only served after the order has been made.[116] This notice contains the excluded person's rights [sic] and the manner of their exercise.[117] There is no statutory right to be informed of the reasons for granting the order or of the evidence used in formulating those reasons. While there is no statutory bar to that information being given, there are no reports of disclosure.

An excluded person who makes representations does so by submitting her or his objections to the order in writing.[118] In addition to this the excluded person may request a personal interview with a person or persons nominated by the Secretary of State.[119] The Secretary of State is then obliged under the Act to reconsider the order, taking into account the written representations, the advice of the persons to whom the matter was referred, and the report of any interview.[120] Following the reconsideration the excluded person is then notified as to whether or not the order has been revoked.[121]

A person can be removed from Great Britain, Northern Ireland or the United Kingdom after the order has been made and notice of making the order has been served, and after that person has either consented, or the period for making representations has expired, or after representations have been made and the order not been revoked.[122]

There are three offences relating to exclusion orders that a person may be charged with: failing to comply with an exclusion order; being knowingly concerned in arrangements for securing or facilitating the entry into Britain, Northern Ireland or the United Kingdom of a person whom s/he knows or has reasonable grounds for believing to be an excluded person; or harbouring an excluded person.[123]

There is a right to trial by jury only in Britain and the maximum sentence is imprisonment for five years or an unlimited fine or both.[124] Up to 1 January 1988 a total of 19 people had been charged with failing to comply with an exclusion order;[125] 17 were found guilty and 2 were not proceeded with. Of the 17 found guilty one received an absolute or conditional discharge, 5 were fined, 2 received suspended prison sentences, 8 were given immediate prison sentences of one year or less and one received a sentence of more than one year and up to 5 years' immediate imprisonment.[126] In addition to those people a further four people have been charged with helping an excluded person to breach the order.[127] Of these, three were found guilty with two of them being fined and one was given an immediate prison sentence of less than one year. The charge against one person was dropped. All four were charged and dealt with before the 1984 PTA came into force.[128]

The potential for abuse of the exclusion order procedure can be seen in two clear instances. First, in extended detention, and second, in the exile of political activists.

Extended detentions can arise in the following way. The powers of detention under section 12 (dealt with in detail later) mean that a person arrested under the PTA can be kept in police custody for seven days. If at the end of that period a detained person is served with an exclusion order, s/he will be detained for a further period of at least seven days unless s/he consents to being removed from the country. Thus, where someone does not consent to being removed, s/he may be held for a total period of 14 days. If during the seven days following the service of the order the detained person exercises her or his rights to make representations, that period of 14 days could be further extended. There is no specified time limit for the Secretary of State to complete the reconsideration of the order, merely the statutory imperative to do it 'as soon as is reasonably practicable'.[129]

This grossly unfair system thus presents a detained person with a dilemma. Having been in the hands of the Special Branch interrogators for up to seven days without private legal advice or family contact, should s/he consent to removal or remain in the company of the Special Branch? As if the prospect of release is not sufficient inducement, the PTA provides for a 14-day time limit, that is, an extra seven days, for the making of representations following removal by consent.[130]

Additional fertile ground for abuse and unfairness is provided by the procedure for making and reconsidering exclusion orders. The entire decision-making process is shrouded in government secrecy. A person is made subject to an exclusion order solely by the operation of executive discretion. There is nothing in the PTA that says an excluded person shall not be told the reasons for exclusion nor the evidence used to support those reasons. It is a legally enforceable order made without warning or the right to make *prior* representations. It thus allows a person to be plucked from society and banished without the right or ability to challenge as false the evidence and reasons.

The right to make representations after the order has been made is of limited value. The burden is on the excluded person to persuade the Secretary of State either in writing or by interview with a government-appointed adviser that unspecified reasons and unknown evidence are either false or capable of innocent explanation.

Who is being excluded? The common charges against alleged terrorists include murder, causing explosions with intent to endanger life, offences under the Firearms Act 1968, or conspiring or attempting to do any of the above or related offences. Excluded persons are not charged with these or any other offence. It must be assumed that if there was any evidence of any offence the police would charge that person. Therefore people are being excluded against whom there is insufficient evidence even to charge, let alone secure a conviction. Often these people are political activists such as Sinn Fein councillors visiting Britain on speaking tours. Furthermore, if there is a genuine fear that such people pose a threat to the stability of society, then why are they quite often excluded from one part of the UK and allowed to remain in another part?

The procedure begins with an application by the police to the Secretary of State. The police application passes through the hands of the Special Branch at New Scotland Yard and then on to civil servants. The police application will include their own 'gradings and assessment', criminal record, intelligence reports on political activity, and any unsupported allegation or statement in the possession of the police. If the application follows a detention during which the detained person enforced her or his 'right to silence', the person may be assessed as a terrorist trained in anti-interrogation techniques.[131] The government officials prepare a submission which is attached to the police application. Senior government officials then consider the matter before a junior minister presents it to the Secretary of State, who signs the order.[132]

In Britain only 13 per cent of applications by the police are refused by the Secretary of State. Up to 1 January 1988 there had been 398 police applications, of which 345 (87 per cent) had been granted, and 53 refused. Despite the 3-year time limit, as well as deaths, revocations and imprisonment since the introduction of the Act, there were still 112 of the 345 orders (32.5 per cent) in force.[133] In Northern Ireland only 6 per cent of applications by the police are refused. Up to 30 June 1987 there had been 32 police applications, of which 30 (94 per cent) had been granted and 2 (6 per cent) refused. At that date 23 (77 per cent) were still in force.

The making of representations against unknown evidence has a Kafkaesque quality unmitigated by the adviser system. In 1985 the advisers, selected by the Secretary of State, were Sir Brian Bailey OBE JP (Chairman of the South West Regional Health Authority and of Television South West Ltd); Henry Brooke QC and Hugh Carlisle QC.[134] There is no requirement that they should have any knowledge about Irish politics, nor any legal qualifications, though two of them did have. The system is a gloss. The Secretary of State can and does ignore the advisers,[135] besides which s/he is likely to choose people who support the establishment view of who should be excluded, and who are discreet and unlikely to embarrass the government.

The government does not publish a comprehensive table of statistics on representations. Colville reports that there are now more representations being made[136] (against up to 50 per cent of the orders made), contrasting with Jellicoe's evidence that by the end of 1982 only 43 people (or 15 per cent) had made representations against 292 orders. Fourteen of these representations resulted in revocation of the order.[137] Colville concludes from this, 'It may be illustrative of some growth in the confidence of those who advise them in the fairness and open mindedness with which their case will be considered.' This conclusion was not drawn from evidence given by an excluded person or legal representatives.

Colville recommends that the power to exclude should not be renewed in the next PTA.[138] He remains satisfied, however, that the power is 'used in a fair and reasonable manner',[139] that the British police would not be able, through lack of resources, to maintain surveillance on all suspect terrorists,[140] that it is an 'effective way of getting rid of people from an area where otherwise they might cause great trouble',[141] and that 'it disrupts terrorist lines of communication and supply of arms, ammunition and explosives'.[142] Even Jellicoe concluded that the power should 'be allowed to lapse as soon as it is no longer considered strictly necessary'.[143]

Why has Colville come to this conclusion? Two reasons are advanced.[144] First, that it is 'correct in terms of civil rights in the United Kingdom' that the power to exclude should lapse. This is indeed true, but the remainder of the PTA also infringes civil liberties without provoking this response. Besides, exclusion is claimed to be an effective measure in preventing terrorism, affecting only a small number of relatively isolated people and not the rights of political expression of a whole class of people as do other sections of the PTA.

The second, and probably the only sincere reason advanced by Colville, is that the country's civil rights reputation is damaged in the eyes of the international community. The exclusion power has prevented the United Kingdom from ratifying Protocol Four of the European Convention on Human Rights which declares the right to move freely and choose where to live in a person's own country.[145] When the government criticises human rights violations in other countries it is no doubt faced with the embarrassment of its own power of internal political exile.

Intelligence Gathering and Short-term Internment — Extended Powers of Arrest and Detention

People are most vulnerable when the state uses force to detain them against their will. Whenever there is an arrest by a police officer there is a restraint not just of the person but also of that person's rights and freedoms. Continued detention and questioning bring with them fears for the safety and treatment of the arrested person. The potential for abuse of an arrested person and her or his rights is immense. That is why 'The basic principle is that police officers can only arrest without a warrant *for offences. Except under the prevention of terrorism legislation no-one may be arrested solely to question him*'.[146] (My emphasis.)

Parliament has seen fit to codify in one statute the Police and Criminal Evidence Act 1984 (PACE), the essential rules governing this area. The preamble to PACE states that it is 'an Act to make further provision in relation to the powers and duties of the police, persons in police detention ... and for connected purposes'. PACE can be said to state what is now the ordinary criminal law on the subject, and it is from this that we can take our norms when assessing whether, and if so, how, the PTA goes beyond the ordinary law. It is a well accepted principle that 'if arrest and charge can take place under the ordinary criminal law this is preferable to any exceptional powers'.[147]

Extended Powers of Arrest

Lord Jellicoe said, 'There can be no clear proof that the arrest powers in the Prevention of Terrorism Act are, or are not, an essential weapon in the fight against terrorism.'[148] Can the extra powers granted under the Act be justified? Is the ordinary criminal law sufficient?

The powers of arrest in the ordinary law are governed by sections 24 and 25 of PACE. In brief, a police officer may arrest someone without first obtaining a warrant where s/he has reasonable grounds for suspecting that an arrestable offence has been committed and reasonable grounds for suspecting that the person arrested committed the offence. An arrestable offence is one where the sentence is fixed by law; or where a person over 21 may be gaoled for five years; or certain other specified offences under the Customs and Excise Management Act 1979, the

Official Secrets Acts 1911 and 1920, the Sexual Offences Act 1956, the Theft Act 1968, the Public Bodies Corrupt Practices Act 1889, and the Prevention of Corruption Act 1906. The definition also includes conspiring, attempting, inciting, aiding, abetting, counselling or procuring any of the above offences. There are a further 21 Acts containing powers of arrest that were unaltered by the introduction of PACE. Further, a person may be arrested under PACE for a non-arrestable offence where the name and address of a person to be summonsed by post for an offence is in doubt, or where a police officer has reasonable grounds for believing arrest is necessary to prevent injury, suffering, loss or damage, an offence against public decency, an unlawful obstruction of the highway, or to protect a child or vulnerable person.

One of the further 21 Acts mentioned above is the PTA which provides for special powers of arrest and detention in addition to those contained in the other statutes. Section 12(1)(a) of the PTA permits a police officer to arrest without warrant[149] a person if s/he has reasonable grounds for suspecting: (a) that person to be guilty of an offence under section 1 (concerning banned organisations), section 9 (offences relating to exclusion orders), or section 10 (contributions to acts of terrorism); (b) that the person 'is or has been concerned in the commission, preparation or instigation of acts of terrorism' in connection with Northern Ireland or international terrorism (but not domestic terrorism); (c) that the person is subject to an exclusion order.[150]

In Britain up to 1 January 1988, 6,430 people had been arrested under the PTA in connection with Northern Ireland related terrorism. Of these people 5,586 (87 per cent) were not charged with any offence nor were any of them excluded; 299 people (4.6 per cent) were excluded; 203 people (3.1 per cent) were charged with a PTA offence; and 342 people (5.3 per cent) were charged with a non-PTA offence.[151]

Arrest under 12(1)(a) is *not* an extended power: as the offences mentioned carry a prison sentence of five years it is covered by the PACE provisions and is thus superfluous. The police have been advised by a Home Office circular[152] to arrest under a lesser power (PACE) where possible. This appears to conflict with another Home Office circular[153] that accepts the PTA arrest power as making available greater powers of detention, and thereby encourages its use. There are no statistics published by the Home Office setting out when or how often the lesser powers are used where the greater powers under the PTA are available.

The powers of arrest under sections 12(1)(b), 12(1)(c) and 13 do represent a genuine extension of arrest powers beyond those contained under the normal criminal law.

An arrest under section 12(1)(b) enables a police officer to arrest *where no actual offence has been committed*, where there is no suspicion that any offence has been committed, and where *the person arrested is not suspected of committing any offence*. Lord Chief Justice Lowry said in the case of *Lynch*,[154] 'no specific crime need be suspected in order to ground a proper arrest under section 12(1)(b) ... it is usually the first step in the investigation of the suspected person's involvement in terrorism'. This stands in stark contrast to the general principle that no one may be arrested solely to be questioned. Being concerned in the commission, preparation or instigation of an act of terrorism is not an offence. A police officer with a suspicion that a person is so concerned, provided the suspicion is on reasonable grounds, can arrest such a person without a warrant.

The phrase, 'being concerned in the commission, preparation or instigation of an act of terrorism', falls short of an act of terrorism constituting a substantive offence (like murder or possession of explosives with intent to endanger life, etc.), and also falls short of an attempt or conspiracy to commit a substantive offence. An example would be a person who writes out a death list of intended victims. This is obviously preparation but is not an attempt as it is not sufficiently proximate to the completed offence. If the person drafted the list on her or his own it could not be a conspiracy as that offence requires someone else, even an unknown person, with whom to conspire.

One of the difficulties with this power is knowing what amounts to reasonable grounds sufficient to raise a suspicion. A suspicion is based on reasonable grounds though the grounds do not prove guilt, do not amount to a case to answer in a court of law, and may even be, at a trial, inadmissible in evidence against the person arrested.[155] Grounds may be unreasonable where there is an 'excess [of] sentimentality, romanticism, bigotry, wild prejudice, caprice, fatuousness or excessive lack of common sense'[156] but this is not an exhaustive list. The Codes of Practice to PACE provide some explanation, by way of unenforceable guidance, on what amounts to reasonable grounds for suspicion.[157]

What in practice amounts to reasonable grounds in PTA arrests is unclear. The opportunities for testing a police officer's suspicions are rare. Criminal charges are often not the result of the arrests and too few people attempt to sue the police for false imprisonment. It could be that information received from other people arrested and interviewed, items found in a search, declared political allegiances, attendance at certain public meetings or demonstrations, destination of travel, or wearing political badges, might trigger a police officer's suspicion.

The essence of the extended power of arrest is the gathering of information. As the statistics go some way to proving, there is no intention to charge the arrested person with any offence, merely to question them.

This is an extraordinary and unparalleled power. Attempts to justify it have included the suggestion that it is necessary to thwart the commission of offences of violence, or where it is believed that an active service unit is being formed. Such beliefs will naturally come from intelligence sources.[158] If such sources are to be believed, then no doubt continued observation and surveillance would lead the security services to evidence of an actual crime, probably in sufficient time to prevent it. If, however, the purpose is something other than the prevention of terrorist acts, then arrests under the extended power of the PTA would not hamper but assist that other purpose.

Those people charged following arrest under the PTA could all have been arrested under ordinary police powers.[159] So who is arrested and why?

The power to arrest under section 12(1)(b) can be described as a power to arrest a suspected terrorist. There are, it seems, at least 5,586 suspected terrorists who were never charged with any offence, nor were they made subject to an exclusion order. This seems to be an exceptionally large number of suspected terrorists to be allowed to walk free from police custody. There are broad powers under the PTA to exclude persons who are or have been concerned 'in the commission, preparation or instigation of acts of terrorism'. In making an exclusion order the Secretary of State is not constrained by the higher test applicable to arrest, that is, 'reasonable grounds for suspicion'. The test is what appears *expedient* to the Secretary of State. In the early years of the use of this extended power of arrest it was probably used against a higher proportion of permanent, mainly Irish, residents. In recent years it has been used mainly against people who have travelled from Ireland or Northern Ireland to Britain, or who have been in Britain for only a short period of time.[160]

If the extended powers of arrest are really necessary to prevent terrorism, and if a person has been arrested on reasonable grounds that s/he is a suspected terrorist, why did successive Secretaries of State not find it 'expedient' to make exclusion orders against 5,586 suspected terrorists? Did all these people have the required 3 years' continuous residence to avoid the exclusion order? Could it be that a large proportion, if not all, of the 5,586 people have had their civil right to freedom from arbitrary arrest infringed for the benefit of the information-gatherers of the Special Branch? Is there an element of racist harassment of Irish people and the victimisation of supporters of Republicanism? There is no known proposal currently under consideration by the government to create any new offences that would have criminalised these 5,586 victims of the PTA.

An arrest under section 12(1)(c) entitles a police officer who has reasonable grounds for suspecting a person to be subject to an exclusion order to arrest that person without a warrant. Thus, if the Secretary of State has signed an exclusion order, the excluded person becomes subject to that order and liable to arrest. The section does not give the power of arrest in anticipation of an order being made. As with section 12(1)(b), a 12(1)(c) arrest is not in connection with an offence and thus represents a power in the hands of the police that goes beyond the ordinary law. This power is not necessary to arrest people who are in breach of an exclusion order. It is an offence under section 9(1) for someone to fail to comply with an order after that person has become liable for removal. It is an offence for which a person may receive a prison sentence of five years.[161] Consequently, there is a power of arrest available under the ordinary law in section 24 of PACE.

The section 12(1)(c) power of arrest is only exercisable in two situations, either where someone is at liberty, or where they are in custody having been arrested under a different power, and in the jurisdiction from which they are excluded but from where they are not yet liable to removal. The fear is that someone already in custody may have their detention further extended by a subsequent arrest while still in custody by a successive arrest under section 12(1)(c). In Britain, up to 1 January 1988, 299 people were excluded following arrest under the PTA. The remaining 46 orders were made against people who were detained under other powers, released from prison, already subject to orders, or outside Britain for another reason.[162] The Home Office does not publish statistics showing under which section 12 power the person was arrested, nor the total time spent in custody by those subjected to arrest under more than one power.

Far from being a redundant power, section 12(1)(c) represents a potential source of oppressive detention by the police. It may in practice represent the final straw for the person who has already been detained for a lengthy period of time under section 12(1)(b). The prospect of such an arrest can also be used as a threat or inducement during interrogation.

The power of a 12(1)(c) arrest is subject to an anomaly. Section 12(2) restricts the power of arrest exercisable in Britain to where the order excludes the person from Britain under section 4, and in Northern Ireland to where the order excludes the person from Northern Ireland under section 5. Where, however, a person is subject to an order excluding them from the United Kingdom, there is no power of arrest.

The consequence of this anomaly is that an Irish citizen who is subject to an exclusion order from the United Kingdom under section 6 cannot be arrested under section 12(1)(c). Sections 7 and 8 give the Irish citizen subject to a UK exclusion order the right to make written representations on the seventh and final day and remain at liberty until there has been an interview with the advisers and a decision by the Secretary of State.

One result of this is that Irish citizens are better placed than British citizens liable to arrest under section 12(1)(c). Alternatively, the police may be tempted to abuse their powers of arrest under section 12(1)(b) and hold a person for up to seven days. This abuse might be used to apply the persuasive force of interrogation by the Special Branch to encourage the person's consent to exclusion, followed by immediate removal from the UK, and release in the Irish Free State (sic).

Section 13 of the PTA allows the Secretary of State to make an order by statutory instrument providing for further powers of arrest, detention, search and questioning at air- and seaports. Statutory instruments were laid before Parliament in 1974 and have been renewed substantially unaltered.[163]

Those further powers of arrest may be exercised where a person is leaving or entering Britain or Northern Ireland and:

(1) where the person is to be *examined* with a view to determining whether: (i) s/he 'appears to be a person who is or has been concerned in the commission, preparation or instigation of acts of terrorism'; or, (ii) s/he is subject to an exclusion order; or, (iii) there are *grounds for suspecting* that s/he has committed an offence in relation to an exclusion order;

(2) pending a decision by the Secretary of State whether or not to make an exclusion order against her or him; and,

(3) pending *removal* following the making of an exclusion order.[164]

With the exception of 1(iii) above, none of the powers are in connection with any offence. These powers are exercised by what the PTA calls 'examining officers' who are police officers, immigration officers and customs and excise officers.[165] In Northern Ireland, solders and other members of the armed forces are included in the definition of 'examining officer'.[166] In addition to the powers of arrest there is a power to search people, ships, aircraft, 'or elsewhere' and confiscate any items that the Secretary of State might use in determining whether or not to make an exclusion order, or for use in criminal proceedings.[167]

In Britain up to 1 January 1988 total detentions *at ports* in connection with Northern Irish terrorism accounted for 70 per cent (4,454 people) of all people detained. The remaining 30 per cent (1,976 people) were detained inland. From 1984 but up to the same date detentions *at ports* in connection with international terrorism accounted for 14 per cent (30 people) of all those detained. The remaining 86 per cent (182 people) were detained inland.[168]

These detentions are only the tip of the iceberg, as the statistics do not include arrest and detentions for the purpose of examination. In recent years at ports on average in excess of 45,000 people are stopped under the PTA from further passage until they have been questioned and searched.[169] Most people are released within one hour but there are supplemental powers enabling an examining officer to keep a person for up to 12 hours.[170]

The figures for examinations for more than one hour but not more than 12 hours make interesting reading. In Britain between 27 March 1984 and 1 January 1988, 177 people were examined but not detained in connection with Northern Irish terrorism; four of these people (2 per cent) were charged with an offence under the PTA, and there were no charges under any other Act, and no exclusion orders. Between the same dates 61 people were examined but not detained in connection with international terrorism; four of these (7 per cent) were charged with an offence under the Immigration Act 1971 and one person was charged with an offence under another Act.[171]

Section 13 provides an extension of powers not only beyond the ordinary law but also beyond the other, already extensive, PTA powers. It is the only power in law that allows for the arrest and/or detention of people at random or on the 'suspicions' of an examining officer – someone who need not even be a trained police officer. As Colville admits and protests, 'there is no room for a "reasonable suspicion" test at this stage'.[172] Colville makes no proposal to change the grounds upon which an initial stop and one hour's detention (examination) takes place. He does, however, propose that examination beyond one hour but less than 12 hours should be on the basis of 'reasonable suspicion'.[173]

The more than 45,000 suspected terrorists who are stopped and examined each year are subject to search and questioning to discover a reason for further detention. There is no limitation to the questioning, as there is no specific offence in mind. It is acknowledged that there are criticisms of the questioning technique which seems to include questions about their 'political affiliations, their activities and their friends; associates and family members'.[174] Colville justifies this on the ground that terrorists are trained to stay silent for long periods of time, or to waste time and impede the progress of an inquiry.[175] It seems that on this basis the innocent and the obstinate attract the same level of suspicion as the highly trained terrorist. The danger posed by Colville's argument is that the terrorist trained in anti-interrogation techniques becomes the excuse for, or the basis of, repressive measures.

Introduced with the PTA was the further measure of landing and embarkation cards for travel between Britain and Ireland.[176] The cards are designed to be completed by the traveller with their personal details, the address of the place they are visiting, and the purpose of the visit. It is unlikely that a terrorist will complete the cards by giving the target as the place to be visited or 'to plant a bomb' as the purpose of the visit. There is no effective check on the truthfulness of the information, nor is this 'carding' procedure even adopted uniformly throughout the United Kingdom. Further, it is claimed that there is 'no computer into which it is all fed'.[177] It is difficult to appreciate the value of the carding procedure and there is no claim that any terrorist has been caught or act of terrorism prevented by its use. The records of all those who purchase tickets for travel is computerised and the names are checked against a list of names of people wanted by the police on warrant. There appears to be no reason why the passage of suspected terrorists cannot be adequately checked against a similar list − if that does not already take place. It is an offence to refuse to complete the cards, punishable with imprisonment for up to three months and a fine.[178] A few prosecutions have been brought.[179]

The carding procedure is superficially of no value but there is great potential for abuse of civil rights. Colville concludes that the procedure would be 'much more acceptable if the same powers applied all round the national coast ... Applicability to all journeys, therefore, not only makes practical sense but also could reduce a grievance.'[180] Colville does not explain how grievances would be reduced by annoying a larger number of people with time-wasting and intrusive card filling, nor how nationwide applicability would be more practicable when there are insufficient resources at existing ports.

Extended Powers of Detention

Under the ordinary law the maximum length of detention is governed, in England and Wales, by PACE. Under PACE 96 hours (four days) is the longest period of custody before charge. A safeguard was thought necessary by Parliament, and so within the first 36 hours (one and a half days) a detainee has to be brought before a Magistrates' Court, wherein the police have to supply a good reason why that person should be kept any longer without charge.[181]

In Northern Ireland a detainee must be brought before a Magistrates' Court within 24 hours of arrest, if practicable, but not later than within 48 hours.[182] In Scotland, a charge must be made within six hours or that person must be released.[183] It is not claimed that vast numbers of criminals go free in Scotland because the police cannot get the required work done in the time allowed.

Having been arrested under the PTA the person detained may be kept in police custody for up to seven days. The initial period of detention is limited to two days by section 12(4) but the police may apply to the Secretary of State for extensions of the period up to a maximum of five days as specified by section 12(5).[184] The result is that the normal safeguard against abuse by the requirement of a charge or bringing the person before a court to justify detention, is waived by the PTA.[185]

In Britain between 1 January 1979 and 1 January 1988, 2,394 people had been arrested under the PTA but released without charge, exclusion, deportation or removal. The figure includes 127 people arrested in connection with international terrorism. Of the 2,394, 70 (3 per cent) were detained for six days or more including 7 detained for the full seven days. A total of 378 people (16 per cent) were detained for two days or more, and 1,045 people (44 per cent) were kept up to 24 hours.[186]

Colville has set out[187] the following reasons given by the police when requesting extensions of detention beyond the two day limit:

(1) checking fingerprints;
(2) forensic tests;
(3) checking the detainees' replies against intelligence;
(4) new lines of inquiry;
(5) interrogation to identify accomplices;
(6) correlating information obtained from one or more than one other detainee in the same case;
(7) awaiting a decision by the Director of Public Prosecutions;
(8) finding and consulting other witnesses;
(9) identification parade;
(10) checking an alibi;
(11) translating documents;
(12) obtaining an interpreter and then carrying out the necessary interviews with his assistance;
(13) communications with foreign police forces, sometimes with time zone and language difficulties;
(14) evaluation of documents once translated and further investigated.

Colville concludes, 'these reasons, individually or, as often, in combination, constitute good grounds for extending the various periods within which otherwise detainees would have to be charged or taken to court'.[188]

The powers of detention are exceptional, yet nowhere does Colville explain how any of the 'good grounds' are exceptional to terrorist cases. The reasons given by the police for extension of detention are *normal* police work carried out in many non-terrorist cases both before and after charging a person with an offence. Further, when there is talk of the 'police', reference in reality is being made to the Special Branch. It is part of their job to investigate terrorism, catching and bringing to trial terrorists responsible for acts of violence and other terrorist offences. This highly specialised unit started life as the Special Irish Branch, and their history of investigating Irish terrorism goes back to 1883;[189] they have had computerised records and information since 1977.[190] No justification is given as to why ordinary police work should take a specialised and highly trained group of police officers such a long time to complete, or why it has all to be completed, unlike most criminal investigations, before charge. Under the PACE Codes of Conduct the police only need sufficient evidence to charge, not all the possible evidence.

There is no requirement that a detained person must be questioned, and consequently, one sinister aspect of such an arrest is that a person may be held in custody with only very little questioning or none at all.[191] Colville notes that the detainee may be trained to say nothing and he points to advice in terrorist training manuals 'which enables him to resist the temptation to answer even the most innocent sounding question'.[192] He further notes that there is now 'no particular period which amounts to a threshold of resistance to questioning'.[193] He does not, however, use this to support the necessity of seven-day detentions as opposed to a shorter period.

The right to silence is, or may be, explained to all detainees. In the familiar form the detainee would be told that s/he 'need say nothing unless they *wish* to do so, but what they say may be taken down and given in evidence' (my emphasis). The PTA does not yet abolish the right to silence, but it does give the right to the police to detain someone in the hope that the pressure of detention induces that person to give up that right. This was the argument used to support extended periods of detention.[194] The introduction of the Codes of Practice[195] in PACE and the existence of similar Force Orders in Scotland and Northern Ireland as well as closed circuit television surveillance in Northern Ireland interrogations has lessened the reliance placed on this argument by the police. Now, assuming the rules are adhered to, the detainees' comfort and protection from violence is better ensured than previously.

There are, however, some important areas where the PTA does affect the treatment of suspects as governed by PACE and the Codes of Practice. For example, under the PTA schedule 3(5) a person may be detained wherever the Secretary of State directs. PACE provides that a detainee may only be kept at a police station or, if necessary, a hospital.

Where a person has been arrested under section 12(1)(b) or (c), that is, where no offence has been committed, s/he may be searched to determine if s/he has possession of 'any document or other article which may constitute evidence that the person is liable to arrest'.[196] No similar power exists under PACE for search where there has been an arrest without an offence, because such an arrest is unlawful.

Where no arrest has been made a similar provision exists under both the PTA and PACE for stopping and searching someone. In both cases reasonable suspicion is required. A police officer acting under PACE must have reasonable grounds for suspecting that s/he will find stolen or prohibited articles.[197] Curiously, under the PTA, where a police officer could arrest a person, but does not, s/he may stop and search that person to discover if that person has 'possession of any document or other article which may constitute evidence that [s/he] is a person liable to arrest'.[198] This power sounds like, and probably is, a charter for harassment. If a person is stopped and searched with the pre-existence of reasonable grounds for arrest, then surely that person should be arrested? Failure to require an arrest in a situation where the power to stop and search is absolute and not dependent on any reasonable grounds for suspecting that the police officer will find any item (contrast PACE), leaves the right of free and unmolested movement in jeopardy. If the power of arrest was abused then the police officer may be sued for false imprisonment. It is, however, virtually impossible to abuse an absolute power in a way that makes a civil action against the police a realistic prospect in the courts. The only recourse would be a complaint to the police, requesting that they investigate their own abuse of power.

When someone is arrested and held in custody by the police they have a right by virtue of section 56 of PACE to have a 'named person' informed of their arrest and a right by virtue of PACE to consult a solicitor in private. These sections apply to arrests under the PTA. The police may withhold those rights for no more than 36 hours,[199] or 48 hours in the case of the PTA arrests, and then only for reasons outlined in sections 56(5) and 58(8) of PACE. Sections 56(5) and 58(8) apply to the PTA arrests and operate to allow an officer (of the rank of superintendent or above[200]) to 'authorise delay where he has reasonable grounds for believing that telling the named person of the arrest or allowing the exercise of the right to consult a solicitor in private:

(a) will lead to interference with or harm to evidence connected with a serious arrestable offence or interference with or physical injury to other persons; or

(b) will lead to the alerting of other persons suspected of having committed such an offence but not yet arrested for it; or

(c) will hinder the recovery of any property obtained as a result of such an offence.'

Sections 56(11) and 58(13) of PACE amend and add to those reasons:

(d) will lead to the interference with the gathering of information about the commission, preparation or instigation of acts of terrorism; or

(e) by alerting any person, will make it more difficult (i) to prevent an act of terrorism; or (ii) to secure the apprehension, prosecution or conviction with the commission, preparation or instigation of an act of terrorism.

A person arrested under the PTA may consult with a solicitor but only within sight and hearing of a uniformed officer of the rank of inspector or above, not in private, and also only upon the direction of a Commander or Assistant Chief Constable.[201]

These lengthy and serious delays are difficult to justify in terms of civil rights, and the courts have taken the limited opportunity available to express their views. In *McVeigh, O'Neill and Evans v. United Kingdom*[202] the European Commission found that where a wife or husband of a detained person was not contacted for 45 hours following arrest, this delay was in breach of Article 8 of the European Convention.[203] In a recent English Court of Appeal decision, *R. v. Samuel* (*The Times*, 19 December 1987), the court held that in order to justify the denial of access to a solicitor the police must believe that the solicitor will commit a criminal offence (probably perverting the course of justice) and prove the belief with evidence concerning that specific solicitor. The court felt that such a genuine belief would be rare. The court further stated that they doubted whether it often happened that intelligent professional solicitors were so naive or lacked sufficient common sense as to pass coded messages from the person detained to someone outside. (See erosion of this decision and attack upon the right of silence in *R. v. Alladyce, The Times* 11 May 1988.)

In the first instance decision of Mr Justice Auld in the case of *R. v. Randhawa and others*[204] the judgment in Samuel's case was applied in an international terrorist case following the holding incommunicado of an alleged Sikh extremist. The decision was based on the evidence of the commander of the anti-terrorist squad who said that he had not addressed his mind to the specific question of access to a solicitor under section 58(13) of PACE as it affected an arrest under the PTA.

How far the *Samuel* case improves the rights of those arrested under the PTA remains unclear, as provision is made in the Act for non-private consultation. It might be that the result is that the Special Branch have a more easily excusable opportunity to hold someone incommunicado for two days, and with very limited contact for a further five days.

International Terrorism

The 1984 Act clarified the powers of arrest and detention in relation to international and domestic terrorism. The 1976 Act did not formally restrict the powers of arrest and detention to Northern Irish terrorism. The position in practice was outlined by the Home Secretary, Leon Brittan, in a written answer to a question in the House of Commons, when he said, 'Arrest is a matter for the chief officer of the force concerned, but an extension of detention under these provisions is granted only where a connection with terrorism related to Northern Irish affairs is established or suspected.'[205] This does not rule out arrests under the PTA for international or domestic terrorism; the circumstances of the passing of the PTA seemed enough, however, to ensure that in effect they were excluded.

Jellicoe recommended an extension of the powers of arrest and detention to allow for their 'use against suspected international terrorists of any group, cause or nationality'.[206] The rationale for the extension had nothing to do with any increase in international terrorist activity in the United Kingdom nor was there any evidence presented to Jellicoe suggesting that there was about to be an increase. Since the extension of the power on 22 March 1984 to 1 January 1988, 212 people have been arrested under these provisions; 30 were arrested at a port or airport, 182 were arrested inland. Another 98 people were subjected to extended detention (beyond 48 hours), 49 people were removed or deported, 36 people were charged with offences (none of these were PTA offences), and 127 were not charged, deported or removed.[207]

The Act, a temporary measure designed to deal with Northern Irish terrorism, has been extended beyond its original purpose. What need does it fulfil? The real objection is that the Act covers those involved in 'terrorist' activities abroad but who are not involved in illegal activity in Britain. Fears that Britain will become a 'friendly spy' for oppressive regimes abroad and that groups such as SWAPO and ANC will be covered by the Act may be realised. Those arrested under the international provisions are likely also to be subject to the Immigration Act 1971. Under section 3(5)(b) a person who is not a British citizen can be deported if the Secretary of State deems the deportation to be conducive to the public good. People stopped at the port of entry *may be refused entry on a similar basis*. These powers are and have been used to keep out or remove terrorists.[208]

In making the decision an immigration officer may detain a person for examination which may include questioning about activities and associates. There is a duty on those examined to answer all questions put to them and silence may result in an adverse inference being taken. The examination should be completed within 12 hours but if the immigration officer cannot decide then the entrant can be served with a notice requiring a further examination of indefinite length. Immigration officers may search luggage and seize or photocopy any relevant document. If a person is to be deported because it would be conducive to the public good but has already entered the country, then s/he can be arrested without a warrant by a police officer or immigration officer, and examined and detained pending removal. There is no right of appeal against a deportation decision *where the deportation is conducive to the public good as being in the interests of national security*, but there is a right to make representations to a three-person panel of advisers as with exclusion orders.

These are substantial powers, some of which were copied into the PTA. It has not been claimed that the Immigration Act powers are in some way defective or weak so the PTA powers appear at best to be superfluous. The only possible reason for this incursion into civil liberties is to allow for more information-gathering by the police and to consequently further dent the principle that it is wrong to arrest someone for the sole purpose of questioning them. Colville recognises the anomaly that domestic terrorism is excluded from these powers and only refrains from recommending this extension because of the danger that 'There might then be apprehensions that the police were being given extra and controversial powers over a range of domestic political activities which warrant no such thing.'[209] It can only be a matter of time before a 'tidying' amendment is recommended and civil liberties are further eroded.

Conclusion

There can be very little doubt that the substantive criminal law is capable of dealing adequately with most of the matters that are the supposed concern of the PTA. What is the Act's real purpose? It was presented as the government's reaction to the Birmingham pub bombings but the reality is that the Act came off the shelf ready for use. It was very similar in form and content to the Prevention of Violence (Temporary Provisions) Act 1939 and the Northern Ireland (Emergency Provisions) Act 1973, and there had been discussions and draft bills for some 18 months before.[210] Within one hour of the Act being passed in 1974 the Special Branch had produced a list of people they wanted made subject to exclusion orders.[211]

Where the PTA amounts to an extension of the law is not in the creation of substantive offences but in the creation of substantial powers. Without reference to any offence a person can be arrested, detained, questioned at length, and then thrown out of the country and stopped from returning. This unchecked power has been used on political activists among others and represents a form of political control and censorship of dangerous proportions. Furthermore, it can be and has been extended to cover international terrorism and thus a wider range of political activists are drawn into the net of the PTA. Still more frightening is the prospect that, as on occasions has been mooted, the Act could be extended to cover industrial or domestic 'terrorism'.

The PTA 1989 will undoubtedly contain major changes. The 'Temporary Provisions' will go, and it will become permanent. The right to silence will probably go. There might be a reduction in the number of days' detention from seven to five if the European Court of Human

Rights follows the decision of the European Commission in July 1987 in the case of *Brogan* and others.[212] Colville has recommended that exclusion orders should be scrapped from the Act but the government's declared intention is to keep them.[213]

The likelihood is that whatever changes are made they will not alter the PTA's fundamental basis of the criminalisation of political opposition to Britain's role in Northern Ireland, the exploitation of anti-Irish racism, and the provision of a ready-made pool of measures to be used as and when required against any other group that the government wishes to silence.

Notes

1. I should like to thank Sharon Jennings for her encouragement and assistance in preparing this chapter. Roy Jenkins, Home Secretary, 25 November 1974, announcing the Prevention of Terrorism (Temporary Provisions) Bill in the House of Commons. Where in this chapter reference is made to 'Hansard' followed by a column number that shall be taken to be House of Commons Debates, vol. 882.

2. Hereinafter referred to as the 'PTA' sometimes followed, if relevant, by the year it received the Royal Assent. See Appendix III for a full copy of the 1984 Act.

3. Those terms of reference were accepted by Lord Jellicoe and Lord Shackleton as well as Viscount Colville, who refers to this in his report at para. 1.1.2 (see note 4 below).

4. *Review of the Operation of the Prevention of Terrorism (Temporary Provisions) Act 1984* (Cmnd. 264, 1987).

5. Hansard, col. 451.

6. Hansard, col. 635.

7. See Appendix III.

8. Hansard, col. 636.

9. *Review of the Operation of the Prevention of Terrorism (Temporary Provisions) Act 1976* (Cmnd. 8803, 1983) (hereafter cited as 'Jellicoe' followed by the paragraph number).

10. Jellicoe, para. 207.

11. Hansard, col. 944.

12. Hansard, col. 943.

13. Interpretation Act 1978 section 5 schedule 1.

14. Northern Ireland has its own legislation passed by the British Parliament which covers the proscription of organisations (NI(EP)A 1978).

15. See the Prevention of Crime Act 1953, section 1, which outlaws the carrying of offensive weapons rather than the expression of political views..

16. Hansard, col. 942. Fitt reported to the House of Commons a newspaper article in which responsibility for 28 recent murders was claimed by a Protestant extremist group.

17. Jellicoe, para. 210.

18. Ibid.

19. Ibid.

20. Colville, para. 13.1.9.
21. Ibid., para. 13.1.5.
22. Ibid., para. 13.1.9.
23. The Home Office issued a circular (number 26/1984) on 22 March 1984 to chief police officers advising them on the use of their powers under the international terrorism provisions of the PTA. See the useful commentary and cogent criticism of this circular in Scorer, C., et al., *The New Prevention of Terrorism Act* (London: NCCL, 1985) referred to hereafter as Scorer. The general criticisms expressed there apply with equal force to any proposed circular giving guidance to the police on the exercise of their powers under sections 1 and 2 of the PTA.
24. Home Office circulars are not delegated legislation and have no force in law. The content of such circulars receives no public discussion or parliamentary scrutiny before they are issued. By the Northern Ireland (Emergency Provisions) Acts 1978 and 1987 sections 32 and 26 respectively, the government has extensive powers to make delegated legislation. Under the PTA the power to make delegated legislation is slightly more limited. The effect is that vague promises of control of discretionary executive powers are issued in a legally unenforceable document, while encroachments of freedoms and rights are extended and given the force of legislation. In this way freedoms and rights become the gift of the police.

   It should be noted that the Emergency Powers Act 1920 section 2 gives the widest possible powers to the executive by Orders in Council. There is, however, no power to order military or industrial conscription or to criminalise participation in a strike or peaceful persuasion of others to do the same.

   The courts will only interfere with an order if 'bad faith' can be proved on the part of the minister or where no reasonable authority could have been satisfied of the grounds for the declaration of an emergency. See *McEldowney v. Forde* (1971) A.C. 632, and *Ross-Clunis v. Papadopollous* (1958) 1 W.L.R. 546. See also the excellent discussion of this topic in Bonner, D., *Emergency Powers in Peacetime* (London: Sweet & Maxwell, 1985) pp. 65–7, referred to hereafter as Bonner.
25. Jellicoe, para. 210.
26. Colville, para. 13.1.6.
27. Jellicoe, para. 211.
28. Ibid.
29. S.1(4).
30. See *Searchlight* no. 107, May 1984, p. 3.
31. Colville, para. 13.1.8.
32. Proscription has at one time or another affected the following groups:
   Sinn Fein: the political wing of the Provisional IRA.
   The Irish Republican Army: the leading military force behind Republicanism.
   Cumann na mBan: the women's section of the IRA.
   Fianna na hEireann: the youth section of the IRA.
   Saor Eire: a Republican splinter group.
   Irish National Liberation Army: military wing of the Irish Republican Socialist Party, formed in 1974.
   Ulster Volunteer Force: a Loyalist paramilitary organisation active from 1966.

Red Hand Commando: a Loyalist paramilitary organisation active from 1972.

Ulster Freedom Fighters: a loyalist paramilitary organisation active from 1972 and responsible for, amongst other things, bomb attacks in Dublin as recent as November 1986 and February 1987.

33. Hereinafter referred to as the NI(EP)A 1973, 1978, or 1987. An 'Amendment' Act was passed in 1975 and shall be referred to as NI(EP)AA 1975.

34. *Review of the Operation of the Northern Ireland (Emergency Provisions) Act 1978* (London: HMSO, 1984) Cmnd. 922, Rt Hon Sir George Baker, para. 419; referred to hereafter as Baker followed by the paragraph number.

35. Farrell, M., *Northern Ireland: The Orange State* (London: Pluto Press, 1980) gives many well documented examples of UDA political violence. See especially pp. 296–8, 303–5, and 313–16.

36. The NI(EP)A 1978 section 31 and the PTA 1984 section 14 employ the same definitions of terrorism: 'the use of violence for political ends and includes any use of violence for the purpose of putting the public or any section of the public in fear'.

37. The *Guardian*, 15 March 1988.

38. *An Phoblacht/Republican News* is the weekly newspaper of the Republican movement.

39. Farrell, M., *Arming the Protestants* (London: Pluto Press, 1983) p. 290.

40. Section 19 of the Offences Against the State Act, 1939.

41. See Appendix III.

42. *Home Office Statistical Bulletin*, 29 January 1987 and 4 February 1988, referred to hereafter as HOSB.

43. Jellicoe, para. 205.

44. Scorer, p.13.

45. Baker, para. 412.

46. See Appendix III.

47. HOSB.

48. S.2(1)(b) and Criminal Justice Act 1982 S.37(2). Under the PTA 1974 the maximum penalty was three months' prison and/or a fine of £200.

49. Home Secretary Roy Jenkins, Hansard, col. 636.

50. Street, H., 'The Prevention of Terrorism (Temporary Provisions) Act 1974', *Criminal Law Review* [1975] p. 192, at 193.

51. Scorer, p. 14.

52. S.1(1) Public Order Act 1936.

53. *O'Moran v. DPP* [1975] Q.B. 864.

54. S.1(1) Public Order Act 1936.

55. Baker, para. 433.

56. Hansard, col. 837.

57. Ibid., col. 838.

58. See Appendix III.

59. Jellicoe, para. 213.

60. Baker, para. 237.

61. HOSB.

62. Jellicoe, para. 213.

63. Colville, para. 14.1.3.

64. Ibid.

65. Baker, para. 239.
66. Jellicoe, para. 213.
67. Ibid., reporting a speech by Sir John Hermon reprinted in *Police* magazine, October 1982.
68. Ibid.
69. S.21 Theft Act 1968 and *R. v. Clear* (1968) 1 All E.R. 74.
70. Colville, para. 14.1.3.
71. Ibid., para. 14.1.4.
72. S.8 Accessories and Abettors Act 1861.
73. Colville, para. 14.1.5.
74. *DPP for Northern Ireland v. Maxwell* (1978) 3 All E.R. 1140.
75. Explosive Substances Act 1883, Firearms Act 1968, etc.
76. Walker, C., *The Prevention of Terrorism in British Law* (Manchester University Press: 1986), p. 96. Referred to hereafter as Walker followed by the page number.
77. Colville, para. 14.1.8.
78. Bunyan, T., *The Political Police in Britain* (London: Quartet, 1977) p. 104. Referred to hereafter as Bunyan..
79. *R. v. Berry* [1984] 2 All E.R. 296, C.A.; [1984] 3 All E.R. 1008, H.L.
80. *R. v. El-Hakkaoui* (1975) 2 All E.R. 146.
81. S.10(4).
82. Colville, paras 14.2.1 to 14.2.8.
83. See Appendix III.
84. Baker, para. 252, Jellicoe, para. 229, Colville, para. 15.1.1.
85. Prevention of Terrorism Bill, Jellicoe, para. 214.
86. Jellicoe, para. 221.
87. Criminal Law Revision Report 1965, 7th report, para. 37.
88. S.11(2).
89. Baker, para. 243.
90. Ibid., para. 245.
91. HOSB. These were the same figures as at 31 December 1986. The figures in the most recent HOSB are suspect and appear to suggest that less people were charged with that offence contradicting previous HOSB's.
92. Jellicoe, Annex D, Table 12.
93. Colville, para. 15.1.2.
94. Jellicoe, para. 220, see also para. 221 for specific examples.
95. Ibid., para. 232.
96. Ibid., para. 229.
97. Ibid., paras 230 to 233
98. See Chapter 3 *The Supergrass* (Concerned Community Organisations: Belfast).
99. Scorer, pp. 58–60.
100. Colville, para. 15.1.4.
101. Ibid.
102. See Chapter 5.
103. Colville, para. 15.1.6.
104. See Appendix III.
105. Jellicoe, para. 175.
106. S.3.
107. Scorer, pp. 24–29 and 32ff for several examples of the gross injustices under the system.

108. S.3(3).
109. S.3(5)(b) Immigration Act 1971 under which a person may be excluded from the United Kingdom on the ground that their presence would not be 'conducive to the public interest'.
110. SS.4, 5 and 6.
111. SS.4(1), 5(1) and 6(1).
112. SS.4(2), 5(2) and 6(2).
113. SS.4(4), 5(4) and 6(4).
114. S.7.
115. S.7(4). Under S.7(5) the time limit is extended to 14 days where before the end of the 7 day period the excluded person consents to being removed from the designated area.
116. S.7(1).
117. S.7(1)(a) and (b).
118. S.7(3)(a) and (b).
119. S.7(3)(b).
120. S.7(12).
121. S.7(13).
122. S.8.
123. S.9(1), (2)(a) and 2(b).
124. S.9(4).
125. S.9(1).
126. HOSB.
127. S.9(2)(a).
128. HOSB.
129. S.7(11).
130. S.7(5).
131. Scorer, p. 31, where the information is credited to the Shackleton Report: *Review of the operation of the Prevention of Terrorism (Temporary Provisions) Acts 1974 and 1976* (Cmnd. 7324, 1978).
132. Jellicoe, para. 162.
133. HOSB.
134. Scorer, p. 20.
135. Jellicoe, para. 169.
136. Colville, para. 11.3.3.
137. Jellicoe, para. 169.
138. Colville, para. 11.6.1.
139. Ibid., para, 11.5.2.
140. Ibid., para. 11.5.1.
141. Ibid., para. 11.6.1.
142. Ibid.
143. Jellicoe, para. 200.
144. Colville, para. 11.6.1.
145. Scorer, p. 32; see also Chapter 1.
146. Baker, para. 258.
147. Colville, para. 4.1.7.
148. Jellicoe, para. 55.
149. A warrant is an order issued by a Magistrate who is satisfied having heard evidence on oàth from a police officer of the necessity for the order..

150. See Appendix III.
151. HOSB.
152. Home Office Circular 90/1983.
153. Home Office Circular 26/1984.
154. *Ex parte Lynch* [1980] N.I. 126.
155. *Halsbury's Laws of England*, vol. 11 4th edn, para. 101.
156. per Lord Hailsham *Re. W* (1971) 2 All E.R. 56.
157. Code 1 Powers of Stop and Search, Annex B..
158. Colville, para. 4.1.7.
159. Scorer, p. 47 quoting Home Secretary Roy Jenkins.
160. Walker, p. 133.
161. Section 9(4)(b).
162. HOSB.
163. The Prevention of Terrorism (Supplemental Temporary Provisions) Order 1984 SI no. 418 and Northern Ireland Order 1984, SI no. 417.
164. See Appendix III.
165. Schedule 3 Part 1 para 1(2).
166. Schedule 3 Part 1 para. 1(4).
167. S.13 (2)(b)(i) and (ii).
168. HOSB.
169. Scorer, p. 36.
170. Article 4 PT(STP)O 1984 SI no. 418.
171. HOSB.
172. Colville, para. 8.2.3.
173. Ibid., para. 8.2.6.
174. Ibid., para. 8.4.1.
175. Ibid., para. 8.4.2.
176. Schedule 3 Part 1 (6)(c)(i) and (ii).
177. Colville, para. 9.2.8.
178. Schedule 3 Part 1 (1)(9).
179. Colville, para. 9.2.5.
180. Ibid., para. 9.2.9.
181. PACE SS. 42, 43, 44.
182. Magistrates' Courts (Northern Ireland) Order 1981 Article 131.
183. Criminal Justice (Scotland) Act 1980 S.2(2).
184. See Appendix III.
185. S.12(6).
186. HOSB.
187. Colville, para. 5.1.6.
188. Ibid., para. 5.1.7.
189. See Allason, R., *The Branch: A History of the Metropolitan Police Special Branch 1883-1983* (London: Secker & Warburg, 1983,) and Bunyan.
190. Allason, p. 166.
191. Scorer, pp. 37ff for individual examples.
192. Colville, para. 5.1.4.
193. Ibid., para. 5.1.4.
194. Ibid., para. 5.1.3.
195. The Codes of Practice cover the questioning and treatment of suspects.
196. Schedule 3 para. 6(2).

197. PACE S.1(3).

198. Schedule 3 Part II para. 6(1).

199. PACE SS.56(3), 58(5).

200. Ibid., SS.56(2)(b), 58(10)(b).

201. Ibid., SS.58(14) (15) (16) and (17).

202. (1981) S EHRR 71, EC of HR.

203. Article 8 of the European 'Convention for the Protection of Human Rights and Fundamental Freedoms', Rome 4 November 1950, states as follows:
    1. Everyone has the right to respect for his private and family life, his home and his correspondence.
    2. There shall be no interference by a public authority with the exercise of this right except such as is in accordance with the law and is necessary in a democratic society in the interests of the security, public safety or the economic well-being of the country, for the prevention of disorder or crime, for the protection of health or morals, or for the protection of the rights and freedoms of others.

204. Unreported, Central Criminal Court April/May 1988.

205. Official Report, 5 November 1980, Written Answers, col. 571, House of Commons. Set out more fully in Jellicoe, para. 75.

206. Jellicoe, para. 77.

207. HOSB.

208. *Puttick v. Secretary of State for the Home Department* [1984] Imm. AR 118, where the Immigration Appeal Tribunal upheld the decision of the Home Secretary to refuse entry to a former but *reformed* member of the Baader Meinhof Gang because her past conduct gave rise to a *present threat* because of the risk to the fundamental interests of society by a disturbance to the social order or the risk that she will act against those interests. It was further held that it was for her to rebut the risk with evidence. For a more detailed discussion of these issues see Macdonald, Ian M., *Immigration Law and Practice* (London: Butterworths, 1987) pp. 40–1, 52–4, 152–4, 345–50.

209. Colville, para. 7.1.4.

210. Scorer, p. 1.

211. Workers' Research Unit, 'Rough Justice: The Law in Northern Ireland', *The Belfast Bulletin* no. 10, Spring 1982, p.17.

212. *Brogan and others v. United Kingdom* Application no. 11209/84.

213. House of Lords Debates, 16 February, vol. 493 no. 77, cols. 567/8.

8

PADDY HILLYARD

Political and Social Dimensions of Emergency Law in Northern Ireland

The chapters in this book have drawn attention to the serious abuses in the operation of the emergency legislation in Northern Ireland. They have shown that no sooner has one abuse been stopped than another springs up in its place. The catalogue of malpractices is long: internment without trial; the abolition of trial by jury; the elimination of common law safeguards on the grounds of being 'merely technical rules'; the use of brutal methods of interrogation; the widespread abuse of army and police powers of arrest, stop and search; the use of supergrasses to obtain convictions; and the adoption of a shoot to kill policy. A generation of youngsters has now grown up experiencing the effects of these 'law and order' policies. Although the level of violence has declined since the early 1970s, these various strategies have not eradicated the violence and there is little to suggest that other law and order measures will achieve any greater success in the future. It is a depressing picture.

This chapter stands back a little from the detail of the abuses dealt with in previous chapters and attempts to highlight the more important characteristics of the law in Northern Ireland. The law, especially in Northern Ireland, cannot be considered in isolation from its political and social context. In the intentions of its authors and in its application, the law is inseparable from the region's profound divisions and from the British government's policies for tackling the political impasse.

This chapter also returns to the issue of whether emergency measures help defeat or sustain political violence. Official reviews of the various aspects of emergency legislation have uniformly recommended that the existing legislation be continued, albeit with minor modifications. But these reviews have either accepted, or been given restricted terms of reference which have forced them to accept, the view that exceptional measures are needed to deal with an exceptional problem. None has considered in any detail whether the exceptional measures themselves create the problems. We conclude by considering the most important issue of all: can this catalogue of malpractices be prevented in the future, or is it so much a part of the conflict in Northern Ireland that nothing can be done until the underlying political issues are resolved?

Characteristics of the Law in Northern Ireland

The Garrison State

Throughout the history of Ireland, north and south, emergency laws have been the authorities' answer to political violence. But legal efforts have by no means been seen as the sole solution: the other side of 'law' is 'order', and in this case, imposing order has meant substantial military force, not only in the size of the security force presence, but in the way in which the Catholic community is policed and the extent to which Catholics are affected by security force activities. It is this use of force, as much as non-jury courts, which characterises the law in Northern Ireland.

If nothing else, the sheer numbers of the security forces make clear the inadequacy of the law on its own in quelling dissent. In 1969, the year the British army was first deployed 'in aid of the civil power', the RUC contained 3,044 officers. The Ulster Special Constabulary held another 8,581 auxiliary members, although only 100 were full-time. At the outbreak of the Troubles, then, the security forces were almost 11,600 strong, with the vast majority of its members (nearly 8,500) working part-time.[1]

By 1973, the figure had tripled. The security forces now included the police and army as well as the newly-formed Ulster Defence Regiment; of their members, 9,301 were part-time and 22,569 — more than a seven-fold increase since 1969 — were full-time. A decade later, in 1984, there were still nearly 23,000 full-time officers, although part-timers had dropped to just over 5,500.[2] In other words, bolstering the emergency laws has required a force of between 21,500 and 23,000. This amounts to a full-time member of the security forces for every 69 people in Northern Ireland.[3]

Not surprisingly, we can see a change in the composition of the security forces as, over the years, the authorities sought to make policing more effective. In 1972, nearly 80 per cent of the total security force was made up of members of the British army. In 1976, Merlyn Rees announced a new policy known as 'primacy of the police', or Ulsterisation.[4] This involved handing over the responsibility for security to the police and greatly strengthening the RUC, RUC Reserve and the UDR while at the same time reducing the number of British army personnel. The result was a fundamental switch in the policing of Northern

Figure 8.1 Total Number of Full and Part-time Members of the Security Forces, 1973–87

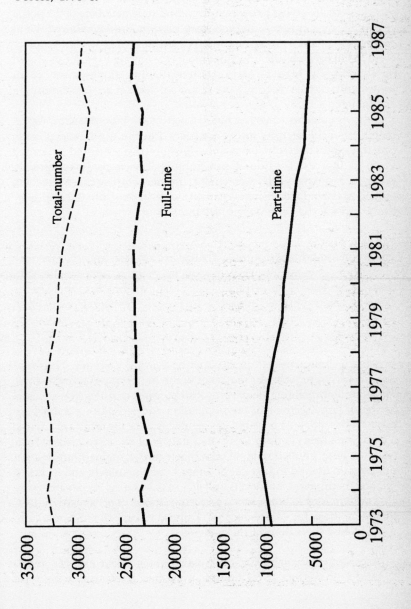

Ireland. Instead of being policed by people from outside Northern Ireland, three-quarters of the police and security forces are now from within Northern Ireland, and the vast majority are Protestant.

Security work is now a major form of Protestant employment. It is estimated that when those employed in the prison service and other security jobs are added to the number of full-time members of the police and UDR, one in ten of all Protestant men in employment works in the security services in some capacity.[5] Without this kind of employment to fall back on, the unemployment rate among Protestants would be significantly higher. At least in relation to employment, then, Protestants can be said to have a vested interest in the continuing emergency.

There is another, more ominous aspect of Ulsterisation. As all members of the security forces are trained in the use of and possess firearms, the policy of Ulsterisation has effectively created an armed Protestant force of considerable magnitude. The crucial issue, recently raised by the Anglo-Irish Agreement, is whether this armed force will remain loyal to the British government in the face of any political solution to which the Protestant community is opposed.

Policing People

The second important feature of the law in Northern Ireland is the way in which policing has always focused on maintaining 'order' rather than on policing crime. In practice this has meant treating the whole of the Catholic community as 'suspect'. At the slightest threat of political violence, a wide range of powers was deployed to police the suspect population.

When the army entered Northern Ireland in 1969, it introduced a new policing technique based on its experience in the colonies. The foundation of its approach was the belief in the importance of intelligence. To gather information, the powers of stop, arrest and search were used to screen large sections of the population and to build up a database on as many people as possible. The centrepiece of the army system was a card personality index. This noted details of all 'suspected subversives' in each unit's operating area. Each card contained information not only on the individual but on other family members and included religion, occupation, car details and lists of associates. These cards were cross-referenced to house cards and to a number of other card indices, including those for vehicle records. Duncan Campbell and Steve Connor describe the extent of the system:

> According to army intelligence training notes, house cards are maintained 'in respect of all houses and small businesses within the

Republican areas'; Protestant areas are not, apparently, included. House cards include a full description of the house, its telephone number if any, cars owned, a list of all occupants, their dates of birth, and schools attended by children. House cards are also opened on all business premises in Republican areas, listing all employees. So far as the Catholic community is concerned, the army's intelligence system is, in theory, at least, total.[6]

House searches were automatically completed by a twelve-page search report. These reports, later filed as annexes to the less detailed house cards, noted everything about a house, from the number of telephone extensions and the type of television set to the colour of the front door and the furnishings and the type of fire in the main room.[7]

At the same time, the police maintained its own intelligence system. The result was often considerable tension between the army and the police over access to each other's information. With the assumption of primary responsibility for security by the police, the tensions have abated, and the intelligence system has grown more sophisticated. The RUC now has one of the largest computer installations of any police force in Europe. It has developed four main systems: a Command and Control system, which at present is available only in the Belfast area but is to be extended; a Criminal Information Retrieval (CIR) system for all criminal records and vehicles; a Criminal Statistics system; and a Data Reference centre 'concerned primarily with the collation and analysis of the terrorist use of firearms'. Details on the size and sophistication of the various systems are difficult to obtain, but it is known that the computer for the Command and Control system is five times more powerful than that of the Metropolitan Police which polices a population five times larger than Northern Ireland's.[8] The CIR system, the most important of the RUC's computer networks, came into operation in 1986. Essentially a database on suspects, it is likely to be similar to, but much more powerful than, British CIR systems, which contain details on a suspect's name, address, date of birth, place of birth, occupation, sex, height, build, colour of hair, race, ethnic group, eye colour and other characteristics. This information would be accessed by the RUC's 38 sub-divisions, all of which have visual display units linked to the central computer.

The policing of 'suspect' populations in Northern Ireland has also involved other agencies apart from the security forces. Evidence now suggests that planners have played an active role: housing estates and other aspects of the environment, such as the siting of roads, warehousing, factories and even flower beds have been designed to facilitate the policing of particular areas. This effort apparently has been directed from Stormont, in consultation with the army and the police via the Belfast Development Office, to the Department of the Environment and the Northern Ireland Housing Executive.[9] The fruits of their labour now dot the landscape. In Belfast, a number of new estates have been built in the shape of islands; all the houses face inwards, and only one or two roads enter the island. This design restricts access and makes the estate easier to seal off in the event of trouble. In other places, roads have been widened and walls built with no other obvious reason than to help police the area.

The Broad Scope of Policing

One of the major indictments of direct rule has been the failure of successive governments to appreciate the impact on the Catholic community of the strategy of 'policing people'. It has not been simply a matter of the widespread curtailment of basic rights through the widespread abuse of the powers of stop, arrest and search, but the constant and systematic harassment of thousands of people within clearly defined areas.

Just how broad is the scope of police activity? No one really knows. The security forces maintain statistics on certain aspects of security such as the number of shooting incidents, deaths, explosions and neutralised bombs, and the government publishes this information. But little systematic information exists on who, and how many, are affected by army and police use of their widespread powers. There are, for instance, no published statistics on stop and searches, and data on arrests under the Northern Ireland (Emergency Provisions) Act have only been made public since 1 June 1978.[10] Nor has any attempt been made to collect statistics using households or individuals, rather than the power, as the basis of analysis. In other words, there is no systematic information on the cumulative and selective impact of the emergency laws.

The various inquiries into emergency legislation have singularly failed to demand such statistics. The Gardiner Report, for example, contained no information whatsoever on the powers to stop and question, arrest and detain, or search and seize, yet it endorsed, with minor qualifications, the use of these powers.[11] With the Baker Report, some new statistics emerged, although stop and search figures were notably absent. More importantly, the Baker Report recommended that more information be made publicly available, and the government published the first of a new series of statistics in August 1987.[12]

These data give us a rough idea of the impact of the arrest and search powers on the Catholic community. A staggering 30,444 arrests were made by the army under section 14 between 1975 and the end of 1986. From 1978 to 1986, the police made a further 13,835 arrests under sections 11 and 13, bringing the total for the ten year period to over 44,000.[13] Another 24,000 or so arrests were made by the police and army between 1972 and 1977. Adding the 6,000 arrests under the Prevention of Terrorism Acts,[14] we arrive at a total of nearly 75,000 arrests in Northern Ireland in the 15 years to the end of 1986.

Note that this calculation gives us the number of arrests, not the number of people arrested. Individuals taken in by the army are often handed over to the RUC, where he or she is rearrested. Although the same person is involved, the arrest is counted twice. The Baker inquiry revealed that between a quarter and half of those arrested by the army were turned over to the RUC.[15] If we allow for this double counting, we come to a figure of 50,000 people − 3 per cent of the total population of Northern Ireland − who have undergone arrest since the early 1970s.

None the less, we are still missing the extent to which the arrest powers are used selectively, and the degree of intensity with which they are applied. The security forces' target group is primarily Catholic, specifically Catholic men between the ages of 16 and 44. Assuming that three-quarters of all arrests were of Catholics (and this is likely to be an underestimation), some 10 per cent of this population group would have been arrested,[16] and *one in four* Catholic men between 16 and 44 would have been subject to at least one arrest during this period. With certain Catholic neighbourhoods not considered 'risk areas' by the security forces, the figure is in reality probably far higher.

The story is the same for house searches. In the period from 1971 to 1986, the security forces searched 338,803 houses, some 75 per cent of all houses in Northern Ireland.[17] Again, as the vast majority of the house searches were in Catholic areas it is more realistic to relate the figures to the 170,000 Catholic dwellings in Northern Ireland.[18] This suggests that the total number of searches is the equivalent of searching every Catholic home on *two* occasions. Many homes would not be under suspicion, so it is reasonable to conclude that certain houses in certain areas would have been searched perhaps as many as ten or more times. As a corporal described:

We did a search this morning. It was the house of a woman with five children. We went in about five thirty. Four of her kids had got measles and we had to tell her to get them up. We didn't wreck the house, but we turned it over properly, we did our job thoroughly. Her husband is a wanted man, and of course we didn't expect to find him there but we thought we might get some ammunition, or evidence he'd been there. On the whole she took it very well: she wasn't very pleased, but she didn't say much, just gave us dirty looks. I mean eight soldiers clumping round her house, and her and the kids standing there in their night clothes in the dark early hours getting cold. I'm surprised she didn't make more fuss: but perhaps she's getting used to it. After all, this is the thirteenth time she's had her house searched in three weeks.[19]

The amount of damage caused by searches has been considerable. Most houses have been, in the corporal's words, 'turned ... over properly'. Under the Emergency Provisions Acts, householders can claim compensation for any personal property which is taken, destroyed or damaged. Since 1973, the government has paid out over £2 million in compensation.[20]

The pattern of harassment, as Figure 8:2 shows, has varied considerably over time. The abuse of the powers was greatest in the early 1970s, when the army was principally responsible for most of the arrests and house searches. Both are now much less frequent, with about 1,000 arrests and 300 house searches being carried out each year. The figures, however, disguise the important switch which has taken place in the use of particular arrest powers. The RUC now mainly uses the seven, rather than the three day arrest power. In other words, although the number of arrests has declined, people are now being detained for longer periods.

Normalisation of Emergency Legislation

Both the Prevention of Terrorism (Temporary Provisions) Act 1974 and the Northern Ireland (Emergency Provisions) Act 1973 were, as their titles suggest, intended as temporary measures designed to deal with an emergency. Both have now become 'normalised' in a number of respects

To begin with, both have been re-enacted and extended: the PTA in 1976 and 1984, and the EPA in 1975, 1978 and 1987. The most important extension to the PTA occurred in 1984 when it was amended to cover international terrorism. It now provides powers to deal with people suspected of involvement in political violence anywhere in the world, even if the violence has no connection with the United Kingdom and could not be dealt with in British courts.[21] The most important extensions to the EPA were made in 1987 when search and seizure powers were extended, two new offences were created concerning proscribed organisations and the scope of the offence of collecting, recording, publishing or communicating or eliciting information which is 'likely to be useful to terrorists' was enlarged.

Secondly, it is apparent that successive governments and some of the independent assessors no longer consider either piece of legislation as

Figure 8:2 Total Number of Houses Searched and Estimated Number of People Arrested, 1971–86

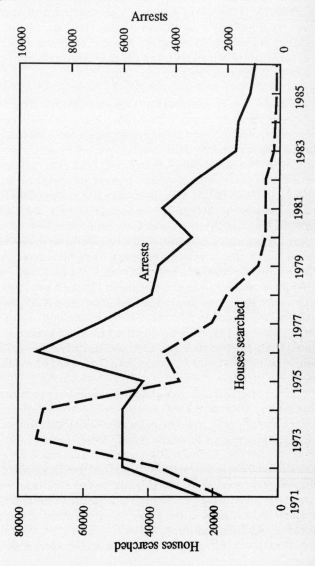

temporary. In his review of the EPA in 1984, Sir George Baker noted that an emergency was defined as a 'sudden and unexpected occurrence' and pointed out that there was something incongruous about an emergency extending over twenty years. He therefore recommended that there should be a new title to the Act — 'The Protection of the People's Act' — because that is 'what it really is'.[22]

Thirdly, the legislation is used in ways in which it was never intended. A good example is the use of emergency powers of arrest and trial for offences which have nothing to do with the Troubles. The most common offence is robbery. Here many ordinary criminals who have no political motivations whatsoever are charged with scheduled offences and processed through the jury-less courts.[23]

Sectarian and Class Dimensions of Law in Northern Ireland

The law in any society tends to be a reflection of the structure of the broader society. In Northern Ireland, deep sectarian, class and gender divisions have been continually reproduced in the administration of justice. One of the major complaints of the civil rights movement was the partisan character of the Northern Ireland judiciary and the police. Of the 20 High Court judges appointed since the independent Northern Ireland courts were established, 15 had been openly associated with the Unionist Party; of the 23 County Court appointments, 14 had been visibly connected with Unionism. By the late 1960s, all the more important echelons of the judiciary and magistracy had strong Unionist associations. In the Northern Ireland Court of Appeal, two out of the three judges were ex-Attorney Generals in Unionist governments. In the High Court, one of the four judges was another ex-Attorney General and one was the son of an Attorney General. Among the twelve Resident Magistrates there was an ex-Unionist MP, an ex-Unionist Senator, a defeated Unionist candidate and a former legal adviser to the Ministry of Home Affairs.[24] In the police, less than 5 per cent of the force was Catholic.

Since 1969 a few Catholics have been appointed to the judiciary and the magistracy. Four of the ten judges in the High Court are now Catholic, although only one out of twelve is Catholic in the County Courts. Both professions therefore remain firmly rooted in Unionism; in any event, the few Catholic appointments have done little to alter the widespread view in Republican circles that the courts and judiciary are still part and parcel of the old Unionist power structure. Similarly, changes in the police have done little to change the Protestant character of the force. In fact, since Ulsterisation the proportion of Catholics in the force has declined still further.[25]

The most important change in the sectarian character of the law has occurred within the legal profession, particularly in the Bar. In 1969, there were 61 barristers, very few of whom were Catholic. By 1984 there were over 200 barristers, a significant but unknown proportion of whom are Catholics.[26] A number of them specialise in the Diplock courts.

The rewards for those employed in the administration of justice in Northern Ireland are considerable. A judge's annual income is now in excess of £50,000 and some of the top criminal lawyers in the Diplock courts are believed to earn as much as £100,000 a year. The take-home pay of police and prison warders is also high, averaging around £15,000 per year.[27] These high earnings and the predominantly Protestant composition of the legal profession contrast sharply with the characteristics of most of the defendants. The majority are working class Catholics, often unemployed and dependent on state benefits. The rhetoric of the administration of justice may emphasise the notion of equality before the law, but the reality of law which is most observable in any Diplock trial are the sectarian, class and income divisions between those who administer the law and those who are directly affected by it.

The Politics of Emergency Law

Since the beginning of the Northern Ireland state, successive Unionist governments have interpreted most violence associated with the Catholic community as politically inspired. Irrespective of the actual cause of the violence (and often it was a reaction to some Protestant outrage), governments claimed that the violence was an attempt to weaken or overthrow the state. It was widely acknowledged that its motivation was political; the reaction was similarly political, with the executive assuming extraordinary powers under the Civil Authorities (Special Powers) Act, which included the ultimate power to detain people without trial. In this context, there was scant regard to notions such as the rule of law or due process. As Michael Farrell has emphasised in his comprehensive analysis of the establishment and consolidation of the state: 'for all the bourgeois respectability of the Unionist leadership ... their commitment to the rule of law was always partial and conditional.'[28]

This approach to violence underpinned the security strategy until the mid-1970s, when the British government introduced a totally new approach. Instead of acknowledging that political violence was part of the basic conflict over national identity, it now defined it as a problem of 'law and order'.[29] There are a number of dimensions to this very deliberate strategy.

To begin with, political violence is now defined by the authorities as a crime no different from any other – in Mrs Thatcher's classic aphorism, 'a crime, is a crime, is a crime'. No distinction is made between the activities of a common burglar and the activities of a self-professed member of the IRA or UVF who plants a bomb or shoots someone, although it is clear that the motivation of those involved in political violence differs substantially from those involved in burglary.

Secondly, by relying upon the courts as the only method of dealing with people involved in political violence, their activities are further depoliticised. Court proceedings are merely between individuals and the state, not between the state and a wider constituency. They place strict limits on what is or is not a legally relevant issue and reconstruct events narrowly, excluding an accused's social and political environment. The confession of the accused is also central. Confessions played a central role in producing convictions prior to the use of supergrasses.[30] But their function is much wider than this. More broadly, confessions help to legitimate the judicial and the penal system by laying the blame for the actions at the feet of the accused, so justifying all subsequent actions by the state.[31]

The government's reconstruction of the nature of violence appears to have little impact on the way people in Northern Ireland conceive of the problem. But it does substantially affect the way people in Britain view the situation. Instead of seeing it as fundamentally a conflict over national identity, the problem is seen as the state insists on defining it: one of 'law and order'. And in Northern Ireland, these are the terms in which the authorities measure progress. As Dermot Walsh has expressed it: 'Success here means being able to produce statistics every three or four months which reveal an increasing number of arrests, charges and convictions as well as the seizure of greater quantities of arms, ammunition and explosives and a decreasing level of violence.'[32]

The upshot of such a standard of success, not surprisingly, is a tremendous pressure on those responsible for 'law and order' to produce the results. The best illustration of this process concerned the abuses which occurred during interrogation in Castlereagh and Gough. It is more than probable that these arose not from the over-zealousness of a few police officers, but from the pressure put on the police by the Northern Ireland Secretary, Roy Mason, to obtain convictions.[33] The absence of any strong opposition to the use of supergrasses by those involved in the administration of justice probably also stems from the political pressures which were put on the system following the widespread criticism of the interrogation procedures.

Defeating or Sustaining Political Violence?

Throughout this book, the question has been raised: have the strategies which the authorities have pursued over the last two decades helped defeat political violence, or have they helped maintain and sustain it? Certainly successive governments have failed to ask this question. In fact, they have actively limited the terms of reference of the various reviews of emergency legislation, so precluding any such discussion. The Baker Committee's terms of reference began: 'Accepting that temporary emergency powers are necessary to combat sustained terrorist violence ...,'[34] while the Jellicoe review began: 'Accepting the continuing need for legislating against terrorism ...'.[35]

The answer to the first part of the question − have the emergency powers helped defeat political violence? − must be no. Although the level of violence is now considerably reduced from that of the early 1970s, no one would argue that the problem has been solved. Both sides are perfectly capable of continuing the struggle. In 1979 the Provisional IRA obtained a top secret report prepared by the Intelligence Staff of the Ministry of Defence. The report concluded that the IRA was still a force with which to be reckoned, that it would have the manpower to sustain violence during the next five years, and that it would show 'more precise targeting and greater expertise'.[36] These predictions have proved correct and are likely to be just as apt in the future.

The pattern of violence, however, has changed. The number of deaths rose rapidly from the start of the Troubles until the imposition of direct rule in 1972, when they began to decline. In the initial years more Catholics than Protestants were killed, but since 1976 the death toll in the Protestant community has been higher.[37] Violence is now more deadly and effective. In 1972, for every 25.6 violent incidents, one person was killed. In 1978, the equivalent figure was 14.9; in 1972, there was a death for every 7.2 violent incidents.[38]

Some commentators argue that an acceptable level of violence has been achieved; life in Northern Ireland has returned to some degree of normality. But this begs the question: what is acceptable and for whom has normality been restored? Since the bombing campaign in the early and mid-1970s, life in the centre of many towns differs little from that of towns and cities in Britain. But in other areas of Northern Ireland, particularly in the working class Catholic areas of Belfast and Derry, life is far from normal.

The second part of the question − have the emergency powers helped maintain and sustain political violence? − is more difficult to answer. It is almost impossible to separate the impact of the various security strategies from other alienating factors and the role which Republicanism has played in encouraging people to take up the armed struggle against the British presence in Ireland. Certain strategies, however, have clearly led to an increase in the level of violence.

The internment strategy coupled with the use of in-depth interrogation consolidated Republican support for the Provisional IRA, which in turn escalated its fight against the security forces. In the period up to 9 August 1971, 30 people were killed. In the following five months, 143 people were killed, including 46 members of the security forces. There were some 729 explosions and 1,437 shooting incidents. Adding to the hostilities were the army's mass house searches, head counts, stop and search and arrests in the early 1970s, and, more recently, the Diplock courts, the adoption of brutal interrogation techniques, the willingness of the authorities to rely upon supergrasses to obtain convictions, the shoot to kill policy and the abolition of special status category. All these practices would have confirmed many Catholics' view that there was little possibility of reform. Despite repeated assurances by successive British governments that they were concerned about correcting the injustices against the minority, the daily reality for large sections of the Catholic population was quite the reverse: their position under the old Unionist regime, as far as law and order was concerned, was probably marginally better than under direct rule.

Whether these policies have encouraged violence is still open to question, but their political consequences are considerable. Sinn Fein has had substantial electoral success since it decided to stand at elections. It has not only eaten into the vote of the constitutional Nationalist parties, but it has also appealed to a section of the Nationalist population who have traditionally abstained. Its support has come mainly, not surprisingly, from the younger voter.[39]

Prospects for Change

After almost 20 years of extraordinary legislation, oppressive practices and abuses, and extensive infringements of human rights, the essential question is: can anything be done about the security and judicial systems in Northern Ireland or is change impossible under the present constitutional arrangements? Can specific reforms, such a return to jury trial, be achieved? Even if they were possible, is there any point in arguing for reforms in the face of other aspects of the security and judicial system in Northern Ireland?

The answer depends on how the problem is conceived. The usual explanation for the abuses suffered by people in detention, in police stations, or even in the courts is that they stem from the failure of certain safeguards in controlling the behaviour of over-zealous individuals. In fact, most of the oppressive practices in Northern Ireland are legal under the emergency legislation. Where abuses of these laws occur, these have been, by and large, a result of deliberate policy measures made at the upper reaches of the executive or the security forces. 'Legality' and 'illegality' in Northern Ireland's liberal democracy have become part of the same institutional structure.[40]

The security forces bear the responsibility for the most overtly oppressive policies. Shoot to kill, the use of plastic bullets, and the mass screening of the Catholic population were developed by either the police or the army, with no apparent dissent from the Northern Ireland Office. For its part, the executive made the decision to rely on the courts rather than internment as the primary method of dealing with paramilitary suspects. It also appears to have initiated the supergrass strategy, and to have made the decision to build two interrogation centres.

Ironically, Parliament, an elected body, has legislated policies which must fly in the face of democratic practice. It approved the abolition of jury trials, the provision for seven days' detention, and internal exile from one part of the UK to another, all on the grounds that the emergency required some curtailment of civil liberties. Parliament has not been privy, however, to much of the executive's internal policy reviews. An exception was the 1975 review of the role of the police which lead to Ulsterisation. While the committee report, *The Way Ahead*, was never published, Parliament was informed of the policy.[41] This was not the case, by contrast, with the supergrass strategy.

Parliamentary, executive and security force actions have institutionalised undemocratic practices and have set the stage for human rights abuses. None the less, within this framework, certain practices could have been curtailed or prevented. But those with the power to do so have remained singularly silent.

The judiciary, as Walsh has shown, has failed to exercise control and, in some cases, extended the powers of arrest. Interpretations by the courts of the arrest provisions under both the EPA and the PTA have allowed the RUC the freedom to decide who to arrest and, due to the judiciary's inactivity, the freedom to arrest for the purpose of bringing a suspect to trial instead of its original purpose of arrest pending the issue of a detention order. The courts made no attempt to control abuses in the interrogation centres in the late 1970s. Similarly, the judiciary initially readily accepted supergrass evidence, despite it being described, on one occasion, as 'bizarre and contradictory'. It made no effort to prevent or restrict the use of accomplice evidence until extensive campaigns by various groups exposed the injustices of the system.

The Director of Public Prosecutions has also failed to exert control over oppressive practices. The majority of those responsible for the 13 plastic bullet deaths have not been charged. Nor did the DPP take action against many of those involved in the shoot to kill policy. In general, it appears that bringing a case against a member of the security forces demands much greater prima facie evidence than for anyone else. This raises the issue of the DPP's independence. The decision to prosecute is, formally speaking, the DPP's. But it is known that the DPP discusses such cases with the Attorney General; there is, therefore, a real possibility of political interference with the DPP's potential influence over these serious abuses – witness the Attorney General's decision not to prosecute, despite the Scarman findings and the DPP's decision not to prosecute after the Stalker/Sampson findings.

The Northern Ireland Police Authority, created in 1970, is another body with the ability to curb or prevent malpractices. Although it cannot interfere with the 'operational decisions' of the Chief Constable, it has other means of overseeing police practices. It has a specific responsibility in relation to complaints against the police, including the duty to require the Chief Constable to refer a complaint to a tribunal where the Authority considers that the matter affects or appears to affect the public interest. In addition, it can call for reports on specific policing matters from the Chief Constable and ultimately call for his retirement. 'On paper, therefore', as Walsh notes, 'it would appear that the police authority is equipped to guard against the development of persistent or oppressive policing policies or practices.'[42] In reality, it has been weak and ineffectual.

If most of the bodies which form part of the administration of justice have failed to counter malpractices,[43] what have non-governmental organisations accomplished? Unfortunately, very little. The first group of potential challengers, the legal profession, has made little public protest despite its close contact with the victims of the security forces. The greatest concern has been the supergrass system, with a number of lawyers active in groups calling for the abolition of supergrass trials, and on one occasion threatening to withdraw their services. Typically, however, lawyers argue that their first and foremost responsibility is to clients; if they receive instructions, they are under a professional obligation to carry them out. A more cynical explanation, which has been suggested by a number of people close to the two professions, is that the main barrier to any real opposition is the considerable earnings which can be made in criminal work in Northern Ireland.

The second group comes from the general community, both within and outside the Catholic population. Catholic groups have mounted campaigns against internment, interrogations, plastic bullets, Diplock courts, the abolition of special category status, and, most recently, supergrass trials and strip searching in Armagh gaol. These campaigns have played a vital role in publicising the abuses, but, with the exception of the internment and supergrass campaigns, they have had limited impact. 'Civil libertarians' form the second, and probably most influential, of these community lobbies. As the civil liberties approach informs this and previous work of the authors of this book it is important to examine its achievements and the criticisms levelled against it.

Its central tenet is that the rule of law can in certain circumstances effectively inhibit the exercise of power to prevent the abuse of civil liberties. Typically, civil libertarians measure existing law against the yardstick of the notion of the 'rule of law', and put forward sets of proposals designed to impose effective control over those in authority. They may explicitly condemn the use of violence for political ends because it claims the lives of innocent people, and may examine the context in which civil liberties are curtailed. Some prefer to avoid the issue of political violence.

The main criticism of the civil liberties lobby is that it is partisan. Tomlinson and Rolston, for example, argue that civil libertarians pose 'as umpires between the agencies of the state and political law-breakers' and 'subscribe to the ideal of the law as non-partisan'. Consequently, rather than see the law in Northern Ireland as an extension of British rule, civil libertarians see it as 'neutral' and therefore 'acceptable'.[44] According to this school of critics, the civil libertarians are a virtual irrelevancy because, finally, the state of Northern Ireland is illegitimate. Their recommendations are therefore seen at best as providing advice to the British government, and at worst as legitimating British repression. By default, civil libertarians become little more than police technocrats.[45]

These criticisms are misplaced. Few in the civil liberties lobby actually subscribe to the view that the law is 'non-partisan'; fewer still are so naive as to ignore the reality that, under the present constitutional arrangements, it is 'British rule' in Northern Ireland. But while accepting that because of British rule the law can never be non-partisan, civil libertarians argue that the law as it is practised can be assessed against certain accepted standards and, moreover, that it is important to challenge the use of arbitrary power as a cause in its own right irrespective of the origins of the law. Abuses of power affect people's daily lives; the struggle to improve their lot is sufficient justification in itself to pursue a civil libertarian approach. In either avoiding a stance on the issue of the armed struggle against British rule or explicitly condemning violence, however, the civil libertarians side-step the difficult questions, and become partisan in relation to the relative claims of Republicanism and Loyalism.

The real weakness of the civil liberties approach is that it has done little to alter the situation radically. Their successful challenge to any particular oppressive strategy usually leads to its replacement by another equally oppressive strategy. This failure stems principally from the marginal position of the civil libertarian lobby in the overall context of the forces which determine policy for Northern Ireland. The majority of policies which affect the lives of people in Northern Ireland are not made in Parliament, but among the higher echelons of the executive, police and the army, where the civil libertarian lobby has no influence whatsoever. Even in relation to Parliament's discussion of Northern Ireland, it is in a weak position. As yet no constituency exists within Parliament which can be mobilised to oppose the development of such policies. Successive governments have been able to draw upon all-party support for the emergency measures.

Its limitations notwithstanding, the civil liberties lobby has made its mark. It has played an important role in exposing oppressive practices and abuses. By carrying out detailed and systematic studies of various aspects of the administration of justice, it has drawn public attention, both in Northern Ireland and more widely, to the abnormality of the system of justice and of the state in Northern Ireland. Without persistent civil libertarian demands, moreover, the repression would no doubt have been greater; internment, for example, would probably have lasted longer, the interrogations in Castlereagh and Gough would been more oppressive, the shoot to kill policy more extensive and the supergrass system more embracive. The critics of the civil libertarian approach, however, would argue that this is not necessarily a good thing; greater repression is beneficial because it helps to precipitate political change in Ireland. Apart from the fact that this position displays a callous disregard for those affected by the oppressive policies, there is no guarantee that the outcome would be better and that repressive strategies would no longer be required in any new arrangements which emerge.

The only way in which the oppressive practices are likely to be altered is either through a realignment of political forces within Northern Ireland or through international pressure. The Anglo-Irish Agreement is an example of the latter. Essentially it was a product of growing fears in the South of Ireland of the threat posed by the IRA and Sinn Fein to the stability of the whole of Ireland. The Irish government pressured the British government and the SDLP in the North to recognise this threat and to take action to deal with the political impasse. How far it will assist in changing the law in Northern Ireland is a matter of conjecture.

When the Agreement was signed in 1985 it was suggested that it potentially benefited both communities as far as 'law and order' was concerned. For the Unionists, there was the prospect of greater cooperation on security matters between the Irish and British governments; for Catholics, there was the prospect of some reform of the judicial and security systems. Yet this view is inherently contradictory: in the context of 'law and order' in Northern Ireland, concessions cannot be delivered to both communities at the same time. After two years it is apparent that the Loyalist community has gained most from the Agreement.

It is clear that there is now far greater cooperation on security between the North and the South. As of 1 December 1987, a new law provided for extradition from the Republic to the UK. Although the Agreement made some changes in the Emergency Provisions Acts, as noted above, these are minor and do little to alter the Diplock courts. Following the British rejection of article 8 of the Agreement proposing mixed courts of Northern and Southern judges, it appeared that Irish government pressure would lead to the introduction of three judges instead of one in the Diplock courts. But the British government rejected this proposal as well. In any event, three judges rather than one are unlikely to inspire greater Nationalist confidence in the administration of justice. Only a return to trial by jury and traditional rules of evidence would help and this change would have to be accompanied by a serious attempt to alter those other aspects of the security system about which the Catholic community have long complained, such as the emphasis upon 'policing people', the normalisation of emergency legislation and the increasing Protestant character of the law enforcement process.

British strategy since the late 1960s has been built on the cultivation of an unequal balance of forces, strongly weighted against the Catholic community. If this balance were to change, peace might eventually come to Northern Ireland. But the prospects are dim. Successive British governments have worked to divide the moderates in the Catholic community — the supporters of constitutional Nationalist politics — from the supporters of militant Republicanism, and, most recently, to present the problem as one of 'law and order'. The success of this strategy has depended in part on the continuing loyalty of the Protestant community. Indeed, the repressiveness of the security policies against Catholics has been as much a reflection of the need to placate Loyalist opinion as a reaction to the situation on the ground.

The first rumblings were heard at the signing of the Anglo-Irish Agreement, when the Unionists, feeling that they had been sold out, mounted a concerted campaign in protest. Mass marches, rallies, withdrawal from local government, intimidation of the RUC, and sectarian attacks on Catholics have been the main signs. As yet, the campaign has posed no real problems for the authorities, but it does serve to indicate what might happen if the balance of power began to tip. The British government would be forced to use the same tactics to control the Unionists as it has on the Catholics; in a community in which the majority of the police are Protestant, this spells a likelihood of mutiny amongst the security forces.

It is, therefore, highly unlikely that the British government will do anything to bring about change in Northern Ireland, including, not least, a confrontation with the Loyalist opposition. At home there is little impetus to do so, since Northern Ireland remains on the political backburner. While the cost of quelling dissent in Northern Ireland is high, both parties have failed to make it an electoral issue.

Sixteen years of direct rule in Northern Ireland have had a direct impact on Britain. The state has become increasingly coercive. Taking a lesson from Northern Ireland, it now defines dissent — such as the miners' strike, the Greenham Common protest, inner city riots and the peace convoy — as issues of 'law and order'.[46] Many of the changes in the criminal justice system in Northern Ireland have now been applied to Britain. Under the Police and Criminal Evidence Act and the Public Order Act, police powers have risen dramatically, and their tactics increasingly resemble those used in Northern Ireland. As in Northern Ireland, the future in Britain will be marked by a new willingness by those in authority to use the criminal law and its agencies to deal with growing divisions in an already deeply divided country.[47]

Notes

I would like to thank Steven Greer, Tom Hadden, Anthony Jennings and Margaret Ward for comments on an early draft of this chapter and Fintan for deciding that the nights are for sleeping.

1.   Northern Ireland Information Service, personal communication.
2.   Police statistics were obtained from *House of Commons Debates*, vol. 72, col. 711 (8 February 1985) and the army figures from Army Headquarters at Lisburn, Northern Ireland.
3.   The total population was estimated at 1.5 million. See *Northern Ireland Annual Abstract of Statistics*, no. 4-1985 (Belfast: HMSO, 1986).
4.   *House of Commons Debates*, vol. 914, cols. 879–88 (2 July 1976).
5.   R. Rowthorn, 'Unemployment: The Widening Sectarian Gap', *Fortnight*, 16 December–26 January 1986.
6.   D. Campbell and S. Connor, *On the Record: Surveillance, Computers and Privacy* (Michael Joseph, 1986) p. 293.
7.   Ibid., p. 293
8.   A. Pollak, 'The Spreading Tentacles of the RUC's Computers', *Fortnight*, 1–28 April 1985.
9.   See Derek Alcorn, 'Who Plans Belfast?', *Scope* (April 1982) and Jim Cusack, 'Sectarian Division of Belfast Reduces Violence', *Irish Times* (8 February 1986).
10. *Review of the operation of the Northern Ireland (Emergency Provisions) Act 1978* Cmnd. 9222 (HMSO, 1984) Appendix M, p. 164.
11. *Report of a Committee to consider, in the context of civil liberties and human rights, measures to deal with terrorism in Northern Ireland*, Cmnd. 5847 (HMSO, 1975) pp. 27–31.
12. Northern Ireland Information Service, *Government Publishes new Statistics on Northern Ireland Emergency Legislation*, 3 August 1987.

13. Ibid., Table 6.
14. Northern Ireland Information Service, *Prevention of Terrorism (Temporary Provisions) Acts 1974, 1976 and 1984 — Statistics for the Second Quarter of 1987*, 11 August 1987.
15. Cmnd. 9222, p. 102.
16. This estimate is based on the 1981 Census of Population and the Continuous Household Survey; see *The NI Census 1981: Housing and Household Composition Report* (Belfast: HMSO, 1983) and Department of Finance and Personnel, *PPRU Monitor*, no. 2/85 (June 1985).
17. *House of Commons Debates*, vol. 92, cols. 637–41 (27 February 1986) and Northern Ireland Information Service, 3 August 1987.
18. This estimate is also based on the 1981 Census of Population and the Continuous Household Survey; see *NI Census 1981* and *PPRU Monitor*.
19. Tony Parker, *Soldier Soldier* (Heinemann, 1985) p. 64.
20. Northern Ireland Information Service, 3 August 1987, Table 8.
21. See Chapter 7.
22. Cmnd. 9222, pp. 7–8.
23. D.P.J. Walsh, *The Use and Abuse of Emergency Legislation in Northern Ireland* (Cobden Trust, 1983) pp. 81–2.
24. K. Boyle, T. Hadden and P. Hillyard, *Law and State: the Case of Northern Ireland* (Martin Robertson, 1975) p. 12.
25. No precise figures are available, but the Police Authority admits that it has been disappointed 'in the failure of sufficient number of Catholics to come forward'. See *Report of the Work of the Police Authority for Northern Ireland 1970–1981* (Belfast, 1982).
26. Anon, 'The Law in Northern Ireland', *Belfast Bulletin*, no.10 (Belfast, 1982) p. 30.
27. In 1984–5, 75 per cent of prison officers in Northern Ireland had gross salaries in excess of £15,000. No comparable figures are available for the RUC.
28. Michael Farrell, *Arming the Protestants* (Pluto Press, 1983) p. 277.
29. The term 'law and order' is misleading. It is possible to produce order by abusing the law; and law is often the adversary of order. See Jerome K. Skolnick, *Justice without Trial: Law Enforcement in Democratic Society* (John Wiley, 1967) ch. 1.
30. See Boyle *et al.*, *Ten Years On*, p. 44.
31. L. Radzinowicz, *History of English Criminal Law and its Administration from 1750* (Stevens, 1968).
32. Walsh, *Emergency Legislation*, p. 123.
33. Boyle *et al.*, p. 40.
34. Cmnd. 9222, p. 1.
35. Cmnd. 8803, p. iv.
36. W.D. Flackes, *Northern Ireland: A Political Directory* (Ariel Books, 1980) p. 194.
37. K. Boyle and T. Hadden, *Ireland: a Positive Proposal* (Penguin, 1985) p. 14.
38. D. Roche, 'The Political Consequences of a Changing Pattern of Violence', *Fortnight*, September 1984, pp. 4–5.
39. W. Rolston, 'The Republican Movement and Elections: An Historical Account', *Working Papers in European Criminology* no. 5 (Bristol, 1985).
40. P. Gilroy and J. Sim, 'Law and Order and the State of the Left', *Capital and Class*, no. 25, Spring 1985, p. 34.
41. See Peter Taylor, *Beating the Terrorists? Interrogation in Omagh, Gough and*

Castlereagh (Penguin, 1980) pp. 40–5. *House of Commons Debates*, vol. 914, cols. 879–88 (2 July 1976).

42.   Walsh, *Emergency Legislation*, p. 116.

43.   There have been a few exceptions. The coroners' courts in Armagh and Derry, for example, have taken strong positions.

44.   W. Rolston and M. Tomlinson, 'Spectators at the "Carnival of Reaction"? Analysing Political Crime in Ireland', in M. Kelly, L. O'Dowd and J. Wickham (eds) *Power, Conflict and Inequality* (Turoe Press, 1982) pp. 21–43.

45.   *Belfast Bulletin*, no. 10, p. 30.

46.   See Paddy Hillyard, 'Lessons from Ireland', in Bob Fine and Robert Millar (eds), *Policing the Miners' Strike* (Lawrence & Wishart, 1985).

47.   See Paddy Hillyard and Janie Percy-Smith, *The Coercive State: The Decline of Democracy in Britain* (Fontana, 1988). See also the provisions of the Criminal Justice Bill.

Appendix I: Extracts from the Northern Ireland (Emergency Provisions) Act 1978 (1978 c 5)

PART I

SCHEDULED OFFENCES

Preliminary enquiries, bail and young persons in custody

1 Preliminary enquiry into scheduled offences

(1) Where in any proceedings before a magistrates' court for a scheduled offence (not being an extra-territorial offence as defined in section 1(3) of the Criminal Jurisdiction Act 1975) the prosecutor requests the court to conduct a preliminary enquiry into the offence under the [Magistrates'Courts (Northern Ireland) Order 1981], the court shall, notwithstanding anything in [Article 31 of that Order of 1981], conduct a preliminary enquiry into the offence unless the court is of opinion that in the interests of justice a preliminary investigation should be conducted into the offence under [that Order of 1981].

(2) Where in any proceedings a person charged with a scheduled offence is also charged with another offence which is not a scheduled offence, that other offence shall be treated as a scheduled offence for the purposes of subsection (1) above.

2 Limitation of power to grant bail in case of scheduled offences

(1) Subject to the provisions of this section, a person to whom this section applies shall not be admitted to bail except –

    (*a*) by a judge [of the High Court or the Court of Appeal]; or

    (*b*) by the judge of the court of trial, on adjourning the trial of a person so charged.

(2) A judge shall not admit any such person to bail unless he is satisfied that the applicant —

    (*a*) will comply with the conditions on which he is admitted to bail; and

    (*b*) will not interfere with any witness; and

    (*c*) will not commit any offence while he is on bail.

(3) Without prejudice to any other power to impose conditions on admission to bail, a judge may impose such conditions on admitting a person to bail under this section as appear to him to be likely to result in that person's appearance at the time and place required or to be necessary in the interests of justice or for the prevention of crime.

(4) Nothing in this section shall prejudice any right of appeal against the refusal of a judge to grant bail.

(5) This section applies, subject to subsection (6) below, to any person —

    (*a*) who is charged with a scheduled offence; and

    (*b*) who has attained the age of 14; and

    (*c*) who is not a serving member of any of Her Majesty's regular naval, military or air forces.

(6) This section does not apply to a person charged with a scheduled offence —

    (*a*) which is being tried summarily; or

    (*b*) which the Director of Public Prosecutions for Northern Ireland certifies is in his opinion suitable to be tried summarily.

7 Mode of trial on indictment of scheduled offences

(1) A trial on indictment of a scheduled offence shall be conducted by the court without a jury.

(2) The court trying a scheduled offence on indictment under this section shall have all the powers, authorities and jurisdiction which the court would have had if it had been sitting with a jury, including power to determine any question and to make any finding which would, apart from this section, be required to be determined or made by a jury, and references in any enactment to a jury or the verdict or finding of a jury shall be construed accordingly in relation to a trial under this section.

(3) Where separate counts of an indictment allege a scheduled offence and an offence which is not a scheduled offence, the trial on indictment shall, without prejudice to section 5 of the Indictments Act (Northern Ireland) 1945 (orders for amendment of indictment, separate trial and postponement of trial), be conducted as if all the offences alleged in the indictment were scheduled offences.

(4) Without prejudice to subsection (2) above, where the court trying a scheduled offence on indictment −

(*a*) is not satisfied that the accused is guilty of that offence but

(*b*) is satisfied that he is guilty of some other offence which is not a scheduled offence, but of which a jury could have found him guilty on a trial for the scheduled offence,

the court may convict him of that other offence.

(5) Where the court trying a scheduled offence convicts the accused of that or some other offence, then, without prejudice to its power apart from this subsection to give a judgment, it shall, at the time of conviction or as soon as practicable thereafter, give a judgment stating the reasons for the conviction.

(6) A person convicted of any offence on a trial under this section without a jury may, notwithstanding anything in [sections 1 and 10(1) of the Criminal Appeal (Northern Ireland) Act 1980 appeal to the Court of Appeal under Part I of that Act] −

(*a*) against his conviction, on any ground, without the leave of the [Court of Appeal] or a certificate of the judge of the court of trial; and

(*b*) against sentence passed on conviction, without that leave, unless the sentence is one fixed by law.

(7) Where a person is so convicted, the time for giving notice of appeal under subsection (1) of [section 16 of that Act of 1980] shall run from the date of judgment, if later than the date from which it would run under that subsection.

Evidence, onus of proof and treatment of convicted young persons

8 Admissions by persons charged with scheduled offences

(1) In any criminal proceedings for a scheduled offence, or two or more offences which are or include scheduled offences, a statement made by the accused may be given in evidence by the prosecution in so far as −

(*a*) it is relevant to any matter in issue in the proceedings; and

(*b*) it is not excluded by the court in pursuance of subsection (2) below.

(2) If, in any such proceedings where the prosecution proposes to give in evidence a statement made by the accused, prima facie evidence is adduced that the accused was subjected to torture or to inhuman or degrading treatment in order to induce him to make the statement, the court shall, unless the prosecution satisfies it that the statement was not so obtained −

(a) exclude the statement, or
(b) if the statement has been received in evidence, either –
  (i) continue the trial disregarding the statement; or
  (ii) direct that the trial shall be restarted before a differently constituted court (before which the statement in question shall be inadmissible).

(3) This section does not apply to a summary trial.

9 Onus of proof in relation to offences of possession

(1) Where a person is charged with possessing a proscribed article in such circumstances as to constitute an offence to which this section applies and it is proved that at the time of the alleged offence –
  (a) he and that article were both present in any premises; or
  (b) the article was in premises of which he was the occupier or which he habitually used otherwise than as a member of the public,

the court may accept the fact proved as sufficient evidence of his possessing (and, if relevant, knowingly possessing) that article at that time unless it is further proved that he did not at that time know of its presence in the premises in question, or, if he did know, that he had no control over it.

(2) This section applies to vessels, aircraft and vehicles as it applies to premises.

(3) In this section 'proscribed article' means an explosive, firearm, ammunition, substance or other thing (being a thing possession of which is an offence under one of the enactments mentioned in subsection (4) below).

(4) This section applies to scheduled offences under the following enactments, that is to say –

The Explosive Substances Act 1883

Section 3, so far as relating to subsection (1)(b) thereof (possessing explosive with intent to endanger life or cause serious damage to property).
Section 4 (possessing explosive in suspicious circumstances).
. . . . .

The Protection of the Person and Property Act (Northern Ireland) 1969

Section 2 (possessing petrol bomb, etc., in suspicious circumstances).

[*The Firearms (Northern Ireland) Order 1981*

Article 3 (possessing firearm or ammunition without, or otherwise than as authorised by, a firearm certificate).

Article 6 (possessing machine gun, or weapon discharging, or ammunition containing, noxious substance).

Article 17 (possessing firearm or ammunition with intent to endanger life or cause serious damage to property).

Article 18(2) (possessing firearm or imitation firearm at time of committing, or being arrested for, a specified offence).

Article 22(1), (2) or (4) (possession of a firearm or ammunition by a person who has been sentenced to imprisonment, etc).

Article 23 (possessing firearm or ammunition in suspicious circumstances).]

(5) This section does not apply to a summary trial.

PART II

POWERS OF ARREST, DETENTION, SEARCH AND SEIZURE, ETC

11 Arrest of terrorists

(1) Any constable may arrest without warrant any person whom he suspects of being a terrorist.

(2) For the purpose of arresting a person under this section a constable may enter and search any premises or other place where that person is or where the constable suspects him of being.

(3) A person arrested under this section shall not be detained in right of the arrest for more than seventy-two hours after his arrest, and [Article 131 of the Magistrates' Courts (Northern Ireland) Order 1981] and section 50(3) of the Children and Young Persons Act (Northern Ireland) 1968 (requirement to bring arrested person before a magistrates' court not later than forty-eight hours after his arrest) shall not apply to any such person.

(4) Where a person is arrested under this section, an officer of the Royal Ulster Constabulary not below the rank of chief inspector may order him to be photographed and to have his finger prints and palm prints taken by a constable, and a constable may use such reasonable force as may be necessary for that purpose.

12 Detention of terrorists, etc

Schedule 1 to this Act shall have effect with respect to the detention of terrorists and persons suspected of being terrorists.

13 Constables' general power of arrest and seizure

(1) Any constable may arrest without warrant any person whom he suspects of committing, having committed or being about to commit a scheduled offence or an offence under this Act which is not a scheduled offence.

(2) For the purposes of arresting a person under this section a constable may enter and search any premises or other place where that person is or where the constable suspects him of being.

(3) A constable may seize anything which he suspects is being, has been or is intended to be used in the commission of a scheduled offence or an offence under this Act which is not a scheduled offence.

14 Powers of arrest of members of Her Majesty's forces

(1) A member of Her Majesty's forces on duty may arrest without warrant, and detain for not more than four hours, a person whom he suspects of committing, having committed or being about to commit any offence.

(2) A person effecting an arrest under this section complies with any rule of law requiring him to state the ground of arrest if he states that he is effecting the arrest as a member of Her Majesty's forces.

(3) For the purpose of arresting a person under this section a member of Her Majesty's forces may enter and search any premises or other place −

    (*a*) where that person is, or

    (*b*) if that person is suspected of being a terrorist or of having committed an offence involving the use or possession of an explosive, explosive substance or firearm, where that person is suspected of being.

15 Power to search for munitions and radio transmitters

(1) Any member of Her Majesty's forces on duty or any constable may enter any premises or other place other than a dwelling-house for the purpose of ascertaining −

    (*a*) whether there are any munitions unlawfully at that place; or

    (*b*) whether there is a transmitter at that place;

and may search the place for any munitions or transmitter with a view to exercising the powers conferred by subsection (4) below.

(2) Any member of Her Majesty's forces on duty authorised by a commissioned officer of those forces or any constable authorised by an officer of the Royal Ulster Constabulary not below the rank of chief inspector may enter any dwelling-house in which it is suspected that there are unlawfully any munitions or that there is a transmitter and may search it for any munitions or transmitter with a view to exercising the said powers.

(3) Any member of Her Majesty's forces on duty or any constable may –

(a) stop any person in any public place and, with a view to exercising the said powers, search him for the purpose of ascertaining whether he has any munitions unlawfully with him or any transmitter with him; and

(b) with a view to exercising the said powers, search any person not in a public place whom he suspects of having any munitions unlawfully with him or any transmitter with him.

(4) A member of Her Majesty's forces or a constable –

(a) authorised to search any premises or other place or any person under this Act, may seize any munitions found in the course of the search unless it appears to the person so authorised that the munitions are being, have been and will be used only for a lawful purpose and may retain and, if necessary, destroy them;

(b) authorised to search any premises or other place or any person, may seize any transmitter found in the course of the search unless it appears to the person so authorised that the transmitter has been, is being and is likely to be used only lawfully and may retain it.

(5) In this section –
'munitions' means –

(a) explosives, explosive substances, firearms and ammunition; and

(b) anything used or capable of being used in the manufacture of any explosive, explosive substance, firearm or ammunition;

'transmitter' means any apparatus for wireless telegraphy designed or adapted for emission, as opposed to reception, and includes part of any such apparatus;

'wireless telegraphy' has the same meaning as in section 19(1) of the Wireless Telegraphy Act 1949.

17 Entry to search for persons unlawfully detained

(1) Where any person is believed to be unlawfully detained in such circumstances that his life is in danger, any member of Her Majesty's forces on duty or any constable may, subject to subsection (2) below, enter any premises or other place for the purpose of ascertaining whether that person is so detained there.

(2) A dwelling-house may be entered in pursuance of subsection (1) above —

(a) by a member of Her Majesty's forces, only when authorised to do so by a commissioned officer of those forces; and

(b) by a constable, only when authorised to do so by an officer of the Royal Ulster Constabulary not below the rank of chief inspector.

18 Power to stop and question

(1) Any member of Her Majesty's forces on duty or any constable may stop and question any person for the purpose of ascertaining —

(a) that person's identity and movements;

(b) what he knows concerning any recent explosion or any other incident endangering life or concerning any person killed or injured in any such explosion or incident; or

(c) any one or more of the matters referred to in paragraphs (a) and (b) above.

(2) Any person who —

(a) fails to stop when required to do so under this section, or

(b) refuses to answer, or fails to answer to the best of his knowledge and ability, any question addressed to him under this section,

shall be liable on summary conviction to imprisonment for a term not exceeding six months or to a fine not exceeding [level 5 on the standard scale], or both.

19 General powers of entry and interference with rights of property and with highways

(1) Any member of Her Majesty's forces on duty or any constable may enter any premises or other place —

(a) if he considers it necessary to do so in the course of operations for the preservation of the peace or the maintenance of order; or

(b) if authorised to do so by or on behalf of the Secretary of State.

(2) Any member of Her Majesty's forces on duty, any constable or

any person specifically authorised to do so by or on behalf of the Secretary of State may, if authorised to do so by or on behalf of the Secretary of State —

    (*a*) take possession of any land or other property;

    (*b*) take steps to place buildings or other structures in a state of defence;

    (*c*) detain any property or cause it to be destroyed or moved;

    (*d*) do any other act interfering with any public right or with any private rights of property, including carrying out any works on any land of which possession has been taken under this subsection.

(3) Any member of Her Majesty's forces on duty, any constable or any person specifically authorised to do so by or on behalf of the Secretary of State may, so far as he considers it immediately necessary for the preservation of the peace or the maintenance of order —

    (*a*) wholly or partly close a highway or divert or otherwise interfere with a highway or the use of a highway; or

    (*b*) prohibit or restrict the exercise of any right of way or the use of any waterway.

(4) Any person who, without lawful authority or reasonable excuse (the proof of which lies on him), interferes with works executed, or any apparatus, equipment or any other thing used, in or in connection with the exercise of powers conferred by this section, shall be liable on summary conviction to imprisonment for a term not exceeding six months or to a fine not exceeding [level 5 on the standard scale], or both.

(5) Any authorisation to exercise any powers under any provision of this section may authorise the exercise of all those powers, or powers of any class or a particular power specified, either by all persons by whom they are capable of being exercised or by persons of any class or a particular person specified.

20 Supplementary provisions

(1) Any power conferred by this Part of this Act —

    (*a*) to enter any premises or other place includes power to enter any vessel, aircraft or vehicle;

    (*b*) to search any premises or other place includes power to stop and search any container;

and in this Part of this Act references to any premises or place shall be construed accordingly.

(2) In this Part of this Act references to a dwelling-house include

references to a vessel or vehicle which is habitually stationary and used as a dwelling.

(3) Any power conferred by this Part of this Act to enter any place, vessel, aircraft or vehicle shall be exercisable, if need be, by force.

(4) Any power conferred by virtue of this section to search a vehicle or vessel shall, in the case of a vehicle or vessel which cannot be conveniently or thoroughly searched at the place where it is, include power to take it or cause it to be taken to any place for the purpose of carrying out the search.

(5) Any power conferred by virtue of this section to search any vessel, aircraft, vehicle or container includes power to examine it.

(6) Any power conferred by this Part of this Act to stop any person includes power to stop a vessel or vehicle or an aircraft which is not airborne.

(7) Any person who, when required by virtue of this section to stop a vessel or vehicle or any aircraft which is not airborne, fails to do so shall be liable on summary conviction to imprisonment to a term not exceeding six months or to a fine not exceeding [level 5 on the standard scale], or both.

(8) A member of Her Majesty's forces exercising any power conferred by this Part of this Act when he is not in uniform shall, if so requested by any person at or about the time of exercising that power, produce to that person documentary evidence that he is such a member.

(9) The Documentary Evidence Act 1868 shall apply to any authorisation given in writing under this Part of this Act by or on behalf of the Secretary of State as it applies to any order made by him.

PART III

OFFENCES AGAINST PUBLIC SECURITY AND PUBLIC ORDER

21 Proscribed organisations

(1) Subject to subsection (7) below, any person who –

(a) belongs or professes to belong to a proscribed organisation; or

(b) solicits or invites financial or other support for a proscribed organisation, or knowingly makes or receives any contribution in money or otherwise to the resources of a proscribed organisation; or

(c) solicits or invites any person to become a member of a proscribed organisation or to carry out on behalf of a proscribed

> organisation orders or directions given, or requests made, by a member of that organisation,

shall be liable on summary conviction to imprisonment for a term not exceeding six months or to a fine not exceeding [level 5 on the standard scale], or both, and on conviction on indictment to imprisonment for a term not exceeding ten years or to a fine, or both.

(2) The court by or before which a person in convicted of an offence under this section may order the forfeiture of any money or other property which at the time of the offence he had in his possession or under his control for the use or benefit of the proscribed organisation.

(3) The organisations specified in Schedule 2 to this Act are proscribed organisations for the purposes of this section; and any organisation which passes under a name mentioned in that Schedule shall be treated as proscribed, whatever relationship (if any) it has to any other organisation of the same name.

(4) The Secretary of State may by order add to Schedule 2 to this Act any organisation that appears to him to be concerned in terrorism or in promoting or encouraging it.

(5) The Secretary of State may also by order remove an organisation from Schedule 2 to this Act.

(6) The possession by a person of a document –

(*a*) addressed to him as a member of a proscribed organisation; or

(*b*) relating or purporting to relate to the affairs of a proscribed organisation; or

(*c*) emanating or purporting to emanate from a proscribed organisation or officer of a proscribed organisation,

shall be evidence of that person belonging to the organisation at the time when he had the document in his possession.

(7) A person belonging to a proscribed organisation shall –

(*a*) if the organisation is a proscribed organisation by virtue of an order under subsection (4) above; or

(*b*) if this section has ceased to be in force but has been subsequently brought into force by an order under section 33(3) below,

not be guilty of an offence under this section by reason of belonging to the organisation if he has not after the coming into force of the order under subsection (4) above or the coming into force again of this section, as the case may be, taken part in any activities of the organisation.

(8) Subsection (7) above shall apply in relation to a person belonging to the Red Hand Commando, the Ulster Freedom Fighters or the Ulster

Volunteer Force as if the organisation were proscribed by virtue of an order under subsection (4) above with the substitution, in subsection (7), for the reference to the coming into force of such an order of a reference —

   (*a*) as respects a person belonging to the Red Hand Commando or the Ulster Freedom Fighters, to 12th November 1973;
   (*b*) as respects a person belonging to the Ulster Volunteer Force, to 4th October 1975.

22 Unlawful collection, etc of information

   (1) No person shall, without lawful authority or reasonable excuse (the proof of which lies on him) —

   (*a*) collect, record, publish, communicate or attempt to elicit any information with respect to any person to whom this paragraph applies which is of such a nature as is likely to be useful to terrorists;
   (*b*) collect or record any information which is of such a nature as is likely to be useful to terrorists in planning or carrying out any act of violence; or
   (*c*) have in his possession any record of or document containing any such information as is mentioned in paragraph (*a*) or (*b*) above.

   (2) Subsection (1)(*a*) above applies to any of the following persons, that is to say —

   (*a*) any constable or member of Her Majesty's forces;
   (*b*) any person holding judicial office;
   (*c*) any officer of any court; and
   (*d*) any person employed for the whole of his time in the prison service in Northern Ireland.

   (3) In subsection (1) above any reference to recording information includes a reference to recording it by means of photography or by any other means.

   (4) If any person contravenes this section, he shall be liable —

   (*a*) on summary conviction, to imprisonment for a term not exceeding six months or to a fine not exceeding [level 5 on the standard scale], or both;
   (*b*) on conviction on indictment, to imprisonment for a term not exceeding ten years or a fine, or both.

   (5) The court by or before which a person is convicted of an offence under this section may order the forfeiture of any record or document

mentioned in subsection (1) above which is found in his possession.

(6) Without prejudice to section 33 of the Interpretation Act 1889 (offences under two or more laws), nothing in this section shall derogate from the operation of the Official Secrets Acts 1911 and 1920.

23 Training in making or use of firearms, explosives or explosive substances

(1) Subject to subsection (2) below, any person who instructs or trains another or receives instruction or training in the making or use of firearms, explosives or explosive substances shall be liable −

  (*a*) on summary conviction, to imprisonment for a term not exceeding six months or to a fine not exceeding [level 5 on the standard scale], or both;

  (*b*) on conviction on indictment, to imprisonment for a term not exceeding ten years or to a fine, or both.

(2) In any prosecution for an offence under this section it shall be a defence for the person charged to prove that the instruction or training was given or received with lawful authority or for industrial, agricultural or sporting purposes only or otherwise with good reason.

(3) The court by or before which a person is convicted of an offence under this section may order the forfeiture of any thing which appears to the court to have been in his possession for purposes connected with the offence.

(4) Without prejudice to section 33 of the Interpretation Act 1889 (offences under two or more laws), nothing in this section shall derogate from the operation of the Unlawful Drilling Act 1819.

24 Failure to disperse when required to do so

(1) Where any commissioned officer of Her Majesty's forces or any officer of the Royal Ulster Constabulary not below the rank of chief inspector is of opinion that any assembly of three or more persons −

  (*a*) may lead to a breach of the peace or public disorder; or

  (*b*) may make undue demands on the police or Her Majesty's forces,

he, or any member of those forces on duty or any constable, may order the persons constituting the assembly to disperse forthwith.

(2) Where an order is given under this section with respect to an assembly, any person who thereafter joins or remains in the assembly or otherwise fails to comply with the order shall be liable on summary

conviction to imprisonment for a term not exceeding six months or to a fine not exceeding [level 5 on the standard scale], or both.

25 Dressing or behaving in a public place like a member of a proscribed organisation

Any person who in a public place dresses or behaves in such a way as to arouse reasonable apprehension that he is a member of a proscribed organisation shall be liable on summary conviction to imprisonment for a term not exceeding six months or to a fine not exceeding [level 5 on the standard scale], or both.

26 Wearing of hoods, etc in public places

Any person who, without lawful authority or reasonable excuse (the proof of which lies on him), wears in a public place or in the curtilage of a dwelling-house (other than one in which he is residing) any hood, mask or other article whatsoever made, adapted or used for concealing the identity or features shall be liable on summary conviction to imprisonment for a term not exceeding six months or to a fine not exceeding [level 5 on the standard scale], or both.

PART IV

MISCELLANEOUS AND GENERAL

27 Supplementary regulations for preserving the peace, etc

(1) The Secretary of State may by regulations make provision additional to the foregoing provisions of this Act for promoting the preservation of the peace and the maintenance of order.

(2) Any person contravening or failing to comply with the provisions of any regulations under this section or any instrument or directions under any such regulations shall be liable on summary conviction to imprisonment for a term not exceeding six months or to a fine not exceeding [level 5 on the standard scale], or both.

(3) The regulations contained in Schedule 3 to this Act shall be deemed to have been made under this section and to have been approved in draft by each House of Parliament, and may be varied or revoked accordingly.

29 Restriction of prosecutions

(1) A prosecution shall not be instituted in respect of any offence under this Act except by or with the consent of the Director of Public Prosecutions for Northern Ireland.

(2) ...

30 The scheduled offences

(1) In this Act 'scheduled offence' means an offence specified in Part I or Part III of Schedule 4 to this Act, subject, however, to any relevant note contained in the said Part I.

(2) Part II of that Schedule shall have effect with respect to offences related to those specified in Part I of that Schedule.

(3) The Secretary of State may by order amend Parts I and II of that Schedule (whether by adding an offence to, or removing an offence from, either of those Parts, or otherwise).

31 Interpretation

(1) In this Act, except so far as the context otherwise requires –

'constable' includes any member of the Royal Naval, Military or Air Force Police;

'dwelling-house' means any building or part of a building used as a dwelling;

'enactment' includes an enactment of the Parliament of Northern Ireland and a Measure of the Northern Ireland Assembly;

'explosive' means any article or substance manufactured for the purpose of producing a practical effect by explosion;

'explosive substance' means any substance for the time being specified in regulations made under section 3 of the Explosives Act (Northern Ireland) 1970;

'firearm' includes an air gun or air pistol;

'proscribed organisation' means an organisation for the time being specified in Schedule 2 to this Act, including an organisation which is to be treated as a proscribed organisation by virtue of section 21(3) above;

'public place' means a place to which for the time being members of the public have or are permitted to have access, whether on payment or otherwise;

'scheduled offence' has the meaning ascribed to it by section 30 above;

'terrorism' means the use of violence for political ends and includes any use of violence for the purpose of putting the public or any section of the public in fear;

'terrorist' means a person who is or has been concerned in the commission or attempted commission of any act of terrorism or in directing, organising or training persons for the purpose of terrorism;

'vehicle' includes a hovercraft.

(2) Any reference in this Act, except so far as the context otherwise requires, to an enactment shall be construed as a reference to that enactment as amended, applied or extended by or under any other enactment, including this Act.

(3) It is hereby declared that in applying section 38(1) of the Interpretation Act 1889 (effect of repeal and re-enactment) for the construction of references in this Act to other Acts or enactments, account is to be taken of repeal and re-enactment by a Measure of the Northern Ireland Assembly or an Order in Council.

32 Orders and regulations

(1) Any power to make orders or regulations conferred by this Act (except the powers to make orders conferred by Schedules 1 and 3 to this Act) shall be exercisable by statutory instrument.

(2) Any power to make an order under any provision of this Act shall include power to vary or revoke any order under that provision.

(3) No order or regulations under this Act (except an order under either of those Schedules) shall be made unless –

(a) a draft of the order or regulations has been approved by resolution of each House of Parliament; or

(b) it is declared in the order or regulations that it appears to the Secretary of State that by reason of urgency it is necessary to make the order or regulations without a draft having been so approved.

(4) Orders and regulations under this Act (except an order under either of those Schedules and except an order or regulations of which a draft has been so approved) shall be laid before Parliament after being made and, if at the end of the period of 40 days (computed in accordance with section 7(1) of the Statutory Instruments Act 1946) after the day on which the Secretary of State made an order or regulations a resolution has not been passed by each House approving the order or regulations in question, the order or regulations shall then cease to have effect

(but without prejudice to anything previously done or to the making of a new order or new regulations).

33 Commencement, duration, expiry and revival of provisions of this Act

(1) This Act (except section 32 above and this section) shall come into operation on 1st June 1978.

(2) The provisions of this Act, except sections 5 and 28 to 36, Part III of Schedule 4 and Schedules 5 and 6 to this Act and, so far as they relate to offences which are scheduled offences by virtue of the said Part III, sections 2, 6 and 7 above, shall expire with 24th July 1978 unless continued in force by an order under this section.

(3) The Secretary of State may by order provide −

- (*a*) that all or any of the said provisions which are for the time being in force (including any in force by virtue of an order under this section) shall continue in force for a period not exceeding six months from the coming into operation of the order;
- (*b*) that all or any of the said provisions which are for the time being in force shall cease to be in force; or
- (*c*) that all or any of the said provisions which are not for the time being in force shall come into force again and remain in force for a period not exceeding six months from the coming into operation of the order.

(4) The coming into force of any provision of sections 6 and 9 above (otherwise than on the commencement of this Act) shall not affect any trial on indictment where the indictment has been presented, or any summary trial which has started, before the coming into force of that provision, and any such trial shall be conducted as if the provision had not come into force.

(5) Where before the coming into force of subsection (1) of section 6 above (otherwise than on the commencement of this Act), a person has been committed for trial for a scheduled offence and the indictment has not been presented, then, on the coming into force of that subsection, he [shall, if he was committed to the Crown Court sitting elsewhere than in Belfast, be treated as having been committed to the Crown Court sitting in Belfast].

(6) The expiry or cesser of any provision mentioned in subsection (4) above shall not affect the application of that provision to any trial on indictment where the indictment has been presented, or any summary trial which has started, before the expiry or cesser.

(7) It is hereby declared that the expiry or cesser of subsection (2) of section 6 above shall not affect any committal of a person for trial under that subsection to [the Crown Court sitting in Belfast] where the indictment has not been presented.

(8) On the expiry or cesser of any provision of this Act, section 38(2) of the Interpretation Act 1889 (effect of repeals) shall apply as if the provision had been repealed by another Act and, in the case of section 27 above, any regulations made thereunder had been enactments.

35 Transitional provisions, savings and repeals

(1) Neither any rule of law nor any enactment other than this Act nor anything contained in a commission issued for the trial of any person shall be construed as limiting or otherwise affecting the operation of any provision of this Act for the time being in force, but −

- (a) subject to the foregoing, any power conferred by this Act shall not derogate from Her Majesty's prerogative or any powers exercisable apart from this Act by virtue of any rule of law or enactment; and
- (b) subject to the foregoing and to section 33(6) above, a provision of this Act shall not affect the operation of any rule of law or enactment at a time when the provision is not in force.

(2) The transitional provisions and savings contained in Schedule 5 to this Act shall have effect.

(3) Subject to Schedule 5, the enactments specified in Schedule 6 to this Act are hereby repealed to the extent specified in column 3 of that Schedule.

36 Short title and extent

(1) This Act may be cited as the Northern Ireland (Emergency Provisions) Act 1978.

(2) This Act extends to Northern Ireland only.

SCHEDULES

SCHEDULE 1

Section 12

DETENTION OF TERRORISTS

Advisers

1. The Secretary of State shall for the purposes of this Act appoint such number of Advisers as he may determine to advise him on matters concerning the detention and release of terrorists.

2. An Adviser shall be a person who holds or has held judicial office in any part of the United Kingdom or is a barrister, advocate or solicitor, in each case of not less than ten years' standing in any part of the United Kingdom.

3. – (1) An Adviser shall hold and vacate his office in accordance with the terms of his appointment and shall, on ceasing to hold office, be eligible for reappointment.

(2) An Adviser may at any time by notice in writing to the Secretary of State resign his office.

(3) The Secretary of State may pay to the Advisers such remuneration and allowances as he may determine.

Interim Custody Orders

4. – (1) Where it appears to the Secretary of State that there are grounds for suspecting that a person has been concerned –

   (*a*) in the commission or attempted commission of any act of terrorism; or

   (*b*) in directing, organising or training persons for the purpose of terrorism,

the Secretary of State may make an interim custody order for the temporary detention of that person.

(2) An interim custody order shall be signed by the Secretary of State or a Minister of State or Under Secretary of State.

5. – (1) The Secretary of State may, at any time before the expiration of the period of fourteen days following the date of an interim custody order, refer the case to an Adviser and, unless the case is so referred, the order shall cease to have effect at the expiration of that period.

(2) A reference to an Adviser under this paragraph shall be by notice in writing signed on behalf of the Secretary of State and a copy of the notice shall be sent to the person detained.

Reference to an Adviser

6. – (1) As soon as possible after a case is referred to an Adviser under paragraph 5 above, the person detained shall be served with a statement in writing as to the nature of the terrorist activities of which he is suspected.

(2) A person detained may, within seven days following the date on which he receives any such statement as is mentioned in sub-paragraph (1) above, send to the Secretary of State –

(*a*) written representations concerning his case; and

(*b*) a written request that he be seen personally by an Adviser;

and the Secretary of State shall send a copy of such representations or request to the Adviser concerned.

(3) The Secretary of State may pay any reasonable costs or expenses incurred by a person detained in obtaining legal advice or legal assistance in connection with the preparation of any representations he may make concerning his case.

7. – (1) Where the case of a person detained under an interim custody order is referred to an Adviser, he shall consider it and report to the Secretary of State whether or not in his opinion –

(*a*) the person detained has been concerned in terrorist activities; and

(*b*) the detention of that person is necessary for the protection of the public.

(2) In considering any case referred to him an Adviser shall have regard to any information (whether oral or in writing) which is made available to, or obtained by, him and to any representations (whether oral or in writing) made by the person detained.

(3) No person shall be present during the consideration by an Adviser of the case of any person referred to him, except –

(*a*) any person who for the time being is being seen by the Adviser;

(*b*) any assistant to the Adviser; and

(*c*) any person who is present in the interests of security.

(4) The Secretary of State may, at the request of an Adviser, pay any reasonable expenses incurred by any person in connection with a reference to the Adviser.

Detention Orders

8. – (1) After receiving a report made by an Adviser under paragraph

7(1) above, the Secretary of State shall consider the case of the person to whom it relates and, if he is satisfied —

(a) that that person has been concerned in the commission or attempted commission of any act of terrorism, or in directing, organising or training persons for the purpose of terrorism; and

(b) that the detention of that person is necessary for the protection of the public,

the Secretary of State may make a detention order for the detention of that person.

(2) If, on considering any case under sub-paragraph (1) above, the Secretary of State is not satisfied as mentioned in that sub-paragraph, he shall direct the release of the person concerned.

(3) Subject to sub-paragraphs (4) and (5) below, where —

(a) a person is detained under an interim custody order; and

(b) a detention order is not made in respect of that person within the period of seven weeks following the date of the interim custody order,

the interim custody order shall cease to have effect.

(4) The Secretary of State may, where a person is required to be detained under an interim custody order, give a direction in writing extending the period of seven weeks mentioned in sub-paragraph (3) above (or that period as extended under this sub-paragraph) for a further period of one week if it is stated in the direction that the report of the Adviser in relation to that person's case has not been received before the sixth day immediately preceding the day on which the interim custody order would, but for the direction, cease to have effect.

(5) Not more than three directions under sub-paragraph (4) above shall be given in respect of any one interim custody order.

(6) A detention order shall be signed by the Secretary of State, and a direction under sub-paragraph (4) above shall be signed by the Secretary of State or a Minister of State or Under Secretary of State.

Supplemental

9. – (1) The Secretary of State may at any time refer the case of a person detained under a detention order to an Adviser and, if so requested in writing in accordance with sub-paragraph (2) below by a person so detained, shall do so within fourteen days beginning with the receipt of the request.

(2) A person detained under a detention order shall not be entitled

to make a request for the purposes of sub-paragraph (1) above —

> (*a*) before the expiration of the period of one year beginning with the date of the detention order; or
>
> (*b*) within a period of six months from the date of the last notification under sub-paragraph (5) below.

(3) On any reference under this paragraph, an Adviser shall consider the case and report to the Secretary of State whether or not the person's continued detention is necessary for the protection of the public.

(4) Paragraphs 6(3) and 7(2) to (4) above shall apply for the purposes of a reference under this paragraph as they apply for the purposes of a reference under paragraph 5 above.

(5) Where a case is referred to an Adviser in consequence of a request made in accordance with this paragraph, the Secretary of State shall, after receiving the report of the Adviser, reconsider the case of the person to whom it relates and, if he decides not to release that person, shall notify him of his decision.

(6) A notification under sub-paragraph (5) above shall be by notice in writing and signed by the Secretary of State.

10. — (1) The Secretary of State may, as respects a person detained under an interim custody order —

> (*a*) direct his discharge unconditionally; or
>
> (*b*) direct his release (whether or not subject to conditions) for a specified period.

(2) The Secretary of State may, as respects a person detained under a detention order, —

> (*a*) direct his discharge unconditionally; or
>
> (*b*) direct his release subject to conditions or for a specified period, or both.

(3) The Secretary of State may recall to detention a person released under sub-paragraph (1)(*b*) or (2)(*b*) above and a person so recalled may be detained under the original interim custody or detention order, as the case may be.

(4) Where a person is released under sub-paragraph (1)(*b*) above, any period during which he is not in detention shall be left out of account for the purposes of paragraphs 5(1), 6(2) and 8(3) above.

11. — (1) A person required to be detained under an interim custody order or a detention order may be detained in a prison or in some other place approved for the purposes of this paragraph by the Secretary of State.

(2) A person for the time being having custody of a person required

to be detained as aforesaid shall have all the powers, authorities, protection and privileges of a constable.

(3) Subject to any directions of the Secretary of State, a person required to be detained as aforesaid shall be treated as nearly as may be as if he were a prisoner detained in a prison on remand and any power of temporary removal for judicial, medical or other purposes shall apply accordingly.

(4) A person required to be detained as aforesaid who is unlawfully at large may be arrested without warrant by any constable or any member of Her Majesty's forces on duty.

12. Where a person required to be detained under an interim custody order is unlawfully at large, the interim custody order shall not cease to have effect under paragraph 5 or 8 above while he remains at large; and, upon his being taken again into custody, those paragraphs shall have effect as if the date of the interim custody order were that of his being taken again into custody.

13. Any person who –

    (*a*) being detained under an interim custody order or detention order, escapes;

    (*b*) rescues any person detained as aforesaid, or assists a person so detained in escaping or attempting to escape;

    (*c*) fails to return to detention at the expiration of a period for which he was released under paragraph 10(1)(*b*) or (2)(*b*) above; or

    (*d*) knowingly harbours any person required to be detained under an interim custody order or detention order, or gives him any assistance with intent to prevent, hinder or interfere with his being taken into custody,

shall be liable on conviction on indictment to imprisonment for a term not exceeding five years or to a fine, or to both.

14. –(1) Any document purporting to be an order, notice or direction made or given by the Secretary of State for the purposes of this Schedule and to be signed in accordance with this Schedule shall be received in evidence and shall, until the contrary is proved, be deemed to be duly made or given and signed.

(2) Prima facie evidence of any such order, notice or direction may, in any legal proceedings, be given by the production of a document bearing a certificate purporting to be signed by or on behalf of the Secretary of State and stating that the document is a true copy of the order, notice or direction; and the certificate shall be received in evidence, and shall, until the contrary is proved, be deemed to be duly made and signed.

15. The Secretary of State may make such payments to persons released or about to be released from detention under this Schedule as he may, with the consent of the Treasury, determine.

SCHEDULE 2

Section 21

Proscribed Organisations

The Irish Republican Army.
Cumann na mBan.
Fianna na hEireann.
The Red Hand Commando.
Saor Eire.
The Ulster Freedom Fighters.
The Ulster Volunteer Force.
[The Irish National Liberation Army.]

SCHEDULE 3

Section 27

The Northern Ireland (Emergency Provisions) Regulations 1978

Title

1. These regulations may be cited as the Northern Ireland (Emergency Provisions) Regulations 1978.

Road Traffic

2. The Secretary of State may by order prohibit, restrict or regulate in any area the use of vehicles or any class of vehicles on highways or the use by vehicles or any class of vehicles of roads or classes of roads specified in the order, either generally or in such circumstances as may be so specified.

Railways

3. The Secretary of State, or any officer of the Royal Ulster Constabulary not below the rank of assistant chief constable, may direct any person having the management of a railway to secure that any train specified in the direction or trains of any class so specified shall stop, or shall not stop, at a station or other place so specified.

Funerals

4. Where it appears to an officer of the Royal Ulster Constabulary not below the rank of chief inspector that a funeral may –

(a) occasion a breach of the peace or serious public disorder, or

(b) cause undue demands to be made on Her Majesty's forces or the police,

he may give directions imposing on the persons organising or taking part in the funeral such conditions as appear to him to be necessary for the preservation of public order including (without prejudice to the generality of the foregoing) conditions –

(i) prescribing the route to be taken by the funeral;

(ii) prohibiting the funeral from entering any place specified in the directions;

(iii) requiring persons taking part in the funeral to travel in vehicles.

Closing of licensed premises, clubs, etc.

5. The Secretary of State may by order required that premises licensed under the Licensing Act (Northern Ireland) 1971, premises registered under the Registration of Clubs Act (Northern Ireland) 1967 or any place of entertainment or public resort –

(a) shall be closed and remain closed, either for an indefinite period or for a period, or until an event, specified in the order, or

(b) shall be closed at a particular time either on all days or on any day so specified.

SCHEDULE 4

Section 30

The Scheduled Offences

Part I
Substantive Offences

Common law offences

1. Murder, subject to note 1 below.
2. Manslaughter, subject to note 1 below.
3. The common law offence of riot.
4. Kidnapping [, subject to note 1 below].
5. False imprisonment [,subject to note 1 below].
6. Assault occasioning actual bodily harm, subject to note 1 below.

Malicious Damage Act 1861

7. Offences under section 35 of the Malicious Damage Act 1861 (interference with railway) [, subject to note 2 below].

Offences against the Person Act 1861

8. Offences under the following provisions of the Offences against the Person Act 1861, subject as mentioned below, −
    (a) section 4 (conspiracy, etc. to murder) subject to note 2 below;
    (b) section 16 (threats to kill) subject to note 2 below;
    (c) section 18 (wounding with intent to cause grievous bodily harm) subject to note 2 below;
    (d) section 20 (causing grievous bodily harm) subject to note 2 below;
    (e) section 28 (causing grievous bodily harm by explosives);
    (f) section 29 (causing explosion or sending explosive substance or throwing corrosive liquid with intent to cause grievous bodily harm);
    (g) section 30 (placing explosive near building or ship with intent to do bodily injury).

Explosive Substances Act 1883

9. Offences under the following provisions of the Explosive Substances Act 1883−
    (a) section 2 (causing explosion likely to endanger life or damage property);
    (b) section 3 (attempting to cause any such explosion, and making or possessing explosives with intent to endanger life or cause serious damage to property);
    (c) section 4 (making or possessing explosives in suspicious circumstances).

Prison Act (Northern Ireland) 1953

10. Offences under the following provisions of the Prison Act (Northern Ireland) 1953, subject to note 2 below, −
    (a) section 25 (being unlawfully at large while under sentence);
    (b) section 26 (escaping from lawful custody and failing to surrender to bail);
    (c) section 27 (attempting to break prison);
    (d) section 28 (breaking prison by force or violence);
    (e) section 29 (rescuing or assisting or permitting to escape from lawful custody persons under sentence of death or life imprisonment);

(*f*) section 30 (rescuing or assisting or permitting to escape from lawful custody persons other than persons under sentence of death or life imprisonment);

(*g*) section 32 (causing discharge of prisoner under pretended authority);

(*h*) section 33 (assisting prisoners to escape by conveying things into prisons).

Firearms Act (Northern Ireland) 1969

11. ...

Theft Act (Northern Ireland) 1969

12. Offences under the following provisions of the Theft Act (Northern Ireland) 1969, subject to *note 4* below, –

(*a*) section 8 (robbery);

(*b*) section 10 (aggravated burglary).

Protection of the Person and Property Act (Northern Ireland) 1969

13. Offences under the following provisions of the Protection of the Person and Property Act (Northern Ireland) 1969 –

(*a*) section 1 (intimidation) [, subject to note 2 below];

(*b*) section 2 (making or possessing petrol bomb, etc. in suspicious circumstances);

(*c*) section 3 (throwing or using petrol bomb, etc.).

Hijacking

14. Offences under section 1 of [the Aviation Security Act 1982] (aircraft).

15. Offences in Northern Ireland under section 2 of the Criminal Jurisdiction Act 1975 (vehicles and ships).

[Prevention of Terrorism (Temporary Provisions) Act 1984]

16. Offences under the following provisions of the [Prevention of Terrorism (Temporary Provisions) Act 1984] –

(*a*) section 9 (breach of exclusion orders);

(*b*) section 10 (contributions towards acts of terrorism);

(*c*) section 11 (information about acts of terrorism).

Criminal Damage (Northern Ireland) Order 1977

17. Offences under the following provisions of the Criminal Damage (Northern Ireland) Order 1977, subject to note 2 below –

(a) Article 3(1) and (3) or Article 3(2) and (3) (arson);
(b) Article 3(2) (destroying or damaging property with intent to endanger life);
(c) Article 4 (threats to destroy or damage property);
(d) Article 5 (possessing anything with intent to destroy or damage property).

Criminal Law (Amendment) (Northern Ireland) Order 1977

18. Offences under Article 3 of the Criminal Law (Amendment) (Northern Ireland) Order 1977 (bomb hoaxes), subject to note 2 below.

This Act

19. Offences under the following provisions of this Act—

(a) section 21;
(b) section 22;
(c) section 23;
(d) paragraph 13 of Schedule 1.

[The Firearms (Northern Ireland) Order 1981

19A. Offences under the following provisions of the Firearms (Northern Ireland) Order 1981—

(a) Article 3(1) (possessing, purchasing or acquiring firearm or ammunition without certificate) [, subject to note 2 below];
(b) Article 4(1), (2), (3) or (4) (manufacturing, dealing in, repairing, etc, firearm or ammunition without being registered) [, subject to note 2 below];
(c) Article 5 (shortening barrel of shot gun or converting imitation firearm into firearm) [, subject to note 2 below];
(d) Article 6(1) (manufacturing, dealing in or possessing machine gun, or weapon discharging, or ammunition containing, noxious substance) [, subject to note 2 below];
(e) Article 17 (possessing firearm or ammunition with intent to endanger life or cause serious damage to property);
(f) Article 18 (use or attempted use of firearm or imitation firearm to prevent arrest of self or another, etc);
(g) Article 19 (carrying firearm or imitation firearm with intent to commit indictable offence or prevent arrest of self or another);
(h) Article 20(1) (carrying firearm, etc, in public place) [, subject to notes 2 and 3 below];
(i) Article 22 (possession of firearm or ammunition by person who has been sentenced to imprisonment, etc, and sale of

firearm or ammunition to such a person) [, subject to note 2 below];

(*j*) Article 23 (possessing firearm or ammunition in suspicious circumstances).]

[*Taking of Hostages Act 1982*

19A. Offences under the Taking of Hostages Act 1982.]

NOTES

1. Murder, manslaughter [, kidnapping, false imprisonment] or an assault occasioning actual bodily harm is not a scheduled offence in any particular case in which the Attorney General for Northern Ireland certifies that it is not to be treated as a scheduled offence.

[2. An offence under—

(*a*) section 35 of the Malicious Damage Act 1861; or

(*b*) section 4, 16, 18 or 20 of the Offences Against the Person Act 1861; or

(*c*) section 25, 26, 27, 28, 29, 30, 32 or 33 of the Prison Act (Northern Ireland) 1953; or

(*d*) section 1 of the Protection of the Person and Property Act (Northern Ireland) 1969; or

(*e*) Article 3, 4 or 5 of the Criminal Damage (Northern Ireland) Order 1977; or

(*f*) Article 3 of the Criminal Law (Amendment) (Northern Ireland) Order 1977; or

(*g*) Article 3, 4, 5, 6, 20 or 22 of the Firearms (Northern Ireland) Order 1981,

is not a scheduled offence in any particular case in which the Attorney General for Northern Ireland certifies that it is not be treated as a scheduled offence.]

3. An offence under [article 20(1) of the Firearms (Northern Ireland) Order 1981] is a scheduled offence only where it is charged that the offence relates to a weapon other than an air weapon.

4. *Robbery and aggravated burglary are scheduled offences only where it is charged that an explosive, firearm, imitation firearm or weapon of offence was used to commit the offence; and expressions defined in section 10 of the Theft Act (Northern Ireland) 1969 have the same meaning when used in this note.*

PART II

INCHOATE AND RELATED OFFENCES

20. Each of the following offences, that is to say—

(*a*) aiding, abetting, counselling, procuring or inciting the commission of an offence specified in Part I of this Schedule (hereafter in this paragraph referred to as a 'substantive offence');

(*b*) attempting or conspiring to commit a substantive offence;

(*c*) an offence under section 4 of the Criminal Law Act (Northern Ireland) 1967 of doing any act with intent to impede the arrest or prosecution of a person who has committed a substantive offence;

(*d*) an offence under section 5(1) of the Criminal Law Act (Northern Ireland) 1967 of failing to give information to a constable which is likely to secure, or to be of material assistance in securing the apprehension, prosecution or conviction of a person for a substantive offence,

shall be treated for the purposes of this Act as if it were the substantive offence.

PART III

EXTRA-TERRITORIAL OFFENCES

21. Any extra-territorial offence as defined in section 1 of the Criminal Jurisdiction Act 1975.

SCHEDULE 5

Section 35(2)

TRANSITIONAL PROVISIONS AND SAVINGS

1. —(1) Subject to sub-paragraph (4) below, any instrument made, any direction or authorisation given or any other thing done under any enactment repealed by this Act or any order, rules or regulations made under any such enactment shall, so far as it could have been made, given or done under any provision of this Act have effect as if it had been made, given or done under that provision.

(2) The Northern Ireland (Emergency Provisions) Regulations 1973 (set out in Schedule 3 to the Northern Ireland (Emergency Provisions) Act 1973) are an enactment repealed by this Act and, accordingly, the reference in sub-paragraph (1) above to anything done under an enact-

ment repealed by this Act includes a reference to anything done under those Regulations.

(3) In sub-paragraph (1) above, references (however expressed) to things done under an enactment repealed by this Act shall be construed, in relation to the Northern Ireland (Emergency Provisions) Act 1973, as including references to things which, by virtue of section 31(5) of that Act, fell to be treated as if done under that Act.

(4) Sub-paragraph (1) above shall not be construed as saving the provisions specified in Part II of Schedule 6 to this Act.

2. Any enactment, instrument or document referring to any enactment repealed by this Act shall, so far as may be necessary for preserving its effect, be construed as referring, or as including a reference, to the corresponding provision of this Act.

3. Nothing in this Act shall affect the enactments repealed by Parts I and II of Schedule 6 to this Act in their operation in relation to offences committed before the commencement of this Act.

4. ...

5. −(1) Paragraph 14 of Schedule 1 to this Act shall have effect in relation to a document purporting to be an order, notice or direction made or given by the Secretary of State for the purposes of Schedule 1 to the Northern Ireland (Emergency Provisions) Act 1973 or Part I of Schedule 1 to the 1975 Act and to be signed in accordance with the said Schedule or Part as it has effect in relation to a document referred to in that paragraph.

(2) In this paragraph 'the 1975 Act' means the Northern Ireland (Emergency Provisions) (Amendment) Act 1975.

6. Nothing in the foregoing paragraphs shall be construed as affecting the operation of section 38 of the Interpretation Act 1889 (effect of repeals).

SCHEDULE 6

ENACTMENT REPEALED

PART I

ACTS, ETC

Chapter or Number	Short Title	Extent of Repeal
1973 c 53	The Northern Ireland (Emergency Provisions) Act 1973	Sections 2 to 4 and 6 to 8. Sections 10 to 8. Section 19(1) to (7). Sections 20 and 21. Sections 23 to 27. In section 28(1),the definitions, except that of 'enactment'. Section 29. In section 30, subsections (1) to (3), in subsections (4) and (5), the words 'whether' and 'or subsequently' and subsections (6) and (7). In section 31, subsections (2), (3) and (5) and in subsection (7), the words 'for the time being in force', paragraph (*b*) and the word 'and' preceding it. Schedules 2 to 5.
1974 c 33	The Northern Ireland (Young Persons) Act 1974	The whole Act.
1975 c 59	The Criminal Jurisdiction Act 1975	In section 4(1), the words from the beginning to 'and'. In Schedule 2, paragraphs 1, 2(1) and 3.
1975 c 62	The Northern Ireland (Emergency Provisions) (Amendent) Act 1975	Sections 2 to 5. Section 6(1) and (2)(*a*). Section 8. Section 9(1) and (3) Sections 10 to 13. In section 14, the words from the beginning to 'and accordingly'. Sections 15 to 19. Sections 21 and 22. Section 23(2). In Schedule 1, Part I. Schedules 2 and 3.
1976 c 8	The Prevention of Terrorism (Temporary Provisions) Act 1976	In Schedule 3, in paragraph 8, the words from 'and accordingly' onwards.
SI 1977 No 426 (NI 4)	The Criminal Damage (Northern Ireland) Order 1977	Article 13(5).
1977 c 34	The Northern Ireland (Emergency Provisions) (Amendment) Act 1977	The whole Act.

PART II

ORDERS

Number	Short Title	Extent of Repeal
SI 1973 No 1880	The Northern Ireland (Emergency Provisions) Act Proscribed Organisations Order 1973 (Amendment) Order 1973	The whole Order.
SI 1974 No 864	The Northern Ireland (Emergency Provisions) Act 1973 (Amendment) Order 1974	In Article 3, the words from the beginning to 'of the Act)'.
SI 1974 No 1212	The Northern Ireland (Emergency Provisions) Act 1973 (Continuance) Order 1974	The whole Order.
SI 1974 No 2162	The Northern Ireland (Various Emergency Provisions) (Continuance) Order 1974	The whole Order.
SI 1975 No 1059	The Northern Ireland (Various Emergency Provisions) (Continuance) Order 1975	The whole Order.
SI 1975 No 1609	The Northern Ireland (Emergency Provisions) Act 1973 (Amendment) Order 1975	The whole Order.
SI 1975 No 2214	The Northern Ireland (Various Emergency Provisions) (Continuance) (No 2) Order 1975	The whole Order
SI 1976 No 1090	The Northern Ireland (Various Emergency Provisions) (Continuance) Order 1976	The whole Order.
SI 1976 No 2238	The Northern Ireland (Various Emergency Provisions) (Continuance) (No 2) Order 1976	The whole Order.
SI 1977 No 1171	The Northern Ireland (Various Emergency Provisions) (Continuance) Order 1977	The whole Order.
SI 1977 No 1265	The Northern Ireland (Emergency Provisions) Act 1973 (Amendment) Order 1977	The whole Order.
SI 1977 No 2142	The Northern Ireland (Various Emergency Provisions) (Continuance) (No 2) Order 1977	The whole Order.

Appendix II: Extracts From the Northern Ireland (Emergency Provisions) Act 1987 (1987 c. 30)

ARRANGEMENT OF SECTIONS

PART I

AMENDMENTS OF THE NORTHERN IRELAND
(EMERGENCY PROVISIONS) ACT 1987

SECT.

PART II

RIGHTS OF PERSONS DETAINED UNDER TERRORISM PROVISIONS IN POLICE CUSTODY

PART III

REGULATION OF THE PROVISION OF SECURITY SERVICES

PART IV

GENERAL

An Act to amend the Northern Ireland (Emergency Provisions) Act 1978; to confer certain rights on persons detained in police custody in Northern Ireland under or by virtue of Part IV of the Prevention of Terrorism (Temporary Provisions) Act 1984; to regulate the provision of security services there; and for connected purposes.

[15th May 1987]

PART I

AMENDMENTS OF THE NORTHERN IRELAND (EMERGENCY PROVISIONS)
ACT 1978

Limitation of power to grant bail in case of scheduled offences

1. The following section shall be substituted for section 2 of the Northern Ireland (Emergency Provisions) Act 1978 (in this Act referred to
as 'the 1978 Act')—

'Limitation of power to grant bail in case of scheduled offences

2.—(1) Subject to subsection (7) below, a person to whom this section applies shall not be admitted to bail except—

(a) by a judge of the High Court or the Court of Appeal; or
(b) by the judge of the court of trial, on adjourning the trial
of a person charged with a scheduled offence.

(2) A judge may, in his discretion, admit to bail in pursuance of
subsection (1) above a person to whom this section applies except
where he is satisfied that there are substantial grounds for believing
that that person, if released on bail (whether subject to conditions
or not), would—

(a) fail to surrender to custody, or
(b) commit an offence while on bail, or
(c) interfere with any witness, or
(d) otherwise obstruct or attempt to obstruct the course of
justice, whether in relation to himself or in relation to any
other person,

or, if released subject to conditions, would fail to comply with all
or any of those conditions.

(3) In exercising his discretion in accordance with subsection (2)
above in relation to a person, a judge shall have regard to such of
the following considerations as appear to him to be relevant,
namely—

(a) the nature and seriousness of the offence with which the
person is charged,
(b) the character, antecedents, associations and community ties
of the person,
(c) the time which the person has already spent in custody
and the time which he is likely to spend in custody if he
is not admitted to bail, and
(d) the strength of the evidence of his having committed the
offence,

as well as to any others which appear to be relevant.

(4) Without prejudice to any other power to impose conditions on

admission to bail, a judge may impose such conditions on admitting a person to bail under this section as appear to him to be likely to result in that person's appearance at the time and place required, or to be necessary in the interests of justice or for the prevention of crime.

(5) This section applies, subject to subsection (6) below, to any person –

(a) who is charged with a scheduled offence; and
(b) who has attained the age of fourteen.

(6) This section does not apply to a person charged with a scheduled offence–

(a) which is being tried summarily, or
(b) which the Director of Public Prosecutions for Northern Ireland certifies is in his opinion suitable to be tried summarily.

(7) Subsection (1) above shall not preclude a resident magistrate from admitting to bail a person to whom this section applies if–

(a) the person is a serving member of any of Her Majesty's forces or a serving member of the Royal Ulster Constabulary or of the Royal Ulster Constabulary Reserve, and
(b) the resident magistrate is satisfied that suitable arrangements have been made for the person to be held in military or (as the case may be) police custody, and imposes a condition on admitting him to bail that he is to be held in such custody.'

Maximum period of remand in custody in case of scheduled offences

2. The following section shall be inserted after section 3 of the 1978 Act –

'Maximum period of remand in custody in case of scheduled offences

3A. Notwithstanding Article 47(2) and (3) of the Magistrates' Courts (Northern Ireland) Order 1981, the period for which a person charged with a scheduled offence may be remanded in custody by a magistrates' court shall be a period of not more than 28 days beginning with the day following that on which he is so remanded.'

Power of Secretary of State to set time limits in relation to preliminary proceedings for scheduled offences

3. The following section shall be inserted after section 5 of the 1978 Act–

'Time limits on preliminary proceedings

Power of Secretary of State to set time limits in relation to preliminary proceedings for scheduled offences

5A. – (1) The Secretary of State may by regulations make provision, with respect to any specified preliminary stage of proceedings for a scheduled offence, as to the maximum period –

    (a) to be allowed to the prosecution to complete that stage;

    (b) during which the accused may, while awaiting completion of that stage, be –

        (i) in the custody of a magistrates' court; or

        (ii) in the custody of the Crown Court, in relation to that offence.

(2) The regulations may, in particular –

    (a) provide for –

        (i) the Magistrates' Courts (Northern Ireland) Order 1981,

        (ii) section 2 above, or

        (iii) any other enactment, or any rule of law, relating to bail,

to apply in relation to cases to which custody or overall time limits apply subject to such modifications as may be specified (being modifications which the Secretary of State considers necessary in consequence of any provision made by the regulations);

    (b) provide for time limits imposed by the regulations to cease to have effect in cases where, after the institution of proceedings for a scheduled offence, the Attorney General for Northern Ireland has certified that the offence in question is not to be treated as a scheduled offence;

    (c) make such provision with respect to the procedure to be followed in criminal proceedings as the Secretary of State considers appropriate in consequence of any other provision of the regulations; and

    (d) make such transitional provision in relation to proceedings instituted before the commencement of any provision of the regulations as the Secretary of State considers appropriate.

(3) Where separate counts of an indictment allege a scheduled offence and an offence which is not a scheduled offence, then (subject to, and in accordance with, the provisions of the regulations) the regulations shall have effect in relation to the latter offence as if it were a scheduled offence.

(4) The Crown Court may, at any time before the expiry of a time limit imposed by the regulations, extend, or further extend, that limit if it is satisfied —

    (a) that there is good and sufficient cause for doing so; and

    (b) that the prosecution has acted with all due expedition.

(5) Where, in relation to any proceedings for a relevant offence, an overall time limit has expired before the completion of the stage of the proceedings to which the limit applies, the accused shall be treated, for all purposes, as having been acquitted of that offence.

(6) Where —

    (a) a person escapes from the custody of a magistrates' court or of the Crown Court before the expiry of a custody time limit which applies in his case; or

    (b) a person who has been released on bail in consequence of the expiry of a custody time limit —

        (i) fails to surrender himself into the custody of the court at the appointed time; or

        (ii) is arrested by a constable in connection with any breach, or apprehended breach, of any condition of his bail,

the regulations shall, so far as they provide for any custody time limit in relation to the preliminary stage in question, be disregarded.

(7) Where —

    (a) a person escapes from the custody of a magistrates' court or of the Crown Court; or

    (b) a person who has been released on bail fails to surrender himself into the custody of the court at the appointed time,

the overall time limit which applies in his case in relation to the stage which the proceedings have reached at the time of the escape or, as the case may be, at the appointed time shall, so far as the relevant offence in question is concerned, cease to have effect.

(8) Where a person is convicted of a relevant offence in any proceedings, the exercise, in relation to any preliminary stage of those proceedings, of the power conferred by subsection (4) above shall not be called into question on any appeal against that conviction.

(9) In this section —

    ''custody of the Crown Court'' includes custody to which a person is committed in pursuance of —

    (a) Article 37 or 40(4) of the Magistrates' Courts (Northern Ireland) Order 1981 (magistrates' court committing accused for trial); or

   (b) section 51(8) of the Judicature (Northern Ireland) Act 1978 (magistrates'court dealing with a person brought before it following his arrest in pursuance of a warrant issued by the Crown Court);

"custody of a magistrates' court" means custody to which a
p e r s o n
   is committed in pursuance of Article 47 or 49 of the Magistrates' Courts (Northern Ireland) Order 1981 (remand);

"custody time limit" means a time limit imposed by the regulations in pursuance of subsection (1)(b) above or, where any such limit has been extended by the Crown Court under subsection (4) above, the limit as so extended;

"preliminary stage", in relation to any proceedings, does not include any stage of the proceedings after the accused has been arraigned in the Crown Court or, in the case of a summary trial, the magistrates' court has begun to hear evidence for the prosecution at the trial;

"overall time limit" means a time limit imposed by the regulations in pursuance of subsection (1)(a) above or, where any such limit has been extended by the Crown Court under subsection (4) above, the limit as so extended;

"relevant offence" means —

   (a) a scheduled offence, or

   (b) an offence in relation to which the regulations have effect in accordance with subsection (3) above; and

"specified " means specified in the regulations.

   (10) For the purposes of the application of any custody time limit in relation to a person who is in the custody of a magistrates' court or of the Crown Court—

   (a) all periods during which he is in the custody of a magistrates' court in respect of the same offence shall be aggregated and treated as a single continuous period; and

   (b) all periods during which he is the custody of the Crown Court in respect of the same offence shall be aggregated and treated similarly.'

Court for trial of scheduled offences

4. The following section shall be substituted for section 6 of the 1978 Act —

'**Court for trial of scheduled offences**

6.—(1) A trial on indictment of a scheduled offence shall be held only at the Crown Court sitting in Belfast, unless the Lord Chancellor after consultation with the Lord Chief Justice of Northern Ireland directs in any particular case that such a trial shall be held at the Crown Court sitting elsewhere.

(2) A person committed for trial for a scheduled offence, or for two or more offences at least one of which is a scheduled offence, shall be committed—

(a) to the Crown Court sitting in Belfast, or

(b) where the Lord Chancellor has given a direction under subsection (1) above with respect to the trial, to the Crown Court sitting at the place specified in the direction;

and section 48 of the Judicature (Northern Ireland) Act 1978 (committal for trial on indictment) shall have effect accordingly.

(3) Where —

(a) in accordance with subsection (2) above any person is committed for trial to the Crown Court sitting in Belfast, and

(b) a direction is subsequently given by the Lord Chancellor under subsection (1) above altering the place of trial,

that person shall be treated as having been committed for trial to the Crown Court sitting at the place specified in the direction.'

Admissions by persons charged with scheduled offences

5. The following section shall be substituted for section 8 of the 1978 Act —

'**Admissions by persons charged with scheduled offences**

8.—(1) In any criminal proceedings for a scheduled offence, or for two or more offences at least one of which is a scheduled offence, a statement made by the accused may be given in evidence by the prosecution in so far as —

(a) it is relevant to any matter in issue in the proceedings, and

(b) it is not excluded by the court in pursuance of subsection

(2) below or in the exercise of its discretion referred to in subsection (3) below (and has not been rendered inadmissible by virtue of such a direction as is mentioned in subsection (2)(iii) below).

(2) Where in any such proceedings —

(a) the prosecution proposes to give, or (as the case may be) has given, in evidence a statement made by the accused, and

(b) prima facie evidence is adduced that the accused was subject to torture, to inhuman or degrading treatment, or to any violence or threat of violence (whether or not amounting to torture), in order to induce him to make the statement,

then, unless the prosecution satisfies the court that the statement was not obtained by so subjecting the accused in the manner indicated by that evidence, the court shall do one of the following things, namely —

(i) in the case of a statement proposed to be given in evidence, exclude the statement;

(ii) in the case of a statement already received in evidence, continue the trial disregarding the statement; or

(iii) in either case, direct that the trial shall be restarted before a differently constituted court (before which the statement in question shall be inadmissible).

(3) It is hereby declared that, in the case of any statement made by the accused and not obtained by so subjecting him as mentioned in subsection (2)(b) above, the court in any such proceedings as are mentioned in subsection (1) above has a discretion to do one of the things mentioned in subsection (2)(1) to (iii) above if it appears to the court that it is appropriate to do so in order to avoid unfairness to the accused or otherwise in the interests of justice.

(4) This section does not apply to a summary trial.'

Entry and search of premises for purpose of arresting terrorists

6. The following section shall be substituted for section 11 of the 1978 Act —

'**Entry and search of premises for purpose of arresting terrorists**

11. For the purpose of arresting a person under section 12(1)(b) of the Prevention of Terrorism (Temporary Provisions) Act 1984 (arrest of persons suspected of being concerned in acts of terrorism) a constable may enter and search any premises or other place where that person is or where the constable has reasonable grounds for suspecting him to be.'

Power to search for scanning receivers

7.—(1) Section 15 of the 1978 Act (power to search for munitions and radio transmitters) shall be amended as follows.

(2) The following subsection shall be inserted after subsection (4) —

'(4A) The preceding provisions of this section shall have effect in relation to scanning receivers as they have effect in relation to transmitters.'

(3) In subsection (5), after the definition of 'munitions' there shall be inserted —

' ''scanning receiver'' means —

(a) any apparatus for wireless telegraphy designed or adapted for the purpose of automatically monitoring selected frequencies, or automatically scanning a selected range of frequencies, so as to enable transmissions on any of those frequencies to be detected or intercepted; or

(b) part of any such apparatus;'.

Power of Secretary of State to direct the closure etc. of roads

8. The following section shall be inserted after section 19 of the 1978 Act —

'Power of Secretary of State to direct the closure etc. of roads

19A.—(1) The Secretary of State may by order direct —

(a) that any highway specified in the order shall either be wholly closed or be closed to such extent, or diverted in such manner, as may be so specified;

(b) that any highway specified in the order, being a highway which has already been wholly or partly closed, or diverted, in the exercise or purported exercise of any power conferred by or under a relevant enactment, shall continue to be so closed or diverted by virtue of the order.

(2) Any person who, without lawful authority or reasonable excuse (the proof of which lies on him), interferes with—

(a) works executed in connection with the closure or diversion of any highway specified in an order under this section (whether executed in pursuance of any such order or in pursuance of the exercise or purported exercise of any such power as is mentioned in subsection (1)(b) above), or

(b) apparatus, equipment or any other thing used in pursuance of any such order in connection with the closure or diversion of any such highway,

shall be liable on summary conviction to imprisonment for a term not exceeding six months or to a fine not exceeding level 5 on the standard scale, or both.

(3) In this section "relevant enactment" means section 19(2) or (3) above, section 17(2) or (3) of the Northern Ireland (Emergency Provisions) Act 1973, or the Civil Authorities (Special Powers) Act (Northern Ireland) 1922.

(4) Nothing in this section shall prejudice the operation of section 19(2) or (3) above.'

Additional offence relating to proscribed organisations

9. After paragraph (c) of section 21(1) of the 1978 Act (proscribed organisations) there shall be inserted 'or

(d) arranges or assists in the arrangement or management of, or addresses, any meeting of three or more persons (whether or not it is a meeting to which the public are admitted) knowing that the meeting —
  (i) is to support a proscribed organisation;
  (ii) is to further the activities of such an organisation; or
  (iii) is to be addressed by a person belonging or professing to belong to such an organisation,'.

Extension of categories of persons about whom it is unlawful to collect information

10. In section 22(2) of the 1978 Act (unlawful collection etc. of information) —

(a) at the end of paragraph (c) 'and' shall be omitted; and
(b) after paragraph (d) there shall be added '; and
(e) any person who has at any time been a person falling within any of the preceding paragraphs.'

Offences relating to behaviour and dress in public places

11.—(1) The following section shall be substituted for section 25 of the 1978 Act —

'Display of support in public for a proscribed organisation

25. Any person who in a public place —

(a) wears any item of dress; or
(b) wears, carries or displays any article,

in such a way or in such circumstances as to arouse reasonable apprehension that he is a member or supporter of a proscribed organisation, shall be liable —

(i) on summary conviction, to imprisonment for a term not exceeding six months or to a fine not exceeding the statutory maximum, or both;

(ii) on conviction on indictment to imprisonment for a term not exceeding one year or to a fine, or both.'

(2) In section 26 of that Act (wearing of hoods etc. in public places), for the words from 'a fine not exceeding' onwards there shall be substituted 'a fine not exceeding the statutory maximum, or both, and on conviction on indictment to imprisonment for a term not exceeding one year or to a fine, or both.'

(3) After sub-paragraph (c) of paragraph 19 of Schedule 4 to the 1978 Act (scheduled offences) there shall be inserted the following sub-paragraphs –

'(ca) section 25;
(cb) section 26;'

(4) Subsections (2) and (3) above shall not have effect in relation to an offence committed before the commencement of this section.

Expiry and eventual repeal of 1978 Act

13. –(1) Section 33 of the 1978 Act (commencement etc. of that Act) shall be amended as follows –

(2) In subsection (2), for '24th July 1978' there shall be substituted '21st March 1988'.

(3) In subsection (3)(a) and (c), for 'six' there shall be substituted 'twelve'.

(4) After subsection (8) there shall be added the following subsection –

'(9) This Act shall, by virtue of this subsection, be repealed as from the end of the period of five years beginning with the date of the passing of the Northern Ireland (Emergency Provisions) Act 1987.'

(5) The amendment made by subsection (2) above does not affect any provision to which section 33(2) of the 1978 Act applies and which is not in force at the commencement of this section, and accordingly that amendment shall not be taken –

(a) to revive any such provision, or
(b) to preclude the making of an order under section 33 with respect to any such provision.

(6) Where, immediately before the repeal of the 1978 Act takes effect under the provision inserted by subsection (4), a person is held in custody in a prison or other place by virtue of a direction under section 4 of that Act (holding in custody of young persons charged with

scheduled offences), it shall be lawful for him to continue to be held in custody in that prison or place until arrangements can be made for him to be held in custody in accordance with the law then applicable to his case.

(7) Nothing in subsection (6) shall be taken to make lawful the holding in custody of any person who would, disregarding that subsection, be entitled to be released from custody.

(8) The repeal of the 1978 Act shall not affect the application of any provision of sections 6 to 9 of that Act to any trial on indictment where the indictment has been presented, or any summary trial which has started, before the repeal takes effect.

(9) It is hereby declared that the repeal of the 1978 Act shall not affect —

(a) any committal of a person for trial in accordance with section 6 of that Act to the Crown Court sitting either in Belfast or elsewhere, or

(b) any committal of a person for trial which, in accordance with that section, has taken effect as a committal for trial to the Crown Court sitting elsewhere than in Belfast,

in a case where the indictment has not been presented before the repeal takes effect.

(10) The repeal of the 1978 Act shall not affect the application of any provision of sections 28 and 28A of that Act in relation to any right to compensation under section 28 which arises before the date when the repeal takes effect.

PART II

RIGHTS OF PERSONS DETAINED UNDER TERRORISM PROVISIONS IN POLICE CUSTODY

Right to have someone informed of detention under terrorism provisions

14. — (1) A person who is detained under the terrorism provisions and is being held in police custody shall be entitled, if he so requests, to have one friend or relative or other person who is known to him or is likely to take an interest in his welfare told that he is being detained under those provisions and where he is being held in police custody.

(2) A person shall be informed of the right conferred on him by subsection (1) as soon as practicable after he has become a person to whom that subsection applies.

(3) A request made by a person under subsection (1), and the time at which it is made, shall be recorded in writing.

(4) If a person makes such a request, it must be complied with as soon as is practicable except to the extent that any delay is permitted by this section.

(5) Any delay in complying with such a request is only permitted if —

(a) it is authorised by an officer of at least the rank of superintendent; and

(b) it does not extend beyond the end of the period referred to in subsection (6).

(6) That period is —

(a) (except where paragraph (b) applies) the period of 48 hours beginning with the time when the detained person was first detained under the terrorism provisions;

(b) Where the detained person was, prior to the time when he was first so detained, being examined in accordance with any order under section 13 of the Prevention of Terrorism (Temporary Provisions) Act 1984, the period of 48 hours beginning with the time when he was first so examined.

(7) An officer may give an authorisation under subsection (5) orally or in writing but, if he gives it orally, he shall confirm it in writing as soon as is practicable.

(8) An officer may only authorise a delay in complying with a request under subsection (1) where he has reasonable grounds for believing that telling the person named in the request of the detention of the detained person —

(a) will lead to interference with or harm to evidence connected with a scheduled offence or interference with or physical injury to any person; or

(b) will lead to the alerting of any person suspected of having committed such an offence but not yet arrested for it; or

(c) will hinder the recovery of any property obtained as a result of such an offence; or

(d) will lead to interference with the gathering of information about the commission, preparation or instigation of acts of terrorism; or

(e) by alerting any person, will make it more difficult —

(i) to prevent an act of terrorism; or

(ii) to secure the apprehension, prosecution or conviction of any person in connection with the commission, preparation or instigation of an act of terrorism.

(9) If any delay is authorised, then, as soon as is practicable —

    (a) the detained person shall be told the reason for authorising it; and

    (b) the reason shall be recorded in writing.

(10) Any authorisation under subsection (5) shall cease to have effect once the reason for giving it ceases to subsist.

(11) The right conferred by subsection (1) may be exercised by a person to whom that subsection applies on each occasion when he is transferred from one place to another; and this section applies to each subsequent occasion on which that right is so exercised as it applies to the first such occasion.

(12) Subsection (11) shall not be construed as prejudicing the operation of a request by a person to whom subsection (1) applies which was made, but not complied with, before he was transferred.

Right of access to legal advice

15. — (1) A person who is detained under the terrorism provisions and is being held in police custody shall be entitled, if he so requests, to consult a solicitor privately.

(2) A person shall be informed of the right conferred on him by subsection (1) as soon as practicable after he has become a person to whom that subsection applies.

(3) A request made by a person under subsection (1), and the time at which it is made, shall be recorded in writing unless it is made by him while at a court after being charged with an offence.

(4) If a person makes such a request, he must be permitted to consult a solicitor as soon as is practicable except to the extent that any delay is permitted by this section.

(5) Any delay in complying with a request under subsection (1) is only permitted if —

    (a) it is authorised by an officer of at least the rank of superintendent; and

    (b) it does not extend beyond the relevant time.

(6) In subsection (5) ''the relevant time'' means —

    (a) where the request is the first request made by the detained person under subsection (1), the end of the period referred to in section 14(16); or

    (b) where the request follows an earlier request made by the detained person under that subsection in pursuance of which he has consulted a solicitor, the end of the period of 48 hours beginning with the time when that consultation began.

(7) An officer may give an authorisation under subsection (5) orally or in writing but, if he gives it orally, he shall confirm it in writing as soon as is practicable.

(8) An officer may only authorise a delay in complying with a request under subsection (1) where he has reasonable grounds for believing that the exercise of the right conferred by that subsection at the time when the detained person desires to exercise it −

(a) will lead to interference with or harm to evidence connected with a scheduled offence or interference with or physical injury to any person; or

(b) will lead to the alerting of any person suspected of having committed such an offence but not yet arrested for it; or

(c) will hinder the recovery of any property obtained as a result of such an offence; or

(d) will lead to interference with the gathering of information about the commission, preparation or instigation of acts of terrorism; or

(e) by alerting any person, will make it more difficult −

 (i) to prevent an act of terrorism; or

 (ii) to secure the apprehension, prosecution or conviction of any person in connection with the commission, preparation or instigation of an act of terrorism.

(9) If any delay is authorised, then, as soon as is practicable−

(a) the detained person shall be told the reason for authorising it; and

(b) the reason shall be recorded in writing.

(10) If an officer of at least the rank of Assistant Chief Constable has reasonable grounds for believing that, unless he gives a direction under subsection (11), the exercise by a person of the right conferred by subsection (1) will have any of the consequences specified in subsection (8), he may give a direction under subsection (11).

(11) A direction under this subsection is a direction that a person desiring to exercise the right conferred by subsection (1) may only consult a solicitor in the sight and hearing of a qualified officer of the uniformed branch of the Royal Ulster Constabulary.

(12) An officer is qualified for the purposes of subsection (11) if−

(a) he is of at least the rank of inspector; and

(b) in the opinion of the officer giving the direction, he has no connection with the case.

(13) Any authorisation under subsection (5) or direction under subsection (11) shall cease to have effect once the reason for giving it ceases to subsist.

Interpretation of Part II

16. — (1) In this Part —

'scheduled offence' and 'terrorism' have the same meaning as in the 1978 Act; and

'the terrorism provisions' means —

(a) section 12 of the Prevention of Terrorism (Temporary Provisions) Act 1984 (powers of arrest and detention); and

(b) any provision conferring a power of detention and contained in an order under section 13 of that Act (control of entry and procedure for removal).

(2) A person is held in police custody for the purposes of this Part if he is detained at a police station or is detained elsewhere in the charge of a constable, except that a person who is at a court after being charged with an offence is not held in police custody for the purposes of section 14.

PART IV

GENERAL

Minor and consequential amendments, repeals and revocation

25. — (1) The enactments mentioned in Schedule 1 shall have effect subject to the minor and consequential amendments there specified.

(2) The enactments mentioned in Part I of Schedule 2 are hereby repealed to the extent specified in the third column of that Schedule, and the enactment mentioned in Part II of that Schedule is hereby revoked to the extent so specified.

(3) Any order in force under section 33 of the 1978 Act at the commencement of section 13 of this Act is hereby revoked.

Commencement, expiry, revival and eventual repeal of Act

26. — (1) This Act, except section 12 and Part III, shall come into force at the end of the period of one month beginning with the day on which it is passed, and section 12 and Part III shall come into force on such day as the Secretary of State may by order appoint.

(2) An order under subsection (1) —

(a) may appoint different days for different provisions, and

(b) shall be made by statutory instrument.

(3) The provisions of Parts II and III shall expire with 21st March 1988 unless continued in force by an order under subsection (4).

(4) The Secretary of State may provide by order made by statutory instrument —

    (a) that all or any of the provisions of Parts II and III which are for the time being in force (including any in force by virtue of an order under this subsection) shall continue in force for a period not exceeding 12 months from the coming into operation of the order;

    (b) that all or any of those provisions which are for the time being in force shall cease to be in force; or

    (c) that all or any of those provisions which are not for the time being in force shall come into force again and remain in force for a period not exceeding 12 months from the coming into operation of the order.

(5) No order under subsection (4) shall be made unless —

    (a) a draft of the order has been approved by resolution of each House of Parliament; or

    (b) it is declared in the order that it appears to the Secretary of State that by reason of urgency it is necessary to make the order without a draft having been so approved.

(6) Every order under subsection (4), except an order of which a draft has been so approved —

    (a) shall be laid before Parliament; and

    (b) unless approved by resolution of each House of Parliament before the end of the period of 40 days beginning with the date on which it was made, shall cease to have effect at the end of that period (but without prejudice to anything previously done or to the making of a new order).

In reckoning for the purposes of this subsection any period of 40 days, no account shall be taken of any period during which Parliament is dissolved or prorogued or during which both Houses are adjourned for more than four days.

(7) With the exception of section 13(6) to (10), this subsection and section 27, this Act shall, by virtue of this subsection, be repealed immediately after the repeal of the 1978 Act takes effect under section 33(9) of that Act (as amended by section 13(4) above).

Short title, construction and extent

27. —(1) This Act may be cited as the Northern Ireland (Emergency Provisions) Act 1987.

(2) In this Act "the 1978 Act" means the Northern Ireland (Emergency Provisions) Act 1978.

(3) This Act extends to Northern Ireland only.

SCHEDULES

SCHEDULE 1

MINOR AND CONSEQUENTIAL AMENDMENTS

NORTHERN IRELAND (EMERGENCY PROVISIONS) ACT 1978 (c.5)

1. In section 13 (constables' general power of arrest and seizure) —

    (a) in subsection (1), for 'whom he suspects of committing, having committed or being' substitute 'who he has reasonable grounds to suspect is committing, has committed or is';

    (b) in subsection (2), for 'suspects him of being ' substitute 'has reasonable grounds for suspecting him to be'; and

    (c) in subsection (3), for 'suspects' substitute 'has reasonable grounds to suspect'.

2. In section 14 (powers of arrest of members of Her Majesty's forces) —

    (a) in subsection (1), for 'whom he suspects of committing, having committed or being' substitute 'who he has reasonable grounds to suspect is committing, has committed or is'; and

    (b) in subsection (3), for paragraph (b) substitute the following paragraph —

    '(b) if there are reasonable grounds for suspecting that that person is a terrorist or has committed an offence involving the use or possession of an explosive substance or firearm, where there are reasonable grounds for suspecting him to be.'

3. In section 15 (power to search for munitions and radio transmitters) —

    (a) in subsection (2), for 'it is suspected' substitute 'there are reasonable grounds for suspecting';

    (b) in subsection (3)(b), for 'whom he suspects of having' substitute 'who he has reasonable grounds to suspect has';

    (c) for subsection (4) substitute —

    '(4) Where a member of Her Majesty's forces or a constable is empowered by virtue of any provision of this Act to search any premises or other place or any person —

    (a) he may seize any munitions found in the course of the search (unless it appears to him that the munitions are being, have been and will be used only lawfully) and may retain and, if necessary, destroy them; and

    (b) he may seize any transmitter found in the course of the search (unless it appears to him that the transmitter has been, is being and is likely to be used only lawfully) and may retain it.'; and

  (d) in subsection (5), in the definition of 'transmitter', for 'and includes' substitute 'or'.

4. In section 18 (power to stop and question) –

  (a) in subsection (1)(b), after 'other' insert 'recent'; and

  (b) in subsection (2), for the words from 'imprisonment' onwards substitute 'a fine not exceeding level 5 on the standard scale.'

5. In section 31(1) (interpretation),omit the definition of 'constable'.

6. In section 32 (orders and regulations) –

  (a) in subsection (1), after 'orders conferred by' insert 'section 19A above and';

  (b) in subsection (3), for the words from the beginning to 'Schedules)' substitute 'Subject to subsection (5) below, no order and regulations under this Act';

  (c) in subsection (4), for the words from the beginning to 'approved) shall' substitute 'Subject to subsection (5) below, orders and regulations under this Act shall, if not so approved in draft,'; and

  (d) after that subsection add –

    '(5) Subsections (3) and (4) above do not apply to –

      (a) any order under section 19A above or under Schedule 1 or 3 to this Act; or

      (b) any regulations under section 5A above;

    but a statutory instrument containing any such regulations shall be subject to annulment in pursuance of a resolution of either House of Parliament.'

7. In section 33 (commencement etc. of provisions of the 1978 Act) –

  (a) in subsection (5), at the end add 'or (where the Lord Chancellor gives a direction under that subsection with respect to the trial) to the Crown Court sitting at the place specified in the direction'; and

  (b) for subsection (7) substitute –

    '(7) It is hereby declared that the expiry or cesser of any provision of section 6 above shall not affect –

      (a) any committal of a person for trial in accordance with that provision to the Crown Court sitting either in Belfast or elsewhere, or

      (b) any committal of a person for trial which, in accordance with that provision, has taken effect as a

committal for trial to the Crown Court sitting
elsewhere than in Belfast,
in a case where the indictment has not been presented.'

8.—(1) In Scheduled 4 (scheduled offences), Part I (substantive offences) shall be amended as follows.

(2) In paragraph 12(f), at the end add ',subject also to note 2 below.'

(3) In note 2, after paragraph (c) insert —

'(cc) section 20 of the Theft Act (Northern Ireland) 1969 (subject to note 5 below); or'.

(4) In note 5 —

(a) for '15 or 20' substitute 'or 15'; and

(b) at the end add '; and the Attorney General for Northern Ireland shall not certify that an offence under section 20 of the said Act of 1969 is not be treated as a scheduled offence in a case where it is charged that the offence was so committed.'

JUDICATURE (NORTHERN IRELAND) ACT 1978 (c.23)

9. In Part II of Schedule 5 (minor and consequential amendments), in the entry relating to section 2(1)(a) of the Northern Ireland (Emergency Provisions) Act 1978, for 'sections 2(1)(a) and' substitute 'section'.

SCHEDULE 2

Section 25(2)

REPEALS AND REVOCATION

PART I

REPEALS

Chapter	Short title	Extent of repeal
1978 c.5.	Northern Ireland (Emergency Provisions) Act 1978.	In section 22(2), the word 'and' at the end of paragraph (c).
1978 c.23.	Judicature (Northern Ireland) Act 1978.	In Part II of Schedule 5, the entries relating to sections 6 and 33(7) of the Northern Ireland (Emergency Provisions) Act 1978.

PART II

REVOCATION

Number	Title	Extent of revocation
S.I. 1981/16 75 (N.I. 26)	Magistrates' Courts (Northern Ireland) Order 1981	In Schedule 6, paragraph 49.

Appendix III: The Prevention of Terrorism (Temporary Provisions) Act 1984 (1984 c 8)

ARRANGEMENT OF SECTIONS

PART I

PROSCRIBED ORGANISATIONS

PART II

EXCLUSION ORDERS

PART III

MISCELLANEOUS OFFENCES

PART IV

ARREST, DETENTION AND PORT POWERS

13 Control of entry and procedure for removal

An Act to repeal and re-enact with amendments the provisions of the Prevention of Terrorism (Temporary Provisions) Act 1976   [22 March 1984]

PART I

PROSCRIBED ORGANISATIONS

1 Proscribed organisations

(1) Subject to subsection (7) below, if any person –

(*a*) belongs or professes to belong to a proscribed organisation;

(*b*) solicits or invites financial or other support for a proscribed organisation, or knowingly makes or receives any contribution in money or otherwise to the resources of a proscribed organisation; or

(*c*) arranges or assists in the arrangement or management of, or addresses, any meeting of three or more persons (whether or not it is a meeting to which the public are admitted) knowing that the meeting –

(i) is to support a proscribed organisation;

(ii) is to further the activities of such an organisation; or

(iii) is to be addressed by a person belonging or professing to belong to such an organisation,

he shall be guilty of an offence.

(2) A person guilty of an offence under subsection (1) above shall be liable –

(*a*) on summary conviction to imprisonment for a term not exceeding six months, or to a fine not exceeding the statutory maximum, or both; or

(*b*) on conviction on indictment to imprisonment for a term not exceeding five years, or to a fine, or both.

(3) Any organisation for the time being specified in Schedule 1 to this Act is a proscribed organisation for the purposes of this Act; and any organisation which passes under a name mentioned in that Schedule shall be treated as proscribed, whatever relationship (if any) it has to any other organisation of the same name.

(4) The Secretary of State may by order made by statutory instrument add to Schedule 1 to this Act any organisation that appears to him to be concerned in terrorism occurring in the United Kingdom and connected with Northern Irish affairs, or in promoting or encouraging it.

(5) The Secretary of State may also by order so made remove an organisation from Schedule 1 to this Act.

(6) In this section and section 2 below 'organisation' includes any association or combination of persons.

(7) A person belonging to a proscribed organisation shall not be guilty of an offence under this section by reason of belonging to the organisation if he shows—

(*a*) that he became a member when it was not a proscribed organisation under the current legislation; and

(*b*) that he has not since he became a member taken part in any of its activities at any time while it was a proscribed organisation under that legislation.

(8) In subsection (7) above 'the current legislation', in relation to any time, means whichever of the following was in force at that time—

(*a*) the Prevention of Terrorism (Temporary Provisions) Act 1974;

(*b*) the Prevention of Terrorism (Temporary Provisions) Act 1976;

(*c*) this Act.

(9) The reference in subsection (7) above to a person becoming a member of an organisation is a reference to the only or last occasion on which he became a member.

(10) The court by or before which a person is convicted of an offence under this section may order the forfeiture of any money or other property which, at the time of the offence, he had in his possession or under his control for the use or benefit of the proscribed organisation.

2 Display of support in public for a proscribed organisation

(1) Any person who in a public place—

(*a*) wears any item of dress; or

(*b*) wears, carries or displays any article,

in such a way or in such circumstances as to arouse reasonable apprehension that he is a member or supporter of a proscribed organisation, shall be guilty of an offence, and shall be liable on summary conviction —

(i) to imprisonment for a term not exceeding six months; or

(ii) to a fine of an amount not exceeding level 5 on the standard scale, or to both.

(2) *A constable may arrest without warrant anyone whom he has reasonable grounds to suspect of being a person guilty of an offence under this section.*

(3) In this section 'public place' includes any highway [, or in Scotland any road within the meaning of the Roads (Scotland) Act 1984,] and any other premises or place to which at the material time the public have, or are permitted to have, access, whether on payment or otherwise.

PART II

EXCLUSION ORDERS

3 Exclusion orders: general

(1) The Secretary of State may exercise the powers conferred on him by this Part of this Act in such way as appears to him expedient to prevent acts of terrorism to which this Part of this Act applies.

(2) An order under section 4, 5 or 6 below is referred to in this Act as an 'exclusion order.'

(3) An exclusion order may be revoked at any time by a further order made by the Secretary of State.

(4) An exclusion order shall, unless revoked earlier, expire at the end of the period of three years beginning with the day on which it is made.

(5) The fact that an exclusion order against a person has been revoked or has expired shall not prevent the making of a further exclusion order against him.

(6) The acts of terrorism to which this Part of this Act applies are acts of terrorism designed to influence public opinion or Government policy with respect to affairs in Northern Ireland.

4 Orders excluding persons from Great Britain

(1) If the Secretary of State is satisfied that any person —

(*a*) is or has been concerned in the commission, preparation or instigation of acts of terrorism to which this Part of this Act applies; or

(b) is attempting or may attempt to enter Great Britain with a view to being concerned in the commission, preparation or instigation of such acts of terrorism,

the Secretary of State may make an exclusion order against him.

(2) An exclusion order under this section is an order prohibiting a person from being in, or entering, Northern Ireland.

(3) In deciding whether to make an exclusion order under this section against a person who is ordinarily resident in Great Britain, the Secretary of State shall have regard to the question whether that person's connection with any country or territory outside Great Britain is such as to make it appropriate that such an order should be made.

(4) An exclusion order shall not be made under this section against a person who is a British citizen and who –

(a) is at the time ordinarily resident in Great Britain, and has then been ordinarily resident in Great Britain throughout the last three years; or

(b) is at the time subject to an order under section 5 below.

(5) Subsection (4)(a) above shall be construed in accordance with Schedule 2 to this Act.

5 Orders excluding persons from Northern Ireland

(1) If the Secretary of State is satisfied that any person –

(a) is or has been concerned in the commission, preparation or instigation of acts of terrorism to which this Part of this Act applies; or

(b) is attempting or may attempt to enter Northern Ireland with a view to being concerned in the commission, preparation or instigation of such acts of terrorism,

the Secretary of State may make an exclusion order against him.

(2) An exclusion order under this section is an order prohibiting a person from being in, or entering, Northern Ireland.

(3) In deciding whether to make an exclusion order under this section against a person who is ordinarily resident in Northern Ireland, the Secretary of State shall have regard to the question whether that person's connection with any country or territory outside Northern Ireland is such as to make it appropriate that such an order should be made.

(4) An exclusion order shall not be made under this section against

a person who is a British citizen and who—

> (*a*) is at the time ordinarily resident in Northern Ireland, and has been ordinarily resident in Northern Ireland throughout the last three years; or
>
> (*b*) is at the time subject to an order under section 4 above.

(5) Subsection (3)(*a*) above shall be construed in accordance with Schedule 2 to this Act.

6 Orders excluding persons from the United Kingdom

(1) If the Secretary of State is satisfied that any person—

> (*a*) is or has been concerned in the commission, preparation or instigation of acts of terrorism to which this Part of this Act applies; or
>
> (*b*) is attempting or may attempt to enter Great Britain or Northern Ireland with a view to being concerned in the commission, preparation or instigation of such acts of terrorism,

the Secretary of State may make an exclusion order against him.

(2) An exclusion order under this section is an order prohibiting a person from being in, or entering, the United Kingdom.

(3) In deciding whether to make an exclusion order under this section against a person who is ordinarily resident in the United Kingdom, the Secretary of State shall have regard to the question whether that person's connection with any country or territory outside the United Kingdom is such as to make it appropriate that such an order should be made.

(4) An exclusion order shall not be made under this section against a person who is a British citizen.

7 Right to make representations to Secretary of State etc

(1) As soon as may be after the making of an exclusion order, notice of the making of the order shall be served on the person against whom it has been made; and the notice—

> (*a*) shall set out the rights afforded to him by this section; and
>
> (*b*) shall specify the manner in which those rights are to be exercised.

(2) Subsection (1) above shall not impose an obligation to take any steps to serve a notice on a person at a time when he is outside the United Kingdom.

(3) After service of the notice, if the person against whom an exclusion order has been made objects to the order—

(a) he may make representations in writing to the Secretary of State setting out the grounds of his objections; and

(b) he may include in those representations a request for a personal interview with the person or persons nominated by the Secretary of State under subsection (6) below.

(4) Subject to subsection (5) below, a person against whom an exclusion order has been made must exercise the rights conferred by subsection (3) above within seven days of the service of the notice.

(5) Where before the expiry of that period—

(a) he has consented to his removal under section 8 below from Great Britain, Northern Ireland or the United Kingdom, as the case may be; and

(b) he has been removed accordingly,

he may exercise the rights conferred by subsection (3) above within fourteen days of his removal.

(6) If he exercises them within the period within which they are required to be exercised, the matter shall be referred for the advice of one or more persons nominated by the Secretary of State.

(7) Where subsection (4) above applies, the person against whom the exclusion order has been made shall be granted a personal interview with the person or persons so nominated.

(8) Where subsection (5) above applies, the person against whom the exclusion order has been made shall be granted a personal interview with the person or persons so nominated if it appears to the Secretary of State that it is reasonably practicable to grant him such an interview in an appropriate country or territory within a reasonable period from the date on which he made his representations.

(9) In subsection (8) above 'an appropriate country or territory' means—

(a) Northern Ireland or the Republic of Ireland, if the exclusion order was made under section 4 above;

(b) Great Britain or the Republic of Ireland, if it was made under section 5 above;

(c) the Republic of Ireland, if it was made under section 6 above.

(10) Where it appears to the Secretary of State that it is reasonably practicable to grant a personal interview in more than one appropriate country or territory, he may grant the interview in whichever of them he thinks fit.

(11) The Secretary of State shall reconsider the matter as soon as is reasonably practicable after he has received representations relating to it under this section and any report of an interview relating to it which is granted under this section.

(12) In reconsidering a matter under subsection (11) above, the Secretary of State shall take into account everything which appears to him to be relevant and in particular—

(a) the representations relating to the matter made to him under this section;

(b) the advice of the person or persons to whom the matter was referred by him under this section; and

(c) the report of any interview relating to the matter granted under this section.

(13) The Secretary of State shall thereafter, if it is reasonably practicable to do so, give notice in writing to the person against whom the exclusion order has been made of any decision which he takes as to whether or not to revoke the order.

8 Powers of removal

Where—

(a) an exclusion order has been made against a person; and

(b) notice of the making of the order has been served upon him,

the Secretary of State may have him removed from Great Britain, Northern Ireland or the United Kingdom, as the case may be—

(i) if he consents;

(ii) if the period mentioned in subsection (4) of section 7 above has expired and he has not made representations relating to the matter in accordance with that section; or

(iii) if he has made such representations but the Secretary of State has notified him that he has decided not to revoke the order.

9 Offences under Part II

(1) If any person who is subject to an exclusion order fails to comply with the order at a time after he has been, or has become liable to be, removed under section 8 above, he shall be guilty of an offence.

(2) If any person—

(a) is knowingly concerned in arrangements for securing or facilitating the entry into Great Britain, Northern Ireland or the United Kingdom of a person whom he knows, or has reasonable grounds for believing, to be an excluded person; or

(b) in Great Britain, Northern Ireland or the United Kingdom knowingly harbours such a person,

he shall be guilty of an offence.

(3) In subsection (2) above 'excluded person' means—

(a) in relation to Great Britain, a person subject to an exclusion order made under section 4 above who has been, or has become liable to be, removed from Great Britain under section 8 above;

(b) in relation to Northern Ireland, a person subject to an exclusion order made under section 5 above who has been, or has become liable to be, removed from Northern Ireland under section 8 above; and

(c) in relation to the United Kingdom, a person subject to an exclusion order made under section 6 above who has been, or has become liable to be, removed from the United Kingdom under section 8 above.

(4) A person guilty of an offence under this section shall be liable —

(a) on summary conviction to imprisonment for a term not exceeding six months, or to a fine not exceeding the statutory maximum, or both; or

(b) on conviction on indictment to imprisonment for a term not exceeding five years, or to a fine, or both.

PART III

MISCELLANEOUS OFFENCES

10 Contributions towards acts of terrorism

(1) If any person —

(a) solicits or invites any other person to give, lend or otherwise make available, whether for consideration or not, any money or other property; or

(b) receives or accepts from any other person, whether for consideration or not, any money or other property,

intending that it shall be applied or used for or in connection with the commission, preparation or instigation of acts of terrorism to which this Part of this Act applies, he shall be guilty of an offence.

(2) If any person gives, lends or otherwise makes available to any other person, whether for consideration or not, any money or other property, knowing or suspecting that it will or may be applied or used for or in connection with the commission, preparation or instigation of acts of terrorism to which this Part of this Act applies, he shall be guilty of an offence.

(3) A person guilty of an offence under subsection (1) or (2) above shall be liable —

    (*a*) on summary conviction to imprisonment for a term not exceeding six months, or to a fine not exceeding the statutory maximum, or both; or

    (*b*) on conviction on indictment to imprisonment for a term not exceeding five years, or to a fine, or both.

(4) The court by or before which a person is convicted of an offence under subsection (1) above may order the forfeiture of any money or other property—

    (*a*) which, at the time of the offence, he had in his possession or under his control; and

    (*b*) which, at that time, he intended should be applied or used for or in connection with the commission, preparation or instigation of acts of terrorism to which this Part of this Act applies.

(5) The acts of terrorism to which this Part of this Act applies are acts of terrorism connected with Northern Irish affairs.

(6) In this section 'property' includes—

    (*a*) in England and Wales and Northern Ireland, both real and personal property; and

    (*b*) in Scotland, both heritable and moveable property.

11 Information about acts of terrorism

(1) If a person who has information which he knows or believes might be of material assistance—

    (*a*) in preventing the commission by any other person of an act of terrorism to which this Part of this Act applies; or

    (*b*) in securing the apprehension, prosecution or conviction of any other person for an offence involving the commission, preparation or instigation of an act of terrorism to which this Part of this Act applies,

fails without reasonable excuse to disclose that information as soon as reasonably practicable—

    (i) in England and Wales, to a constable;

    (ii) in Scotland, to a constable or the procurator fiscal; or

    (iii) in Northern Ireland, to a constable or a member of Her Majesty's forces,

he shall be guilty of an offence.

(2) A person guilty of an offence under subsection (1) above shall be liable—

    (*a*) on summary conviction to imprisonment for a term not

exceeding six months, or to a fine not exceeding the statutory maximum, or both;

(b) on conviction on indictment to imprisonment for a term not exceeding five years, or to a fine, or both.

(3) Proceedings for an offence under this section may be taken, and the offence may for the purpose of those proceedings be treated as having been committed, in any place where the person to be charged is or has at any time been since he first knew or believed that the information might be of material assistance as mentioned in subsection (1) above.

Part IV

Arrest, Detention and Port Powers

12 Powers of arrest and detention

(1) Subject to subsection (2) below, a constable may arrest without warrant a person whom he has reasonable grounds for suspecting to be –

(a) a person guilty of an offence under section 1, 9 or 10 above;

(b) a person who is or has been concerned in the commission, preparation or instigation of acts of terrorism to which this Part of this Act applies;

(c) a person subject to an exclusion order.

(2) The power of arrest conferred by subsection (1)(c) above is exercisable only –

(a) In Great Britain, if the exclusion order was made under section 4 above; and

(b) in Northern Ireland, if it was made under section 5 above.

(3) The acts of terrorism to which this Part of this Act applies are –

(a) acts of terrorism connected with the affairs of Northern Ireland; and

(b) acts of terrorism of any other description except acts connected solely with the affairs of the United Kingdom or any part of the United Kingdom other than Northern Ireland.

(4) A person arrested under this section shall not be detained in right of the arrest for more than forty-eight hours after his arrest; but the Secretary of State may, in any particular case, extend the period of forty-eight hours by a period or periods specified by him.

(5) Any such further period or periods shall not exceed five days in all.

(6) The following provisions (requirement to bring accused person before the court after his arrest) shall not apply to a person detained in right of the arrest —

(a) section 43 of the Magistrates' Courts Act 1980;

(b) section 29 of the Children and Young Persons Act 1969;

(c) *(applies to Scotland only)*;

(d) Article 131 of the Magistrates' Courts (Northern Ireland) Order 1981; and

(e) section 50(3) of the Children and Young Persons Act (Northern Ireland) 1968.

(7) *(Applies to Scotland only.)*

(8) The provisions of this section are without prejudice to any power of arrest exercisable apart from this section.

13 Control of entry and procedure for removal

(1) The Secretary of State may by order made by statutory instrument provide for —

(a) the examination of persons arriving in, or leaving, Great Britain or Northern Ireland, with a view to determining —

(i) whether any such person appears to be a person who is or has been concerned in the commission, preparation or instigation of acts of terrorism to which this Part of this Act applies;

(ii) whether any such person is subject to an exclusion order; or

(iii) whether there are grounds for suspecting that any such person has committed an offence under section 9 above;

(b) the arrest and detention of persons subject to exclusion orders, pending their removal pursuant to section 8 above; and

(c) arrangements for the removal of persons pursuant to that section.

(2) An order under this section may confer powers on the examining officers specified in paragraph 1(2) of Schedule 3 to this Act including —

(a) the power of arresting and detaining any person pending —

(i) his examination;

(ii) a decision by the Secretary of State whether or not to make an exclusion order against him; or

(iii) his removal pursuant to section 8 above;

(b) the power of searching persons, of boarding ships or aircraft, of searching in ships or aircraft or elsewhere and of detaining articles —

    (i) for use in connection with the taking of a decision by the Secretary of State as to whether or not to make an exclusion order; or

    (ii) for use as evidence in criminal proceedings.

PART V

GENERAL

14 Supplementary

(1) In this Act, unless the context otherwise requires—

'aircraft' includes hovercraft;

'captain' means master (of a ship) or commander (of an aircraft);

'exclusion order' has the meaning given by section 3(2) above;

'port' includes airport and hoverport;

'ship' includes every description of vessel used in navigation;

'terrorism' means the use of violence for political ends, and includes any use of violence for the purpose of putting the public or any section of the public in fear.

(2) In this Act 'statutory maximum' has the meaning given by section 74 of the Criminal Justice Act 1982 *and for the purposes of this Act—*

    (a) section 32 of the Magistrates' Courts Act 1980; and

    (b) an order made under section 143 of that Act which alters the sum specified in the definition of 'the prescribed sum' in subsection (9) of the said section 32,

shall extend to Northern Ireland and subsection (1) of the said section 74 shall have effect as if after the words 'England and Wales' there were inserted the words 'or Northern Ireland'.

(3) In this Act 'the standard scale' has the meaning given by section 75 of the Criminal Justice Act 1982 *and for the purposes of this Act—*

    (a) section 37 of that Act; and

    (b) an order under section 143 of the Magistrates' Courts Act 1980 which alters the sums specified in subsection (2) of the said section 37,

shall extend to Northern Ireland and the said section 75 shall have effect as if after the words 'England and Wales' there were inserted the words 'or Northern Ireland'.

(4) The powers conferred by Part II of this Act and section 13 above shall be exercisable notwithstanding the rights conferred by section 1 of the Immigration Act 1971 (general principles regulating entry into and staying in the United Kingdom).

(5) Any reference in a provision of this Act to a person's having been concerned in the commission, preparation or instigation of acts of terrorism shall be taken to be a reference to his having been so concerned at any time, whether before or after the passing of this Act.

(6) When any question arises under this Act whether or not a person is exempted from the provisions of section 4, 5 or 6 above, it shall lie on the person asserting it to prove that he is.

(7) The provisions of Schedule 3 to this Act shall have effect for supplementing sections 1 to 13 above.

(8) An order made under section 13 above varying or revoking a previous order so made may contain such transitional provisions and savings as appear to the Secretary of State to be necessary or expedient.

(9) An order made under section 13 above shall be subject to annulment in pursuance of a resolution of either House of Parliament.

(10) No order under section 1 above or section 17 below shall be made unless –

(a) a draft of the order has been approved by resolution of each House of Parliament; or

(b) it is declared in the order that it appears to the Secretary of State that by reason of urgency it is necessary to make the order without a draft having been so approved.

(11) Every order under section 1 above or section 17 below (except such an order of which a draft has been so approved) –

(a) shall be laid before Parliament; and

(b) shall cease to have effect at the end of a period of forty days beginning with the date on which it was made unless, before the end of that period, the order has been approved by resolution of each House of Parliament, but without prejudice to anything previously done or to the making of a new order.

(12) In reckoning for the purposes of subsection (11) above any period of forty days, no account shall be taken of any period during which Parliament is dissolved or prorogued or during which both Houses are adjourned for more than four days.

15 Financial provisions

Any expenses incurred by the Secretary of State under, or by virtue of, this Act shall be paid out of money provided by Parliament.

16 Power to extend to Channel Islands and Isle of Man

Her Majesty may by Order in Council direct that any of the provisions of this Act shall extend, with such exceptions, adaptations and modifications, if any, as may be specified in the Order, to any of the Channel Islands and the Isle of Man.

17 Duration, expiry and revival of certain provisions

(1) The following provisions of this Act—

section 1 to 13;

section 14 except in so far as it relates to orders under subsection (2)(*a*) or (*b*) below;

subsection (2)(*c*) below; and

the Schedules,

shall remain in force until the end of the period of twelve months beginning with the passing of this Act and shall then expire unless continued in force by an order under subsection (2)(*a*) below.

(2) The Secretary of State may by order made by statutory instrument provide—

(*a*) that all or any of the said provisions which are for the time being in force (including any in force by virtue of an order under this paragraph or paragraph (*c*) below) shall continue in force for a period not exceeding twelve months from the coming into operation of the order;

(*b*) that all or any of the said provisions which are for the time being in force shall cease to be in force; or

(*c*) that all or any of the said provisions which are not for the time being in force shall come into force again and remain in force for a period not exceeding twelve months from the coming into operation of the order.

(3) This Act shall cease to have effect at the end of the period of five years beginning with the date on which it is passed.

18 Repeal of Act of 1976 etc

(1) The Prevention of Terrorism (Temporary Provisions) Act 1976 (in this section referred to as 'the Act of 1976') is hereby repealed.

(2) An exclusion order made or deemed to have been made against a person under Part II of the Act of 1976 and in force on the date on which this act is passed shall, unless it is revoked earlier, expire at the end of a period of three years beginning with that date, but the Secretary of State may make an exclusion order against him under Part II of this Act.

(3) The repeal of the Act of 1976 shall not affect the operation of any Order in Council extending it to any of the Channel Islands or the Isle of Man; but any such Order may be revoked by an Order in Council

under section 16 above as if made under that section.

(4) The Prevention of Terrorism (Temporary Provisions) Act 1976 (Amendment) Order 1979 is hereby revoked.

19 Short title and extent

(1) This Act may be cited as the Prevention of Terrorism (Temporary Provisions) Act 1984.

(2) Part I of this Act shall not extend to Northern Ireland.

SCHEDULES

SCHEDULE 1

Section 1

PROSCRIBED ORGANISATIONS
Irish Republican Army
Irish National Liberation Army

SCHEDULE 2

Sections 4 and 5

EXCLUSION ORDERS: CALCULATION OF PERIOD OF RESIDENCE

1. − (1) It is hereby declared that a person is not to be treated −

   (a) as ordinarily resident in Great Britain for the purpose of the exemption in section 4(4)(a) of this Act; or
   (b) as ordinarily resident in Northern Ireland for the purpose of the exemption in section 5(4)(a) of this Act.

at a time when he is there in breach of −

   (i) an exclusion order;
   (ii) the Immigration Act 1971; or
   (iii) any law for purposes similar to that Act in force in the United Kingdom after the passing of this Act.

(2) In each of those exemptions 'the three years' is to be taken as a period amounting in total to three years exclusive of any time during which the person claiming exemption was undergoing imprisonment or detention for a period of six months or more by virtue of a sentence passed for an offence on a conviction in the United Kingdom and Islands.

2. In this Schedule −

   (a) 'exclusion order' means an order under section 4, 5 or 6 of this Act or the corresponding provisions of the Prevention of Terrorism (Temporary Provisions) Act 1974 or the Prevention of Terrorism (Temporary Provisions) Act 1976;

(b) 'sentence' includes any order made on conviction of an offence;

(c) two or more sentences for consecutive (or partly consecutive) terms shall be treated as a single sentence;

(d) a person shall be deemed to be detained by virtue of a sentence —

(i) at any time when he is liable to imprisonment or detention by virtue of the sentence, but is unlawfully at large; and

(ii) during any period of custody by which under any relevant enactment the term to be served under the sentence is reduced;

(e) 'Islands' means the Channel Islands and the Isle of Man.

3. In paragraph 2(d)(ii) above 'relevant enactment' means section 67 of the Criminal Justice Act 1967 (or, before that section operated, section 17(2) of the Criminal Justice Adminstration Act 1962) and any similar enactment which is for the time being or has (before or after the passing of this Act) been in force in any part of the United Kingdom or Islands.

SCHEDULE 3

Section 14

SUPPLEMENTAL PROVISIONS FOR SECTIONS 1 TO 13

PART I

ORDERS UNDER SECTION 13

1. —(1) In this Part of this Schedule references to an order are to an order made under section 13 of this Act.

(2) The following shall be examining officers —

(a) constables;

(b) immigration officers appointed for the purposes of the Immigration Act 1971 under paragraph 1 of Schedule 2 to that Act; and

(c) officers of customs and excise who are the subject of arrangements for their employment as immigration officers, made under that paragraph by the Secretary of State.

(3) (*Applies to Scotland only.*)

(4) In Northern Ireland members of Her Majesty's forces may perform such functions conferred on examining officers as are specified in an order.

(5) Where, by virtue of section 13(2)(*b*) of this Act, an order confers powers of search and of detaining articles on an examining officer, the order may also confer power on the examining officer to authorise any other person to exercise, on his behalf, any of the powers conferred by virtue of that paragraph.

(6) An order may—

    (*a*) in the case of ships and aircraft—

        (i) coming to Great Britain from the Republic of Ireland, Northern Ireland, the Channel Islands or the Isle of Man; or

        (ii) going from Great Britain to any other of those places,

restrict the ports, areas or places in Great Britain which they may use;

    (*b*) in the case of ships and aircraft—

        (i) coming to Northern Ireland from the Republic of Ireland, Great Britain, the Channel Islands or the Isle of Man; or

        (ii) going from Northern Ireland to any other of those places,

restrict the ports, areas or places in Northern Ireland which they may use; and

    (*c*) provide for the supply and use of—

        (i) landing cards by passengers disembarking in Great Britain or Northern Ireland from ships or aircraft; and

        (ii) embarkation cards by passengers boarding ships or aircraft about to leave either of those places.

(7) The persons on whom duties may be imposed by an order shall include persons arriving in, or leaving, Great Britain or Northern Ireland, whether as passengers or otherwise, and captains, owners or agents of ships or aircraft.

(8) Without prejudice to the generality of section 13 of this Act or of the preceding provisions of this paragraph, an order may contain such supplemental or incidental provisions as appear to the Secretary of State to be expedient, and may contain provisions comparable to those contained in or made under the following administrative provisions of the Immigration Act 1971, that is to say, section 33(3) (designation of ports of entry and exit) and the following paragraphs of Schedule 2: —

Paragraph

4	Duties of persons being examined, and powers to search them and their belongings.
5	Orders about landing and embarkation cards.
8, 10 and 11	Arrangements for the removal of persons.
16,17 and 18(3)	Detention of persons liable to examination or removal.
26 and 27	Supplemental duties of those connected with ships or aircraft or with ports.

(9) A person who knowingly contravenes or fails to comply with an order shall be guilty of an offence, and shall be liable on summary conviction—

> (*a*) to imprisonment for a term not exceeding three months; or
> (*b*) to a fine of an amount not exceeding level 4 on the standard scale,

or to both.

(10) Examining officers shall exercise their functions under this Act in accordance with such instructions as may from time to time be given them by the Secretary of State.

2. An order may make such provision as appears to the Secretary of State expedient as respects persons who enter or leave Northern Ireland by land, or who seek to do so.

PART II
OFFENCES, DETENTION ETC

Prosecution of offences

3. Proceedings shall not be instituted—

> (*a*) in England and Wales for an offence under section 1, 2, 9, 10 or 11 of this Act, except by, or with the consent of, the Attorney General; or
> (*b*) in Northern Ireland for an offence under section 9, 10 or 11 of this Act, except by, or with the consent of, the Attorney General for Northern Ireland.

Search warrants

4.—(1) If a justice of the peace is satisfied that there is reasonable ground for suspecting that—

    (*a*) evidence of the commission of an offence under section 1, 9
    or 10 of this Act; or

    (*b*) evidence sufficient to justify the making of an order under sec-
    tion 1 of this Act or an exclusion order,

is to be found at any premises or place, he may grant a search warrant
authorising entry to the premises or place.

(2) An application for a warrant under sub-paragraph (1) above shall
be made by a member of a police force of a rank not lower than inspector, and he shall give his information to the justice on oath.

(3) The warrant shall authorise the applicant, and any other member
of any police force, to enter the premises or place, if necessary by force,
and to search the premises or place and every person found therein
and to seize anything found on the premises or place, or on any such
person, which any member of a police force acting under the warrant
has reasonable grounds for suspecting to be evidence falling within sub-
paragraph (1) above.

(4) [Subject to sub-paragraph (4A) below, if] a member of a police
force of a rank not lower than superintendent has reasonable grounds
for believing that the case is one of great emergency and that in the
interests of the State immediate action is necessary, he may by a written order signed by him give to any member of a police force the
authority which may be given by a search warrant under this paragraph
[or which could have been so given but for section 9(2) of the Police
and Criminal Evidence Act 1984].

[(4A) An order given under sub-paragraph (4) above may not
authorise a search for items subject to legal privilege within the meaning of section 10 of the Police and Criminal Evidence Act 1984.]

(5) Where an authority is given under sub-paragraph (4) above, particulars of the case shall be notified as soon as may be to the Secretary
of State.

(6) A search of a person under this paragraph may only be carried
out —

    (*a*) by a person of the same sex as the person searched; or

    (*b*) by a medical practitioner.

(7) (*Applies to Scotland only.*)

(8) In the application of this paragraph to Northern Ireland —

    (*a*) for any reference to a justice of the peace there shall be
    substituted a reference to a resident magistrate;

    (*b*) references to a police force shall be substituted as follows —

        (i) for the reference in sub-paragraph (2) and the first

reference in sub-paragraph (4) there shall be substituted references to the Royal Ulster Constabulary; and

(ii) for all other references there shall be substituted references to the Royal Ulster Constabulary, including the Royal Ulster Constabulary Reserve; and

(c) for any reference to information on oath there shall be substituted a reference to complaint on oath.

Detention: supplemental provisions

5. – (1) A person may be detained –

(a) in right of an arrest under section 12 of this Act; or

(b) under any provision contained in or made under section 13 of this Act, or Part I of this Schedule,

in such place as the Secretary of State may from time to time direct (when not detained in accordance with an order under section 13 of this Act on board a ship or aircraft).

(2) A person shall be deemed to be in legal custody at any time when he is so detained.

(3) Where a person is so detained, any examining officer, constable or prison officer, or any other person authorised by the Secretary of State, may take all such steps as may be reasonably necessary for photographing, measuring or otherwise identifying him.

Powers of search without warrant

6. – (1) In any circumstances in which a constable has power under section 12 of this Act to arrest a person, he may also, for the purpose of ascertaining whether he has in his possession any document or other article which may constitute evidence that he is a person liable to arrest, stop that person, and search him.

(2) Where a constable has arrested a person under that section, for any reason other than for the commission of a criminal offence, he or any other constable, may search him for the purpose of ascertaining whether he has in his possession any document or other article which may constitute evidence that he is a person liable to arrest.

(3) A search under this paragraph may only be carried out –

(a) by a person of the same sex as the person searched; or

(b) by a medical practitioner.

Evidence in proceedings

7. – (1) Any document purporting to be an order, notice or direction made or given by the Secretary of State for the purposes of any provision

contained in or made under this Act and to be signed by him or on his behalf shall be received in evidence, and shall, until the contrary is proved, be deemed to be made or given by him.

(2) Prima facie evidence of any such order, notice or direction may, in any legal proceedings, be given by the production of a document bearing a certificate purporting to be signed by or on behalf of the Secretary of State and stating that the document is a true copy of the order, notice or direction.

8. *(Amends the Northern Ireland (Emergency Provisions) Act 1978, Sch 4, para 16 ante.)*

Appendix IV: The Prevention of Terrorism (Temporary Provisions) Act 1989 (1989 c. 4)

ARRANGEMENT OF SECTIONS

PART I

PROSCRIBED ORGANISATIONS

PART II

EXCLUSION ORDERS

PART III

FINANCIAL ASSISTANCE FOR TERRORISM

An Act to make provision in place of the Prevention of Terrorism (Temporary Provisions) Act 1984; to make further provision in relation to powers of search under, and persons convicted of scheduled offences within the meaning of, the Northern Ireland (Emergency Provisions) Act 1978; and to enable the Secretary of State to prevent the establishment of new explosive factories, magazines and stores in Northern Ireland. [15th March 1989]

PART I

PROSCRIBED ORGANISATIONS

Proscribed organisations

1.—(1) Any organisation for the time being specified in Schedule 1 to this Act is a proscribed organisation for the purposes of this Act; and any organisation which passes under a name mentioned in that Schedule shall be treated as proscribed whatever relationship (if any) it has to any other organisation of the same name.

(2) The Secretary of State may by order made by statutory instrument—

(a) add to Schedule 1 to this Act any organisation that appears to him to be concerned in, or in promoting or encouraging, terrorism occurring in the United Kingdom and connected with the affairs of Northern Ireland;

(b) remove an organisation from that Schedule.

(3) No order shall be made under this section unless—

(a) a draft of the order has been laid before and approved by a resolution of each House of Parliament; or

(b) it is declared in the order that it appears to the Secretary of State that by reason of urgency it is necessary to make the order without a draft having been so approved.

(4) An order under this section of which a draft has not been approved under subsection (3) above—

(a) shall be laid before Parliament; and

(b) shall cease to have effect at the end of the period of forty days beginning with the day on which it was made unless, before the end of that period, the order has been approved by a resolution of each House of Parliament, but without prejudice to anything previously done or to the making of a new order.

(5) In reckoning for the purposes of subsection (4) above any period of forty days, no account shall be taken of any period during which Parliament is dissolved or prorogued or during which both Houses are adjourned for more than four days.

(6) In this section 'organisation' includes any association or combination of persons.

Membership, support and meetings

2.—(1) Subject to subsection (3) below, a person is guilty of an offence if he—

(a) belongs or professes to belong to a proscribed organisation;

(b) solicits or invites support for a proscribed organisation other than support with money or other property; or

(c) arranges or assists in the arrangement or management of, or addresses, any meeting of three or more persons (whether or not it is a meeting to which the public are admitted) knowing that the meeting is—

   (i) to support a proscribed organisation,

   (ii) to further the activities of such an organisation; or

   (iii) to be addressed by a person belonging or professing to belong to such an organisation.

(2) A person guilty of an offence under subsection (1) above is liable—

(a) on conviction on indictment, to imprisonment for a term not exceeding ten years or a fine or both;

(b) on summary conviction, to imprisonment for a term not exceeding six months or a fine not exceeding the statutory maximum or both.

(3) A person belonging to a proscribed organisation is not guilty

of an offence under this section by reason of belonging to the organisation if he shows—

    (a) that he became a member when it was not a proscribed organisation under the current legislation; and

    (b) that he has not since he became a member taken part in any of its activities at any time while it was a proscribed organisation under that legislation.

(4) In subsection (3) above 'the current legislation', in relation to any time, means whichever of the following was in force at that time—

    (a) the Prevention of Terrorism (Temporary Provisions) Act 1974;

    (b) the Prevention of Terrorism (Temporary Provisions) Act 1976;

    (c) the Prevention of Terrorism (Temporary Provisions) Act 1984; or

    (d) this Act.

(5) The reference in subsection (3) above to a person becoming a member of an organisation is a reference to the only or last occasion on which he became a member.

Display of support in public

3.—(1) Any person who in a public place—

    (a) wears any item of dress; or

    (b) wears, carries or displays any article,

in such a way or in such circumstances as to arouse reasonable apprehension that he is a member or supporter of a proscribed organisation, is guilty of an offence and liable on summary conviction to imprisonment for a term not exceeding six months or a fine not exceeding level 5 on the standard scale or both.

(2) In Scotland a constable may arrest without warrant anyone whom he has reasonable grounds to suspect of being a person guilty of an offence under this section.

(3) In this section 'public place' includes any highway or, in Scotland, any road within the meaning of the Roads (Scotland) Act 1984 and any premises to which at the material time the public have, or are permitted to have, access, whether on payment or otherwise.

PART II

EXCLUSION ORDERS

Exclusion orders: general

4.—(1) The Secretary of State may exercise the powers conferred on him by this Part of this Act in such a way as appears to him expedient to prevent acts of terrorism to which this Part of this Act applies.

(2) The acts of terrorism to which this Part of this Act applies are acts of terrorism connected with the affairs of Northern Ireland.

(3) An order under section 5, 6 or 7 below is referred to in this Act as an 'exclusion order'.

(4) Schedule 2 to this Act shall have effect with respect to the duration of exclusion orders, the giving of notices, the right to make representations, powers of removal and detention and other supplementary matters for this Part of this Act.

(5) The exercise of the detention powers conferred by that Schedule shall be subject to supervision in accordance with Schedule 3 to this Act.

Orders excluding persons from Great Britain

5.—(1) If the Secretary of State is satisfied that any person—

  (a) is or has been concerned in the commission, preparation or instigation of acts of terrorism to which this Part of this Act applies; or

  (b) is attempting or may attempt to enter Great Britain with a view to being concerned in the commission, preparation or instigation of such acts of terrorism,

the Secretary of State may make an exclusion order against him.

(2) An exclusion order under this section is an order prohibiting a person from being in, or entering, Great Britain.

(3) In deciding whether to make an exclusion order under this section against a person who is ordinarily resident in Great Britain, the Secretary of State shall have regard to the question whether that person's connection with any country or territory outside Great Britain is such as to make it appropriate that such an order should be made.

(4) An exclusion order shall not be made under this section against a person who is a British citizen and who—

  (a) is at the time ordinarily resident in Great Britain and has then been ordinarily resident in Great Britain throughout the last three years; or

  (b) is at the time subject to an order under section 6 below.

Orders excluding persons from Northern Ireland

6.—(1) If the Secretary of State is satisfied that any person—

  (a) is or has been concerned in the commission, preparation or instigation of acts of terrorism to which this Part of this Act applies; or

(b) is attempting or may attempt to enter Northern Ireland with a view to being concerned in the commission, preparation or instigation of such acts of terrorism,

the Secretary of State may make an exclusion order against him.

(2) An exclusion order under this section is an order prohibiting a person from being in, or entering, Northern Ireland.

(3) In deciding whether to make an exclusion order under this section against a person who is ordinarily resident in Northern Ireland, the Secretary of State shall have regard to the question whether that person's connection with any country or territory outside Northern Ireland is such as to make it appropriate that such an order should be made.

(4) An exclusion order shall not be made under this section against a person who is a British citizen and who—

(a) is at the time ordinarily resident in Northern Ireland and has then been ordinarily resident in Northern Ireland throughout the last three years; or

(b) is at the time subject to an order under section 5 above.

Orders excluding persons from the United Kingdom

7.—(1) If the Secretary of State is satisfied that any person—

(a) is or has been concerned in the commission, preparation or instigation of acts of terrorism to which this Part of this Act applies; or

(b) is attempting or may attempt to enter Great Britain or Northern Ireland with a view to being concerned in the commission, preparation or instigation of such acts of terrorism,

the Secretary of State may make an exclusion order against him.

(2) An exclusion order under this section is an order prohibiting a person from being in, or entering, the United Kingdom.

(3) In deciding whether to make an exclusion order under this section against a person who is ordinarily resident in the United Kingdom, the Secretary of State shall have regard to the question whether that person's connection with any country or territory outside the United Kingdom is such as to make it appropriate that such an order should be made.

(4) An exclusion order shall not be made under this section against a person who is a British citizen.

Offences in respect of exclusion orders

8.—(1) A person who is subject to an exclusion order is guilty of an offence if he fails to comply with the order at a time after he has been, or has become liable to be, removed under Schedule 2 to this Act.

(2) A person is guilty of an offence—

  (a) if he is knowingly concerned in arrangements for securing or facilitating the entry into Great Britain, Northern Ireland or the United Kingdom of a person whom he knows, or has reasonable grounds for believing, to be an excluded person; or

  (b) if he knowingly harbours such a person in Great Britain, Northern Ireland or the United Kingdom.

(3) In subsection (2) above 'excluded person' means—

  (a) in relation to Great Britain, a person subject to an exclusion order made under section 5 above who has been, or has become liable to be, removed from Great Britain under Schedule 2 to this Act;

  (b) in relation to Northern Ireland, a person subject to an exclusion order made under section 6 above who has been, or has become liable to be, removed from Northern Ireland under that Schedule; and

  (c) in relation to the United Kingdom, a person subject to an exclusion order made under section 7 above who has been, or has become liable to be, removed from the United Kingdom under that Schedule.

(4) A person guilty of an offence under this section is liable—

  (a) on conviction on indictment, to imprisonment for a term not exceeding five years or a fine or both;

  (b) on summary conviction, to imprisonment for a term not exceeding six months or a fine not exceeding the statutory maximum or both.

Part III

Financial Assistance for Terrorism

Contributions towards acts of terrorism

9.—(1) A person is guilty of an offence if he—

  (a) solicits or invites any other person to give, lend or otherwise make available, whether for consideration or not, any money or other property; or

  (b) receives or accepts from any other person, whether for consideration or not, any money or other property,

intending that it shall be applied or used for the commission of, or in furtherance of or in connection with, acts of terrorism to which this section applies or having reasonable cause to suspect that it may be so used or applied.

(2) A person is guilty of an offence if he—

(a) gives, lends or otherwise makes available to any other person, whether for consideration or not, any money or other property; or

(b) enters into or is otherwise concerned in an arrangement whereby money or other property is or is to be made available to another person,

knowing or having reasonable cause to suspect that it will or may be applied or used as mentioned in subsection (1) above.

(3) The acts of terrorism to which this section applies are—

(a) acts of terrorism connected with the affairs of Northern Ireland; and

(b) subject to subsection (4) below, acts of terrorism of any other description except acts connected solely with the affairs of the United Kingdom or any part of the United Kingdom other than Northern Ireland.

(4) Subsection (3)(b) above does not apply to an act done or to be done outside the United Kingdom unless it constitutes or would constitute an offence triable in the United Kingdom.

(5) In proceedings against a person for an offence under this section in relation to an act within subsection (3)(b) above done or to be done outside the United Kingdom—

(a) the prosecution need not prove that that person knew or had reasonable cause to suspect that the act constituted or would constitute such an offence as is mentioned in subsection (4) above; but

(b) it shall be a defence to prove that he did not know and had no reasonable cause to suspect that the facts were such that the act constituted or would constitute such an offence.

Contributions to resources of proscribed organisations

10.—(1) A person is guilty of an offence if he—

(a) solicits or invites any other person to give, lend or otherwise make available, whether for consideration or not, any money or other property for the benefit of a proscribed organisation;

(b) gives, lends or otherwise makes available or receives or accepts, whether for consideration or not, any money or other property for the benefit of such an organisation; or

(c) enters into or is otherwise concerned in an arrangement whereby money or other property is or is to be made available for the benefit of such an organisation.

(2) In proceedings against a person for an offence under subsection (1)(b) above it is a defence to prove that he did not know and had no reasonable cause to suspect that the money or property was for the benefit of a proscribed organisation; and in proceedings against a person for an offence under subsection (1)(c) above it is a defence to prove that he did not know and had no reasonable cause to suspect that the arrangement related to a proscribed organisation.

(3) In this section and sections 11 and 13 below 'proscribed organisation' includes a proscribed organisation for the purposes of section 21 of the Northern Ireland (Emergency Provisions) Act 1978.

Assisting in retention or control of terrorist funds

11.—(1) A person is guilty of an offence if he enters into or is otherwise concerned in an arrangement whereby the retention or control by or on behalf of another person of terrorist funds is facilitated, whether by concealment, removal from the jurisdiction, transfer to nominees or otherwise.

(2) In proceedings against a person for an offence under this section it is a defence to prove that he did not know and had no reasonable cause to suspect that the arrangement related to terrorist funds.

(3) In this section and section 12 below 'terrorist funds' means—

(a) funds which may be applied or used for the commission of, or in furtherance of or in connection with, acts of terrorism to which section 9 above applies;

(b) the proceeds of the commission of such acts of terrorism or of activities engaged in furtherance of or in connection with such acts; and

(c) the resources of a proscribed organisation.

(4) Paragraph (b) of subsection (3) includes any property which in whole or in part directly or indirectly represents such proceeds as are mentioned in that paragraph; and paragraph (c) of that subsection includes any money or other property which is or is to be applied or made available for the benefit of a proscribed organisation.

Disclosure of information about terrorist funds

12.—(1) A person may notwithstanding any restriction on the disclosure of information imposed by contract disclose to a constable a suspicion or belief that any money or other property is or is derived from terrorist funds or any matter on which such a suspicion or belief is based.

(2) A person who enters into or is otherwise concerned in any such transaction or arrangement as is mentioned in section 9, 10 or 11 above does not commit an offence under that section if he is acting with the express consent of a constable or if—

(a) he discloses to a constable his suspicion or belief that the money or other property concerned is or is derived from terrorist funds or any matter on which such a suspicion or belief is based; and

(b) the disclosure is made after he enters into or otherwise becomes concerned in the transaction or arrangement in question but is made on his own initiative and as soon as it is reasonable for him to make it,

but paragraphs (a) and (b) above do not apply in a case where, having disclosed any such suspicion, belief or matter to a constable and having been forbidden by a constable to enter into or otherwise be concerned in the transaction or arrangement in question, he nevertheless does so.

(3) In proceedings against a person for an offence under section 9(1)(b) or (2), 10(1)(b) or (c) or 11 above it is a defence to prove—

(a) that he intended to disclose to a constable such a suspicion, belief or matter as is mentioned in paragraph (a) of subsection (2) above; and

(b) that there is a reasonable excuse for his failure to make the disclosure as mentioned in paragraph (b) of that subsection.

Penalties and forfeiture

13.—(1) A person guilty of an offence under section 9, 10 or 11 above is liable—

(a) on conviction on indictment, to imprisonment for a term not exceeding fourteen years or a fine or both;

(b) on summary conviction, to imprisonment for a term not exceeding six months or a fine not exceeding the statutory maximum or both.

(2) Subject to the provisions of this section, the court by or before which a person is convicted of an offence under section 9(1) or (2)(a) above may order the forfeiture of any money or other property—

(a) which, at the time of the offence, he had in his possession or under his control; and

(b) which, at that time—

(i) in the case of an offence under subsection (1) of

section 9, he intended should be applied or used, or had
reasonable cause to suspect might be applied or used,
as mentioned in that subsection;

(ii) in the case of an offence under subsection (2)(a) of that
section, he knew or had reasonable cause to suspect
would or might be applied or used as mentioned in subsection (1) of that section.

(3) Subject to the provisions of this section, the court by or before
which a person is convicted of an offence under section 9(2)(b), 10(1)(c)
or 11 above may order the forfeiture of the money or other property
to which the arrangement in question related and which, in the case
of an offence under section 9(2)(b), he knew or had reasonable cause
to suspect would or might be applied or used as mentioned in section
9(1) above.

(4) Subject to the provisions of this section, the court by or before
which a person is convicted of an offence under section 10(1)(a) or
(b) above may order the forfeiture of any money or other property
which, at the time of the offence, he had in his possession or under
his control for the use or benefit of a proscribed organisation.

(5) The court shall not under this section make an order forfeiting
any money or other property unless the court considers that the money
or property may, unless forfeited, be applied or used as mentioned
in section 9(1) above but the court may, in the absence of evidence
to the contrary, assume that any money or property may be applied
or used as there mentioned.

(6) Where a person other than the convicted person claims to be
the owner of or otherwise interested in anything which can be forfeited
by an order under this section, the court shall, before making such
an order in respect of it, give him an opportunity to be heard.

(7) A court in Scotland shall not make an order under subsection
(2), (3) or (4) above except on the application of the prosecutor when
he moves for sentence; and for the purposes of any appeal or review
an order under any of those subsections made by a court in Scotland
is a sentence.

(8) Schedule 4 to this Act shall have effect in relation to orders under
this section.

PART IV

ARREST, DETENTION AND CONTROL OF ENTRY

Arrest and detention of suspected persons
   14.—(1) Subject to subsection (2) below, a constable may arrest

without warrant a person whom he has reasonable grounds for suspecting to be—

    (a) a person guilty of an offence under section 2, 8, 9, 10 or 11 above;

    (b) a person who is or has been concerned in the commission, preparation or instigation of acts of terrorism to which this section applies; or

    (c) a person subject to an exclusion order.

  (2) The acts of terrorism to which this section applies are—

    (a) acts of terrorism connected with the affairs of Northern Ireland; and

    (b) acts of terrorism of any other description except acts connected solely with the affairs of the United Kingdom or any part of the United Kingdom other than Northern Ireland.

  (3) The power of arrest conferred by subsection (1)(c) above is exercisable only—

    (a) in Great Britain if the exclusion order was made under section 5 above; and

    (b) in Northern Ireland if it was made under section 6 above.

  (4) Subject to subsection (5) below, a person arrested under this section shall not be detained in right of the arrest for more than forty-eight hours after his arrest.

  (5) The Secretary of State may, in any particular case, extend the period of forty-eight hours mentioned in subsection (4) above by a period or periods specified by him, but any such further period or periods shall not exceed five days in all and if an application for such an extension is made the person detained shall as soon as practicable be given written notice of that fact and of the time when the application was made.

  (6) The exercise of the detention powers conferred by this section shall be subject to supervision in accordance with Schedule 3 to this Act.

  (7) The provisions of this section are without prejudice to any power of arrest exercisable apart from this section.

Provisions supplementary to s.14

  15.—(1) If a justice of the peace is satisfied that there are reasonable grounds for suspecting that a person whom a constable believes to be liable to arrest under section 14(1)(b) above is to be found on any premises he may grant a search warrant authorising any constable to enter those premises for the purpose of searching for and arresting that person.

(2) In Scotland the power to issue a warrant under subsection (1) above shall be exercised by a sheriff or a justice of the peace, an application for such a warrant shall be supported by evidence on oath and a warrant shall not authorise a constable to enter any premises unless he is a constable for the police area in which they are situated.

(3) In any circumstances in which a constable has power under section 14 above to arrest a person, he may also, for the purpose of ascertaining whether he has in his possession any document or other article which may constitute evidence that he is a person liable to arrest, stop that person and search him.

(4) Where a constable has arrested a person under that section for any reason other than the commission of a criminal offence, he, or any other constable, may search him for the purpose of ascertaining whether he has in his possession any document or other article which may constitute evidence that he is a person liable to arrest.

(5) A search of a person under subsection (3) or (4) above may only be carried out by a person of the same sex.

(6) A person detained under section 14 above shall be deemed to be in legal custody at any time when he is so detained and may be detained in such a place as the Secretary of State may from time to time direct.

(7) The following provisions (requirement to bring accused person before the court after his arrest) shall not apply to a person detained in right of an arrest under section 14 above—

    (a) section 321(3) of the Criminal Procedure (Scotland) Act 1975;

    (b) Article 131 of the Magistrates' Courts (Northern Ireland) Order 1981;

    (c) section 50(3) of the Children and Young Persons Act (Northern Ireland) 1968.

(8) Section 295(1) of the Criminal Procedure (Scotland) Act 1975 (interim liberation by officer in charge of police station) shall not apply to a person detained in right of an arrest under section 14 above.

(9) Where a person is detained under section 14 above, any constable or prison officer, or any other person authorised by the Secretary of State, may take all such steps as may be reasonably necessary for photographing, measuring or otherwise identifying him.

(10) Section 61(1) to (8) of the Police and Criminal Evidence Act 1984 (fingerprinting) shall apply to the taking of a person's fingerprints by a constable under subsection (9) above as if for subsection (4) there were substituted—

        '(4) An officer may only give an authorisation under

subsection (3)(a) above for the taking of a person's fingerprints if he is satisfied that it is necessary to do so in order to assist in determining—

(a) whether that person is or has been concerned in the commission, preparation or instigation of acts of terrorism to which section 14 of the Prevention of Terrorism (Temporary Provisions) Act 1989 applies; or

(b) whether he is subject to an exclusion order under that Act;

or if the officer has reasonable grounds for suspecting that person's involvement in an offence under any of the provisions mentioned in subsection (1)(a) of that section and for believing that his fingerprints will tend to confirm or disprove his involvement.'

Port and border controls

16.—(1) Schedule 5 to this Act shall have effect for conferring powers to examine persons arriving in or leaving Great Britain or Northern Ireland and for connected purposes.

(2) The exercise of the examination and detention powers conferred by paragraphs 2 and 6 of that Schedule shall be subject to supervision in accordance with Schedule 3 to this Act.

(3) The designated ports for the purposes of paragraph 8 of Schedule 5 to this Act shall be those specified in Schedule 6 to this Act but the Secretary of State may by order add any port to, or remove any port from, that Schedule.

(4) Without prejudice to the provisions of Schedule 5 to this Act with respect to persons who enter or leave Northern Ireland by land or who seek to do so, the Secretary of State may by order make such further provision with respect to those persons as appears to him to be expedient.

(5) The power to make orders under this section shall be exercisable by statutory instrument.

(6) An order under subsection (4) above may contain transitional provisions and savings and shall be subject to annulment in pursuance of a resolution of either House of Parliament.

PART V

INFORMATION, PROCEEDINGS AND INTERPRETATION

Investigation of terrorist activities

17.—(1) Schedule 7 to this Act shall have effect for conferring powers to obtain information for the purposes of terrorist investigations, that is to say—

    (a) investigations into—

        (i) the commission, preparation or instigation of acts of terrorism to which section 14 above applies; or

        (ii) any other act which appears to have been done in furtherance of or in connection with such acts of terrorism, including any act which appears to constitute an offence under section 2, 9, 10 or 11 above or section 21 of the Northern Ireland (Emergency Provisions) Act 1978; or

        (iii) without prejudice to sub-paragraph (ii) above, the resources of a proscribed organisation within the meaning of this Act or a proscribed organisation for the purposes of section 21 of the said Act of 1978; and

    (b) investigations into whether there are grounds justifying the making of an order under section 1(2)(a) above or section 21(4) of that Act.

(2) Where in relation to a terrorist investigation a warrant or order under Schedule 7 to this Act has been issued or made or has been applied for and not refused, a person is guilty of an offence if, knowing or having reasonable cause to suspect that the investigation is taking place, he—

    (a) makes any disclosure which is likely to prejudice the investigation; or

    (b) falsifies, conceals or destroys or otherwise disposes of, or causes or permits the falsification, concealment, destruction or disposal of, material which is or is likely to be relevant to the investigation.

(3) In proceedings against a person for an offence under subsection (2)(a) above it is a defence to prove—

    (a) that he did not know and had no reasonable cause to suspect that the disclosure was likely to prejudice the investigation; or

    (b) that he had lawful authority or reasonable excuse for making the disclosure.

(4) In proceedings against a person for an offence under subsection (2)(b) above it is a defence to prove that he had no intention of concealing any information contained in the material in question from the persons carrying out the investigation.

(5) A person guilty of an offence under subsection (2) above is liable—

(a) on conviction on indictment, to imprisonment for a term not exceeding five years or a fine or both;

(b) on summary conviction, to imprisonment for a term not exceeding six months or a fine not exceeding the statutory maximum or both.

Information about acts of terrorism

18.—(1) A person is guilty of an offence if he has information which he knows or believes might be of material assistance—

(a) in preventing the commission by any other person of an act of terrorism connected with the affairs of Northern Ireland; or

(b) in securing the apprehension, prosecution or conviction of any other person for an offence involving the commission, preparation or instigation of such an act,

and fails without reasonable excuse to disclose that information as soon as reasonably practicable—

   (i) in England and Wales, to a constable;

  (ii) in Scotland, to a constable or the procurator fiscal; or

 (iii) in Northern Ireland, to a constable or a member of Her Majesty's Forces.

 (2) A person guilty of an offence under this section is liable—

(a) on conviction on indictment, to imprisonment for a term not exceeding five years or a fine or both;

(b) on summary conviction, to imprisonment for a term not exceeding six months or a fine not exceeding the statutory maximum or both.

 (3) Proceedings for an offence under this section may be taken, and the offence may for the purposes of those proceedings be treated as having been committed, in any place where the person to be charged is or has at any time been since he first knew or believed that the information might be of material assistance as mentioned in subsection (1) above.

Prosecutions and evidence

19.—(1) Proceedings shall not be instituted—

(a) in England and Wales for an offence under section 2, 3, 8, 9, 10, 11, 17 or 18 above or Schedule 7 to this Act except by or with the consent of the Attorney General; or

    (b) in Northern Ireland for an offence under section 8, 9, 10, 11, 17 or 18 above or Schedule 7 to this Act except by or with the consent of the Attorney General for Northern Ireland.

(2) Any document purporting to be an order, notice or direction made or given by the Secretary of State for the purposes of any provision of this Act and to be signed by him or on his behalf shall be received in evidence, and shall, until the contrary is proved, be deemed to be made or given by him.

(3) A document bearing a certificate purporting to be signed by or on behalf of the Secretary of State and stating that the document is a true copy of such an order, notice or direction shall, in any legal proceedings, be evidence, and in Scotland sufficient evidence, of the order, notice or direction.

Interpretation

20.—(1) In this Act—

    'aircraft' includes hovercraft;

    'captain' means master of a ship or commander of an aircraft;

    'examining officer' has the meaning given in paragraph 1 of Schedule 5 to this Act;

    'exclusion order' has the meaning given by section 4(3) above but subject to section 25(3) below;

    'the Islands' means the Channel Islands or the Isle of Man;

    'port' includes airport and hoverport;

    'premises' includes any place and in particular includes—

        (a) any vehicle, vessel or aircraft;

        (b) any offshore installation as defined in section 1 of the Mineral Workings (Offshore Installations) Act 1971; and

        (c) any tent or moveable structure;

    'property' includes property wherever situated and whether real or personal, heritable or moveable and things in action and other intangible or incorporeal property'

    'ship' inclues every description of vessel used in navigation;

    'terrorism' means the use of violence for political ends, and includes any use of violence for the purpose of putting the public or any section of the public in fear;

    'vehicle' includes a train and carriage forming part of a train.

(2) A constable or examining officer may, if necessary, use reasonable force for the purpose of exercising any powers conferred on him under or by virtue of any provision of this Act other than paragraph 2 of Schedule 5; but this subsection is without prejudice to any provision of this Act, or of any instrument made under it, which implies that a person may use reasonable force in connection with that provision.

(3) The powers conferred by Part II and section 16 of, and Schedules 2 and 5 to, this Act shall be exercisable notwithstanding the rights conferred by section 1 of the Immigration Act 1971 (general principles regulating entry into and stay in the United Kingdom).

(4) Any reference in a provision of this Act to a person having been concerned in the commission, preparation or instigation of acts of terrorism shall be taken to be a reference to his having been so concerned at any time, whether before or after the passing of this Act.

PART VI

FURTHER PROVISIONS FOR NORTHERN IRELAND

Search for munitions etc.

21.—(1) The powers conferred by this section shall be exercisable by a person (whether a member of Her Majesty's forces or a constable) carrying out a search under section 15(1) or (2) of the Northern Ireland (Emergency Provisions) Act 1978 (search for munitions, radio transmitters and scanning receivers).

(2) If the person carrying out the search reasonably believes that it is necessary to do so for the purpose of effectively carrying out the search or of preventing the frustration of its object he may—

(a) require any person who when the search begins is on, or during the search enters, the premises or other place where the search is carried out ('the place of search') to remain in, or in a specified part of, that place, to refrain from entering a specified part of it or to go from one specified part of it to another specified part;

(b) require any person who is not resident in the place of search to refrain from entering it; and

(c) use reasonable force to secure compliance with any such requirement.

(3) Where by virtue of section 20 of the said Act of 1978 a search under section 15(1) or (2) of that Act is carried out in relation to a vessel, aircraft or vehicle, the person carrying out the search may, if he reasonably believes that it is necessary to do so for the purpose mentioned in subsection (2) above—

  (a) require any person in or on the vessel, aircraft or vehicle to remain with it or, in the case of a vessel or vehicle which by virtue of section 20(4) of that Act is removed for the purpose of the search, to go to and remain at the place to which it is removed; and

  (b) use reasonable force to secure compliance with any such requirement.

(4) No requirement imposed under this section shall have effect after the conclusion of the search in relation to which it was imposed; and no such requirement shall be imposed or have effect after the end of the period of four hours beginning with the time when that or any other requirement was first imposed under this section in relation to the search in question but a police officer of at least the rank of superintendent may extend that period by a further period of four hours if he reasonably believes that it is necessary to do so for the purpose mentioned in subsection (2) above.

(5) A person who wilfully fails to comply with a requirement imposed under this section or wilfully obstructs, or seeks to frustrate the object of, a search in relation to which such a requirement has been or could be imposed is guilty of an offence and liable—

  (a) on conviction on indictment, to imprisonment for a term not exceeding two years or a fine or both;

  (b) on summary conviction, to imprisonment for a term not exceeding six months or a fine not exceeding the statutory maximum or both.

(6) Sections 13 and 14 of the said Act of 1978 (powers of arrest) and section 29 of that Act (restriction of prosecutions) shall apply to an offence under subsection (5) above.

(7) At the end of section 15(3)(b) of the said Act of 1978 (power to search persons) there shall be inserted the words 'and search any person entering or found in a dwelling-house entered under subsection (2) above'.

(8) The powers conferred by this section are without prejudice to any powers exercisable apart from this section where a member of Her Majesty's forces or a constable is exercising a power of search.

Restricted remission for persons sentenced for scheduled offences

22.—(1) The remission granted under prison rules in respect of a sentence of imprisonment passed in Northern Ireland for a scheduled offence within the meaning of the Northern Ireland (Emergency Provisions) Act 1978 shall not, where it is for a term of five years or more, exceed one-third of that term.

(2) Where a person is sentenced on the same occasion for two or more such offences to terms which are consecutive subsection (1) above shall apply as if those terms were a single term.

(3) Where a person is serving two or more terms which are consecutive but not all subject to subsection (1) above, the maximum remission granted under prison rules in respect of those terms taken together shall be arrived at by calculating the maximum remission for each term separately and aggregating the result.

(4) In this section 'prison rules' means rules made under section 13 of the Prison Act (Northern Ireland) 1953.

(5) The Secretary of State may by order made by statutory instrument substitute a different length of sentence and a different maximum period of remission for those mentioned in subsection (1) above; and any such order shall be subject to annulment in pursuance of a resolution of either House of Parliament.

(6) This section applies where the scheduled offence is committed while this section is in force.

Conviction of scheduled offence during period of remission

23.—(1) This section applies where a person who has been sentenced to imprisonment or a term of detention in a young offenders centre for a period exceeding one year—

(a) is discharged from prison or the centre in pursuance of prison rules; and

(b) before that sentence or term of detention would (but for that discharge) have expired he commits, and is convicted on indictment of, a scheduled offence within the meaning of the Northern Ireland (Emergency Provisions) Act 1978.

(2) If the court before which he is convicted of the scheduled offence sentences him to imprisonment or a term of detention it shall in addition order him to be returned to prison or, where appropriate, to a young offenders centre for the period between the date of the order and the date on which the sentence of imprisonment or term of detention mentioned in subsection (1) above would have expired but for his discharge.

(3) No order shall be made under subsection (2) above if the sentence imposed by the court is a suspended sentence or a sentence of life imprisonment or of detention during the Secretary of State's pleasure under section 73(1) of the Children and Young Persons Act (Northern Ireland) 1968; and any order made by a court under that subsection shall cease to have effect if an appeal results in the acquittal of the person concerned or in the substitution of a sentence other than one in respect of which the duty imposed by that subsection applies.

(4) The period for which a person is ordered under this section to be returned to prison or a young offenders centre—

(a) shall be taken to be a sentence of imprisonment or term of detention for the purposes of the Prison Act (Northern Ireland) 1953 and for the purposes of the Treatment of Offenders Act (Northern Ireland) 1968 other than section 26(2) (reduction for time spent in custody);

(b) shall not be subject to any provision of prison rules for discharge before expiry; and

(c) shall be served before, and be followed by, the sentence or term imposed for the scheduled offence and be disregarded in determining the appropriate length of that sentence or term.

(5) For the purposes of this section a certificate purporting to be signed by the governor or deputy governor of a prison or young offenders centre which specifies—

(a) the date on which a person was discharged from prison or a young offenders centre;

(b) the sentence or term which the person was serving at the time of his discharge, the offence in respect of which the sentence or term was imposed and the date on which he was convicted of that offence;

(c) the date on which the person would, but for his discharge in pursuance of prison rules, have been discharged from prison or a young offenders centre,

shall be evidence of the matters so specified.

(6) In this section—

'prison rules' means rules made under section 13 of the Prison Act (Northern Ireland) 1953;

'sentence of imprisonment' does not include a committal in default of payment of any sum of money or for want of sufficient distress to satisfy any sum of money or for failure to do or abstain from doing anything required to be done or left undone;

'young offenders centre' has the meaning assigned to it by section 2(a) of the Treatment of Offenders Act (Northern Ireland) 1968.

(7) For the purposes of subsection (1) above consecutive terms of imprisonment or of detention in a young offenders centre shall be treated as a single term and a sentence of imprisonment or detention in a young offenders centre includes—

(a) a sentence or term passed by a court in the United Kingdom, the Channel Islands or the Isle of Man;

(b) in the case of imprisonment, a sentence passed by a court-martial on a person found guilty of a civil offence within the meaning of the Army Act 1955, the Air Force Act 1955 and the Naval Discipline Act 1957.

(8) The Secretary of State may by order made by statutory instrument substitute a different period for the period of one year mentioned in subsection (1) above; and any such order shall be subject to annulment in pursuance of a resolution of either House of Parliament.

(9) This section applies where the scheduled offence is committed while this section is in force but irrespective of when the discharge from prison or a young offenders centre took place.

Explosives factories, magazines and stores

24.—(1) The grounds on which the Secretary of State may reject an application for a licence under section 6 of the Explosives Act 1875 (new explosives factories and magazines) shall include the ground that the establishment of the factory or magazine in question is undesirable in the interests of safeguarding national security or protecting public safety; and a licence granted under that section may be withdrawn by him on that ground at any time before it comes into force.

(2) The Secretary of State may also refuse a licence under section 15 or registration under section 21 of that Act (explosives stores and other premises for keeping explosives) on the ground that the establishment of the store or, as the case may be, the keeping of explosives on the premises in question is undesirable in the interests of safeguarding national security or protecting public safety.

PART VII

SUPPLEMENTARY

Consequential amendments, repeals and transitional provisions

25.—(1) The enactments mentioned in Schedule 8 to this Act shall have effect with the amendments there specified, being amendments consequential on the provisions of this Act.

(2) The enactments mentioned in Part I of Schedule 9 to this Act are hereby repealed to the extent specified in the third column of that Schedule; and the Orders mentioned in Part II of that Schedule are hereby revoked.

(3) Any exclusion order in force under any provision of Part II of the Prevention of Terrorism (Temporary Provisions) Act 1984 ('the former Act') shall have effect as if made under the corresponding provision of Part II of this Act and references in this Act to an exclusion order shall be construed accordingly.

(4) Any person who immediately before 22nd March 1989 is being detained under any provision of the former Act or of an order made under section 13 of that Act shall be treated as lawfully detained under the corresponding provision of this Act.

(5) Paragraph 2 of Schedule 5 to this Act shall not apply in relation to a person whose examination under any corresponding provision of an order made under section 13 of the former Act has begun but has not been concluded before the coming into force of that paragraph, and that provision shall continue to apply to him but any reference in this Act to examination under that paragraph shall include a reference to examination under that corresponding provision.

(6) The expiry of the former Act and its repeal by this Act shall not affect the operation of any Order in Council extending it to any of the Channel Islands or the Isle of Man; but any such Order may be revoked as if made under section 28(3) below and, notwithstanding anything contained in any such Order, shall continue in operation until revoked.

Expenses and receipts

26.   There shall be paid out of money provided by Parliament—

(a) any expenses incurred under this Act by the 'Secretary of State or the Lord Advocate; and

(b) any increase attributable to this Act in the sums payable out of such money under any other Act;

and any sums received by the Secretary of State under this Act shall be paid into the Consolidated Fund.

Commencement and duration

27.—(1) Subject to subsections (2), (3) and (4) below, this Act shall come into force on 22nd March 1989.

(2) Sections 22 to 24 shall come into force on the day after that on which this Act is passed.

(3) Schedule 3 and paragraphs 8 to 10, 18 to 20, 28 to 30 and 34 of Schedule 4 shall come into force on such day as the Secretary of State may appoint by an order made by statutory instrument; and different days may be appointed for different provisions or different purposes and for England and Wales, for Scotland and for Northern Ireland.

(4) The repeal by Schedule 9 of paragraph 9 of Schedule 7 shall come into force on the coming into force of the Land Registration Act 1988.

(5) The provisions of Parts I to V of this Act and of subsection (6)(c) below shall remain in force until 22nd March 1990 and shall then expire unless continued in force by an order under subsection (6) below.

(6) The Secretary of State may by order made by statutory instrument provide—

- (a) that all or any of those provisions which are for the time being in force (including any in force by virtue of an order under this paragraph or paragraph (c) below) shall continue in force for a period not exceeding twelve months from the coming into operation of the order;
- (b) that all or any of those provisions which are for the time being in force shall cease to be in force; or
- (c) that all or any of those provisions which are not for the time being in force shall come into force again and remain in force for a period not exceeding twelve months from the coming into operation of the order.

(7) No order shall be made under subsection (6) above unless—

- (a) a draft of the order has been laid before and approved by a resolution of each House of Parliament; or
- (b) it is declared in the order that it appears to the Secretary of State that by reason of urgency it is necessary to make the order without a draft having been so approved.

(8) An order under that subsection of which a draft has not been approved under section (7) above—

- (a) shall be laid before Parliament; and
- (b) shall cease to have effect at the end of the period of forty days beginning with the day on which it was made unless, before the end of that period, the order has been approved by a resolution of each House of Parliament, but without prejudice to anything previously done or to the making of a new order.

(9) In reckoning for the purposes of subsection (8) above the period

of forty days no account shall be taken of any period during which Parliament is dissolved or prorogued or during which both Houses are adjourned for more than four days.

(10) In subsection (5) above the reference to Parts I to V of this Act does not include a reference to the provisions of Parts III and V so far as they have effect in Northern Ireland and relate to proscribed organisations for the purposes of section 21 of the Northern Ireland (Emergency Provisions) Act 1978 or offences or orders under that section.

(11) The provisions excluded by subsection (10) above from subsection (5) and the provisions of sections 21 to 24 above shall remain in force until 22nd March 1990 and then expire but shall be—

- (a) included in the provisions to which subsection (3) of section 33 of the said Act of 1978 applies (provisions that can be continued in force, repealed or revived by order); and
- (b) treated as part of that Act for the purposes of subsection (9) of that Act (repeal on 14th May 1992).

(12) The expiry or cesser of sections 22 and 23 above shall not affect the operation of those sections in relation to an offence committed while they were in force.

Short title and extent

28.—(1) This Act may be cited as the Prevention of Terrorism (Temporary Provisions) Act 1989.

(2) This Act extends to the whole of the United Kingdom except that—

- (a) Part I and section 15(1) do not extend to Northern Ireland and sections 21 to 24, Part III of Schedule 4 and the repeal in Schedule 9 relating to the Explosives Act 1875 extend only to Northern Ireland;
- (b) section 15(10), Part I of Schedule 4 and paragraph 7(6) of Schedule 5 extend only to England and Wales;
- (c) Part II of Schedule 4 and Part II of Schedule 7 extend only to Scotland;
- (d) Part I of Schedule 7 extends only to England, Wales and Northern Ireland; and
- (e) subject to paragraph (a) above, the amendments and repeals in Schedules 8 and 9 have the same extent as the enactments to which they refer.

(3) Her Majesty may by Order in Council direct that any of the provisions of this Act shall extend, with such exceptions, adaptations and

modifications, if any, as may be specified in the Order, to any of the Channel Islands and the Isle of Man.

SCHEDULES

Section 1 ## SCHEDULE 1

PROSCRIBED ORGANISATIONS

Irish Republican Army
Irish National Liberation Army

Section 4(4) ## SCHEDULE 2

EXCLUSION ORDERS

Duration

1.—(1) An exclusion order may be revoked at any time by a further order made by the Secretary of State.

(2) An exclusion order shall, unless revoked earlier, expire at the end of the period of three years beginning with the day on which it is made.

(3) The fact that an exclusion order against a person has been revoked or has expired shall not prevent the making of a further exclusion order against him.

Notice of making of order

2.—(1) As soon as may be after the making of an exclusion order, notice of the making of the order shall be served on the person against whom it has been made; and the notice shall—

    (a) set out the rights afforded to him by paragraph 3 below; and

    (b) specify the manner in which those rights are to be exercised.

(2) Sub-paragraph (1) above shall not impose an obligation to take any steps to serve a notice on a person at a time when he is outside the United Kingdom.

(3) Where the person against whom an exclusion order is made is

not for the time being detained by virtue of this Act, the notice of the making of the order may be served on him by posting it to him at his last known address.

Right to make representations

3.—(1) If after being served with notice of the making of an exclusion order the person against whom it is made objects to the order he may—

(a) make representations in writing to the Secretary of State setting out the grounds of his objections; and

(b) include in those representations a request for a personal interview with the person or persons nominated by the Secretary of State under sub-paragraph (5) below.

(2) Subject to sub-paragraphs (3) and (4) below, a person against whom an exclusion order has been made must exercise the rights conferred by sub-paragraph (1) above within seven days of the service of the notice.

(3) Where before the end of that period—

(a) he has consented to his removal under paragraph 5 below from Great Britain, Northern Ireland or the United Kingdom, as the case may be; and

(b) he has been removed accordingly,

he may exercise the rights conferred by sub-paragraph (1) above within fourteen days of his removal.

(4) Where at the time when the notice of an exclusion order is served on a person he is in a part of the United Kingdom other than that from which the order excludes him he may exercise the rights conferred by sub-paragraph (1) above within fourteen days of the service of the notice.

(5) If a person exercises those rights within the period within which they are required to be exercised by him, the matter shall be referred for the advice of one or more persons nominated by the Secretary of State.

(6) Where sub-paragraph (2) above applies, the person against whom the exclusion order has been made shall be granted a personal interview with the person or persons so nominated.

(7) Where sub-paragraph (3) or (4) above applies, the person against whom the exclusion order has been made shall be granted a personal interview with the person or persons so nominated if it appears to the Secretary of State that it is reasonably practicable to grant him such an interview in an appropriate country or territory within a reasonable period from the date on which he made his representations.

(8) In sub-paragraph (7) above 'an appropriate country or territory' means—

- (a) Northern Ireland or the Republic of Ireland if the exclusion order was made under section 5 of this Act;
- (b) Great Britain or the Republic of Ireland if it was made under section 6 of this Act;
- (c) the Republic of Ireland if it was made under section 7 of this Act.

(9) Where it appears to the Secretary of State that it is reasonably practicable to grant a personal interview in more than one appropriate country or territory he may grant the interview in whichever of them he thinks fit.

(10) It shall be for the Secretary of State to determine the place in any country or territory at which an interview under this paragraph is to be granted.

Reconsideration of exclusion order following representations

4.—(1) Where the Secretary of State receives representations in respect of an exclusion order under paragraph 3 above he shall reconsider the matter as soon as reasonably practicable after receiving the representations and any report of an interview relating to the matter which has been granted under that paragraph.

(2) In reconsidering a matter under this paragraph the Secretary of State shall take into account everything which appears to him to be relevant and in particular—

- (a) the representations relating to the matter made to him under paragraph 3 above;
- (b) the advice of the person or persons to whom the matter was referred by him under that paragraph; and
- (c) the report of any interview relating to the matter granted under that paragraph.

(3) The Secretary of State shall thereafter, if it is reasonably practicable to do so, give notice in writing to the person against whom the exclusion order has been made of any decision he takes as to whether or not to revoke the order.

Powers of removal

5. Where an exclusion order has been made against a person and notice of the making of the order has been served on him, the Secretary of State may have him removed from the relevant territory—

- (a) if he consents;

   (b) if the period mentioned in paragraph 3(2) above has expired and he has not made representations relating to the matter in accordance with the paragraph; or

   (c) if he has made such representations but the Secretary of State has notified him that he has decided not to revoke the order.

Removal directions .

6.—(1) The Secretary of State may in accordance with the following provisions of this paragraph give directions for the removal from the relevant territory of any person subject to an exclusion order; but a person shall not be removed in pursuance of the directions until notice of the making of the order has been served on him and one of the conditions in paragraph 5(a), (b) and (c) above is fulfilled.

(2) Directions under this paragraph above may be—

   (a) directions given to the captain of a ship or aircraft about to leave the relevant territory requiring him to remove the person in question from that territory in that ship or aircraft; or

   (b) directions given to the owners or agents of any ship or aircraft requiring them to make arrangements for the removal from the relevant territory of the person in question in a ship or aircraft specified or indicated in the directions; or

   (c) directions for the removal from the relevant territory of the person in question in accordance with arrangements to be made by the Secretary of State;

and any such directions shall specify the country or territory to which the person in question is to be removed.

(3) Directions under this paragraph may also be given for the removal of a person by land to the Republic of Ireland; and those directions may be—

   (a) directions given to the driver or owner of any vehicle (being, in the case of a private vehicle, one in which that person arrived in Northern Ireland) requiring him to remove the person in question to the Republic of Ireland in a vehicle specified in the directions; or

   (b) directions for the removal of the person in question in accordance with arrangements to be made by the Secretary of State.

(4) No directions under this paragraph shall be for the removal of a person to any country or territory other than one—

   (a) of which the person in question is a national or citizen;

(b) in which he obtained a passport or other document of identity; or

(c) to which there is reason to believe that he will be admitted;

and no such directions shall be given for the removal of a British citizen, a British Dependent Territories citizen, a British Overseas citizen or a British National (Overseas) to a country or territory outside the United Kingdom unless he is also a national or citizen of, or has indicated that he is willing to be removed to, that country or territory.

(5) Where—

(a) a person is found on examination under Schedule 5 to this Act to be subject to an exclusion order; or

(b) an exclusion order is made against a person following such an examination,

the power to give directions for his removal under any provision of this paragraph except sub-paragraphs (2)(c) and (3)(b) shall be exercisable by an examining officer as well as by the Secretary of State; and where any such person has arrived in a ship or aircraft (including arrival as a transit passenger, member of the crew or other person not seeking to enter Great Britain or Northern Ireland) the countries or territories to which he may be directed to be removed under subparagraph (2) above include the country or territory in which he embarked on that ship or aircraft.

(6) A person in respect of whom directions are given under this paragraph may be placed under the authority of the Secretary of State or an examining officer on board any ship or aircraft or, as the case may be, in or on any vehicle in which he is to be removed in accordance with the directions.

(7) The cost of complying with any directions under this paragraph shall be defrayed by the Secretary of State.

(8) Any person who without reasonable excuse fails to comply with directions given to him under this paragraph is guilty of an offence and liable on summary conviction to imprisonment for a term not exceeding three months or a fine not exceeding level 4 on the standard scale or both.

(9) In this paragraph 'the relevant territory' means—

(a) in relation to a person subject to an exclusion order made under section 5 of this Act, Great Britain;

(b) in relation to a person subject to an exclusion order made under section 6 of this Act, Northern Ireland; and

(c) in relation to a person subject to an exclusion order made under section 7 of this Act, the United Kingdom.

Detention pending removal

7.—(1) A person in respect of whom directions for removal may be given under paragraph 6 above may be detained pending the giving of such directions and pending removal in pursuance of the directions under the authority of the Secretary of State or, if the directions are to be or have been given by an examining officer, of such an officer.

(2) A person liable to be detained under this paragraph may be arrested without warrant by an examining officer.

(3) The captain of a ship or aircraft, if so required by an examining officer, shall prevent any person placed on board the ship or aircraft under paragraph 6 above from disembarking in the relevant territory or, before the directions for his removal have been fulfilled, elsewhere.

(4) Where under sub-paragraph (3) above the captain of a ship or aircraft is required to prevent a person from disembarking he may for that purpose detain him in custody on board the ship or aircraft.

(5) The captain of a ship or aircraft who fails to take reasonable steps to comply with a requirement imposed under sub-paragraph (3) above is guilty of an offence and liable on summary conviction to imprisonment for a term not exceeding six months or a fine not exceeding level 4 on the standard scale or both.

(6) A person may be removed from a vehicle for detention under this paragraph.

(7) In this paragraph 'relevant territory' has the same meaning as in paragraph 6 above.

Detention: supplementary provisions

8.—(1) If a justice of the peace is satisfied that there are reasonable grounds for suspecting that a person liable to be arrested under paragraph 7(2) above is to be found on any premises he may grant a search warrant authorising any constable to enter those premises for the purpose of searching for and arresting that person.

(2) In Scotland the power to issue a warrant under sub-paragraph (1) above shall be exercised by a sheriff or a justice of the peace, an application for such a warrant shall be supported by evidence on oath and a warrant shall not authorise a constable to enter any premises unless he is a constable for the police area in which they are situated.

(3) In Northern Ireland an application for a warrant under sub-paragraph (1) above shall be made by a complaint on oath.

(4) A person detained under this Schedule shall be deemed to be in legal custody at any time when he is so detained and, if detained

otherwise than on board a ship or aircraft, may be detained in such a place as the Secretary of State may from time to time direct.

(5) Where a person is detained under this Schedule, any examining officer, constable or prison officer, or any other person authorised by the Secretary of State, may take all such steps as may be reasonably necessary for photographing, measuring or otherwise identifying him.

(6) Any person detained under this Schedule may be taken in the custody of a constable or an examining officer, or of any person acting under the authority of an examining officer, to and from any place where his attendance is required for the purpose of establishing his nationality or citizenship or for making arrangements for his admission to a country or territory outside the United Kingdom or where he is required to be for any other purpose connected with the operation of this Act.

Exemption from exclusion orders

9.—(1) When any question arises under this Act whether a person is exempted from the provisions of section 5, 6 or 7 of this Act it shall be for the person asserting that he is exempt to prove it.

(2) A person is not to be treated as ordinarily resident in Great Britain for the purposes of the exemption in section 5(4)(a) of this Act or in Northern Ireland for the purpose of the exemption in section 6(4)(a) of this Act at a time when he is there in breach of—

    (a) an exclusion order; or

    (b) the Immigration Act 1971 or any law for purposes similar to that Act in force in the United Kingdom after the passing of this Act.

(3) In each of those exemptions 'the last three years' is to be taken as a period amounting in total to three years exclusive of any time during which the person claiming exemption was undergoing imprisonment or detention for a period of six months or more by virtue of a sentence passed for an offence on a conviction in the United Kingdom or in any of the Islands.

(4) In sub-paragraph (3) above—

    (a) 'sentence' includes any order made on conviction of an offence;

    (b) two or more sentences for consecutive (or partly consecutive) terms shall be treated as a single sentence;

    (c) a person shall be deemed to be detained by virtue of a sentence

      (i) at any time when he is liable to imprisonment or detention by virtue of the sentence but is unlawfully at large; and

     (ii) during any period of custody by which under any relevant enactment the term to be served under the sentence is reduced.

(5) In sub-paragraph (4)(c)(ii) above 'relevant enactment' means section 67 of the Criminal Justice Act 1967 and any similar enactment which is for the time being or has (before or after the passing of this Act) been in force in any part of the United Kingdom or in any of the Islands.

SCHEDULE 3
Sections 4(5), 14(6) and 16(2)

SUPERVISION OF DETENTION AND EXAMINATION POWERS

Detention pending removal

1.—(1) Where a person is detained under paragraph 7 of Schedule 2 to this Act under the authority of an examining officer his detention shall be periodically reviewed in accordance with this paragraph by a review officer and shall not continue unless that officer has authorised it to continue.

(2) The reviews shall be carried out as follows—

    (a) the first review shall be as soon as practicable after the beginning of the detention; and

    (b) the subsequent reviews shall be at intervals of not more than twelve hours.

(3) On any such review the review officer shall authorise the continued detention of the person in question if, and only if, he is satisfied that steps for giving directions for his removal or for removing him in pursuance of the directions are being taken diligently and expeditiously.

Examination without detention

2.—(1) Where a person has been required by a notice under paragraph 2(4) of Schedule 5 to this Act to submit to further examination but is not detained under paragraph 6 of that Schedule his further examination shall be reviewed by a review officer not later than twelve hours after the beginning of the examination and shall not continue unless that officer has authorised it to continue.

(2) The review officer shall authorise the examination to continue if, and only if, he is satisfied that the enquiries necessary to complete the examination are being carried out diligently and expeditiously.

Detention for examination or as suspected person

3.—(1) Where a person is detained under section 14 of this Act or under paragraph 6 of Schedule 5 to this Act his detention shall be periodically reviewed in accordance with this paragraph by a review officer and shall not continue unless—

(a) that officer has authorised it to continue; or

(b) an application has been made to the Secretary of State for an extension of the period of detention under subsection (5) of that section or sub-paragraph (3) of that paragraph.

(2) The reviews shall be carried out as follows—

(a) the first review shall be as soon as practicable after the beginning of the detention; and

(b) the subsequent reviews shall be at intervals of not more than twelve hours;

and no review shall be carried out after such an application as is mentioned in sub-paragraph (1)(b) above has been made.

(3) Subject to sub-paragraph (4) below, on any such review the review officer shall authorise the continued detention of the person in question if, and only if, he is satisfied—

(a) that his continued detention is necessary in order to obtain (whether by questioning him or otherwise) or to preserve evidence which—

(i) relates to an offence under section 2, 8, 9, 10 or 11 of this Act (in the case of detention under section 14) or under section 8 (in the case of detention under paragraph 6 of Schedule 5);

(ii) indicates that he is or has been concerned in the commission, preparation or instigation of acts of terrorism to which section 14 of this Act applies; or

(iii) indicates that he is subject to an exclusion order; and

(b) that the investigation in connection with which that person is detained is being conducted diligently and expeditiously.

(4) The review officer may also authorise the continued detention of the person in question—

(a) pending consideration of the question whether he is subject to an exclusion order;

(b) pending consideration by the Secretary of State whether to make an exclusion order against him or to serve him with notice of a decision to make a deportation order under the Immigration Act 1971;

(c) pending a decision by the Director of Public Prosecutions or Attorney General or, as the case may be, the Lord Advocate or the Director of Public Prosecutions or Attorney General for Northern Ireland whether proceedings for an offence should be instituted against him; or

(d) if he is satisfied as to the matters specified in sub-paragraph (5) below.

(5) The matters referred to in sub-paragraph (4)(d) above are—

(a) that the continued detention of the person in question is necessary—

    (i) pending a decision whether to apply to the Secretary of State for an exclusion order to be made in respect of him or for notice of a decision to make a deportation order under the Immigration Act 1971 to be served on him; or

    (ii) pending the making of such an application; and

(b) that consideration of that question is being undertaken, or preparation of the application is being proceeded with, diligently and expeditiously.

The review officer

4. The review officer shall be an officer who has not been directly involved in the matter in connection with which the person in question is detained or examined and—

(a) in the case of a review carried out within twenty-four hours of the beginning of that person's detention or in the case of a review under paragraph 2 above, shall be an officer of at least the rank of inspector;

(b) in the case of any other review, shall be an officer of at least the rank of superintendent.

Postponement of reviews

5.—(1) A review may be postponed—

(a) if, having regard to all the circumstances prevailing at the latest time specified in paragraph 1(2), 2(1) or 3(2) above, it is not practicable to carry out the review at that time;

(b) without prejudice to the generality of paragraph (a) above—

    (i) if at that time the person in detention or being examined is being questioned by a police officer or an examining officer and the review officer is satisfied that an interruption of the questioning for the purpose of carrying out the review would prejudice the investigation in connection with which the person is being detained or examined; or

    (ii) if at that time no review officer is readily available.

(2) If a review is postponed under this paragraph it shall be carried out as soon as practicable after the latest time specified for it under the relevant provision mentioned in sub-paragraph (1)(a) above.

(3) If a review is carried out after postponement under this paragraph, the fact that it was so carried out shall not affect any requirement of this Schedule as to the time at which any subsequent review is to be carried out.

Representation about detention

6.—(1) Before determining whether to authorise a person's continued detention the review officer shall give—

(a) that person (unless he is asleep); or

(b) any solicitor representing him who is available at the time of the review,

an opportunity to make representations to him about the detention.

(2) Subject to sub-paragraph (3) below, the person whose detention is under review or his solicitor may make representations under this paragraph either orally or in writing.

(3) The review officer may refuse to hear oral representations from the person whose detention is under review if he considers that he is unfit to make such representations by reason of his condition or behaviour.

Rights of detained persons

7.—(1) Where the review officer authorises a person's continued detention and at that time that person has not yet exercised a right conferred on him by section 56 or 58 of the Police and Criminal Evidence Act 1984 (right of arrested person to have someone informed and to have access to legal advice) the review officer shall inform him of that right and, if its exercise is being delayed in accordance with the provisions of the section in question, that it is being so delayed.

(2) Where a review of a person's detention is carried out under paragraph 1 or 3 above at a time when his exercise of a right conferred by either of those sections is being delayed—

    (a) the review officer shall consider whether the reason or reasons for which the delay was authorised continue to subsist; and

    (b) if he is not himself the officer who authorised the delay and is of the opinion that the reason or reasons have ceased to subsist, he shall inform that officer of his opinion.

(3) In the application of this paragraph to Scotland for the references to sections 56 and 58 of the said Act of 1984 there shall be substituted a reference to section 3A of the Criminal Justice (Scotland) Act 1980.

(4) In the application of this paragraph to Northern Ireland for the references to sections 56 and 58 of the said Act of 1984 there shall be substituted references to sections 14 and 15 of the Northern Ireland (Emergency Provisions) Act 1987.

Records of review

8.—(1) The review officer carrying out a review under this Schedule shall make a written record of the outcome of the review, including, where the continued detention or examination of the person in question is authorised, the grounds for authorisation and, where a review is postponed, the reason for the postponement.

(2) The record required by this paragraph shall be made in the presence of the person detained or examined and, where his continued detention or examination is authorised, he shall at that time be told the grounds for the authorisation.

(3) Sub-paragraph (2) above shall not apply where the person detained or examined is, at the time when the written record is made—

    (a) incapable of understanding what is said to him;

    (b) violent or likely to become violent; or

    (c) in urgent need of medical attention.

(4) Where the review officer informs a detained person of the matters mentioned in sub-paragraph (1) of paragraph 7 above he shall make a written record of the fact that he has done so.

(5) The review officer shall also make a written record of his conclusion on the matter which he is required to consider under sub-paragraph (2)(a) of that paragraph, and, if he has taken action in accordance with sub-paragraph (2)(b) of that paragraph, of the fact that he has done so.

Intervention by superior officer

9. Where the review officer is of a rank lower than superintendent and—

  (a) an officer of higher rank than the review officer gives directions relating to the person detained or examined; and
  (b) the directions are at variance—

    (i) with any decision made or action taken by the review officer in the performance of a duty imposed on him by this Schedule; or
    (ii) with any decision or action which would but for the directions have been made or taken by him in the performance of that duty,

the review officer shall refer the matter at once to an officer of the rank of superintendent or above.

Section 13(8)   SCHEDULE 4

FORFEITURE ORDERS

PART I

ENGLAND AND WALES

Implementation of forfeiture orders

1.—(1) Where a court in England and Wales makes an order under section 13(2), (3) or (4) of this Act (in this Part of this Schedule referred to as a 'forfeiture order') it may make an order—

  (a) requiring any money or other property to which the forfeiture order applies to be paid or handed over to the proper officer or to a constable designated for the purpose by the chief officer of police of a police force specified in the order;
  (b) directing any such property other than money or land to be sold or otherwise disposed of in such manner as the court may direct and the proceeds to be paid to the proper officer;
  (c) appointing a receiver to take possession, subject to such conditions and exceptions as may be specified by the court, of any such property which is land, to realise it in such manner as the court may direct and to pay the proceeds to the proper officer;
  (d) directing a specified part of any money, or of the proceeds of the sale, disposal or realisation of any property, to which

the forfeiture order applies to be paid by the proper officer to or for a specified person falling within section 13(6) of this Act.

(e) making such other provision as appears to the court to be necessary for giving effect to the forfeiture order or to any order made by virtue of paragraph (a), (b), (c) or (d) above.

(2) A forfeiture order shall not come into force until (disregarding any power of a court to grant leave to appeal out of time) there is no further possibility of the order being set aside.

(3) Any balance in the hands of the proper officer after making any payment required under sub-paragraph (1)(d) above or paragraph 2 below shall be treated for the purposes of section 61 of the Justices of the Peace Act 1979 (application of fines etc.) as if it were a fine imposed by a magistrates' court.

(4) The proper officer shall, on the application of the prosecutor or defendant in the proceedings in which a forfeiture order is made, certify in writing the extent (if any) to which, at the date of the certificate, effect has been given to the order in respect of the money or other property to which it applies.

(5) In this paragraph 'the proper officer' means, where the forfeiture order is made by a magistrates' court, the clerk of that court and, where the order is made by the Crown Court—

(a) the clerk of the magistrates' court by which the defendant was committed to the Crown Court; or

(b) if the proceedings were instituted by a bill of indictment preferred by virtue of section 2(2)(b) of the Administration of Justice (Miscellaneous Provisions) Act 1933, the clerk of the magistrates' court for the place where the trial took place;

and in this sub-paragraph references to the clerk of a magistrates' court shall be construed in accordance with section 141 of the Magistrates' Courts Act 1980 taking references to that Act as references to this Act.

(6) In this paragraph references to the proceeds of the sale, disposal or realisation of property are references to the proceeds after deduction of the costs of sale, disposal or realisation.

(7) This paragraph has effect to the exclusion of section 140 of the said Act of 1980.

2.—(1) Where a receiver appointed under paragraph 1 above takes any action—

(a) in relation to property which is not subject to forfeiture, being action which he would be entitled to take if it were such property;

(b) believing, and having reasonable grounds for believing, that he is entitled to take that action in relation to that property,

he shall not be liable to any person in respect of any loss or damage resulting from his action except in so far as the loss or damage is caused by his negligence.

(2) A receiver appointed under paragraph 1 above shall be entitled to be paid his remuneration and expenses out of the proceeds of the property realised by him or, if and so far as those proceeds are insufficient, by the prosecutor.

Restraint orders

3.—(1) The High Court may in accordance with this paragraph by an order (referred to in this Part of this Schedule as a 'restraint order') prohibit any person, subject to such conditions and exceptions as may be specified in the order, from dealing with any property liable to forfeiture, that is to say, any property in respect of which a forfeiture order has been made or in respect of which such an order could be made in the proceedings referred to in sub-paragraph (2) or (3) below.

(2) A restraint order may be made where—

(a) proceedings have been instituted against a defendant in England or Wales for an offence under Part III of this Act;

(b) the proceedings have not been concluded; and

(c) either a forfeiture order has been made or it appears to the court that there are reasonable grounds for thinking that a forfeiture order may be made in those proceedings.

(3) A restraint order may also be made where—

(a) the court is satisfied that, whether by the laying of an information or otherwise, a person is to be charged in England and Wales with an offence under Part III of this Act; and

(b) it appears to the court that a forfeiture order may be made in proceedings for the offence.

(4) In the application of the provisions of this Part of this Schedule at a time when a restraint order may be made by virtue of sub-paragraph (3) above references to the prosecutor shall be construed as references to the person who the High Court is satisfied is to have the conduct of the proposed proceedings.

(5) Where the court has made an order under this paragraph by virtue of sub-paragraph (3) above the court may discharge the order if proceedings in respect of the offence are not instituted (whether by the laying of an information or otherwise) within such time as the court considers reasonable.

(6) For the purposes of this paragraph, dealing with property includes, without prejudice to the generality of that expression—

    (a) where a debt is owed to the person concerned, making a payment to any person in reduction of the amount of the debt; and

    (b) removing the property from the jurisdiction of the High Court.

(7) In exercising the powers conferred by this paragraph the court shall not take account of any obligations of any person having an interest in the property subject to the restraint order which might frustrate the making of a forfeiture order.

(8) For the purposes of this paragraph proceedings for an offence are instituted—

    (a) when a justice of the peace issues a summons or warrant under section 1 of the Magistrates' Courts Act 1980 in respect of that offence;

    (b) when a person is charged with the offence after being taken into custody without a warrant;

    (c) when a bill of indictment is preferred by virtue of section 2(2)(b) of the Administration of Justice (Miscellaneous Provisions) Act 1933;

and where the application of this sub-paragraph would result in there being more than one time for the institution of proceedings they shall be taken to be instituted at the earliest of those times.

(9) For the purposes of this paragraph and paragraph 4 below proceedings are concluded—

    (a) when a forfeiture order has been made in those proceedings and effect has been given to it in respect of all the money or other property to which it applies; or

    (b) when (disregarding any power of a court to grant leave to appeal out of time) there is no further possibility of a forfeiture order being made in the proceedings.

4.—(1) A restraint order—

    (a) may be made only on an application by the prosecutor;

    (b) may be made on an ex parte application to a judge in chambers; and

    (c) shall provide for notice to be given to persons affected by the order.

(2) A restraint order—

    (a) may be discharged or varied in relation to any property; and

(b) shall be discharged when proceedings for the offence are concluded.

(3) An application for the discharge or variation of a restraint order may be made by any person affected by it.

5.—(1) Where the High Court has made a restraint order a constable may for the purpose of preventing any property subject to the order being removed from the jurisdiction of the court seize that property.

(2) Property seized under this paragraph shall be dealt with in accordance with the court's directions.

6.—(1) The Land Charges Act 1972 and the Land Registration Act 1925 shall apply—

(a) in relation to restraint orders as they apply in relation to orders affecting land made by the court for the purpose of enforcing judgments or recognizances; and

(b) in relation to applications for restraint orders as they apply in relation to other pending land actions.

(2) The prosecutor shall be treated for the purposes of section 57 of the Land Registration Act 1925 (inhibitions) as a person interested in relation to any registered land to which a restraint order or an application for such an order relates.

Compensation

7.—(1) If proceedings are instituted against a person for an offence under Part III of this Act and either—

(a) the proceedings do not result in his conviction for any such offence; or

(b) where he is convicted of one or more such offences—

(i) the conviction or convictions concerned are quashed; or

(ii) he is pardoned by Her Majesty in respect of the conviction or convictions concerned,

the High Court may, on an application by a person who had an interest in any property which was subject to a forfeiture or restraint order made in or in relation to those proceedings, order compensation to be paid to the applicant if, having regard to all the circumstances, it considers it appropriate to do so.

(2) The High Court shall not order compensation to be paid in any case unless it is satisfied—

(a) that there is some serious default on the part of a person concerned in the investigation or prosecution of the offence concerned, being a person mentioned in sub-paragraph (5) below; and

(b) that the applicant has suffered loss in consequence of anything done in relation to the property by or in pursuance of an order under this Part of this Schedule.

(3) The court shall not order compensation to be paid in any case where it appears to it that the proceedings would have been instituted even if the serious default had not occurred.

(4) The amount of compensation to be paid under this paragraph shall be such as the High Court thinks just in all the circumstances of the case.

(5) Compensation payable under this paragraph shall be paid—

(a) where the person in default was or was acting as a member of a police force, out of the police fund out of which the expenses of that police force are met,

(b) where the person in default was a member of the Crown Prosecution Service or acting on behalf of the Service, by the Director of Public Prosecutions.

(6) Sub-paragraph (8) of paragraph 3 above applies for the purposes of this paragraph as it applies for the purposes of that paragraph.

Enforcement of orders made elsewhere in the British Islands

8.—(1) In the following provisions of this Part of this Schedule 'a Scottish order' means—

(a) an order made in Scotland under section 13(2), (3) or (4) of this Act ('a Scottish forfeiture order');

(b) an order made under paragraph 13 below ('a Scottish restraint order'); or

(c) an order made under any other provision of Part II of this Schedule in relation to a Scottish forfeiture or restraint order;

'a Northern Ireland' order means—

(a) an order made in Northern Ireland under section 13(2), (3) or (4) of this Act ('a Northern Ireland forfeiture order');

(b) an order made under paragraph 23 below ('a Northern Ireland restraint order'); or

(c) an order made under any other provision of Part III of this Schedule in relation to a Northern Ireland forfeiture or restraint order;

'an Islands order' means—

(a) an order made in any of the Islands under section 13(2), (3) or (4) of this Act as extended to that Island under section 28(3) of this Act ('an Islands forfeiture order');

(b) an order under paragraph 3 above as so extended ('an Islands restraint order'); or

(c) an order made under any other provision of this Part of this Schedule as so extended in relation to an Islands forfeiture or restraint order.

(2) In paragraphs (a), (b) and (c) of the definition of 'an Islands order' the reference to a provision of this Act as extended to an Island under section 28(3) of this Act includes a reference to any provision of the law of that Island for purposes corresponding to that provision.

9.—(1) A Scottish order, Northern Ireland order or Islands order shall, subject to the provisions of this paragraph, have effect in the law of England and Wales but shall be enforced in England and Wales only in accordance with the provisions of this paragraph and any provision made by rules of court as to the manner in which and the conditions subject to which such orders are to be enforced there.

(2) The High Court shall, on an application made to it in accordance with rules of court for registration of a Scottish order, Northern Ireland order or Islands order, direct that the order shall, in accordance with such rules, be registered in that court.

(3) Rules of court shall also make provision—

(a) for cancelling or varying the registration of a Scottish, Northern Ireland or Islands forfeiture order when effect has been given to it (whether in England and Wales or elsewhere) in respect of all or, as the case may be, part of the money or other property to which the order applies;

(b) for cancelling or varying the registration of a Scottish, Northern Ireland or Islands restraint order which has been discharged or varied by the court by which it was made.

(4) If a Scottish, Northern Ireland or Islands forfeiture order is registered under this paragraph the High Court shall have, in relation to that order, the same powers as a court has under paragraph 1(1) above in relation to a forfeiture order made by it (and paragraph 2 above applies accordingly) but any functions of the clerk of a magistrates' court shall be exercised by the appropriate officer of the High Court.

(5) After making any payment required by virtue of paragraph 1(1)(d) or 2 above, the balance of any sums received by the appropriate officer of the High Court by virtue of an order made under subparagraph (4) above shall be paid by him to the Secretary of State.

(6) Paragraph 3(7), 5 and 6 above shall apply to a registered Scottish, Northern Ireland or Islands restraint order as they apply to a restraint order and the High Court shall have the like power to make an order

under section 33 of the Supreme Court Act 1981 (extended power to order inspection of property etc.) in relation to proceedings brought or likely to be brought for a Scottish, Northern Ireland or Islands restraint order as if those proceedings had been brought or were likely to be brought in the High Court.

(7) Without prejudice to the foregoing provisions, if a Scottish order, Northern Ireland order or Islands order is registered under this paragraph—

    (a) the High Court shall have, in relation to its enforcement, the same power;

    (b) proceedings for or with respect to its enforcement may be taken; and

    (c) proceedings for or with respect to any contravention of such an order (whether before or after such registration) may be taken,

as if the order had originally been made in the High Court.

(8) The High Court may, additionally, for the purpose of—

    (a) assisting the achievement in England and Wales of the purposes of a Scottish order, Northern Ireland order or Islands order; or

    (b) assisting any receiver or other person directed by any such order to sell or otherwise dispose of property,

make such orders or do otherwise as seems to it appropriate.

(9) A document purporting to be a copy of a Scottish order, Northern Ireland order or Islands order and to be certified as such by a proper officer of the court by which it was made or purporting to be a certificate for purposes corresponding to those of paragraph 1(4) above and to be certified by a proper officer of the court concerned shall, in England and Wales, be received in evidence without further proof.

Enforcement of orders made in designated countries

10.—(1) Her Majesty may by Order in Council make such provision as appears to Her Majesty to be appropriate for the purpose of enabling the enforcement in England and Wales of orders to which this paragraph applies.

(2) This paragraph applies to any order ('an external order') which is made in a country or territory designated for the purposes of this paragraph by the Order in Council and—

    (a) provides for the forfeiture of terrorist funds within the meaning of section 11(3)(a) or (b) of this Act ('an external forfeiture order'); or

(b) makes provision prohibiting dealing with property which is subject to an external forfeiture order or in respect of which such an order could be made in proceedings which have been or are to be instituted in that country or territory ('an external restraint order').

(3) Without prejudice to the generality of sub-paragraph (1) above, an Order in Council under this paragraph may make provision for matters corresponding to those for which provision is made by, or can be made under, paragraph 9(1) to (8) above in relation to the orders to which that paragraph applies and for the proof of any matter relevant for the purposes of anything falling to be done in pursuance of the Order in Council.

(4) An Order in Council under this paragraph may also make such provision as appears to Her Majesty to be appropriate with respect to anything falling to be done on behalf of the United Kingdom in a designated country or territory in relation to proceedings in that country or territory for or in connection with the making of an external order.

(5) An Order under this paragraph may make different provision for different cases.

(6) No Order shall be made under this paragraph unless a draft of it has been laid before and approved by a resolution of each House of Parliament.

PART II

SCOTLAND

Implementation of forfeiture orders

11.—(1) Where a court in Scotland makes an order under section 13(2), (3) or (4) of this Act (in this Part of this Schedule referred to as a 'forfeiture order') it may make an order—

(a) directing any property to which the forfeiture order applies other than money or land to be sold or otherwise disposed of in such manner as the court may direct;

(b) appointing an administrator to take possession, subject to such conditions and exceptions as may be specified by the court, of any such property which is land and to realise it in such manner as the court may direct;

(c) directing a specified part of any money, or of the proceeds of the sale, disposal or realisation of any property, to which the forfeiture order applies to be paid to or for a specified person falling within section 13(6) of this Act;

(d) making such other provision as appears to the court to be necessary for giving effect to the forfeiture order or to any order made by virtue of paragraph (a), (b) or (c) above.

(2) The Court of Session may by rules of court prescribe the powers and duties of an administrator appointed under sub-paragraph (1)(b) above.

(3) A forfeiture order shall not come into force so long as an appeal is pending against the order or against the conviction on which it was made; and for this purpose where an appeal is competent but has not been brought it shall be treated as pending until the expiry of a period of fourteen days from the date when the order was made.

(4) Any balance remaining after making any payment required under sub-paragraph (1)(c) above or paragraph 12 below shall be treated for the purposes of section 203 of the Criminal Procedure (Scotland) Act 1975 (fines payable to HM Exchequer) as if it were a fine imposed in the High Court.

(5) The clerk of court shall, on the application of the prosecutor or defender in the proceedings in which a forfeiture order is made, certify in writing the extent (if any) to which, at the date of the certificate, effect has been given to the order in respect of the money or other property to which it applies.

(6) In this paragraph references to the proceeds of the sale, disposal or realisation of property are references to the proceeds after deduction of the costs of sale, disposal or realisation.

12.—(1) Where an administrator appointed under paragraph 11 above takes any action—

(a) in relation to property which is not subject to forfeiture, being action which he would be entitled to take if it were such property;

(b) believing, and having reasonable grounds for believing, that he is entitled to take that action in relation to that property,

he shall not be liable to any person in respect of any loss or damage resulting from his action except in so far as the loss or damage is caused by his negligence.

(2) An administrator appointed under paragraph 11 above shall be entitled to be paid his remuneration and expenses out of the proceeds of the property realised by him or, if and so far as those proceeds are insufficient, by the Lord Advocate.

(3) The accountant of court shall supervise an administrator

appointed under paragraph 11 above in the exercise of the powers conferred, and discharge of the duties imposed, on him under or by virtue of that paragraph.

Restraint orders

13.—(1) The Court of Session may in accordance with this paragraph by an order (referred to in this Part of this Schedule as a 'restraint order') prohibit any person specified in the order, subject to such conditions and exceptions as may be so specified, from dealing with any property liable to forfeiture, that is to say, any property in respect of which a forfeiture order has been made or in respect of which such an order could be made in the proceedings referred to in sub-paragraph (2) or (3) below.

(2) A restraint order may be made in respect of a person where—

(a) proceedings have been instituted against him in Scotland for an offence under Part III of this Act;

(b) the proceedings have not been concluded; and

(c) either a forfeiture order has been made or it appears to the court that there are reasonable grounds for thinking that a forfeiture order may be made in those proceedings.

(3) A restraint order may also be made where—

(a) the court is satisfied that a procurator fiscal proposes to apply for a warrant to arrest and commit a person suspected of an offence under Part III of this Act or to charge such a person with such an offence and that in either case the suspicion is reasonable; and

(b) it appears to the court that a forfeiture order may be made in proceedings for the offence.

(4) Where the court has made an order under this paragraph by virtue of sub-paragraph (3) above the court may discharge the order if proceedings in respect of the offence are not instituted within such time as the court considers reasonable.

(5) For the purposes of this paragraph, dealing with property includes, without prejudice to the generality of that expression—

(a) where a debt is owed to the person concerned, making a payment to any person in reduction of the amount of the debt; and

(b) removing the property from the jurisdiction of the Court of Session.

(6) In exercising the powers conferred by this paragraph the court shall not take account of any obligations of any person having an

interest in the property subject to the restraint order which might frustrate the making of a forfeiture order.

(7) For the purposes of this paragraph proceedings for an offence are instituted—

(a) when warrant to arrest a person suspected of or charged with such an offence is granted;

(b) when a person is charged with the offence after being taken into custody without a warrant;

(c) when a person is charged with the offence without being arrested,

and where the application of this sub-paragraph would result in there being more than one time for the institution of proceedings they shall be taken to be instituted at the earliest of those times.

(8) For the purposes of this paragraph and paragraph 14 below proceedings are concluded—

(a) when a forfeiture order has been made in those proceedings and effect has been given to it in respect of all the money or other property to which it applies; or

(b) when (disregarding any power of a court to extend the period within which an appeal may be made) there is no further possibility of a forfeiture order being made in the proceedings.

14.—(1) A restraint order—

(a) may be made only on an application by the Lord Advocate;

(b) may be made on an ex parte application which shall be heard in chambers; and

(c) shall provide for notice to be given to persons affected by the order.

(2) On an application made by any person affected by a restraint order, the order—

(a) may be recalled or varied in relation to any property; and

(b) shall be recalled when proceedings for the offence are concluded.

(3) Where proceedings for the offence are concluded the Lord Advocate shall forthwith apply to the court for recall of the order and the court shall grant the application.

15.—(1) Where the Court of Session has made a restraint order a constable may for the purpose of preventing any property subject to the order being removed from the jurisdiction of the court seize that property.

(2) Property seized under this paragraph shall be dealt with in accordance with the court's directions.

16.—(1) On the application of the Lord Advocate, the Court of Session may, in respect of—

(a) heritable property in Scotland affected by a restraint order (whether such property generally or particular such property) grant warrant for inhibition against any person interdicted by the order; and

(b) moveable property so affected (whether such property generally or particular such property) grant warrant for arrestment if the property would be arrestable were the person entitled to it a debtor.

(2) Subject to the provisions of this Part of this Schedule, a warrant under sub-paragraph (1) above—

(a) shall have effect as if granted on the dependence of an action for debt at the instance of the Lord Advocate against the person and may be executed, recalled, loosed or restricted accordingly;

(b) where granted under sub-paragraph (1)(a) above, shall have the effect of letters of inhibition and shall forthwith be registered by the Lord Advocate in the register of inhibitions and adjudications.

(3) Section 155 of the Titles to Land Consolidation (Scotland) Act 1868 (effective date of inhibition) shall apply in relation to an inhibition for which warrant has been granted under sub-paragraph (1)(a) above as that section applies to an inhibition by separate letters or contained in a summons.

(4) In the application of section 158 of the said Act of 1868 (recall of inhibition) to such inhibition as is mentioned in sub-paragraph (3) above, references in that section to a particular Lord Ordinary shall be construed as references to any Lord Ordinary.

(5) That an inhibition or arrestment has been executed under sub-paragraph (2) above in respect of property shall not prejudice the exercise of an administrator's powers under or for the purposes of this Part of this Schedule in respect of that property.

(6) No inhibition or arrestment executed under sub-paragraph (2) above shall have effect once, or in so far as, the restraint order affecting the property in respect of which the warrant for such inhibition or arrestment has been granted has ceased to have effect in respect of that property, and the Lord Advocate shall—

(a) apply for the recall, or as the case may be restriction, of the inhibition or arrestment accordingly; and

(b) ensure that recall, or restriction, of an inhibition on such application is reflected in the register of inhibitions and adjudications.

Compensation

17.—(1) If proceedings are instituted against a person for an offence under Part III of this Act and either—

(a) the proceedings do not result in his conviction for any such offence; or

(b) where he is convicted of one or more such offences—

(i) the conviction or convictions concerned are quashed; or

(ii) he is pardoned by Her Majesty in respect of the conviction or convictions concerned,

the Court of Session may, on an application by a person who had an interest in any property which was subject to a forfeiture or restraint order made in or in relation to those proceedings, order compensation to be paid to the applicant if, having regard to all the circumstances, it considers it appropriate to do so.

(2) Sub-paragraph (1) above is without prejudice to any right which may otherwise exist to institute proceedings in respect of delictual liability disclosed by such circumstances as are mentioned in paragraphs (a) and (b) of that sub-paragraph.

(3) The court shall not order compensation to be paid in any case unless it is satisfied—

(a) that there is some serious default on the part of a person concerned in the investigation or prosecution of the offence concerned, being a person mentioned in sub-paragraph (6) below; and

(b) that the applicant has suffered loss in consequence of anything done in relation to the property by or in pursuance of an order under this Part of this Schedule.

(4) The court shall not order compensation to be paid in any case where it appears to it that the proceedings would have been instituted even if the serious default had not occurred.

(5) The amount of compensation to be paid under this paragraph shall be such as the court thinks just in all the circumstances of the case.

(6) Compensation payable under this paragraph shall be paid—

(a) where the person in default was a constable of a police force, out of the police fund out of which the expenses of that police force are met;

(b) where the person in default was a constable other than is mentioned in paragraph (a) above, but with the powers of such a constable, by the body under whose authority he acts; and

(c) where the person in default was a procurator fiscal or was acting on behalf of the Lord Advocate, by the Lord Advocate.

(7) Sub-paragraph (7) of paragraph 13 above applies for the purposes of this paragraph as it applies for the purposes of that paragraph.

Enforcement of orders made elsewhere in the British Islands

18.—(1) In the following provisions of this Part of this Schedule—

'an England and Wales order' means—

(a) an order made in England and Wales under section 13(2), (3) or (4) of this Act ('an England and Wales forfeiture order');

(b) an order made under paragraph 3 above ('an England and Wales restraint order'); or

(c) an order made under any other provision of Part I of this Schedule in relation to an England and Wales forfeiture or restraint order;

'a Northern Ireland order' means—

(a) an order made in Northern Ireland under section 13(2), (3) or (4) of this Act ('a Northern Ireland forfeiture order');

(b) an order made under paragraph 23 below ('a Northern Ireland restraint order'); or

(c) an order made under any other provision of Part III of this Schedule in relation to a Northern Ireland forfeiture or restraint order;

'an Islands order' means—

(a) an order made in any of the Islands under section 13(2), (3) or (4) of this Act as extended to that Island under section 28(3) of this Act ('an Islands forfeiture order');

(b) an order under paragraph 3 above as so extended ('an Islands restraint order'); or

(c) an order made under any provision of Part I of this Schedule as so extended in relation to an Islands forfeiture or restraint order.

(2) In paragraphs (a), (b) and (c) of the definition of 'an Islands order' the reference to a provision of this Act as extended to an Island under section 28(3) of this Act includes a reference to any other

provision of the law of that Island for purposes corresponding to that provision.

19.—(1) An England and Wales order, Northern Ireland order or Islands order shall, subject to the provisions of this paragraph, have effect in the law of Scotland but shall be enforced in Scotland only in accordance with the provisions of this paragraph and any provision made by rules of court as to the manner in which and the conditions subject to which such orders are to be enforced there.

(2) The Court of Session shall, on an application made to it in accordance with rules of court for registration of an England and Wales order, Northern Ireland order or Islands order, direct that the order shall, in accordance with such rules, be registered in that court.

(3) Rules of court shall also make provision—

(a) for cancelling or varying the registration of an England and Wales, Northern Ireland or Islands forfeiture order when effect has been given to it (whether in Scotland or elsewhere) in respect of all or, as the case may be, part of the money or other property to which the order applies;

(b) for cancelling or varying the registration of an England and Wales, Northern Ireland or Islands restraint order which has been discharged or varied by the court by which it was made.

(4) If an England and Wales, Northern Ireland or Islands forfeiture order is registered under this paragraph the Court of Session shall have, in relation to that order, the same powers as a court has under paragraph 11(1) above in relation to a forfeiture order made by it and paragraphs 11(4) to (6) and 12 above apply accordingly.

(5) Paragraphs 13(6), 15 and 16 above shall apply to a registered England and Wales, Northern Ireland or Islands restraint order as they apply to a restraint order and the Court of Session shall have the like power to make an order under section 1 of the Administration of Justice (Scotland) Act 1972 (extended power to order inspection of documents etc.) in relation to proceedings brought or likely to be brought for an England and Wales, Northern Ireland or Islands restraint order as if those proceedings had been brought or were likely to be brought in the Court of Session.

(6) Without prejudice to the foregoing provisions, if an England and Wales order, Northern Ireland order or Islands order is registered under this paragraph—

(a) the Court of Session shall have, in relation to its enforcement, the same power;

(b) proceedings for or with respect to its enforcement may be taken; and

(c) proceedings for or with respect to any contravention of such an order (whether before or after such registration) may be taken,

as if the order had originally been made in the Court of Session.

(7) The Court of Session may, additionally, for the purpose of—

(a) assisting the achievement in Scotland of the purposes of an England and Wales order, Northern Ireland order or Islands order; or

(b) assisting any receiver or other person directed by any such order to sell or otherwise dispose of property,

make such orders or do otherwise as seems to it appropriate.

(8) A document purporting to be a copy of an England and Wales order, Northern Ireland order or Islands order and to be certified as such by a proper officer of the court by which it was made or purporting to be a certificate for purposes corresponding to those of paragraph 11(5) above and to be certified by a proper officer of the court concerned shall, in Scotland, be sufficient evidence of the order.

(9) Nothing in any England and Wales order, Northern Ireland order or Islands order prejudices any enactment or rule of law in respect of the recording of deeds relating to heritable property in Scotland or the registration of interests in such property.

Enforcement of orders made in designated countries

20.—(1) Her Majesty may by Order in Council make such provision as appears to Her Majesty to be appropriate for the purpose of enabling the enforcement in Scotland of orders to which this paragraph applies.

(2) This paragraph applies to an order ('an external order') which is made in a country or territory designated for the purposes of this paragraph by the Order in Council and—

(a) provides for the forfeiture of terrorist funds within the meaning of section 11(3)(a) or (b) of this Act ('an external forfeiture order'); or

(b) makes provision prohibiting dealing with property which is subject to an external forfeiture order or in respect of which such an order could be made in proceedings which have been or are to be instituted in that country or territory ('an external restraint order').

(3) Without prejudice to the generality of sub-paragraph (1) above, an Order in Council under this paragraph may make provision for

matters corresponding to those for which provision is made by, or can be made under, paragraph 19(1) to (7) above in relation to the orders to which that paragraph applies and for the proof of any matter relevant for the purposes of anything falling to be done in pursuance of the Order in Council.

(4) An Order in Council under this paragraph may also make such provision as appears to Her Majesty to be appropriate with respect to anything falling to be done on behalf of the United Kingdom in a designated country or territory in relation to proceedings in that country or territory for or in connection with the making of an external order.

(5) An Order under this paragraph may make different provision for different cases.

(6) No Order shall be made under this paragraph unless a draft of it has been laid before and approved by a resolution of each House of Parliament.

PART III

NORTHERN IRELAND

Implementation of forfeiture orders

21.—(1) Where a court in Northern Ireland makes an order under section 13(2), (3) or (4) of this Act (in this Part of this Schedule referred to as a 'forfeiture order') it may make an order—

- (a) requiring any money or other property to which the forfeiture order applies to be paid or handed over to the proper officer or to a member of the Royal Ulster Constabulary designated for the purpose by the Chief Constable;
- (b) directing any such property other than money or land to be sold or otherwise disposed of in such manner as the court may direct and the proceeds to be paid to the proper officer;
- (c) appointing a receiver to take possession, subject to such conditions and exceptions as may be specified by the court, of any such property which is land, to realise it in such manner as the court may direct and to pay the proceeds to the proper officer;
- (d) directing a specified part of any money, or of the proceeds of the sale, disposal or realisation of any property, to which the forfeiture order applies to be paid by the proper officer to or for a specified person falling within section 13(6) of this Act;

(e) making such other provision (including provision as to the manner of conveyance or transfer of property which is land) as appears to the court to be necessary for giving effect to the forfeiture order or to any order made by virtue of paragraph (a), (b), (c) or (d) above.

(2) A forfeiture order shall not come into force until (disregarding any power of a court to grant leave to appeal out of time) there is no further possibility of the order being set aside.

(3) Any balance in the hands of the proper officer after making any payment required under sub-paragraph (1)(d) above or paragraph 22 below shall be treated for the purposes of section 20 of the Administration of Justice (Northern Ireland) Act 1954 (application of fines etc.) as if it were a fine.

(4) The proper officer shall, on the application of the prosecution or defendant in the proceedings in which a forfeiture order is made, certify in writing the extent (if any) to which, at the date of the certificate, effect has been given to the order in respect of the money or other property to which it applies.

(5) In this paragraph 'the proper officer' means, where the forfeiture order is made by a court of summary jurisdiction, the clerk of petty sessions and, where the order is made by the Crown Court, the appropriate officer of the Crown Court.

(6) In this paragraph references to the proceeds of the sale, disposal or realisation of property are references to the proceeds after deduction of the costs of sale, disposal or realisation.

(7) This paragraph has effect to the exclusion of Article 58 of the Magistrates' Courts (Northern Ireland) Order 1981.

22.—(1) Where a receiver appointed under paragraph 21 above takes any action—

(a) in relation to property which is not subject to forfeiture, being action which he would be entitled to take if it were such property;
(b) believing, and having reasonable grounds for believing, that he is entitled to take that action in relation to that property,

he shall not be liable to any person in respect of any loss or damage resulting from his action except in so far as the loss or damage is caused by his negligence.

(2) A receiver appointed under paragraph 21 above shall be entitled to be paid his remuneration and expenses out of the proceeds of the property realised by him or, if and so far as those proceeds are insufficient, by the prosecution.

Restraint orders

23.—(1) The High Court may in accordance with this paragraph by an order (referred to in this Part of this Schedule as a 'restraint order') prohibit any person, subject to such conditions and exceptions as may be specified in the order, from dealing with any property liable to forfeiture, that is to say, any property in respect of which a forfeiture order has been made or in respect of which such an order could be made in the proceedings referred to in sub-paragraph (2) or (3) below.

(2) A restraint order may be made where—

(a) proceedings have been instituted against a defendant in Northern Ireland for an offence under Part III of this Act;

(b) the proceedings have not been concluded; and

(c) either a forfeiture order has been made or it appears to the court that there are reasonable grounds for thinking that a forfeiture order may be made in those proceedings.

(3) A restraint order may also be made where—

(a) the High Court is satisfied that, whether by the making of a complaint or otherwise, a person is to be charged in Northern Ireland with an offence under Part III of this Act; and

(b) it appears to the court that a forfeiture order may be made in proceedings for the offence.

(4) In the application of the provisions of this Part of this Schedule at a time when a restraint order may be made by virtue of sub-paragraph (3) above references to the prosecution shall be construed as references to the person who the High Court is satisfied is to have the conduct of the proposed proceedings.

(5) Where the High Court has made an order under this paragraph by virtue of sub-paragraph (3) above the court may discharge the order if proceedings in respect of the offence are not instituted (whether by the making of a complaint or otherwise) within such time as the court considers reasonable.

(6) For the purposes of this paragraph, dealing with property includes, without prejudice to the generality of that expression—

(a) where a debt is owed to the person concerned, making a payment to any person in reduction of the amount of the debt; and

(b) removing the property from the jurisdiction of the High Court.

(7) In exercising the powers conferred by this paragraph the High Court shall not take account of any obligations of any person having

an interest in the property subject to the restraint order which might frustrate the making of a forfeiture order.

(8) For the purposes of this paragraph proceedings for an offence are instituted—

> (a) when a summons or a warrant is issued under Article 20 of the Magistrates' Courts (Northern Ireland) Order 1981 in respect of that offence;
>
> (b) when a person is charged with the offence after being taken into custody without a warrant;
>
> (c) when an indictment is presented under section 2(2)(c), (e) or (f) of the Grand Jury (Abolition) Act (Northern Ireland) 1969;

and where the application of this sub-paragraph would result in there being more than one time for the institution of proceedings they shall be taken to be instituted at the earliest of those times.

(9) For the purposes of this paragraph and paragraph 24 below proceedings are concluded—

> (a) when a forfeiture order has been made in those proceedings and effect has been given to it in respect of all the money or other property to which it applies; or
>
> (b) when (disregarding any power of a court to grant leave to appeal out of time) there is no further possibility of a forfeiture order being made in the proceedings.

24.—(1) A restraint order—

> (a) may be made only on an application by the prosecution;
>
> (b) may be made on an ex parte application to a judge in chambers; and
>
> (c) shall provide for notice to be given to persons affected by the order.

(2) A restraint order—

> (a) may be discharged or varied in relation to any property; and
>
> (b) shall be discharged when proceedings for the offence are concluded.

(3) An application for the discharge or variation of a restraint order may be made by any person affected by it.

25.—(1) Where the High Court has made a restraint order a constable may for the purpose of preventing any property subject to the order being removed from the jurisdiction of the court seize that property.

(2) Property seized under this paragraph shall be dealt with in accordance with the court's directions.

26.—(1) The prosecution shall be treated for the purposes of section 66 of the Land Registration Act (Northern Ireland) 1970 (cautions) as a person interested in relation to any registered land to which a restraint order or an application for such an order relates.

(2) On the application of the prosecution, the Registrar of Titles shall, in respect of any registered land to which a restraint order or an application for such order relates, make an entry inhibiting any dealing with the land without the consent of the High Court.

(3) Subsections (2) and (4) of section 67 of the Land Registration Act (Northern Ireland) 1970 (inhibitions) shall apply to an entry made on the application of the prosecution under sub-paragraph (2) above as they apply to an entry made on the application of any person interested in the registered land under subsection (1) of that section.

(4) In this paragraph—

> 'registered land' has the meaning assigned to it by section 45(1)(a) of the Interpretation Act (Northern Ireland) 1954; and
>
> 'Registrar of Titles' and 'entry' have the same meanings as in the Land Registration Act (Northern Ireland) 1970.

Compensation

27.—(1) If proceedings are instituted against a person for an offence under Part III of this Act and either—

(a) the proceedings do not result in his conviction for any such offence; or

(b) where he is convicted of one or more such offences—

  (i) the conviction or convictions concerned are quashed; or

  (ii) he is pardoned by Her Majesty in respect of the conviction or convictions concerned,

the High Court may, on an application by a person who had an interest in any property which was subject to a forfeiture or restraint order made in or in relation to those proceedings order compensation to be paid to the applicant if, having regard to all the circumstances, it considers it appropriate to do so.

(2) The High Court shall not order compensation to be paid in any case unless it is satisfied—

(a) that there is some serious default on the part of a person concerned in the investigation or prosecution of the offence concerned, being a person mentioned in sub-paragraph (5) below; and

(b) that the applicant has suffered loss in consequence of

anything done in relation to the property by or in pursuance of an order under this Part of this Schedule.

(3) The High Court shall not order compensation to be paid in any case where it appears to it that the proceedings would have been instituted even if the serious default had not occurred.

(4) The amount of compensation to be paid under this paragraph shall be such as the High Court thinks just in all the circumstances of the case.

(5) Compensation payable under this paragraph shall be paid—

(a) where the person in default was or was acting as a member of the Royal Ulster Constabulary, by the Police Authority for Northern Ireland;

(b) where the person in default was a member of the Office of the Director of Public Prosecutions for Northern Ireland, by the Director of Public Prosecutions for Northern Ireland.

(6) Sub-paragraph (8) of paragraph 23 above applies for the purposes of this paragraph as it applies for the purposes of that paragraph.

Enforcement of orders made elsewhere in the British Islands

28.—(1) In the following provisions of this Part of this Schedule— 'an England and Wales order' means—

(a) an order made in England and Wales under section 13(2), (3), or (4) of this Act ('an England and Wales forfeiture order');

(b) an order made under paragraph 3 above ('an England and Wales restraint order'); or

(c) an order made under any other provision of Part I of this Schedule in relation to an England and Wales forfeiture or restraint order;

'a Scottish order' means—

(a) an order made in Scotland under section 13(2), (3) or (4) of this Act ('a Scottish forfeiture order');

(b) an order made under paragraph 13 above ('a Scottish restraint order'); or

(c) an order made under any other provision of Part II of this Schedule in relation to a Scottish forfeiture or restraint order;

'an Islands order' means—

(a) an order made in any of the Islands under section 13(2), (3) or (4) of this Act as extended to that Island under section 28(3) of this Act ('an Islands forfeiture order');

(b) an order under paragraph 3 above as so extended ('an Islands restraint order'); or

(c) an order made under any other provision of Part I of this Schedule as so extended in relation to an Islands forfeiture or restraint order.

(2) In paragraphs (a), (b) and (c) of the definition of 'an Islands order' the reference to a provision of this Act as extended to an Island under section 28(3) of this Act includes a reference to any other provision of the law of that Island for purposes corresponding to that provision.

29.—(1) An England and Wales order, Scottish order or Islands order shall, subject to the provisions of this paragraph, have effect in the law of Northern Ireland but shall be enforced in Northern Ireland only in accordance with the provisions of this paragraph and any provision made by rules of court as to the manner in which and the conditions subject to which such orders are to be enforced there.

(2) The High Court shall, on an application made to it in accordance with rules of court for registration of an England and Wales order, Scottish order or Islands order, direct that the order shall, in accordance with such rules, be registered in that court.

(3) Rules of court shall also make provision—

(a) for cancelling or varying the registration of an England and Wales, Scottish or Islands forfeiture order when effect has been given to it (whether in Northern Ireland or elsewhere) in respect of all or, as the case may be, part of the money or other property to which the order applies;

(b) for cancelling or varying the registration of an England and Wales, Scottish or Islands restraint order which has been discharged or varied by the court by which it was made.

(4) If an England and Wales, Scottish or Islands forfeiture order is registered under this paragraph the High Court shall have, in relation to that order, the same powers as a court has under paragraph 21(1) above in relation to a forfeiture order made by it (and paragraph 22 above applies accordingly) but any functions of the clerk of petty sessions or the appropriate officer of the Crown Court shall be exercised by the appropriate officer of the High Court.

(5) After making any payment required by virtue of paragraph 21(1)(d) or 22 above, the balance of any sums received by the appropriate officer of the High Court by virtue of an order made under sub-paragraph (4) above shall be paid into or disposed for the benefit of the Consolidated Fund.

(6) Paragraphs 23(7), 25 and 26 above and the Land Registration Act (Northern Ireland) 1970 and the Registration of Deeds Act

(Northern Ireland) 1970 shall apply to a registered England and Wales, Scottish or Islands restraint order as they apply to a restraint order and the High Court shall have the like power to make an order under section 21 of the Administration of Justice Act 1969 (extended power to order inspection of property etc.) in relation to proceedings brought or likely to be brought for an England and Wales, Scottish or Islands restraint order as if those proceedings had been brought or were likely to be brought in the High Court.

(7) Without prejudice to the foregoing provisions, if an England and Wales order, Scottish order or Islands order is registered under this paragraph—

    (a) the High Court shall have, in relation to its enforcement, the same power;

    (b) proceedings for or with respect to its enforcement may be taken; and

    (c) proceedings for or with respect to any contravention of such an order (whether before or after such registration) may be taken,

as if the order had originally been made in the High Court.

(8) The High Court may, additionally, for the purpose of—

    (a) assisting the achievement in Northern Ireland of the purposes of an England and Wales order, Scottish order or Islands order; or

    (b) assisting any receiver or other person directed by any such order to sell or otherwise dispose of property,

make such orders or do otherwise as seems to it appropriate.

(9) A document purporting to be a copy of an England and Wales order, Scottish order or Islands order and to be certified as such by a proper officer of the court by which it was made or purporting to be a certificate for purposes corresponding to those of paragraph 21(4) above and to be certified by a proper officer of the court concerned shall, in Northern Ireland, be received in evidence without further proof.

Enforcement of orders made in designated countries

30.—(1) Her Majesty may by Order in Council make such provision as appears to Her Majesty to be appropriate for the purpose of enabling the enforcement in Northern Ireland of orders to which this paragraph applies.

(2) This paragraph applies to any order ('an external order') which is made in a country or territory designated for the purposes of this paragraph by the Order in Council and—

(a) provides for the forfeiture of terrorist funds within the meaning of section 11(3)(a) or (b) of this Act ('an external forfeiture order'); or

(b) makes provision prohibiting dealing with property which is subject to an external forfeiture order in respect of which such an order could be made in proceedings which have been or are to be instituted in that country or territory ('an external restraint order').

(3) Without prejudice to the generality of sub-paragraph (1) above, an Order in Council under this paragraph may make provision for matters corresponding to those for which provision is made by, or can be made under, paragraph 29(1) to (8) above in relation to the orders to which that paragraph applies and for the proof of any matter relevant for the purposes of anything falling to be done in pursuance of the Order in Council.

(4) An Order in Council under this paragraph may also make such provision as appears to Her Majesty to be appropriate with respect to anything falling to be done on behalf of the United Kingdom in a designated country or territory in relation to proceedings in that country or territory for or in connection with the making of an external order.

(5) An Order under this paragraph may make different provision for different cases.

(6) No Order shall be made under this paragraph unless a draft of it has been laid before and approved by a resolution of each House of Parliament.

PART IV

INSOLVENCY: UNITED KINGDOM PROVISIONS

Proceedings of creditors against forfeiture

31.—(1) During the period of six months following the making of a forfeiture order no money which is subject to the order, or which represents any property subject to it, shall be finally disposed of under this Schedule.

(2) If, in a case where any money or other property is subject to a forfeiture order—

(a) the commencement of an insolvency occurs, or has occurred, in the course of any qualifying insolvency proceedings,

(b) any functions in relation to that property would (apart from

the forfeiture order) be exercisable by an insolvency practitioner acting in those proceedings, and

(c) during the period of six months following the making of
the forfeiture order any such insolvency practitioner gives
written notice to the relevant officer of the matters referred
to in paragraphs (a) and (b) above,

then sub-paragraph (3) below shall apply in relation to the property
in question.

(3) Where this sub-paragraph applies then, subject to the following
provisions of this Part of this Schedule, the property in question or,
if it has been sold, the proceeds of sale—

(a) shall cease to be subject to the forfeiture order and any ancillary order; and

(b) shall fall to be dealt with in the insolvency proceedings as
if the forfeiture order had never been made.

(4) In any case where—

(a) sub-paragraph (30 above would, apart from this sub-
paragraph, apply in relation to any property, but

(b) the relevant officer, or any person acting in pursuance of
an ancillary order, has entered into a contract for the sale
of that property or has incurred any other obligations in relation to it,

that sub-paragraph shall not take effect in relation to that property,
or its proceeds of sale, unless and until those obligations have been
discharged.

(5) Where in consequence of sub-paragraph (3) above any money
or other property falls to be dealt with in insolvency proceedings, the
Secretary of State shall be taken to be a creditor in those proceedings
to the amount or value of that property but, notwithstanding any provision contained in or made under any other enactment—

(a) except in sequestration proceedings, his debt shall rank after
the debts of all other creditors and shall not be paid until
they have been paid in full with interest under section 189(2)
or, as the case may be, section 328(4) of the 1986 Act or Article
25 of the Bankruptcy Amendment (Northern Ireland) Order
1980; and

(b) in sequestration proceedings, his debt shall rank after all the
debts mentioned in section 51(1) of the Bankruptcy (Scotland)
Act 1985 and shall not be paid until they have been paid
in full.

(6) In any case where—

    (a) by virtue of sub-paragraph (3) above any property ceases to be subject to a forfeiture order in consequence of the making of a bankruptcy order or an award of sequestration, and

    (b) subsequently the bankruptcy order is annulled or the award of sequestration is recalled or reduced,

the property shall again become subject to the forfeiture order and, if applicable, any ancillary orders.

(7) If any of the property referred to in sub-paragraph (6) above is money, or has been converted into money, then—

    (a) the court which ordered the annulment, or which recalled or reduced the award of sequestration, shall make an order specifying, for the purposes of paragraph (b) below, property comprised in the estate of the bankrupt or debtor to the amount or value of the property in question; and

    (b) the property so specified shall become subject to the forfeiture order, and any applicable ancillary orders, in place of the property in question.

(8) In this paragraph—

'the commencement of an insolvency' means—

    (a) the making of a bankruptcy order;

    (b) the date of sequestration of a person's estate, within the meaning of section 12(4) of the Bankruptcy (Scotland) Act 1985;

    (c) in England and Wales, in the case of the insolvent estate of a deceased person, the making of an insolvency administration order;

    (d) in the case of a company—

        (i) the passing of a resolution for its winding up; or

        (ii) the making of an order by the court for the winding up of the company where no such resolution has been passed;

'final disposal under this Schedule', in relation to any money, means—

    (a) in England and Wales, its payment to the Secretary of State in accordance with paragraph 1(3) or 9(5) above;

    (b) in Scotland, its payment to the proper officer in Exchequer under section 203 of the Criminal Procedure (Scotland) Act 1975;

    (c) in Northern Ireland, its payment into, or its disposal for the benefit of, the Consolidated Fund in accordance with paragraph 21(3) or 29(5) above;

and 'finally dispose' shall be construed accordingly.

Expenses incurred in connection with the forfeiture

32.—(1) Where any money or other property would, apart from this paragraph, fall to be dealt with in accordance with paragraph 31(3) above, the relevant officer may—

(a) deduct from that money any allowable forfeiture expenses; or

(b) retain so much of that property as he considers necessary for the purpose of realising it and deducting any such expenses from the proceeds or realisation;

and paragraph 31(3) above shall apply only in relation to any balance remaining after making provision for those expenses.

(2) If any money or other property is delivered up in pursuance of paragraph 31(3) above and provision has not been made for any allowable forfeiture expenses, then—

(a) the person who incurred them shall have a claim to their value in the insolvency proceedings; and

(b) the expenses in question shall be treated for the purposes of the insolvency proceedings as if they were expenses of those proceedings.

(3) In this paragraph 'allowable forfeiture expenses'—

(a) means any expenses incurred in relation to property subject to the forfeiture order—

(i) by the relevant officer;

(ii) by any receiver, administrator or other person appointed by the relevant officer; or

(iii) by any person appointed or directed to deal with any property by an order under paragraph 11(1) above; and

(b) includes any amount paid, or required to be paid, under paragraph 1(1)(d), 11(1)(c) or 21(1)(d) above.

Protection of insolvency practitioners

33.—(1) In any case where—

(a) an insolvency practitioner seizes or disposes of any property in relation to which his functions are not exercisable because it is for the time being subject to a forfeiture or restraint order, and

(b) at the time of the seizure or disposal he believes and has reasonable grounds for believing that he is entitled (whether in pursuance of a court order or otherwise) to seize or dispose of that property,

he shall not be liable to any person in respect of any loss or damage resulting from the seizure or disposal except in so far as the loss or damage is caused by his negligence in so acting.

(2) An insolvency practitioner shall have a lien on the property mentioned in sub-paragraph (1) above or the proceeds of its sale—

(a) for such of his expenses as were incurred in connection with insolvency proceedings in relation to which the seizure or disposal purported to take place; and

(b) for so much of his remuneration as may reasonably be assigned for his acting in connection with those proceedings.

(3) Sub-paragraphs (1) and (2) above are without prejudice to the generality of any provision contained in the 1986 Act or the Bankruptcy (Scotland) Act 1985 or any other Act or the Bankruptcy Acts (Northern Ireland) 1857 to 1980 or the Companies (Northern Ireland) Order 1986.

(4) In this paragraph 'insolvency practitioner', in any part of the United Kingdom, means a person acting as an insolvency practitioner in that or any other part of the United Kingdom; and for this purpose—

(a) any question whether a person is acting as an insolvency practitioner in England and Wales or in Scotland shall be determined in accordance with section 388 of the 1986 Act, except that—

(i) the reference in subsection (2)(a) to a permanent or interim trustee in a sequestration shall be taken to include a reference to a trustee in sequestration;

(ii) subsection (5) shall be disregarded; and

(iii) the expression shall also include the Official Receiver acting as receiver or manager of property; and

(b) a person acts as an insolvency practitioner in Northern Ireland if he acts as an Official Assignee, trustee, liquidator, receiver or manager of a company, provisional liquidator or a receiver or manager under section 68 of the Bankruptcy (Ireland) Amendment Act 1872.

Insolvency practitioners in the Islands and designated countries

34.—(1) The Secretary of State may by order make provision for securing that an Islands or external insolvency practitioner has, with such modifications as may be specified in the order, the same rights under this Part of this Schedule in relation to property situated in any part of the United Kingdom as he would have if he were an insolvency practitioner in that or any other part of the United Kingdom.

(2) An order under this paragraph may make provision as to the manner in which, and the conditions subject to which, an Islands or external insolvency practitioner may exercise the rights conferred under sub-paragraph (1) above; and any such order may, in particular make provision—

    (a) for requiring him to obtain leave of a court as a condition of exercising any such rights; and

    (b) for empowering a court granting any such leave to impose such conditions as it thinks fit.

(3) An order under this paragraph may make different provision for different cases.

(4) The power to make an order under this paragraph shall be exercisable by statutory instrument and, in relation to property situated in England and Wales, shall be so exercisable with the concurrence of the Lord Chancellor.

(5) A statutory instrument containing an order under this paragraph shall be subject to annulment in pursuance of a resolution of either House of Parliament.

(6) In this paragraph—

    'Islands or external insolvency practitioner' means a person exercising under the insolvency law of a relevant country or territory functions corresponding to those exercised by insolvency practitioners under the insolvency law of any part of the United Kingdom;

    'insolvency law' has the meaning given by section 426(10) of the 1986 Act, except that the reference to a relevant country or territory shall be construed in accordance with this paragraph;

    'relevant country or territory' means—

        (a) any of the Channel Islands or the Isle of Man; or

        (b) any country or territory designated as mentioned in paragraph 10, 20 or 30 above.

Interpretation of Part IV

35.—(1) In this Part of this Schedule—

    'the 1986 Act' means the Insolvency Act 1986;

    'ancillary order' means any order made in connection with the forfeiture in question, other than the forfeiture order;

    'forfeiture or restraint order' means a forfeiture or restraint order, as the case may be, of any of the descriptions referred to in Parts I to III of this Schedule;

'insolvency practitioner', except in paragraph 33 above, means a person acting in any qualifying insolvency proceedings in any part of the United Kingdom as—

(a) a liquidator of a company or partnership;

(b) a trustee in bankruptcy;

(c) an interim or permanent trustee in sequestration;

(d) an administrator of the insolvent estate of a deceased person;

(e) a receiver or manager of any property;

'qualifying insolvency proceedings' means—

(a) any proceedings under the 1986 Act or the Companies (Northern Ireland) Order 1986 for the winding up of a company or an unregistered company and includes any voluntary winding up of a company under Part IV of that Act of Part XX of that Order;

(b) any proceedings in England and Wales under or by virtue of section 420 of the 1986 Act for the winding up of an insolvent partnership;

(c) any proceedings in bankruptcy or, in Scotland, any sequestration proceedings;

(d) any proceedings in England and Wales under or by virtue of section 421 of the 1986 Act in relation to the insolvent estate of a deceased person;

'the relevant officer' means—

(a) in Scotland—

(i) where the forfeiture order in question is made by a court in Scotland, the clerk of that court;

(ii) in any other case, the Principal Clerk of Session and Justiciary;

(b) in any other part of the United Kingdom—

(i) where the forfeiture order in question is made by a court in that part, the proper office within the meanings of paragraph 1 or, as the case may be, paragraph 21 above;

(ii) in any other case, the appropriate officer of the High Court.

(2) Any reference in this Part of this Schedule to the proceeds of the sale or realisation of any property are references to those proceeds after deduction of the costs of sale or realisation.

Section 16(1), (3) and (4)   SCHEDULE 5

PORT AND BORDER CONTROL

Examining officers

1.—(1) The following shall be examining officers for the purposes of this Act—

(a) constables;

(b) immigration officers appointed for the purposes of the Immigration Act 1971 under paragraph 1 of Schedule 2 to that Act; and

(c) officers of customs and excise who are the subject of arrangements for their employment as immigration officers made under that paragraph by the Secretary of State.

(2) In Northern Ireland members of Her Majesty's Forces may perform such functions conferred on examining officers as the Secretary of State may by order specify.

(3) The power to make orders under sub-paragraph (2) above shall be exercisable by statutory instrument subject to annulment in pursuance of a resolution of either House of Parliament.

(4) Examining officers shall exercise their functions under this Act in accordance with such instructions as may from time to time be given to them by the Secretary of State.

Examination on arrival or departure

2.—(1) Any person who has arrived in, or is seeking to leave, Great Britain or Northern Ireland by ship or aircraft may be examined by an examining officer for the purpose of determining—

(a) whether that person appears to be a person who is or has been concerned in the commission, preparation or instigation of acts of terrorism to which this paragraph applies; or

(b) whether any such person is subject to an exclusion order; or

(c) whether there are grounds for suspecting that any such person has committed an offence under section 8 of this Act.

(2) This paragraph applies to—

(a) acts of terrorism connected with the affairs of Northern Ireland; and

(b) acts of terrorism of any other description except acts connected solely with the affairs of the United Kingdom or any part of the United Kingdom other than Northern Ireland.

(3) An examining officer may—

(a) examine any person who is entering or seeking to enter or leave Northern Ireland by land from, or to go to, the Republic of Ireland for the purpose of determining whether that person is such a person as is mentioned in any of paragraphs (a) to (c) of sub-paragraph (1) above;

(b) examine any person found in Northern Ireland within a distance of one mile from the border with the Republic of Ireland for the purpose of ascertaining whether he is in the course of entering or leaving Northern Ireland by land;

(c) examine any person entering Northern Ireland by train when he arrives at the first place where the train is scheduled to stop for the purpose of allowing passengers to alight.

(4) The period of a person's examination under this paragraph shall not exceed twenty-four hours unless he is detained under paragraph 6 below, and may only exceed twelve hours if an examining officer—

(a) has reasonable grounds for suspecting that the person examined is or has been concerned in the commission, preparation or instigation of acts of terrorism to which this paragraph applies; and

(b) gives him a notice in writing requiring him to submit to further examination.

(5) In sub-paragraph (1) above the reference to arrival by ship or aircraft includes a reference to arrival as a transit passenger, member of the crew or other person not seeking to enter Great Britain or Northern Ireland.

Production of information and documents

3.—(1) It shall be the duty of any person examined under paragraph 2 above to furnish to the person carrying out the examination all such information in his possession as that person may require for the purpose of his functions under that paragraph.

(2) A person on his examination under paragraph 2 above by an examining officer shall, if so required by the examining officer—

(a) produce either a valid passport with photograph or some other document satisfactorily establishing his identity and nationality or citizenship; and

(b) declare whether or not he is carrying or conveying documents of any relevant description specified by the examining officer, and produce any documents of that description which he is carrying or conveying.

(3) In sub-paragraph (2)(b) above 'relevant description' means any description appearing to the examining officer to be relevant for the purposes of the examination.

Powers of search, etc.

4.—(1) An examining officer may, for the purpose of satisfying himself whether there are persons he may wish to examine under paragraph 2 above, search any ship or aircraft and anything on board it or anything taken off or about to be taken aboard a ship or aircraft.

(2) An examining officer who examines any person under paragraph 2 above may, for the purpose of determining whether he is such a person as is mentioned in any of paragraphs (a) to (c) of sub-paragraph (1) of that paragraph, search that person and any baggage belonging to him or any ship or aircraft and anything on board it or anything taken off or about to be taken aboard a ship or aircraft.

(3) Without prejudice to sub-paragraphs (1) and (2) above, an examining officer who examines any person in Northern Ireland under paragraph 2 above may, for the purpose mentioned in sub-paragraph (2) above, search any vehicle and anything in or on it or anything taken out of or off it or about to be placed in or on it.

(4) An examining officer may detain for the purpose of examining it anything produced pursuant to paragraph (3)(2)(b) above or found on a search under this paragraph for a period not exceeding seven days; and if on examination of anything so produced or found the examining officer is of the opinion that it may be needed—

    (a) in connection with the taking of a decision by the Secretary of State as to whether or not to make an exclusion order or a deportation order under the Immigration Act 1971; or

    (b) for use as evidence in criminal proceedings,

he may detain it until he is satisfied that it will not be so needed.

(5) A search of a person under this paragraph may only be carried out by a person of the same sex.

(6) An examining officer may board any ship or aircraft or enter any vehicle for the purpose of exercising any of his functions under this Act.

(7) Where an examining officer has power to search under this paragraph, he may, instead, authorise the search to be carried out on his behalf by a person who is not an examining officer.

(8) Where a person who is not an examining officer carries out a search in accordance with sub-paragraph (7) above, he may—

(a) for that purpose, board any ship or aircraft or enter any vehicle; and

(b) exercise the power of detaining articles conferred by sub-paragraph (4) above;

and he may, if necessary, use reasonable force for the purpose of carrying out his functions under this paragraph.

(9) In Scotland any person employed by a police authority for the assistance of constables under section 9 of the Police (Scotland) Act 1967 may perform any functions conferred on examining officers by this paragraph, and may, if necessary, use reasonable force for the purpose of performing those functions.

Landing, embarkation, entry and departure cards

5.—(1) Subject to sub-paragraph (2) below, any person who disembarks from, or embarks on—

(a) a ship or aircraft in Great Britain which has come from, or is going to, the Republic of Ireland, Northern Ireland or any of the Islands, or

(b) a ship or aircraft in Northern Ireland which has come from, or is going to Great Britain, the Republic of Ireland or any of the Islands,

shall, if so required by an examining officer, complete and produce to that officer a landing or, as the case may be, an embarkation card in such form as the Secretary of State may direct, which, where the ship or aircraft is employed to carry passengers for reward, shall be supplied for the purpose to that person by the owners or agents of that ship or aircraft.

(2) Sub-paragraph (1) above shall not apply to a person disembarking from a ship or aircraft coming from the Republic of Ireland if that person is required to produce a landing card under any order for the time being in force under paragraph 5 of Schedule 2 to the Immigration Act 1971.

(3) Any person who may be examined under paragraph 2(3)(a) or (c) above shall, if so required by an examining officer, complete and produce to that officer an entry or, as the case may be, a departure card in such form as the Secretary of State may direct.

Detention pending examination etc.

6.—(1) A person who is examined under this Schedule may be detained under the authority of an examining officer—

(a) pending conclusion of his examination;

(b) pending consideration by the Secretary of State whether to make an exclusion order against him; or

(c) pending a decision by the Director of Public Prosecutions or Attorney General or, as the case may be, the Lord Advocate or the Director of Public Prosecutions or Attorney General for Northern Ireland whether proceedings for an offence should be instituted against him.

(2) Subject to sub-paragraph (3) below, a person shall not be detained under sub-paragraph (1) above for more than forty-eight hours from the time when he is first examined.

(3) The Secretary of State may, in any particular case, extend the period of forty-eight hours mentioned in sub-paragraph (2) above by a period or periods specified by him, but any such further period or periods shall not exceed five days in all and if an application for such an extension is made the person detained shall as soon as practicable be given written notice of that fact and of the time when the application was made.

(4) A person liable to be detained under this paragraph may be arrested without warrant by an examining officer.

(5) A person on board a ship or aircraft may, under the authority of an examining officer, be removed from the ship or aircraft for detention under this paragraph; but if an examining officer so requires, the captain of the ship or aircraft shall prevent from disembarking in the relevant territory any person who has arrived in the ship or aircraft if the examining officer notifies him either that that person is the subject of an exclusion order or that consideration is being given by the Secretary of State to the making of an exclusion order against that person.

(6) Where under sub-paragraph (5) above the captain of a ship or aircraft is required to prevent a person from disembarking he may for that purpose detain him in custody on board the ship or aircraft.

(7) A person may be removed from a vehicle for detention under this paragraph.

(8) In sub-paragraph (5) above 'the relevant territory' has the same meaning as in paragraph 6 of Schedule 2 to this Act.

Detention supplementary provisions

7.—(1) If a justice of the peace is satisfied that there are reasonable grounds for suspecting that a person liable to be arrested under paragraph 6(4) above is to be found on any premises he may grant a search warrant authorising any constable to enter those premises for the purpose of searching for and arresting that person.

(2) In Scotland the power to issue a warrant under sub-paragraph (1) above shall be exercised by a sheriff or a justice of the peace, an application for such a warrant shall be supported by evidence on oath and a warrant shall not authorise a constable to enter any premises unless he is a constable for the police area in which they are situated.

(3) In Northern Ireland an application for a warrant under sub-paragraph (1) above shall be made by a complaint on oath.

(4) A person detained under this Schedule shall be deemed to be in legal custody at any time when he is so detained and, if detained otherwise than on board a ship or aircraft, may be detained in such a place as the Secretary of State may from time to time direct.

(5) Where a person is detained under this Schedule, any examining office, constable or prison officer, or any other person authorised by the Secretary of State, may take all such steps as may be reasonably necessary for photographing, measuring or otherwise identifying him.

(6) Section 61(1) to (8) of the Police and Criminal Evidence Act 1984 (fingerprinting) shall apply to the taking of a person's fingerprints by a constable under sub-paragraph (5) above as if for subsection (4) there were substituted—

'(4) An officer may only give an authorisation under subsection (3)(a) above for the taking of a person's fingerprints if he is satisfied that it is necessary to do so in order to assist in determining—

(a) whether that person is or has been concerned in the commission, preparation or instigation of acts of terrorism to which paragraph 2 of Schedule 5 to the Prevention of Terrorism (Temporary Provisions) Act 1989 applies;
(b) whether he is subject to an exclusion order under that Act; or
(c) whether there are grounds for suspecting that he has committed an offence under section 8 of that Act.'

(7) Any person detained under this Schedule may be taken in the custody of an examining officer, or of any person acting under the authority of such an officer, to and from any place where his attendance is required for the purpose of establishing his nationality or citizenship or for making arrangements for his admission to a country or territory outside the United Kingdom or where he is required to be for any other purpose connected with the operation of this Act.

Designated ports

8.—(1) The owners or agents of a ship or aircraft employed to carry passengers for reward and coming to Great Britain from the Republic of Ireland, Northern Ireland or any of the Islands or going from Great Britain to any other of those places shall not, without the approval of an examining officer, arrange for the ship or aircraft to call at a port in Great Britain other than a designated port for the purpose of disembarking or embarking passengers.

(2) The captain of an aircraft not employed to carry passengers for reward and coming to Great Britain from the Republic of Ireland, Northern Ireland or any of the Islands or going from Great Britain to any other of those places shall not, without the approval of an examining officer, permit the aircraft to call at or leave a port in Great Britain other than a designated port.

(3) The owners or agents of a ship or aircraft employed to carry passengers for reward and coming to Northern Ireland from Great Britain, the Republic of Ireland or any of the Islands or going from Northern Ireland to any other of those places shall not, without the approval of an examining officer, arrange for the ship or aircraft to call at a port in Northern Ireland other than a designated port for the purpose of disembarking or embarking passengers.

(4) The captain of an aircraft not employed to carry passengers for reward and coming to Northern Ireland from Great Britain, the Republic of Ireland or any of the Islands or going from Northern Ireland to any other of those places shall not, without the approval of an examining officer, permit the aircraft to call at or leave a port in Northern Ireland other than a designated port.

Control areas

9.—(1) The Secretary of State may from time to time give written notice to the owners or agents of any ships or aircraft designating control areas for the disembarkation or embarkation of passengers in any port in the United Kingdom and specifying the conditions and restrictions (if any) to be observed in any control area; and where by notice given to any owners or agents a control area is for the time being so designated at any port, the owners or agents shall take all reasonable steps to ensure that, in the case of their ships or aircraft, passengers do not disembark or, as the case may be, embark at the port outside the control area and that any conditions or restrictions notified to them are observed.

(2) The Secretary of State may also from time to time give to any persons concerned with the management of a port in the United Kingdom written notice designating control areas in the port and specifying facilities to be provided and conditions and restrictions to be observed in any control area; and any such person shall take all

reasonable steps to secure that any facilities, conditions or restrictions notified to him are provided or observed.

Requirements with respect to embarkation and disembarkation of passengers and crew

10.—(1) The captain of a ship or aircraft employed to carry passengers for reward arriving in Great Britain from the Republic of Ireland, Northern Ireland or any of the Islands or arriving in Northern Ireland from Great Britain, the Republic of Ireland or any of the Islands—

(a) shall, except so far as he may be otherwise required to do so under paragraph 27(1) of Schedule 2 to the Immigration Act 1971, take such steps as may be necessary to secure that passengers on board and members of the crew do not disembark there unless either they have been examined by an examining officer or they disembark in accordance with arrangements approved by an examining officer; and

(b) where any examination of persons on board is to be carried out on the ship or aircraft, shall take such steps as may be necessary to secure that those to be examined are presented for the purpose in an orderly manner.

(2) The captain of a ship or aircraft employed to carry passengers for reward going from Great Britain to the Republic of Ireland, Northern Ireland or any of the Islands or going from Northern Ireland to Great Britain, the Republic of Ireland or any of the Islands shall take such steps as may be necessary to secure that—

(a) passengers and members of the crew do not embark except in accordance with arrangements approved by an examining officer; and

(b) if persons embarking are to be examined on board the ship or aircraft, they are presented for the purpose in an orderly manner.

(3) Sub-paragraphs (1) and (2) above apply also to aircraft not employed to carry passengers for reward.

(4) The captain of a ship or aircraft arriving in Great Britain from the Republic of Ireland, Northern Ireland or any of the Islands or arriving in Northern Ireland from Great Britain, the Republic of Ireland or any of the Islands shall, unless he is subject to the requirements of an order under paragraph 27(2) of Schedule 2 to the Immigration Act 1971 and subject to sub-paragraph (6) below, comply with the requirements of sub-paragraph (5) below with respect to the furnishing

to the examining officer of the particulars of the passengers on and crew of the ship or aircraft.

(5) The requirements referred to in sub-paragraph (4) above are—

(a) in the case of a ship employed to carry passengers for reward or an aircraft, to furnish to the examining officer, as soon as reasonably practicable after the arrival of the ship or aircraft, a list of the names and of the dates and places of birth of all passengers and members of the crew arriving on the ship or aircraft; and

(b) in the case of a ship not employed to carry passengers for reward, to furnish to the examining officer, within twelve hours of the arrival of the ship, a list of the names, the dates and places of birth and the addresses of the destinations in Great Britain or Northern Ireland of all passengers and members of the crew arriving on the ship.

(6) An examining officer may dispense with all, or any, of the requirements of sub-paragraph (5) above either generally or in respect of such classes of persons as he may specify.

(7) Any passenger on a ship or aircraft shall furnish to the captain of the ship or aircraft as the case may be, any information required by him for the purpose of complying with the provisions of sub-paragraph (5) above.

Offences

11. A person who knowingly contravenes any prohibition or fails to comply with any duty or requirement imposed by or under this Schedule is guilty of an offence and liable on summary conviction to imprisonment for a term not exceeding three months or a fine not exceeding level 4 on the standard scale or both.

Section 16(3)   SCHEDULE 6

DESIGNATED PORTS

PART I

GREAT BRITAIN

Seaports	Airports
Ardrossan	Aberdeen
Cairnryan	Biggin Hill
Fishguard	Birmingham
Fleetwood	Blackpool
Heysham	Bournemouth (Hurn)
Holyhead	Bristol
Pembroke Dock	Cambridge
Plymouth	Cardiff
Port of Liverpool	Carlisle
Poole Harbour	Coventry
Portsmouth Continental Ferry Port	East Midlands
Southampton	Edinburgh
Stranraer	Exeter
Swansea	Glasgow
Torquay	Gloucester/Cheltenham (Staverton)
Weymouth	Humberside
	Leeds/Bradford
	Liverpool
	London-City
	London-Gatwick
	London-Heathrow
	Luton
	Lydd
	Manchester
	Manston
	Newcastle
	Norwich
	Plymouth
	Prestwick
	Southampton
	Southend
	Stansted
	Teesside

PART II

NORTHERN IRELAND

Seaports	Airports
Belfast	Aldergrove
Larne	Sydenham
Warrenpoint	

Section 17   SCHEDULE 7

TERRORIST INVESTIGATIONS

PART I

ENGLAND, WALES AND NORTHERN IRELAND

Interpretation

1. In this Part of this Schedule a "terrorist investigation" means any investigation to which section 17(1) of this Act applies and "items subject to legal privilege", "excluded material" and "special procedure material" have the meanings given in sections 10 to 14 of the Police and Criminal Evidence Act 1984.

Search for material other than excluded or special procedure material

2.—(1) A justice of the peace may, on an application made by a constable, issue a warrant under this paragraph if satisfied that a terrorist investigation is being carried out and that there are reasonable grounds for believing—

    (a) that there is material on premises specified in the application which is likely to be of substantial value (whether by itself or together with other material) to the investigation;

    (b) that the material does not consist of or include items subject to legal privilege, excluded material or special procedure material; and

    (c) that any of the conditions in sub-paragraph (2) below are fulfilled.

(2) The conditions referred to in sub-paragraph (1)(c) above are—

    (a) that it is not practicable to communicate with any person entitled to grant entry to the premises;

    (b) that it is practicable to communicate with a person entitled to grant entry to the premises but it is not practicable to communicate with any person entitled to grant access to the material;

    (c) that entry to the premises will not be granted unless a warrant is produced;

    (d) that the purpose of a search may be frustrated or seriously prejudiced unless a constable arriving at the premises can secure immediate entry to them.

(3) A warrant under this paragraph shall authorise a constable to enter the premises specified in the warrant and to search the premises and any person found there and to seize and retain anything found there or on any such person, other than items subject to legal privilege,

if he has reasonable grounds for believing—

> (a) that it is likely to be of substantial value (whether by itself or together with other material) to the investigation; and
>
> (b) that it is necessary to seize it in order to prevent it being concealed, lost, damaged, altered or destroyed.

(4) In Nothern Ireland an application for a warrant under this paragraph shall be made by a complaint on oath.

Order for production of excluded or special procedure material

3.—(1) A constable may, for the purposes of a terrorist investigation, apply to a Circuit judge for an order under sub-paragraph (2) below in relation to particular material or material of a particular description, being, material consisting of or including excluded material or special procedure material.

(2) If on such an application the judge is satisfied that the material consists of or includes such material as is mentioned in sub-paragraph (1) above, that it does not include items subject to legal privilege and that the conditions in sub-paragraph (5) below are fulfilled, he may make an order that the person who appears to him to be in possession of the material to which the application relates shall—

> (a) produce it to a constable for him to take away; or
>
> (b) give a constanble access to it,

within such period as the order may specify and if the material is not in that person's possession (and will not come into his possession within that period) to state to the best of his knowledge and belief where it is.

(3) An order under sub-paragraph (2) above may relate to material of a particular description which is expected to come into existence or become available to the person concerned in the period of twenty-eight days beginning with the date of the order; and an order made in relation to such material shall require that person to notify a named constable as soon as possible after the material comes into existence or becomes available to that person.

(4) The period to be specified in an order under sub-paragraph (2) above shall be seven days from the date of the order or, in the case of an order made by virtue of sub-paragraph (3) above, from the notification to the constable unless it appears to the judge that a longer or shorter period would be appropriate in the particular circumstances of the application.

(5) The conditions referred to in sub-paragraph (2) above are—

> (a) that a terrorist investigation is being carried out and that there are reasonable grounds for believing that the material

is likely to be of substantial value (whether by itself or together with other material) to the investigation for the purposes of which the application is made; and

(b) that there are reasonable grounds for believing that it is in the public interest, having regard—

 (i) to the benefit likely to accrue to the investigation if the material is obtained; and

(ii) to the circumstances under which the person in possession of the material holds it,

that the material should be produced or that access to it should be given.

(6) Where the judge makes an order under sub-paragraph (2)(b) above in relation to material on any premises he may, on the application of a constable, order any person who appears to him to be entitled to grant entry to the premises to allow a constable to enter the premises to obtain access to the material.

(7) In Northern Ireland the power to make an order under this paragraph shall be exercised by a county court judge.

4.—(1) Provision may be made by Crown Court Rules as to—

(a) the discharge and variation of orders under paragraph 3 above; and

(b) proceedings relating to such orders.

(2) The following provisions shall have effect pending the coming into force of Crown Court Rules under sub-paragraph (1) above—

(a) an order under paragraph 3 above may be discharged or varied by a Circuit judge on a written application made to the appropriate officer of the Crown Court by any person subject to the order;

(b) unless a Circuit judge otherwise directs on grounds of urgency, the applicant shall, not less than forty-eight hours before making the application, send a copy of it and a notice in writing of the time and place where the application is to be made to the constable on whose application the order to be discharged or varied was made or on any other constable serving in the same police station.

(3) An order of a Circuit judge under paragraph 3 above shall have effect as if it were an order of the Crown Court.

(4) Where the material to which an application under that paragraph relates consists of information contained in a computer—

(a) an order under sub-paragraph (2)(a) of that paragraph shall
have effect as an order to produce the material in a form
in which it can be taken away and in which it is visible and
legible; and

(b) an order under sub-paragraph (2)(b) of that paragraph shall
have effect as an order to give access to the material in a
form in which it is visible and legible.

(5) An order under paragraph 3 above—

(a) shall not confer any right to production of, or access to, items
subject to legal privilege;

(b) shall have effect notwithstanding any obligation as to secrecy
or other restriction on the disclosure of information imposed
by statute or otherwise.

(6) An order may be made under paragraph 3 above in relation to
material in the possession of a government department which is an
authorised government department for the purposes of the Crown
Proceedings Act 1947; and any such order (which shall be served as
if the proceedings were civil proceedings against the department) may
require any officer of the department, whether named in the order
or not, who may for the time being be in possession of the material
concerned to comply with it.

(7) In the application of this paragraph to Northern Ireland for
references to a Circuit judge there shall be substituted references to
a county court judge and for references to a government department
or authorised government department there shall be substituted
references to a Northern Ireland department or authorised Northern
Ireland department.

Search for excluded or special procedure material

5.—(1) A constable may apply to a Circuit judge for a warrant under
this paragraph in relation to specified premises.

(2) On such an application the judge may issue a warrant under
this paragraph if satisfied—

(a) that an order made under paragraph 3 above in relation to
material on the premises has not been complied with; or

(b) that there are reasonable grounds for believing that there
is on the premises material consisting of or including
excluded material or special procedure material, that it does
not include items subject to legal privilege and that the conditions in sub-paragraph (5) of that paragraph and the condition in sub-paragraph (3) below are fulfilled in respect of
that material.

(3) The condition referred to in sub-paragraph (2)(b) above is that it would not be appropriate to make an order under paragraph 3 above in relation to the material because—

    (a) it is not practicable to communicate with any person entitled to produce the material; or

    (b) it is not practicable to communicate with any person entitled to grant access to the material or entitled to grant entry to the premises on which the material is situated; or

    (c) the investigation for the purposes of which the application is made might be seriously prejudiced unless a constable could secure immediate access to the material.

(4) A warrant under this paragraph shall authorise a constable to enter the premises specified in the warrant and to search the premises and any person found there and to seize and retain anything found there or on any such person, other than items subject to legal privilege, if he has reasonable grounds for believing that it is likely to be of substantial value (whether by itself or together with other material) to the investigation for the purposes of which the application was made.

(5) In Northern Ireland the power to issue a warrant under this paragraph shall be exercised by a county court judge.

Explanation of seized or produced material

6.—(1) A Circuit judge may, on an application made by a constable, order any person specified in the order to provide an explanation of any material seized in pursuance of a warrant under paragraph 2 or 5 above or produced or made available to a constable under paragraph 3 above.

(2) A person shall not under this paragraph be required to disclose any information which he would be entitled to refuse to disclose on grounds of legal professional privilege in proceedings in the High Court, except that a lawyer may be required to furnish the name and address of his client.

(3) A statement by a person in response to a requirement imposed by virtue of this paragraph may only be used in evidence against him—

    (a) on a prosecution for an offence under sub-paragraph (4) below; or

    (b) on a prosecution for some other offence where in giving evidence he makes a statement inconsistent with it.

(4) A person who, in purported compliance with a requirement under this paragraph—

    (a) makes a statement which he knows to be false or misleading in a material particular; or

    (b) recklessly makes a statement which is false or misleading in a material particular,

is guilty of an offence.

(5) A person guilty of an offence under sub-paragraph (4) above is liable—

    (a) on conviction on indictment, to imprisonment for a term not exceeding two years or a fine or both;

    (b) on summary conviction, to imprisonment for a term not exceeding six months or a fine not exceeding the statutory maximum or both.

(6) In Northern Ireland the power to make an order under this paragraph shall be exercised by a county court judge.

(7) Paragraph 4(1), (2), (3) and (6) above shall apply to orders under this paragraph as they apply to orders under paragraph 3.

Urgent cases

7.—(1) If a police officer of at least the rank of superintendent has reasonable grounds for believing that the case is one of great emergency and that in the interests of the State immediate action is necessary, he may by a written order signed by him give to any constable the authority which may be given by a search warrant under paragraph 2 or 5 above.

(2) Where an authority is given under this paragraph particulars of the case shall be notified as soon as may be to the Secretary of State.

(3) An order under this paragraph may not authorise a search for items subject to legal privilege.

(4) If such a police officer as is mentioned in sub-paragraph (1) above has reasonable grounds for believing that the case is such as is there mentioned he may by a notice in writing signed by him require any person specified in the notice to provide an explanation of any material seized in pursuance of an order under this paragraph.

(5) Any person who without reasonable excuse fails to comply with a notice under sub-paragraph (4) above is guilty of an offence and liable on summary conviction to imprisonment for a term not exceeding six months or a fine not exceeding level 5 on the standard scale or both.

(6) Sub-paragraphs (2) to (5) of paragraph 6 above shall apply to a requirement imposed under sub-paragraph (4) above as they apply to a requirement under that paragraph.

Orders by Secretary of State in relation to certain investigations

8.—(1) This paragraph has effect in relation to a terrorist investigation concerning any act which appears to the Secretary of State to constitute an offence under Part III of this Act.

(2) Without prejudice to the foregoing provisions of this Part of this Schedule, the Secretary of State may by a written order signed by him or on his behalf give to any constable in Northern Ireland the authority which may be given by a search warrant under paragraph 2 or 5 above or impose on any person in Northern Ireland any such requirement as may be imposed by an order under paragraph 3 above if—

    (a) he is satisfied as to the matters specified in those paragraphs respectively for the issue of a warrant by a justice of the peace or the making of an order by a county court judge; and

    (b) it appears to him that the disclosure of information that would be necessary for an application under those provisions would be likely to prejudice the capability of members of the Royal Ulster Constabulary in relation to the investigation of offences under Part III of this Act or otherwise prejudice the safety of, or of persons in, Northern Ireland.

(3) A person who disobeys an order under this paragraph which corresponds to an order under paragraph 3 above (a 'Secretary of State's production order') is liable—

    (a) on conviction on indictment, to imprisonment for a term not exceeding two years or a fine or both;

    (b) on summary conviction, to imprisonment for a term not exceeding six months or a fine not exceeding the statutory maximum or both.

(4) A Secretary of State's production order may be varied or revoked by the Secretary of State and references in paragraphs 4(4), (5) and (6) and 5 above to an order under paragraph 3 above shall include references to a Secretary of State's production order.

(5) The Secretary of State may by a written order signed by him or on his behalf require any person in Northern Ireland to provide an explanation of any material seized or produced in pursuance of an order under the foregoing provisions of this paragraph; and paragraphs 6(2) to (5) and 7(5) above shall apply to an order under this sub-paragraph as they apply to an order or notice under those paragraphs.

Access to Land Register

9.—(1) The Chief Land Registrar shall, on an application made by a police officer of at least the rank of superintendent, in relation to a person specified in the application or to property so specified, provide the applicant with any information kept by the Registrar under the Land Registration Act 1925 which relates to that person or property.

(2) On any such application there shall be given to the Registrar a certificate stating that there are reasonable grounds for suspecting that there is information kept by him which is likely to be of substantial value (whether by itself or together with other information) to a terrorist investigation.

(3) The information to be provided by the Registrar under this paragraph shall be provided in documentary form.

Supplementary

10.—(1) Any power of seizure conferred by this Schedule is without prejudice to the powers conferred by section 19 of the Police and Criminal Evidence Act 1984 and for the purposes of sections 21 and 22 of that Act (access to, and copying and retention of, seized material)—

    (a) a terrorist investigation shall be treated as an investigation of or in connection with an offence; and

    (b) material produced in pursuance of an order under paragraph 3 or 8 above shall be treated as if it were material seized by a constable.

(2) A search of a person under this Part of this Schedule may only be carried out by a person of the same sex.

Part II

Scotland

Interpretation

11. In this Part of this Schedule a 'terrorist investigation' means any investigation to which section 17(1) of this Act applies.

Order for production of material

12.—(1) A procurator fiscal may, for the purpose of a terrorist investigation, apply to a sheriff for an order under sub-paragraph (2) below in relation to particular material or material of a particular description.

(2) If on such an application the sheriff is satisfied that the conditions in sub-paragraph (5) below are fulfilled, he may make an order that the person who appears to him to be in possession of the material to which the application relates shall—

(a) produce it to a constable for him to take away; or

(b) give a constable access to it,

within such period as the order may specify and if the material is not in that person's possession (and will not come into his possession within that period) to state to the best of his knowledge and belief where it is.

(3) An order under sub-paragraph (2) above may relate to material of a particular description which is expected to come into existence or become available to the person concerned in the period of twenty-eight days beginning with the date of the order; and an order made in relation to such material shall require that person to notify a named constable as soon as possible after the material comes into existence or becomes available to that person.

(4) The period to be specified in an order under sub-paragraph (2) above shall be seven days from the date of the order or, in the case of an order made by virtue of sub-paragraph (3) above, from the notification to the constable unless it appears to the sheriff that a longer or shorter period would be appropriate in the particular circumstances of the application.

(5) The conditions referred to in sub-paragraph (2) above are—

(a) that a terrorist investigation is being carried out and that there are reasonable grounds for believing that the material to which the application relates is likely to be of substantial value (whether by itself or together with other material) to the investigation; and

(b) that there are reasonable grounds for believing that it is in the public interest, having regard—

(i) to the benefit likely to accrue to the investigation if the material is obtained; and

(ii) to the circumstances under which the person in possession of the material holds it,

that the material should be produced or that access to it should be given.

(6) Where the sheriff makes an order under sub-paragraph (2)(b) above in relation to material on any premises he may, on the application of the procurator fiscal, order any person who appears to him to be entitled to grant entry to the premises to allow a constable to enter the premises to obtain access to the material.

13.—(1) Provision may be made by Act of Adjournal as to—

    (a) the discharge and variation of orders under paragraph 12 above; and

    (b) proceedings relating to such orders.

(2) The following provisions shall have effect pending the coming into force of an Act of Adjournal under sub-paragraph (1) above—

    (a) an order under paragraph 12 above may be discharged or varied by a sheriff on a written application made to him by any person subject to the order;

    (b) unless the sheriff otherwise directs on grounds of urgency, the applicant shall, not less than forty-eight hours before making the application, send a copy of it and a notice in writing of the time and place where the application is to be made to the procurator fiscal on whose application the order to be discharged or varied was made.

(3) Where the material to which an application under paragraph 12 above relates consists of information contained in a computer—

    (a) an order under sub-paragraph (2)(a) of that paragraph shall have effect as an order to produce the material in a form in which it can be taken away and in which it is visible and legible; and

    (b) an order under sub-paragraph (2)(b) of that paragraph shall have effect as an order to give access to the material in a form in which it is visible and legible.

(4) Subject to paragraph 17(1)(b) below, an order under paragraph 12 above shall have effect notwithstanding any obligation as to secrecy or other restriction on the disclosure of information imposed by statute or otherwise.

(5) An order may be made under paragraph 12 above in relation to material in the possession of a government department which is an authorised government department for the purposes of the Crown Proceedings Act 1947; and any such order (which shall be served as if the proceedings were civil proceedings against the department) may require any officer of the department, whether named in the order or not, who may for the time being be in possession of the material concerned to comply with such order.

Warrant for search of premises

14.—(1) A procurator fiscal may, for the purpose of a terrorist investigation, apply to a sheriff for a warrant under this paragraph in relation to specified premises.

(2) On such application the sheriff may issue a warrant authorising a constable to enter and search the premises if the sheriff if satisfied—

    (a) that an order made under paragraph 12 above in relation to material on the premises has not been complied with; or

    (b) that the conditions in sub-paragraph (3) below are fulfilled.

(3) The conditions referred to in sub-paragraph (2)(b) above are—

    (a) that there are reasonable grounds for believing that there is material on the premises specified in the application in respect of which the conditions in sub-paragraph (5) of paragraph 12 above are fulfilled; and

    (b) that it would not be appropriate to make an order under that paragraph in relation to the material because—

        (i) it is not practicable to communicate with any person entitled to produce the material; or

        (ii) it is not practicable to communicate with any person entitled to grant access to the material or entitled to grant entry to the premises on which the material is situated; or

        (iii) the investigation for the purposes of which the application is made may be seriously prejudiced unless a constable can secure immediate access to the material.

(4) A warrant under this paragraph shall authorise a constable to enter the premises specified in the warrant and to search the premises and any persons found there and to seize and retain any material found there or on any such person, if he has reasonable grounds for believing that it is likely to be of substantial value (whether by itself or together with other material) to the investigation for the purpose of which the warrant was issued.

(5) A warrant under this paragraph may authorise persons named in the warrant to accompany a constable who is executing it.

Explanation of seized or produced material

15.—(1) A sheriff may, on an application made by a procurator fiscal, order any person specified in the order to provide an explanation of any material produced or made available to a constable under paragraph 12 above or seized in pursuance of a warrant under paragraph 14 above.

(2) A person shall not under this paragraph be required to disclose any information which he would be entitled to refuse to disclose on grounds of confidentiality in legal proceedings as being—

    (a) communications between a professional legal adviser and his client, or

    (b) communications made in connection with or in contemplation of legal proceedings and for the purposes of those proceedings,

except that a lawyer may be required to furnish the name and address of his client.

    (3) A statement by a person in response to a requirement imposed by virtue of this section may only be used in evidence against him—

    (a) on a prosecution for an offence under section 2 of the False Oaths (Scotland) Act 1933; or

    (b) on a prosecution for some other offence where in giving evidence he makes a statement inconsistent with it.

    (4) Sub-paragraphs (1), (2) and (5) of paragraph 13 above shall apply to orders under this paragraph as they apply to orders under paragraph 12 above.

Urgent cases

    16.—(1) If a police officer of at least the rank of superintendent has reasonable grounds for believing that the case is one of great emergency and that in the interests of the State immediate action is necessary, he may by a written order signed by him give to any constable the authority which may be given by a search warrant under paragraph 14 above.

    (2) Where an authority is given under this paragraph particulars of the case shall be notified as soon as may be to the Secretary of State.

    (3) If such a police officer as is mentioned in sub-paragraph (1) above has reasonable grounds for believing that the case is such as is there mentioned he may by a notice in writing signed by him require any person specified in the notice to provide an explanation of any materials seized in pursuance of an order under this paragraph.

    (4) Any person who without reasonable excuse fails to comply with a notice under sub-paragraph (3) above is guilty of an offence and liable on summary conviction to imprisonment for a term not exceeding six months or a fine not exceeding level 5 on the standard scale or both.

    (5) Sub-paragraphs (2) and (3) of paragraph 15 above shall apply to a requirement under sub-paragraph (3) above as they apply to an order under that paragraph.

Supplementary

17.—(1) This Part of this Schedule is without prejudice to—

(a) any power of entry or search or any power to seize or retain property which is otherwise exercisable by a constable;

(b) any rule of law whereby—

(i) communications between a professional legal adviser and his client, or

(ii) communications made in connection with or in contemplation of legal proceedings and for the purposes of those proceedings,

are in legal proceedings protected from disclosure on the ground of confidentiality.

(2) For the purpose of exercising any powers conferred on him under this Part of this Schedule a constable may, if necessary, open lockfast places on premises specified in an order under paragraph 12 or 16 above or a warrant under paragraph 14 above.

(3) A search of a person under this Part of this Schedule may only be carried out by a person of the same sex.

Section 25(1)   SCHEDULE 8

CONSEQUENTIAL AMENDMENTS

The Extradition Act 1870 (c.52)

1.— There shall be deemed to be included in the list of extradition crimes in Schedule 1 to the Extradition Act 1870 any offence under Part III of this Act.

The Criminal Justice Act 1967 (c.80)

2. In section 67(7)(b) of the Criminal Justice Act 1967 for the words 'section 12 of the Prevention of Terrorism (Temporary Provisions) Act 1984' there shall be substituted the words 'section 14 of the Prevention of Terrorism (Temporary Provisions) Act 1989'.

The Northern Ireland (Emergency Provisions) Act 1978 (c.5)

3.—(1) The Northern Ireland (Emergency Provisions) Act 1978 shall be amended as follows.

(2) In section 11 for the words 'section 12(1)(b) of the Prevention of Terrorism (Temporary Provisions) Act 1984' there shall be

substituted the words 'section 14(1)(b) of the Prevention of Terrorism (Temporary Provisions) Act 1989'.

    (3) For section 21(1)(b) there shall be substituted—

        '(b) solicits or invites support for a proscribed organisation other than support with money or other property;'.

    (4) For paragraph 16 of Schedule 4 there shall be substituted—

'Prevention of Terrorism (Temporary Provisions) Act 1989

16. Offences under the following provisions of the Prevention of Terrorism (Temporary Provisions) Act 1989—

    (a) section 8 (breach of exclusion order);

    (b) sections 9, 10 and 11 (financial assistance for terrorism);

    (c) section 17 and Schedule 7 (terrorist investigations);

    (d) section 18 (information about acts of terrorism);

    (e) section 21(5) (obstruction etc. of searches).'

The Suppression of Terrorism Act 1978 (c.26)

4. In Schedule 1 to the Suppression of Terrorism Act 1978 after paragraph 19 there shall be inserted—

'Financing terrorism

19A. An offence under Part III of the Prevention of Terrorism (Temporary Provisions) Act 1989.'

The Criminal Justice (Scotland) Act 1980 (c.62)

5. In section 3D(1) of the Criminal Justice (Scotland) Act 1980 for paragraph (a) there shall be substituted—

    '(a) 'terrorism provisions' means section 14(1) of the Prevention of Terrorism (Temporary Provisions) Act 1989 and any provision of Schedule 2 or 5 to that Act conferring a power of arrest or detention;'.

The Police and Criminal Evidence Act 1984 (c.60)

6.—(1) The Police and Criminal Evidence Act 1984 shall be amended as follows.

    (2) In section 30(12) for paragraph (c) there shall be substituted—

        '(c) section 15(6) and (9) of the Prevention of Terrorism (Temporary Provisions) Act 1989 and paragraphs 7(4) and 8(4) and (5) of Schedule 2 and paragraphs 6(6) and 7(4) and (5) of Schedule 5 to that Act.'

(3) In section 32(10)for the words 'paragraph 6 of Schedule 3 to the Prevention of Terrorism (Temporary Provisions) Act 1984' there shall be substituted the words 'section 15(3), (4) and (5) of the Prevention of Terrorism (Temporary Provisions) Act 1989'.

(4) In section 51(b) for the words 'section 12 or 13 of the Prevention of Terrorism (Temporary Provisions) Act 1984' there shall be substituted the words 'section 14 of the Prevention of Terrorism (Temporary Provisions) Act 1989 or Schedule 2 or 5 to that Act'.

(5) In section 61(9)(b) after '(b)' there shall be inserted the words 'except as provided in section 15(10) of, and paragraph 7(6) of Schedule 5 to, the Prevention of Terrorism (Temporary Provisions) Act 1989,'.

(6) In section 65 for the definition of 'the terrorism provisions' and 'terrorism' there shall be substituted respectively—

> 'the terrorism provisions' means section 14(1) of the Prevention of Terrorism (Temporary Provisions) Act 1989 and any provision of Schedule 2 or 5 to that Act conferring a power of arrest or detention; and
> 'terrorism' has the meaning assigned to it by section 20(1) of that Act.'

(7) In section 116(5) for the words 'section 1, 9 or 10 of the Prevention of Terrorism (Temporary Provisions) Act 1984' there shall be substituted the words 'section 2, 8, 9, 10 or 11 of the Prevention of Terrorism (Temporary Provisions) Act 1989'.

(8) In section 118(2)(a) after the word 'offence' there shall be inserted the words 'or after being arrested under section 14 of the Prevention of Terrorism (Temporary Provisions) Act 1989 or under paragraph 6 of Schedule 5 to that Act by an examining officer who is a constable'.

The Drug Trafficking Offences Act 1986 (c.32)

7. In section 5(2) of the Drug Trafficking Offences Act 1986 the word 'or' at the end of paragraph (b) shall be omitted and at the end of paragraph (c) there shall be inserted the words', or

> (d) an order under section 13(2), (3) or (4) of the Prevention of Terrorism (Temporary Provisions) Act 1989 (forfeiture orders),'.

The Northern Ireland (Emergency Provisions) Act 1987 (c.30)

8. In section 16(1) of the Northern Ireland (Emergency Provisions) Act 1987 for the definition of 'the terrorism provisions' there shall be substituted—

'the terrorism provisions' means section 14(1) of the Prevention of Terrorism (Temporary Provisions) Act 1989 and any provision of Schedule 2 or 5 to that Act conferring a power of arrest or detention'.

The Criminal Justice (Scotland) Act 1987 (c.41)

9. In section 5(3)(b) of the Criminal Justice (Scotland) Act 1987 at the end of sub-paragraph (iii) there shall be inserted the words 'or

(iiia) section 13(2), (3) or (4) of the Prevention of Terrorism (Temporary Provisions) Act 1989 (forfeiture orders),'.

The Criminal Justice Act 1988 (c.33)

10.—(1) The Criminal Justice Act 1988 shall be amended as follows.

(2) In section 71(9)(c) after the words 'other than a drug trafficking offence' there shall be inserted the words 'or an offence under Part III of the Prevention of Terrorism (Temporary Provisions) Act 1989'.

(3) In section 74(2) the word 'or' at the end of paragraph (b) shall be omitted and at the end of paragraph (c) there shall be inserted the words '; or

(d) an order under section 13(2), (3) or (4) of the Prevention of Terrorism (Temporary Provisions) Act 1989 (forfeiture orders),'.

(4) In Schedule 14—

(a) in paragraph 5, for the words 'section 12(1)(b) of the Prevention of Terrorism (Temporary Provisions) Act 1984' there shall be substituted the words 'section 14(1)(b) of the Prevention of Terrorism (Temporary Provisions) Act 1989'; and

(b) in paragraph 6, for the definition of 'the terrorism provisions', there shall be substituted—

' 'the terrorism provision' means section 14(1) of the Prevention of Terrorism (Temporary Provisions) Act 1989 and any provision of Schedule 2 or 5 to that Act conferring a power of arrest or detention.'.

SCHEDULE 9

REPEALS AND REVOCATIONS

PART I

ENACTMENTS

Chapter	Short title	Extent of repeal
38 and 39 Vict. c.17	The Explosives Act 1875.	In section 7, the paragraph beginning 'Upon the hearing of the application'.
1978 c.5.	The Northern Ireland (Emergency Provisions) Act 1978.	Section 21(2).
1984 c.8	The Prevention of Terrorism (Temporary Provisions) Act 1984.	The whole Act.
1984 c.54.	The Roads (Scotland) Act 1984.	In Schedule 9, paragraph 91.
1984 c.60.	The Police and Criminal Evidence Act 1984.	Section 53(2). In Schedule 2, the entry relating to the Prevention of Terrorism (Temporary Provisions) Act 1984. In Schedule 6, paragraph 27. In Schedule 7, paragraph 9.
1989 c.4.	The Prevention of Terrorism (Temporary Provision) Act 1989.	

PART II

ORDERS

Number	Title
S.I. 1984/417.	The Prevention of Terrorism (Supplemental Temporary Provisions) (Northern Ireland) Order 1984.
S.I. 1984/418.	The Prevention of Terrorism (Supplemental Temporary Provisions) Order 1984.
S.I. 1987/119.	The Prevention of Terrorism (Supplemental Temporary Provisions) (Amendment) Order 1987.
S.I. 1987/1209.	The Prevention of Terrorism (Supplemental Temporary Provision) (Amendment No. 2) Order 1987.

Bibliography

Ackroyd, C., K. Margolis, J. Rosenhead and T. Shallice *The Technology of Political Control* (London: Penguin, 1977).

Archbold, *Pleading, Evidence and Practice in Criminal Cases* (London: Sweet & Maxwell, 1985).

Asmal, K.(chairman) *Shoot to Kill? International Lawyers' Inquiry* (Dublin: Mercier, 1985).

Baldwin, J. and M. McConville *Jury Trials* (London: Clarendon Press, 1979).

Baxton, J. and L. Koffman *Police: the Constitution and the Community* (Guildford: Professional Books, 1985).

Beddard, R. *Human Rights and Europe* (London: Sweet & Maxwell, 1980).

Bell, G. *The Protestants of Ulster* (London: Pluto, 1976).

——. *Troublesome Business* (London: Pluto, 1982).

Benyon, J. and C. Bourn *The Police Powers, Procedures and Proprieties* (Oxford: Pergamon, 1986).

Beresford, D. *Ten Men Dead* (Dublin: Grafton Books, 1987).

Bew, P., P. Gibbon and H. Patterson *The State in Northern Ireland* (Manchester University Press, 1979).

Bishop, P. and E. Mallie *The Provisional I.R.A.* (London: Heinemann, 1987).

Bloch, J. and P. Fitzgerald *British Intelligence and Covert Action* (Dingle: Brandon, 1983).

Boyd, A. *Holy War in Belfast* (Tralee: Anvil, 1969).

——. *Northern Ireland: Who is to Blame?* (Dublin: Mercier, 1984).

——. *The Informers* (Cork: Mercier, 1984).

Boyle, K. and T. Hadden *Ireland: A Positive Proposal* (London: Penguin, 1985).

Boyle, K., T. Hadden and P. Hillyard *Law and State: the Case of Northern Ireland* (London: Martin Robertson, 1975).

——. *Ten Years On in Northern Ireland: the Legal Control of Political Violence* (London: Cobden Trust, 1980).

Buckland, P. *A History of Northern Ireland* (Dublin: Gill & Macmillan, 1981).

Bunyon, T. *Political Police in Britain* (London: Quartet Books, 1977).

Campbell, C.M. *Do We Need a Bill of Rights?* (London: Maurice Temple Smith, 1980).

Chamblis, W.J. and R.B. Seidman *Law, Order and Power* (London: Addison-Wesley, 1971).

Collins, M. (ed) *Ireland After Britain* (London: Pluto, 1984).

Collins, T. *The Irish Hunger Strike* (Dublin: White Island, 1986).

Coogan, T.P. *Ireland Since the Rising* (London: Pall Mall, 1966).

——. *On the Blanket: The H-Block Story* (Dublin: Ward River Press, 1980).

——. *The I.R.A.* (London: Fontana, 1980).

Cornish, W.R. *The Jury* (London: Penguin, 1968).

Coulter, J., S. Miller and M. Walker *State of Siege* (London: Canary Press, 1984).

Curtis, L. *Ireland: The Propaganda War* (London: Pluto, 1984).

Darby, J. (ed) *Northern Ireland: the Background to the Conflict* (Belfast: Appletree Press, 1983).

De Paor, L. *Divided Ulster* (Middlesex: Penguin, 1970).

Denning, A.T. *What Next in the Law* (London: Butterworths, 1982).

Devlin, P. *Trial by Jury* (London: Stevens, 1956).

Dillon, M. and D. Lehane *Political Murder in Northern Ireland* (London: Penguin, 1973).

Doherty, F. *The Stalker Affair* (Dublin: Mercier, 1986).

Evelegh, R. *Peace Keeping in a Democratic Society: The Lessons of Northern Ireland* (London: Hurst, 1978).

Farrell, M. *Northern Ireland: The Orange State* (London: Pluto, 1976).

——. *Arming the Protestants* (London: Pluto, 1983).

Fine, B. *Democracy and the Rule of Law* (London: Pluto, 1984).

Flackes, W.F. *Northern Ireland: A Political Directory* (Dublin: Gill & Macmillan, 1980).

Geraghty, T. *Who Dares Wins: The Story of the S.A.S. 1950–1980* (London: Fontana, 1980).

Gifford, T. *Supergrasses: the Use of Accomplice Evidence in Northern Ireland* (London: Cobden Trust, 1984).

Greer, S.C. and A. White *Abolishing the Diplock Courts: the Case for Restoring Jury Trial to Scheduled Offences in Northern Ireland* (London: Cobden Trust, 1986).

Griffith, J.A.G. *The Politics of the Judiciary* (Glasgow: Fontana, 1985).

Hadden, T. and P. Hillyard *Justice in Northern Ireland: A Study in Social Confidence* (London: Cobden Trust, 1973).

Hain, P. *Political Trials in Britain: From the Past to the Present Day* (London: Pelican, 1984).

Hamill, D. *Pig in the Middle: The Army in Northern Ireland 1969–1985* (London: Methuen, 1986).

Harvey, R. *Diplock and the Assault on Civil Liberties* (London: Haldane Society, 1981).

Jackson, T.A. *Ireland Her Own* (London: Lawrence & Wishart, 1947).

Kee, R. *Trial and Error* (London: Hamish Hamilton, 1986).

Kitson, F. *Low Intensity Operations: Subversion, Insurgency and Peace Keeping* (London: Faber & Faber, 1971).

Leigh, L.H. *Police Powers in England and Wales* (London: Butterworths, 1985).

Lindsay, K. *The British Intelligence Service in Action* (Dundalk: Dundrod, 1980).

Lodge, J. (ed) *Terrorism: a Challenge to the State* (London: Martin Robertson, 1981).

Lyons, F.S.H. *Ireland Since the Famine* (London: Weidenfeld & Nicolson, 1971).

Macardle, D. *The Irish Republic: A Documented Chronicle* (London: Corgi, 1968).

McCann, E. *War and an Irish Town* (London: Pluto, 1980).

McGuffin, J. *The Guinea Pigs* (London: Penguin, 1974).

Magee, J. *Northern Ireland, Crisis and Conflict* (London: Routledge & Kegan Paul, 1974).

Mullin, C. *Error of Judgment: the Truth about the Birmingham Bombings* (London: Chatto & Windus, 1986).

Nicholas, E. *International Terrorism: A Chronology of Events 1968–1979* (London: Aldwych, 1980).

O'Dowd, L., B. Rolston and B. Tomlinson *Northern Ireland: Between Civil Rights and Civil War* (London: C.S.E. Books, 1980).

O'Malley, P. *The Uncivil Wars* (Belfast: Blackstaff, 1983).

Poulantzas, N. *State, Power and Socialism* (London: New Left Books, 1978).

Powell, G. and C. McGrath *Police and Criminal Evidence Act 1984* (London: Longman Professional, 1985).

Probert, B. *Beyond Orange and Green: The Political Economy of the Northern Ireland Crisis* (London: Zed Press, 1978).

Scorer, C. and P. Hewitt *The Prevention of Terrorism Act: The Case For Repeal* (London: N.C.C.L., 1981).

Scorer, C., S. Spencer and P. Hewitt *The New Prevention of Terrorism Act: The Case For Repeal* (London: Cobden Trust, 1985).

Smith, J. and B. Hogan *Criminal Law* (London: Butterworths, 1983).

Sobel, L. (ed) *Political Terrorism* (Oxford: Clio Press, 1979).

Stalker, J. *Stalker* (London: Harrap, 1988).

Taylor, P. *Beating the Terrorists? Interrogation in Omagh, Gough and Castlereagh* (Middlesex: Penguin, 1980).

——. *Stalker* (London: Faber, 1987).

Townshend, C. *Britain's Civil Wars* (London: Faber & Faber, 1986).

Walsh, D. *The Use and Abuse of Emergency Legislation in Northern Ireland* (London: Cobden Trust, 1983).

Williams, G. *Textbook of Criminal Law* (London: Stevens & Sons, 1983).
Winchester, S. *In Holy Terror: Reporting the Ulster Troubles* (London: Faber, 1974).

Index